RESEARCH AND SUPERVISION
IN MATHEMATICS AND
SCIENCE EDUCATION

RESEARCH AND SUPERVISION IN MATHEMATICS AND SCIENCE EDUCATION

Edited by

John A. Malone
Curtin University of Technology

Bill Atweh
Queensland University of Technology

Jeffrey R. Northfield
Monash University

LEA LAWRENCE ERLBAUM ASSOCIATES, PUBLISHERS
1998   Mahwah, New Jersey   London

Lawrence Erlbaum Associates, Inc., Publishers
10 Industrial Avenue
Mahwah, New Jersey 07430

Cover design by Kathryn Houghtaling Lacey

Library of Congress Cataloging-in-Publication Data

Research and supervision in mathematics and science education / edited
by John A. Malone, Bill Atweh, Jeffrey R. Northfield.
   p.   cm.
   Includes bibliographical references and index.
   ISBN 0-8058-2968-7 (cloth : alk. paper). — ISBN 0-8058-2969-5
(pbk. : alk. paper).
   1. Science—Study and teaching—Research. 2. Mathematics—Study
and teaching—Research. I. Malone, John A. II. Atweh, Bill.
III. Northfield, Jeffrey R.
Q181.R39 1998
507.1—dc21   98-26310
                                                                CIP

Books published by Lawrence Erlbaum Associates are printed on acid-free paper,
and their bindings are chosen for strength and durability.

Printed in the United States of America
10 9 8 7 6 5 4 3 2 1

Contents

Preface

At least four recent and significant changes in the context of research in mathematics and science education were influential in the decision to produce this book. First, mathematics and science education researchers now have access to a much wider choice of research methodologies than they had two decades ago. These so called "emerging" methodologies are being increasingly used by researchers in the social sciences, and although general research texts dealing with these new methodologies are plentiful, very rarely are the principles and methods used problematized with particular reference to actual examples set within a research context. We believe that new researchers generally, and those in mathematics and science education in particular, will benefit from the contextualized discussion of the more common alternative methodologies appearing in this book.

Second, there has been a significant increase in the number of novice researchers now working in the fields of mathematics and science education. This increase in numbers has stemmed, in many countries around the world, from the transfer of these disciplines from colleges and teacher training institutions to the university sector. This phenomenon has been accompanied by the changing emphasis, in a significant number of these institutions, away from undergraduate preparation toward the provision of higher degrees, and by the increasing demand for highly qualified mathematics and science teachers in schools. Coupled with the shrinking job market worldwide and an aggressive recruitment marketing strategy adopted by many tertiary institutions, postgraduate enrollments in mathematics and science education have shifted from a steady-state situation in the recent past to a present growth state.

Third, this rapid increase in the number of postgraduate students in universities has placed considerable pressure on those institutions to hire staff qualified to supervise, and to maintain the quality of that supervision. The number of academics who are experienced in research planning and supervision is alarmingly small in many universities, especially in disciplines that are relatively new to the postgraduate research scene (e.g., the health sciences and others that make use of social research paradigms), and in those that are struggling to establish a research culture—an attribute that requires considerable time to develop. As a result, many universities world-wide employ a sizeable group of novice postgraduate supervisors at the present time—academics conscious of their lack of experience who are seeking support in order to provide their students with quality assistance including not only information on aspects of project and thesis supervision, but also assistance in the form of information on research design and analysis. Again, the literature discussing these problems in mathematics and science education has been scarce. We believe that this is an opportune time to initiate discussion dealing with problems that may arise as alternative methodologies and models of supervision are introduced.

Fourth, the current availability of information technology in higher education has changed many of the practices utilized by researchers. Tasks that were once lengthy and cumbersome are now readily available and easily achieved. Information technologies have the potential to change the processes of conducting literature reviews, analyzing data, writing-up and disseminating research results. Too often today, postgraduate courses assume that students already possess, or will quickly develop, sufficient expertise in the use of such technology to facilitate their personal research program. At the same time, other more experienced researchers are finding it difficult to keep up-to-date with the ever-changing technology. We believe that all mathematics and science education researchers will benefit from the discussion included here on the use of technology in the research and writing process.

The targeting of this book at both novice and more experienced researchers is arguably ambitious; yet it is deliberate. We believe that within the changing contexts just identified, all researchers are placed in a new learning situation. Further, our conception of the supervisory contract as a collaborative engagement between individuals implies that issues related to research and supervision should be mutually accessible to both parties entering into such a relationship. Several of the chapters in this volume have been written by teams of postgraduate students and their supervisors; others by individual students speaking to fellow students, still others by experienced supervisors speaking to students or to their academic colleagues. Consequently, some chapters may be more relevant to readers than others. However, we are hopeful that all researchers in mathematics and science education will find portions useful to their practice.

This volume is an initiative of the Mathematics Education Research Group of Australasia (MERGA), a professional body consisting of many hundreds of mathematics educators and teachers, university academics, and post-graduate research students from Australia, New Zealand, countries on both the Indian and Pacific Ocean rims, and some 20 other countries around the world. Among its functions, MERGA provides a venue for researchers to share the findings from their research efforts. This is achieved through the Group's annual conference, through its international publication (the Mathematics Education Research Journal), a four yearly review of research conducted in the Australasian region, and through various monographs published on specific areas of research. MERGA also provides leadership in the training and development of researchers, an activity which, in the past, has been accomplished through research workshops conducted during the annual conference. This book was initiated under that latter function of MERGA. Its chapters provide a collection of ideas and advice from both experienced and novice researchers from around the world, dealing with their knowledge and experience in conducting research and with the process of supervising and being supervised.

The book opens with an overview chapter describing the different approaches to research in mathematics and science education. Several other chapters then direct the reader's attention to the book's central focus—ethnography—and ways to establish the authenticity of this approach to research are treated, along with details on specific techniques associated with this methodology. Chapters on the student–supervisor relationship follow, and these lead naturally into other chapters dealing with supervision structures. Further chapters are concerned with scholarly writing, and the book concludes with two chapters that address the use of technology in conducting and supervising research.

The opening chapter by Dylan Wiliam entitled "A Framework for Thinking About Research in Mathematics and Science Education" (pp. 1–18) presents an overview of research paradigms beginning with a discussion of some of the different classifications of educational research that have been proposed in the past—for example, basic vs. applied, conclusion-oriented vs. decision-oriented, qualitative vs. quantitative, and systemic vs. analytic. Dylan illustrates the relationship between different approaches to research in terms of the different emphases accorded to the hermeneutic notions of *text*, *context*, and *reader*. He defines the process of knowledge-building in mathematics and science education as the dual process of establishing warrants for particular beliefs, while at the same time eliminating plausible rival hypotheses, where "plausibility" is established either by explicit reference to a theoretical frame or implicitly within a discourse. Dylan then integrates these different approaches to educational research by means of Churchman's classification of *Inquiry Systems*, based on whether the primary source of evidence is taken to be reason, observation, representation, dialectic, or ethical values. He argues that the process of educational research, as well as the process of building knowledge, requires subjecting the consequences of the research to the ethical judgments of the community.

This last point is picked up by Robyn Zevenbergen in her chapter called "Ethnography in the Classroom" (pp. 19–38), which addresses some of the processes and key decisions in conducting ethnographic research in schools. Robyn does not provide an extensive overview of the ethnographic research process, but rather locates the implementation of ethnography in classrooms, with a particular emphasis on some of the critical decisions the researcher will be compelled to make during the research process. A brief overview of what constitutes ethnography follows, and then two of the main tools for qualitative data collection—participant observation and the interview—are described and discussed. Robyn concludes with a discussion of the problems, dilemmas, and critical decisions associated with the implementation of ethnography in mathematics classrooms.

John Schaller and Ken Tobin's chapter, "Quality Criteria for the Genres of Interpretive Research" (pp. 39–60), complements Robyn's chapter in that it provides a fuller discussion of the complexities of communicating classroom experiences. The chapter also discusses innovative approaches to interpretive research—approaches appropriate for that group who the authors refer to as "the new generation" of researchers and supervisors—while conforming to established quality criteria related to the production of a scholarly research product. The controversial issue of fictive stories as interpretive research is raised, and their use is endorsed as a method of rhetorically heightening the narrative and enhancing meaning by conveying a contrived message to the reader. This chapter is sure to generate spirited debate in any doctoral colloquium.

John and Kathleen Truran then introduce the first of two chapters examining the use of clinical interviews as a research tool. In their chapter, "Using Clinical Interviews in Qualitative Research" (pp. 61–83), they examine the general principles behind interview use, then discuss practical matters necessary to ensure that the accompanying fieldwork goes smoothly. Their chapter addresses a number of aspects of ethnography and, in doing so, adds to the information provided in the two preceding chapters. Their contribution is an important one in view of the pivotal role the interview plays in interpretive research. After addressing the analysis and interpretation of data collected by this technique, they conclude with a comment on the presentation and preservation of results. Their arguments throughout the chapter are illustrated with relevant examples and instances where a supervisor's assistance may be of special value.

The technical aspects of analyzing verbal communication between interviewer and interviewee is a feature of Bob Bleicher's chapter, "Classroom

Interactions: Using Interactional Sociolinguistics to Make Sense of Recorded Classroom Talk" (pp. 85–104). His contribution complements that of the Truran's by looking particularly at ways to make sense of the information interviewees provide when they are "thinking on their feet." He not only examines in considerable detail *why* the technique of interactional sociolinguistics is useful for analyzing interviews or any recorded conversations between teachers and students, but he also explains *how* it is useful. Bob explains the technicalities of this process in the limited space available, and illustrates the methodology involved through references to actual interviews and more casual conversations he has recorded.

Peter Taylor and Vaille Dawson's chapter, "Critical Reflections on a Problematic Student–Supervisor Relationship" (pp. 105–127), is the first of three chapters addressing the student–supervisor relationship. Their chapter presents the voices of both the research–supervisor (Peter) and student (Vaille) in a critical self-reflective account of the supportive role adopted by Peter in an action research study in science education carried out in Vaille's classroom. This critical account of their relationship was prompted by a sense of disquiet and lack of harmony that developed during the year-long action research study. Vaille, in the role of a teacher–researcher with a critical constructivist perspective, attempted to transform radically the epistemology of her Grade 10 Bioethics class. Despite Peter's emancipatory intentions, Vaille felt that she was being disempowered as a result of his demands to conform to normative expectations and standards. The chapter is·a fascinating account of how the student and supervisor worked together to conduct a joint, critical inquiry in an effort to resolve the problematic aspects of their relationship.

In the chapter entitled "Higher Degree Supervision: Why It Worked" (pp. 129–150), Gilah Leder, the supervisor, with Helen Forgasz and Julie Landvogt, her students, discuss their collaborative efforts in the students' quest for a doctorate. They discuss higher degree supervision issues from two approaches—first, a formal overview of the "ideal model" and second, personalized accounts of their own experiences. The expected roles and responsibilities of supervisors and students open the chapter, then Helen's and Julie's reflections about their candidature as doctoral students in mathematics education follow. Similarities are evident in their experiences—their candidatures coincided, but their circumstances and motivations differed. Both discerned that the intellectual and personal skills of their supervisor were critical to the success of the supervision process, and each student describes how they went about accommodating the demands Gilah required of them. Events that challenged notions of an ideal model of PhD supervision are discussed, and the chapter concludes with a personal response from Gilah.

Loren White's chapter, "Teacher, Researcher, Collaborator, Student: Multiple Roles and Multiple Dilemmas" (pp. 151–172), also describes the pressures placed on research students as the author reflects on his own attempts as a doctoral student to address problems inherent in the collaborative process. His story touches on many issues that are important for PhD students—for example, the role of research, assumptions about teaching, about research methods, about one's student and professional colleagues, and about theory and practice. Through a series of reflective episodes in his early teaching career, Loren describes the conflict of being both a professional educator and postgraduate student as personified by a power struggle within oneself—between the institutions of university and school, and between supervisor and student.

Supervisor–student experiences are of central concern in Frank Crawley's chapter entitled "Guiding Collaborative Action Research in Science Education Contexts" (pp. 173–198). In it, Frank describes the experiences of graduate students in science education and their instructor too as they both learn about collaborative action research (CAR) and engage in CAR in public schools, colleges, and universities. The perspective taken in CAR is that of the "teacher as researcher." Frank begins with a review of current U.S. efforts to reform science education. One such effort is the CAR process. He follows this up with an overview of studies on life history, action research, and teacher reflection, which are the elements of the CAR course and its assignments. He documents the four-step recursive process involved in CAR and he invites the reader to experience CAR from the perspective of participants—from problematizing existing teaching practice to reflecting on the outcomes of the actions taken by researcher–students and teacher–collaborators—as they progress through their course. His chapter concludes with a description of the struggles and tensions that team members experienced while participating in CAR, and what they learned about the process while actually performing it.

John Malone's chapter, "On Supervising and Being Supervised at a Distance" (pp. 199–214), is the first of three that examine supervision structures. John considers the special problems facing both the supervisor and research student when they are operating on a distance-education basis. He explains how the burgeoning number of part-time postgraduate students in universities worldwide has created a major need for programs that relate to the requirements of these professionals, and that this means that traditional forms of regular on-campus study are often impractical. Research conducted at the student's workplace, wherever that may be, is now recognized as a fact of university postgraduate study, and is a mode of study to which universities must respond. John describes and discusses strategies for overcoming the absence of a host of supporting facilities available to the on-campus student, the personal support networks generally available to them, and resources that the internal student takes for granted.

In the following chapter, "Legitimate Peripheral Participation in the Training of Researchers in Mathematics and Science Education" (pp. 215–230),

Wolff-Michael Roth and Michelle McGinn outline a conception of learning to do research in mathematics and science education that takes *practice* as its core theoretical notion. The authors describe the locus of practice as being within communities where newcomers learn by participating in a craft—such as social science research—with more experienced others in legitimate and initially peripheral ways. They develop a theoretical framework of practice on the basis of existing work in sociology, ethnomethodology, and anthropology, and use examples from their own work to show how their theoretical framework is played out in the practices of teaching, conducting research, and supervising. Their notion of the student serving a type of apprenticeship under the supervisor mirrors the "junior colleague" concept discussed by John Malone in the preceding chapter.

Andy Begg, Beverley Bell, Vicki Compton, and Elizabeth McKinley's chapter describing another supervision structure is entitled "Supervision in a Graduate Center" (pp. 231–248). In it they explain their model for the supervision of graduate research—a model that focuses on avoiding undue duplication of effort while ensuring that a number of key components of supervision (regular supervision meetings, research methods courses, supervision support meetings, regular subject seminars, professional development seminars, writing assistance, and networking by students within and beyond the university) are maintained. The authors provide some details of how their model was developed and the contents of the various components. It is an interesting exercise to compare the operation of the Center these authors describe with the one described by John Malone, located in a different country.

Tom Cooper, Annette Baturo, and Leonie Harris' chapter, "Scholarly Writing in Mathematics and Science Education Higher Degree Courses" (pp. 249–276), is the first of two chapters addressing one of the more daunting tasks facing students and graduates in the early stages of their careers: how to write up their scholarly work. Theirs is a "nuts and bolts" contribution aimed particularly at students who are writing up research. It considers many aspects of writing that we *should* know about, but which do not seem to be taught nowadays. These include common grammatical errors as well as others we all make as a result of our falling standards in writing—a byproduct of our own (often untrained) efforts at word processing. The authors describe scholarly writing at three levels: one addressing the need for the author to be familiar with criteria regarding the mechanics of writing; the second related to the flow of arguments within various sections of a dissertation (the "microstructure" of writing), and the third related to the integration of the entire scholarly work (the "macrostructure" of writing). This will be a handy reference for everyone engaged in the writing process.

In "Writing for Publication" (pp. 277–298), Jack Hourcade and Holly Anderson extend the presentation in chapter 13. Their chapter refers to the process of writing in a general sense. It includes a host of different arguments on why we should write, explanations of why we don't write more, and hints on ways to increase our productivity. In addition, Jack and Holly provide an interesting insight into the thinking by prospective publishers of the work we produce—how important it is to them that we contribute to professional journals—and they explain how the journals function, offering a number of proven strategies and tips for helping prospective authors become successful in publishing their work.

The two final chapters are focused specifically on the way that information technology can be harnessed to assist those engaged in research and supervision. In the penultimate chapter, "The Impact of New Developments in Information Technology on Postgraduate Research and Supervision" (pp. 299–322), David Squires draws the attention of the reader to the ways in which the practicalities of thesis preparation have changed so dramatically in recent times through advances in information technology (IT). He describes the wide range of IT-assisted information systems, how the information explosion fostered by these systems will have significant effects on how research is conducted and reported, and what the implications are for postgraduate research students and their supervisors. David demonstrates how the use of IT-assisted information systems can help students to be more informed when choosing a research area, help them develop a comprehensive awareness of a chosen field, clarify methodological issues, and check the accuracy of information. He concludes by explaining how developments in IT enable student and supervisor to spend more time in quality interaction and how they can enhance personal productivity.

In the final chapter, Peter Rillero and Bee Gallegos complement the Squires chapter with theirs, entitled "Databases: A Gateway to Literature in Mathematics and Science Education Research" (pp. 323–349). In it they stress the point that mathematics and science education researchers and their supervisors need to know the important bibliographic databases for their research interests, and should develop the ability to efficiently access information in these databases. They describe the structure of databases and present strategies for their efficient search, illustrating these ideas with examples from the ERIC database—the world's largest. The Internet is discussed as a disorganized database of databases, and strategies for locating resources on the Internet are also presented. Two appendices to the chapter—annotated bibliographies of worldwide databases and internet sites—will be of considerable interest to the reader.

Although books on research methodology abound, there are few suitable texts in existence that focus on methodology appropriate for mathematics and science education students and those in related disciplines. Even fewer texts address problems associated with the supervision of research students. The editors hope that this volume will go some way toward filling this void. Its particular appeal should stem from its practical approach, its creative future perspective, and the wide generalizability of the thinking and ideas presented by each of its chapter authors.

John A. Malone
Bill Atweh
Jeffrey R. Northfield

1

A Framework for Thinking About Research in Mathematics and Science Education

Dylan Wiliam
King's College London

In the opening chapter of the NCTM handbook on *Research in Mathematics Education*, Begle and Gibb (1980) gave their view of the main purpose of research in that discipline: "Simply stated, there is a need to understand better how, where and why people learn or do not learn mathematics" (p. 8). The crucial word in this definition is, of course, "understand." In this chapter, I discuss some of the different ways that have been developed for thinking about what it means to "understand" something in mathematics or science education. The chapter begins with a discussion of some of the ways in which approaches to research in education have been classified (for example, "basic" vs. "applied" and "qualitative" vs. "quantitative"). This then leads on to considerations of what counts as "knowledge" in the field of education, and what happens as a result of that knowledge.

In the final part of the chapter, these ideas are drawn together in a five-fold classification of different methods of inquiring in education, based on whether the principal source of evidence is reasoning, observation, representation, dispute, or ethical values.

THE NATURE OF RESEARCH IN MATHEMATICS AND SCIENCE EDUCATION

It is common to classify research in most fields as either "basic" or "applied." The fact that these labels are applied as if the categories were distinct types of research obscures the fact that what we really have is a continuum. At

1

one end, basic research questions are typically formulated by researchers and are not driven by the needs of any immediate application. However, much research that would have been described as "basic" at the time it was undertaken has subsequently found fruitful application, and has had a major impact on educational practice.

The other end of the continuum—applied research—focuses much more clearly on situations that arise in practice. However, the fact that the research concerns "real" settings does not necessarily mean that it has to be driven by the need to solve the problem: Just understanding the problem better can often be a worthwhile goal. For example, there has been a radical shift in mathematics and science education research over the last 30 years in the way that pupils errors are treated. In the past, these were often considered as if they were random failures to implement an algorithm properly. More recently, it has been realized that such mistakes arise primarily because the pupils hold alternative conceptions of the subject matter, which then changes our understanding of the problem and how we might choose to tackle it.

This distinction between "pure" and "applied" research was explored by Cronbach and Suppes (1969), who proposed that a more useful way of thinking about educational research was as a continuum from "conclusion-oriented inquiry" to "decision-oriented inquiry." Conclusion-oriented inquiry takes its direction from the intuition of the researchers, and can often change direction as the research proceeds. By contrast, decision-oriented enquiry is tied to a particular decision or set of decisions to be made, and the scope for redirecting the research while it is in progress is limited.

For most of this century, the predominant way of finding out and understanding in education has been based on a way of researching that has attempted to emulate the successes of the physical sciences. The successes of the physical sciences stem largely from the fact that the meanings of the results of experimental data are likely to be agreed across a wide range of contexts and by a large proportion of the research community. In the writing up of such research, it is assumed that the text produced will have the same meaning to the vast majority of readers, and will apply across a wide range of contexts. These "objective" methods are much more difficult to apply in social science research, and, even where the methods have been possible to apply, their success has been extremely limited.

For some, this lack of success can be attributed to the fact that educational research has not yet developed into a fully mature science. Kuhn (1962), in his classic study *The Structure of Scientific Revolutions*, described natural philosophy (that is, the study of nature) before the Renaissance as a "pre-science," indicating a period in which there was no agreement about basic principles and ways of working. During the Renaissance, however, agreement grew about methods of inquiry and basic principles, leading to a period of stability that Kuhn called "normal science." It is certainly the case that research in the social sciences currently shares many of the features of a pre-science and so some researchers look forward to the time when there is widespread (if not complete) agreement about ways of working and basic principles. At this point, educational research will join the elite club of sciences producing "reliable knowledge."

A conflicting view is that the very nature of the educational research—the complexity of the things that it studies—means that educational research will never become a "science" in the traditional sense. (In this context, it is interesting to note that it is becoming increasingly recognized, through work in chaos and complexity theory, that many physical systems show the kind of unpredictability prevalent in the social sciences.) In particular, the sensitivity of educational phenomena to changes in contexts suggests that we need a different way of thinking about educational research.

In the physical sciences, reliable knowledge is typically produced by averaging across a large number of cases. Although the behavior of individual particles, such as the molecules in a gas, is impossible to predict, the aggregate behavior of large numbers of such molecules can be predicted quite well. This is similar to the actuarial sciences, in which it is impossible to predict which particular people will die in a given year, but the *numbers* of people dying of particular causes can usually be predicted quite accurately.

In education, such an approach yields stable results only when the sample sizes are sufficiently large to average out all the effects of particular contexts. Research in this tradition often ends up producing only bland platitudes, which seem only to "tell us what we already knew."

In the 1960s and 1970s, partly as a response to the failure of educational research to have much impact on practice, there was a surge in interest in different ways of finding out about and understanding educational processes, principally derived from the more qualitative approaches that had been developed in sociology and anthropology. In particular, many studies addressed the problem of context by looking in detail at a single educational site (see, for example, Lacey, 1970). In such a study, the problem of context is tackled not by trying to average out across all contexts, but by attending to the details of the particular context. The actual setting for the research is laid out in considerable detail, and readers can make up their own minds about how convincing is the argument presented. However, this does not absolve the researcher from any responsibility about how the research is conducted. It is still incumbent on the researcher to inquire and to report in such a way that the meanings of such research findings will be shared, to a greater or lesser extent, by different readers.

QUALITATIVE AND QUANTITATIVE METHODS

Ever since its emergence as a field of inquiry distinct from, for example, educational psychology, research in education has often been polarized between qualitative and quantitative research. Quantitative data are, simply, data that can be represented in terms of numbers, whether they be measurements, grades on some sort of a scale, or even simply counts of people in different categories. By contrast, the responses of individuals to an open-ended questionnaire, their answers in an interview, or notes on their behavior taken by a researcher "in the field," are examples of qualitative data.

Although we frequently talk about quantitative and qualitative data analysis (and researchers often describe themselves as qualitative or quantitative researchers), these terms are not very helpful ways of dividing up data analysis. It needs to be borne in mind that quantitative and qualitative data are means to answering research questions, rather than ends in themselves. Asking whether qualitative or quantitative research is "better" makes no more sense than asking whether a hammer is better than a screwdriver. It depends on what you are trying to do. Unfortunately, there is still a tendency for researchers in education to be much more confident with one or other of these ways of researching, which then influences the kinds of research they choose to do. As Abraham Maslow once said, someone who is good with a hammer tends to think that everything is a nail.

More importantly, the differences between the "qualitative" and "quantitative" camps are much less to do with what kinds of data they generate (that is, is it in the form of numbers or not?), and much more to do with how the research is conducted. For this reason, Salomon (1991) chose instead to distinguish between *analytic* and *systemic* approaches to educational research.

Analytic approaches are those that attempt to control all variables apart from those under study. For example, if we wanted to look at the characteristics of "effective" mathematics or science teachers, we might give a test to a cohort of students at the end of a school year, and see which teacher's classes obtained the highest scores. Of course, this would not be very sensible, because the students in our cohort would have started the year at different levels, so that we would not be able to ascribe differences in performance at the end of the year to the work of the teachers. Those students who obtained the highest marks at the end of the year could simply be those that knew most at the beginning of the year. To control for this, we might also test the students at the beginning of the year, and look at the *gain* in scores over the year (there are technical problems with gain scores—see Cronbach & Furby, 1970—but we shall ignore them here).

However, it is unlikely that we would be satisfied with just a list of the names of the teachers who were good at producing "gain." We should want to know something about them. For example, one obvious question is whether teachers get better as they get older. To look at this we might collect information on the teachers' ages and correlate them with the average gain score for their classes. If we did find that there was a strong correlation between the age of the teacher and the average gain score for the class, would we be entitled to conclude that older teachers were better? Well, in one sense, clearly "yes." We would have found that the average gain scores of older teachers were, in fact, higher than those for younger teachers, but we would not be able to conclude that it was age that was *causing* this improvement. It is more likely that the improvement in gain scores is more strongly related to the number of years of teaching experience, which itself is closely related to age.

We might therefore collect information on both age and teaching experience, and other background factors such as qualifications, sex, ethnicity, and so on. We could then use a statistical technique such as multiple regression to find out which of these variables is the most closely related to the average gain score. If we found that years of teaching experience was the variable most strongly related to average gain score, we would still not have shown that this experience *causes* improved gain scores—merely that there is an association between the two. Nevertheless, in much quantitative research, there is a tendency to regard the variable that we are interested in as the *dependent* variable, implying in some way that its value depends on the values of the other variables. These other variables are often called *independent* variables, implying that their values can be manipulated to affect the value of the dependent variable, and sometimes they are called *explanatory* variables, even though they may not actually explain anything! Because of the misleading impression created by this terminology, I prefer to describe the variables in which we are interested (called the dependent variable earlier) the *focal* variable, and the others as *reference* variables. Much quantitative research is therefore a process of seeing how changes in a focal variable are related to changes in the reference variables.

In this example, although we are not manipulating the values of the reference variables (for example, we do not try to age the teachers in order to see the effect on their teaching!), we do attempt to control their effect. For instance, we might ensure that the number of teachers in each age category was sufficiently large for us to have faith in any results we get.

The result of this is, of course, that our analysis can only lead to indirect conclusions. Cronbach (1957) termed this kind of study *correlational* (even though statistical techniques other than correlation may be used). We may find that two variables are associated, but we can never be sure that one causes the other.

There are three basic reasons why an observed correlation might not be a causal relationship. The first is due to the presence of what is generally called a *third variable*. Two variables are associated, not because either has influence on the other, but because both are causally influenced by an underlying third variable that has not been identified. A classic example of this is the relationship observed in England between the proportion of students in a school eating school lunches (rather than, say, going home, bringing their own food, or buying lunch locally) and the academic success of pupils in a school. The observed relationship between these two variables is very clear: The greater the proportion of children in the school that eat the school's lunches, the worse will be that school's academic record. The "commonsense" interpretation of this is that eating school food is bad for one's academic attainment, so that if you want to do well, stay away from school food! The real cause of this correlation is, of course, due to an underlying third variable—socioeconomic status. It is well known that socioeconomic disadvantage has a negative effect on academic success, and schools in socioeconomically disadvantaged areas will have a greater proportion of students entitled to, and taking advantage of, free school meals.

The second reason for an observed relationship failing to be causal, at least in the direction we suppose, is an "ambiguous direction of causation." A recent analysis of the thousands of school inspections undertaken in England by the U.K. government's Office for Standards in Education (OFSTED, 1995) shows that higher standards of academic achievement are found in larger classes—a result that has been observed in many countries around the world. This led the government to conclude that children did better when taught in larger classes!

In fact, the causal influence runs the other way. Within fixed resources, schools have to decide how best to teach students of different attainment, and a very common solution is to group by attainment or ability. Because they tend to be highly motivated, higher attaining students can be taught in relatively large groups, whereas those with learning disabilities tend to need more individual attention. Therefore, it is not large classes that cause high attainment, but high attainment that causes large classes!

The third situation arises when an observed correlation arises by chance. For example, in most Western societies, there has been, over the last few decades, a strong correlation between teachers' salaries (in real terms) and the incidence of violent crime (both have risen steadily). It might be possible to argue that this is an example of a very deeply hidden third variable, but it is probably safer to regard the correlation as entirely spurious.

Although analytic approaches to research often involve the collection of quantitative data, it is important to note that they need not do so. A common method in studies of children's mathematical cognition involves taking the child out of the mathematics classroom, away from all the distractions, and talking to him or her in a separate room. If we were interested only in cognitive, rather than affective issues, we might also choose only those students who like mathematics. In this particular example, the data that we generate might be entirely qualitative (in the form of an interview transcript), but the important point is that the approach to the research has attempted to isolate particular features of interest, and to control others, which is why this approach would be regarded as more analytic than systemic.

Because the results of purely correlational studies are so difficult to interpret, some experimenters (i.e., Games, 1990) have argued that using data from correlational studies to make causative conclusions is not defensible, either logically or statistically. Such analyses can only suggest hypotheses that then should be tested by *experimental* studies such as those that manipulate the values of reference variables to see their impact on the focal variable.

An example of such a direct experiment is a study by Swift and Gooding (1983) that used feedback devices to get teachers to increase their wait time in classroom questioning. It is well know that most teachers' wait times (that is, the amount of silence that they allow after questions and responses before speaking themselves) are very short (typically of the order of one second). In this study, red and green lights were installed at the back of teachers' classrooms. After the teacher asked a question, or during a pupil's answer, the red light would stay on until 3 seconds had passed, then the green light would glow. The effect of increasing teachers' wait time on students' achievement could then be measured.

The strength of such direct experiments is that we can be reasonably sure that the effects we observe are due to the variables that we have been manipulating. Their weakness is that because they change the situations they investigate, the results are often rather artificial and of limited usefulness.

By contrast, *systemic* research investigates phenomena in their natural settings. Rather than trying to extract certain features and study them out of context, systemic research prioritizes authenticity. The fact that different effects interact with each other and this makes it very difficult to figure out what is going on merely strengthens the argument for this kind of research. Many educational phenomena arise precisely because of the complex interaction between different effects (in the language of chaos theory, they are *emergent* phenomena). Studying them in isolation fails to yield any insight, because the whole is much greater than the sum of the parts. In this sense, even the best classrooms are essentially chaotic places!

Kilpatrick (1993) noted that "the systemic approach currently dominates research in mathematics education" (p. 17), and, indeed, the fact that the following chapters in this volume are primarily concerned with systemic research bears witness to our current concerns with authenticity. Nevertheless, we should also bear in mind that if we only allow ourselves to study natural settings, we can be seriously misled. For example, if, in investigating the relationship between class size and attainment discussed earlier, we had restricted ourselves to naturalistic settings (whether we used quantitative or qualitative techniques), we might well have concluded that children do better in larger classes. This kind of question is much better studied by large-scale direct experiment such as the "Tennessee study," which explored the impact of class size on the achievement of over 6,000 (aged 5–8) in 76 schools. In a random sample of schools, pairs of classes were assigned a third teacher, so that classes of 22–25 students were reduced to 13–17 students per class. The smaller classes produced significantly higher achievement in mathematics and reading, and the beneficial effects were more marked for minority students. Those who had been taught in smaller classes for a single year continued to outperform their peers in subsequent years (Finn & Achilles, 1990).

Because of the randomized design of the experiment, and the fact that steps were taken to ensure that, as far as possible, the only differences between the experimental and control groups was the class size, we can be reasonably confident that we can attribute the improvements to the smaller class sizes (although there have been critiques of the study, such as Prais, 1996, that call even these conclusions into question).

EVIDENCE AND INFERENCE

The relationship between different approaches to research can be clarified by the use of some ideas from *hermeneutics*, the name given to the study of interpretation (named after Hermes, the messenger god of classical Greek mythology). Originally developed in theology for the interpretation of biblical texts, hermeneutics was applied by Thomas Dilthey in the 19th century to philosophy in the wider sense.

Traditionally, it had been assumed that an utterance, picture, piece of writing, and so on (collectively referred to as *text*) has an absolute meaning. In hermeneutics, it is acknowledged that the same text has a different meaning when presented in a different context, and has different meanings when presented to different readers. For example, when a student says that the work that she has been asked to do is "boring" in one context, to a particular teacher, this might be an informed comment that the work was too repetitive, not sufficiently challenging, and unlikely to effect any meaningful learning. In another context, or to another person, "boring" might mean almost the opposite—work that is too challenging, or even threatening. The text (in this case, "It's boring") will be interpreted differently in different contexts, and by different "readers" (for example, teachers). These three key ideas—text, context, and reader—are said to form the *hermeneutic circle*.

In educational research, the text is usually just data. Harding (1987) has suggested, "One could reasonably argue that all evidence-gathering techniques fall into one of the following three categories: listening to (or interrogating) informants, observing behaviour, or examining historical traces and records" (p. 2).

Sometimes the fact that the data have to be *elicited* is obvious, as when we sit down with someone, ask some questions, and tape-record responses. At other times this elicitation process is less obvious. If I am in a classroom observing and making notes on a teacher's actions, it does not feel as if I am eliciting evidence. It feels much more like the evidence presenting itself to me. However, it is important to realize that the things I choose to make notes about, and even the things that I observe (as opposed to those I *see*), depend on my personal theories about what is important. In other words, all data are, in some sense, *elicited*. This is true even in the physical sciences, where the famous physicist von Heisenberg remarked that "what we learn about is not nature itself, but nature exposed to our methods of questioning" (quoted in Johnson, 1996, p. 147).

For some forms of evidence, the process of elicitation is the same as the process of recording the evidence. If I ask a school for copies of its policy documents in a particular area, all the evidence I elicit comes to me in permanent form. However, much of the evidence that is elicited in educational research is ephemeral, and only some of it gets recorded. I might be interviewing someone who is uncomfortable with the idea of speaking into a tape recorder, and so I have to rely on note taking. Even if I do tape-record an interview, this will not record changes in the interviewee's posture that might suggest a different interpretation of what is being said from that which might be made without the visual evidence. The important point here is that it is very rare for all the evidence that is *elicited* to be *recorded*.

During the process of elicitation and recording, and afterwards, the evidence is *interpreted*. Research based on approaches derived from the physical sciences (often called the *positivistic approach*, after a school of philosophy of science popular in the second quarter of this century), emphasizes text at the expense of context and reader. The same educational experiment is either assumed to yield substantially the same results were it to be repeated elsewhere (for example, in another school), or is repeated over so many schools that individual variation is averaged out. Furthermore, it is generally assumed that different people reading the results would be in substantial agreement about how they should be interpreted. Other approaches will give more or less weight to the role played by *context* and *reader*. For example, an ethnography will place much greater weight on the *context* in which the evidence is generated than would be the case for more positivistic approaches to educational research, but would build in safeguards, so that different readers would share, as far as possible, the same interpretations. By contrast, a teacher researching in her own classroom might pay relatively little attention to the need for the meanings of her findings to be shared by others. For her, the meaning of the evidence in her own classroom might well be paramount.

In what sense, therefore, can the results of educational research be regarded as knowledge? The traditional definition of knowledge is that it is simply "justified true belief" (Griffiths, 1967). In other words, we can be said to know something if we believe it, if it is true, and if we have a justification for our belief. There are at least two difficulties with applying this definition in educational research.

The first is that even within a subject as precisely defined as mathematics or science, it is now acknowledged that there are severe difficulties in establishing what, exactly, constitutes a justification or a "warrant" for belief (Kitcher, 1984). The second is that these problems are compounded in the social sciences because the chain of inference might have to be probabilistic, rather than deterministic. In this case, our inference may be justified, but not true!

An alternative view of knowledge, based on Goldman's (1976) proposals for the basis of perceptual knowledge, offers a partial solution to the problem. The central feature is that knowing something is, in essence, the ability to eliminate other rival possibilities. For example, if a person (let us call her "Chris") sees a book in a school, then we are likely to say that Chris knows it is a book. However, if we know (but Chris does not) that students at this school are expert in making replica books that, to all external appearances, look like books but are solid and cannot be opened, then with a justified-true-belief view of knowledge, we would say that Chris does not *know* it is a book, even if it happens to be one. In other words, Chris' knowledge depends on what *we* know.

Goldman's solution to this dilemma is that Chris knows that the object she is looking at is a book if she can distinguish it from a relevant possible state of affairs in which it is not a book. In most cases, the possibility that the book-like object in front of Chris might not be a book is not a relevant state of affairs, and so we would say that Chris does know it is a book.

However, in our particular case there *is* a relevant alternative state of affairs—the book might be a dummy or it might be genuine. Because Chris cannot distinguish between these two possibilities, we would say that Chris does not know (even though she might think that she does!).

Within educational research, therefore, we can view the task of producing knowledge as having two requirements. The first is establishing that the inferences that are made from the evidence are warranted. This is something at which most researchers are relatively good. The second requirement, honored more in its breach than its observance, is establishing that the chosen interpretation is more warranted than plausible rival interpretations.

Such a process can never be completed and there are no off-the-peg methods; only a never-ending process of marshaling evidence that the chosen interpretation is (a) *supported by the available evidence*, and (b) *more warranted than plausible rival interpretations*.

This solution to the problem of knowledge in education is only partial, because it leaves open what counts as a *plausible* rival hypothesis. In practice, even in the physical sciences, this is decided by the consensus of a community of researchers. For example, Collins and Pinch (1993) described the investigations following Joseph Weber's claim in 1969 to have discovered gravitational radiation. The traditional view of the philosophy of science would have us believe that the claim was subjected rigorously to investigation and refutation but, as Collins and Pinch observed, "Theory and experiment alone did not settle the question of the existence of gravitational radiation" (p. 91).

Between 1969 and 1975, six major attempts were made by experimenters around the world to replicate the original findings. All were unsuccessful, and each of these experimenters concluded from their negative results that Weber's original results must have been wrong. In reply, Weber pointed out flaws in each of the unsuccessful attempts, thus, in effect, providing plausible rival hypotheses: in other words, that the null results were due to defects in the experimental procedure. Perhaps more important, Weber's own critics found flaws in five out of the six null results. A "rational" view of science would, at this stage, require that the flaws that were clearly present in the six null studies be rectified, and the experiments repeated, but this did not happen. Ultimately, the scientific community seems to have decided that Weber's alternative explanations of the null results were simply not plausible, and now regards gravitational radiation as a dead issue, although Weber himself continues to publish papers with new evidence and arguments in favor of his view (Collins & Pinch, 1993).

In the social sciences, the job of deciding what counts as a plausible rival hypothesis is also left to a community of researchers. Sometimes what is and is not plausible is made absolutely explicit, in the form of a theoretical stance. In other words, a researcher might say, "Because I am working from this theoretical basis, I interpret these results in the following way, and I do not consider that alternative interpretation to be plausible." More often, communities of researchers operate within a shared discourse that rules out some alternative hypotheses, although these tend to be implicit and are often unrecognized.

To sum up, evidence is elicited, and, if necessary, recorded in some form and interpreted (not necessarily in that order!). The interpretations are validated by the elimination of plausible rival interpretations of the evidence, and the definition of what counts as plausible is determined by the discourse within which the validation takes place.

MEANINGS AND CONSEQUENCES

The earlier discussion dealt with the production of "educational knowledge," which, although it acknowledges the role of context in interpreting text, still places substantial emphasis on the production of shared meanings within a community of researchers.

During the 1980s, this concern with sharing of meanings across readers was questioned in what is sometimes called *action research*. In action research, what is important is the potential of the research to transform practice for the individual school or even for the individual teacher. Even if the research has different meanings (or is meaningless) for those in different contexts, this is not a problem, as long as it has meaning for the teacher doing the research. There is no doubt that action research has huge transformative potential for the individuals involved, but many have argued that it cannot be classed as research per se, because the research makes no effort to produce meanings that are shared beyond the immediate context and readers.

My concern here is not, however, with whether action research is valid research or not, but to show how it can fit into a theoretical framework and to examine how it differs from other approaches to research.

In all research, there is a tension between the *meanings* and *consequences* of research. For example, it would not be unusual for a researcher to discover something about a teacher's practice (perhaps through interviews with students) that appeared to be preventing the students from learning effectively. The question is, therefore, should the researcher communicate this to the teacher? In the traditional research paradigm, the answer would be a resounding "no." Feedback by the researcher to the teacher might change the teacher's subsequent behavior, thus rendering the results of the research much more difficult to interpret. At the other extreme, many advocates of action research would say that such important evidence should be fed back to the teacher, and if this changes what is being investigated, then so be it. Put crudely, in traditional text- and context focused research, unfortunate (or nonexistent!) consequences are frequently justified and legitimated by the need for shared meanings. In action research, any weaknesses in the extent to which meanings of the research findings are shared are justified and legitimated by the consequences of the research.

A full consideration of the nature of educational research must, therefore, take account of the consequences, as well as the meanings of the research. The importance of consequences in the validation of research is made much more explicit in the classification of inquiry systems developed by Churchman and his associates, to which I now turn.

INQUIRY SYSTEMS

Different methods of inquiry in the natural, physical, and social sciences were investigated by Churchman (1971), who regarded all kinds of inquiry as capable of being classified in five broad categories, each of which he labeled with the name of a philosopher (Leibniz, Locke, Kant, Hegel, Singer) whom he felt best exemplified the stance involved in adopting the system, and in particular, what is to be regarded as *evidence*.

More detailed accounts of the systems can be found in the work of Churchman (1971) and his colleagues (Mitroff & Kilmann, 1978; Mitroff & Sagasti, 1973), and Messick (1989). However, it is perhaps easier to understand the framework when it is applied to a "real" research question in mathematics or science education—should students be taught these subjects in mixed-ability groups?

One approach to this problem (and one far too common in the popular media) is to use only rhetorical tools to attempt to establish the truth of the proposition. The following argument is typical:

> Restricting the range of attainment within a class allows teachers a far greater range of possible approaches than would be the case if they had to teach a class with the full range of attainment. A teacher of a "setted" class can do whatever a teacher of a mixed-attainment class would do, but in addition can use a wide range of approaches that would not be appropriate for a mixed-attainment class. Therefore, by definition, setting can be no worse, and has the potential to be better than mixed-attainment grouping.

This would be an example of what Churchman (1971) called a *Leibnizian* inquiry system, in which certain fundamental assumptions are made, from which deductions are drawn by the use of formal reasoning rather than by using empirical data (evidence from the situation under study). In a Leibnizian system, reason and rationality are held to be the most important sources of evidence. Although there are occasions in educational research when such methods are appropriate, it is usually far more appropriate to use some sort of empirical data in the inquiry.

The most common use of data in inquiry in both the physical and social sciences is via what Churchman (1971) called a *Lockean* inquiry system. In such an inquiry, evidence is derived principally from the observations of the physical world. Empirical data are collected, and then an attempt is made to build a theory that accounts for the data. This corresponds to what is sometimes called a "naive inductivist" paradigm in the physical sciences (Chalmers, 1978), and is most appropriate for well-structured problems.

In the context of our investigation into mixed-ability grouping, we might design an experiment in which students were tested on their mathematical attainment, randomly assigned to either mixed-ability groups or homogenous-ability groups, and then retested after some period of teaching. From the resulting data, we would then attempt to build a coherent account of what was going on. An example of this is provided by Pallas, Entwisle, Alexander, and Stluka (1994), who proposed three mechanisms for the effects of ability grouping: instructional, social, and institutional effects. For each of the three mechanisms, they worked out what patterns one would expect to find in the data if that mechanism were predominant, and they then investigated the patterns found in an already existing data set, in order to select the most convincing theory.

The major difficulty with a Lockean approach is that, because observations are regarded as the most important form of evidence, it is necessary for all observers to agree on what they have observed. Because what we observe is based on the personal theories we hold, different people will observe different things, even in the same classroom.

Thus, for less well-structured problems, or problems where different people are likely to disagree what precisely *is* the problem, a *Kantian* inquiry system is more appropriate. This involves the deliberate framing of multiple alternative perspectives on both theory and data (thus subsuming both Leibnizian and Lockean systems). One way of doing this is to build different theories on the basis of the same set of data. Alternatively, we could build two theories related to the problem, and then for each theory, generate appropriate data (it might well be that different kinds of data were collected for the two theories).

For the issue of mixed-ability teaching, this could involve development of two alternative theories. For example, we might examine the relative effectiveness of mixed-ability and homogenous-ability teaching in terms of achievement (Slavin & Karweit, 1985), or in terms of socialization (Abraham, 1989; Ball, 1981). It is not immediately apparent where these two theories overlap and where they conflict, but by attempting to reconcile the alternative conceptualizations, new theories can develop.

This idea of reconciling two (or more) rival theories is more fully developed in a *Hegelian* inquiry system, where antithetical and mutually inconsistent theories are developed. Not content with building plausible theories, the Hegelian inquirer takes the most plausible theory, and then investigates what would have to be different about the world for the *exact opposite* of the most plausible theory itself to be plausible (if the answer is "not very much," then this raises serious questions about the justification for our beliefs!). The tension produced by confrontation between conflicting theories forces the assumptions of each theory to be questioned, thus possibly creating a synthesis of the rival theories at a higher level of abstraction.

A Hegelian approach to our ability-grouping inquiry would involve researchers who have adopted a socialization perspective to think through what would have to be different about the world for the exact opposite of their theory to be true. Those who adopt the achievement perspective would do the same, which might then result in sufficient clarification of the issues to make a synthesis of the two perspectives, at a higher level of abstraction, possible.

The differences among Lockean, Kantian, and Hegelian inquiry systems were summed up by Churchman (1971):

> The Lockean inquirer displays the "fundamental" data that all experts agree are accurate and relevant, and then builds a consistent story out of these. The Kantian inquirer displays the same story from different points of view, emphasizing thereby that what is put into the story by the internal mode of representation is not given from the outside. But the Hegelian inquirer, using the same data, tells two stories, one supporting the most prominent policy on one side, the other supporting the most promising story on the other side. (p. 177)

However, the most important feature of Churchman's typology is that we can inquire about inquiry systems, questioning the values and ethical assumptions that these systems themselves embody. This inquiry of inquiry systems is itself, of course, an inquiry system, termed *Singerian* by Churchman after the philosopher E. A. Singer (see Singer, 1959). Such an approach entails a constant questioning of the assumptions of inquiry systems. Tenets, no matter how fundamental they appear to be, are themselves to be challenged in order to cast a new light on the situation under investigation. This leads directly and naturally onto examination of the values and ethical considerations inherent in theory building.

In a Singerian inquiry, there is no solid foundation. Instead, everything is "permanently tentative"; instead of asking what "is," we ask what are the implications and consequences of different assumptions about what "is taken to be":

> The "is taken to be" is a self-imposed imperative of the community. Taken in the context of the whole Singerian theory of inquiry and progress, the imperative has the status of an ethical judgment. That is, the community judges that to accept its instruction is to bring about a suitable tactic or strategy.... The acceptance may lead to social actions outside of inquiry, or to new kinds of inquiry, or whatever. Part of the community's judgment is concerned with the *appropriateness of these actions from an ethical point of view*. Hence the linguistic puzzle which bothered some empiricists—how the inquiring system can pass linguistically from "is" statements to "ought" statements—is no puzzle at all in the Singerian inquirer: the inquiring system speaks exclusively in the "ought," the "is" being only a convenient *façon de parler* when one wants to block out

the uncertainty in the discourse. (Churchman, 1971, p. 202; my emphasis in fourth sentence)

The important point about adopting a Singerian perspective is that with such an inquiry system, one can never absolve oneself from the consequences of one's research. Educational research is a process of *modeling* educational processes, and the models are never right or wrong, merely more or less appropriate for a particular purpose.

A Singerian approach to ability grouping in mathematics would then look at not only all possible perspectives, but also at the ethical and value positions underlying such perspectives. Even if homogenous ability grouping advantages higher attainers more than it disadvantages low attainers (as argued by Allan, 1991), we would also have to ask whether it is ethical to create a situation in which the consequences are likely to be that lower attaining students are taught by less skilled and less qualified teachers (Oakes, 1985). Such difficult questions can be avoided within Leibnizian, Lockean, Kantian, and Hegelian inquiry systems, but must be confronted within a Singerian inquiry system.

Educational research can therefore be characterized as an never-ending process of assembling evidence that:

- Particular inferences are warranted on the basis of the available evidence.
- Such inferences are more warranted than plausible rival inferences.
- The consequences of such inferences are ethically defensible.

In addition, the basis for warrants, other plausible interpretations, and the ethical bases for defending the consequences are constantly open to scrutiny and question.

CONCLUSION

In this chapter, different approaches to educational inquiry have been characterized in terms of the hermeneutic notions of text, context, and reader. Traditional positivistic forms of research seek to produce texts (for example, data, research findings, and so on) the meanings of which are shared by different readers, and across a variety of contexts. Other approaches (particularly those labeled "qualitative") acknowledge the context-dependent nature of the research findings, but nevertheless seek to produce texts with widely shared meaning. However, research results that have widely shared meanings appear to be more difficult for teachers to make sense of and to make use of in improving their practice.

The approach sometimes called "action research" addresses this by not even trying to generalize meanings across readers—what matters is the meaning of the research findings for the teacher in her own classroom. This lack of generalizable meaning for action research is justified by its potential to transform the practice of the individual teacher. There appears, therefore, to be a trade-off between meanings and consequences. Put crudely, in action research the lack of shared meanings is justified by the consequences, whereas in other kinds of research the lack of consequences is justified by more widely shared meanings.

The tension between meanings and consequences was then further explored in terms of Churchman's fivefold classification of inquiry systems, based on what is taken to be the primary source of evidence:

Inquiry system	Source of evidence
Leibnizian	Reasoning
Lockean	Observation
Kantian	Representation
Hegelian	Dialectic
Singerian	Ethical values

Adopting a Singerian perspective, it was argued that educational research involved marshaling evidence that:

- The interpretations made of the data were warranted.
- The interpretations were more warranted than plausible rival interpretations.
- The consequences of such interpretations were ethically defensible.

From the point of view of the individual researcher, the important message is that nothing that is written about the process of research relieves the individual researcher of the responsibility for the research undertaken, and what happens as a result of that research.

REFERENCES

Abraham, J. (1989). Testing Hargreaves' and Lacey's differentiation–polarisation theory in a setted comprehensive. *British Journal of Sociology, 40*(1), 46–81.

Allan, S. D. (1991, March). Ability-grouping research reviews: What do they say about grouping and the gifted? *Educational Leadership, 48*, 60–65.

Ball, S. J. (1981). *Beachside comprehensive*. Cambridge, England: Cambridge University Press.

Begle, E. G., & Gibb, E. G. (1980). Why do research? In R. J. Shumway (Ed.), *Research in mathematics education* (pp. 3–19). Washington, DC: National Council of Teachers of Mathematics.

Chalmers, A. F. (1978). *What is this thing called science?* Milton Keynes, England: Open University Press.

Churchman, C. W. (1971). *The design of inquiring systems: Basic concepts of system and organization.* New York: Basic Books.

Collins, H. M., & Pinch, T. (1993). *The golem: What everyone should know about science.* Cambridge, England: Cambridge University Press.

Cronbach, L. J. (1957). The two disciplines of scientific psychology. *American Psychologist, 12,* 671–684.

Cronbach, L. J., & Furby, L. (1970). How should we measure "change"—or should we? *Psychological Bulletin, 74*(1), 68–80.

Cronbach, L. J., & Suppes, P. (Eds.). (1969). *Research for tomorrow's schools: Disciplined enquiry for education.* New York: Macmillan.

Finn, J. D., & Achilles, C. M. (1990). Answers and questions about class size: A statewide experiment. *American Educational Research Journal, 27*(3), 557–577.

Games, P. A. (1990). Correlation and causation: a logical snafu. *Journal of Experimental Education, 58*(3), 239–246.

Goldman, A. I. (1976). Discrimination and perceptual knowledge. *Journal of Philosophy, 73*(20), 771–791.

Griffiths, A. P. (Ed.). (1967). *Knowledge and belief.* Oxford, England: Oxford University Press.

Harding, S. (1987). Introduction: is there a feminist method? In S. Harding (Ed.), *Feminism and methodology: Social science issues* (pp. 1–14). Bloomington, IL, and Milton Keynes, England: Indiana University Press/Open University Press.

Johnson, G. (1996). *Fire in the mind: Science, faith and the search for order.* London: Viking.

Kilpatrick, J. (1993). Beyond face value: Assessing research in mathematics education. In G. Nissen & M. Blomhøj (Eds.), *Criteria for scientific quality and relevance in the didactics of mathematics* (pp. 15–34). Roskilde, Denmark: University of Roskilde.

Kitcher, P. (1984). *The nature of mathematical knowledge.* New York: Oxford University Press.

Kuhn, T. S. (1962). *The structure of scientific revolutions.* Chicago: University of Chicago Press.

Lacey, C. (1970). *Hightown Grammar: The school as a social system.* Manchester, England: Manchester University Press.

Messick, S. (1989). Validity. In R. L. Linn (Ed.), *Educational measurement* (pp. 13–103). Washington, DC: American Council on Education/Macmillan.

Mitroff, I. I., & Kilmann, R. H. (1978). *Methodological approaches to social science.* San Francisco: Jossey-Bass.

Mitroff, I. I., & Sagasti, F. R. (1973). Epistemology as general systems theory: An approach to the design of complex decision-making experiments. *Philosophy of Social Sciences, 3,* 117–134.

Oakes, J. (1985). *Keeping track: How schools structure inequality.* New Haven, CT: Yale University Press.

Office for Standards in Education (OFSTED). (1995). *Class size and the quality of education: A report from the Office of Her Majesty's Chief Inspector of Schools.* London: Author.

Pallas, A. M., Entwisle, D. R., Alexander, K. L., & Stluka, M. F. (1994). Ability-group effects: Instructional, social, or institutional? *Sociology of Education, 67*(1), 27–46.

Prais, S. (1996). Class size and learning. *Oxford Review of Education, 22*(4), 319–414.

Salomon, G. (1991). Transcending the qualitative–quantitative debate: The analytic and systemic approaches to educational research. *Educational Researcher, 20*(6), 10–18.

Singer, E. A, Jr. (1959). *Experience and reflection.* Philadelphia: University of Pennsylvania Press.

Slavin, R. E., & Karweit, N. L. (1985). Effects of whole class, ability grouped, and individualized learning on mathematics achievement. *American Educational Research Journal, 22*(3), 351–367.

Swift, J. N., & Gooding, C. T. (1983). Interaction of wait time feedback and questioning instruction on middle school science teaching. *Journal of Research in Science Teaching, 20*(8), 721–730.

2

Ethnography in the Classroom

Robyn Zevenbergen
Griffith University, Gold Coast, Queensland

WHAT IS ETHNOGRAPHY?

Ethnography represents a distinct break from the more traditional forms of research found in educational research, a point that Eisenhart (1988) actively encourages within mathematics education. In its simplest form, ethnography refers to "writing about a way of life ... [which] involves the researcher in describing the way of life of a group of people" (McNeil, 1990, p. 64). The methodology has been adapted by various researchers to suit their particular needs (Hammersley, 1992b), but there are a number of principles that define what is characteristic of the ethnographic tradition. Shimahara (1990) argued that the following three premises underpin the tradition of ethnography:

- [There is an interest] in sociocultural patterns of human behavior, rather than the quantification of human events.
- Cultural events are understood and categorized in terms of the cultural actor's definition of human events.
- [There is a focus] on on-going settings in sociocultural contexts, such as communities, educational institutions, and classrooms where events occur as human interaction takes place. (pp. 80–82)

The purpose of ethnography is to describe the culture of the people under study in a manner that it is acceptable to them as a true repre-

sentation of their way of life (McNeil, 1990). It seeks to describe and illumi-
nate "the fine grained details of school life . . . [that] often contrast sharply
with official accounts of the schooling process" (Woods, 1988, p. 91). Essentially it is a phenomenological approach to research in which the researcher
acts as a fly on the wall, taking in everything and presenting the data in an
objective form. The task of the researcher is to get inside the heads of the
participants until it is possible to see the world from their perspective.
Ethnography permits the observation of daily life in classrooms, the collection of data on classroom life, and interviews to inform further the data that
have been collected. Accordingly, this methodological approach enables
some description of the lived experiences of the target schools, classrooms,
or selected sites. It is particularly useful for identifying and understanding
social and cultural norms in mathematics classrooms. The knowledge
gained from ethnographic studies can complement the enormous amount
of research conducted under the broad umbrella of cognitive psychology
to provide a richer and more complete understanding of the teaching and
learning of mathematics.

METHODS OF DATA COLLECTION

Two main techniques of data collection found in ethnography are participant
observation and interviews. A third form of data collection, document or
artifact analysis, is also employed. It is recognized that this third form has
application in the mathematics classroom, where documents such as books,
students' work, mathematics posters, and so on constitute materials that
can be used to inform the research. However, participant observation and
interviews are discussed in greater detail here later, as these can incorporate
aspects of document analysis.

Participant Observation

A distinction needs to be made between the nonparticipant and participant
roles open to the ethnographer/researcher. When researchers enter the field
and attempt to be unobtrusive, keeping the social milieu as little informed
as possible so that the true nature of the research will not be affected or
polluted by such knowledge, they assume a nonparticipatory role. The
school ethnographies of McLaren (1980) and Jackson (1990) are of a nonparticipant type—they entered the field and tried to have as little effect as
possible. McLaren's (1989, 1993) later studies are of the participant-observer
form, in which he becomes implicated in the life of the school, asking
questions and becoming involved with the students. In considering which
role the researcher will take, it is necessary to decide whether it is possible

to sit in a classroom, observe the daily grind of school life, and be unobtrusive, or whether it is a better option to be a participant in that context and observe and ask questions on the run.

For many contemporary mathematics teachers there is immense pressure to teach a crowded curriculum to a diverse range of students. In numerous cases, the stretched resources (human and material) of classrooms mean that teachers are appreciative of any assistance that an involved participant observer can provide. Associated with this is the reaction of students to having a silent observer in the classroom. This is a potential distraction, whereas another "teacher" in the room would not impact on the teaching and learning of mathematics in any significant way. This factor is important when considering the learning environments of many mathematics classrooms, wherein a resistance to the subject already exists among the students. A stranger sitting and observing is a potential distracter for teachers and students, having the capacity to inhibit good practice and disturb the learning environment. To this end, in most cases, the role of participant observer is a more appropriate role for contemporary mathematics classrooms.

The goal of participant observation is to make the familiar strange, and the strange familiar (Erickson, 1973). It is not to impose the view of the researcher, but to learn from the participants. For the researcher entering the mathematics classroom, the purpose of the observation is to develop an understanding of the ways in which a mathematics culture is being constructed and reproduced within the context of that classroom or school. By being part of the context, the researcher, through intense and prolonged observation, is expected to "understand the research setting, its participants, and their behaviour" (Glesne & Peshkin, 1992, p. 42). Glesne and Peshkin suggested that "you are not in the research to preach or evaluate, nor to compete for prestige or status. Your focus is on others, and you work to stay out of the limelight."

The role of the participant observer is to observe the "natural" setting, so it is seen as imperative that the presence of the researcher not alter the setting. When observing mathematics classrooms as a participant observer, the ethnographer is likely to assume a role such as a teacher's assistant. Such a role enables the researcher to observe such things as the delivery of content and instructions used by the teacher; the ways in which students work or avoid work; teachers interacting with students; the tactics that students use to negotiate the mathematical tasks set by the teacher; the strategies students use to negotiate meanings with their peers or their teacher; and the types and forms of artifacts (such as books and equipment) present in a classroom and how they are used by students and teachers. Being an active participant in that environment, the researcher can ask spontaneous questions as they arise without being seen as threatening or invasive. As a perceived member of that community, the ethnographer takes on a role that is not dysfunctional within that context.

Interviews

The other principal technique for ethnographic data collection is that of the interview (see chap. 4 also). Most often interviews are used to supplement the information gleaned from observations. Spradley (1979) supports the use of ethnographic interviews to complement the data collected through observation. Such data can be used to increase the understanding of the phenomenon under investigation, to incorporate different perspectives, and to make effective use of time (Glesne & Peshkin, 1992). Two major forms of interviews are available—the unstructured and informal interview, or the more formal and structured interview. These techniques provide a useful mechanism through which it is possible to ascertain teachers' views about issues arising out of the research and to address issues of validity. Taking the role of participant observer allows the researcher to ask informal and unstructured questions as they arise. Such questions can be asked in the context of the classroom, while teachers and students are involved in the lesson, or in the informal discussions that arise after lessons. Typically, the questions arise spontaneously from the environment and may be focused on the mathematical content that is being addressed, the processes that are being used, the rationale behind some actions, and so forth.

The more formal interviews may be conducted at various points in the research process. The questions may be used to clarify points that are emerging from the research in order to develop a more complete picture. In most instances the more formal interviews will be conducted away from the research site—either in a geographical sense, when the participants are interviewed away from the classroom, or in a temporal sense, when the interview is conducted outside of class time.

The use of data collected from interviews allows different perspectives to be brought to the research process. It is expected that students will have different perspectives from teachers and researchers, so the role of interviews is to bring forward these different perspectives in order to develop a better understanding of the mathematics classroom. The students' perspective as to why the teacher adopts a rote-and-drill method for teaching about area, rather than what could be described broadly as an constructivist approach, is often quite different from that of the teacher or even the researcher. Similarly, a broad question such as "What is mathematics?" would yield substantially different responses from different cohorts of participants. Yet it is important that such differences (or similarities) be made known through the research process if a deep understanding of the culture of mathematics classrooms is to be achieved.

In developing an ethnography of a mathematics classroom, it is possible that the questions asked of the various participants will be different. In interviewing students, it may be necessary to access information through a variety of questions, because students will not have well-formed or articulated concepts related to the focus of the research. Hence, to access what students experience as the culture of mathematics, questions which ask them to describe a typical mathematics lesson will be needed: what students see as the reason for studying mathematics; how long they expect to study mathematics for; and so on. By contrast, other participants may have more articulate responses and hence more direct questions can be posed.

Interviews can be used to supplement, clarify, or validate the data gained from other sources. Accordingly, they can be employed to gain access to teachers' and students' impressions, beliefs, assumptions, and justifications of observed events. For example, the use of manipulatives in early childhood classrooms is a relatively common phenomenon, but less common in junior secondary schools. The researcher may observe this "fact," but needs to ascertain why teachers adopt this practice, or why they think that this is an appropriate action (or inappropriate, as the case may be). Similarly, teachers may adopt practices that are teacher-directed pedagogies. By asking questions regarding the rationale for such actions, access to information about teaching, learning, knowledge, history, and so on can be accessed. Having conducted such interviews, it is then possible to represent participants in a way which will be seen as fair and true.

CONDUCTING THE RESEARCH

In the following sections I discuss the process of commencing the research and, perhaps more important, its continuation.

Negotiating Access and Gatekeeping

Before beginning classroom or school ethnographies, the researcher must negotiate access to schools and classrooms. The process is fraught with power relationships, some of which will be known (as formal procedures) and others will be hidden. Power can be exerted by bureaucrats, heads of schools, teachers, and students, and can have insidious effects on the research and its progress.

Early consideration must be given to bureaucratic and legal restrictions. For example, in the 1990s Australian context, to gain access to government schools in Queensland required researchers to obtain permission from the State Education Department. This involved a very detailed application that was aimed at protecting staff and students, and required a full description of the research process before consideration would be given to allowing access. By contrast, school principals in the state of Victoria were responsible for any research undertaken within the school environment, so it was necessary to deal with individual principals to negotiate access to schools. Independent schools could be negotiated directly with the head of the school, or, in the case of the Catholic system, through the regional Catholic Education Office.

Having complied with government requirements, negotiating access to individual schools and classrooms is fraught with the need for many decisions, because this part of the ethnography is very much a "people process" that can have effects on whether or not one actually gains access to the desired school. This process also influences the quality of the relationships, and hence the data, that will be obtained during the study.

Gaining access to schools is a process that:

> Refers to your acquisition of consent to go where you want, observe what you want, talk to whomever you want, obtain and read whatever documents you require, and do all of this for whatever period of time you need to satisfy you research purposes. (Glesne & Peshkin, 1992, p. 33)

At a formal level, the degree of access that is gained will determine the type of data that can be collected and as such, it may be necessary to consider whether the type of access granted is adequate to complete the research satisfactorily. At a more human level, the access that is granted may be enhanced or sabotaged by the people with whom the researcher may come in contact.

In the initial stage of negotiating access to schools/classrooms, the researcher is compelled to talk to a range of people including school secretaries, school principals, teachers, and students, all of whom are able to exert some control over the access that one gains. Each of these people can be seen to be exercising power and they will often act as a gatekeeper, influencing the forms of access, and hence data. Glesne and Peshkin (1992) recommended that this process begins at the top of the hierarchy so that acceptance filters down. They argued that if acceptance is gained within the lower ranks, it may be negated by those higher up. Gaining access to mathematics classrooms under this model necessitates permission being granted by the principal initially, as this will then filter through heads of departments (as in the secondary school sector) or deputy principals (in primary schools) through to the individual classroom teachers.

Gatekeeping

Even when it is possible to negotiate with teachers in an informal context, at some time it is necessary to gain official access to the school. The first formal point of contact with schools usually will be through the school secretary. This may be achieved through telephoning, writing a letter, or visiting the school. Having passed this point of entry, the process of negotiation access will be greatly enhanced or inhibited by particular contacts. The form of contact will depend on the context and the relationship that exists between the researcher and the researched.

The access that is negotiated has a powerful influence on the data that are collected, the rapport that is established, and the reflexivity of the research. These issues are discussed in greater detail in later sections.

Levels of Negotiation and Access

Having gained the principal's permission to enter the school, it is then necessary to negotiate access with the participating teachers, and through them, access to their classrooms. Depending on how teachers are selected for the study, varying degrees of access will be granted. For example, if there is a strong managerial line within a school and teachers are instructed to participate in a study, then effective access is likely to be minimal. Teachers in this situation are able to exert a more covert form of resistance to the research by displaying a disinterest in the project and by withholding information from the researcher. Furthermore, teachers are not at liberty to willingly participate in the study (or to exit from the project), thus creating a dilemma for the researcher. By contrast, where teachers self-select to participate in a study, access is likely to be greater and richer.

At these initial meetings, it is important that teachers be given an outline of the principles of procedure developed for the project (see, i.e., Kemmis & Robottom, 1981). Such documents or discussions outline the mutual rights and obligations of each party and the research process, and may include such issues as the ethics of the research; anonymity; rights to read, alter, or veto writings; expectations of input into the work; verification of transcripts; and input to the research; and may stress the intrusive nature of the research. At such meetings, teachers should be given the opportunity to withdraw from the project if they do not want to participate. However, although this right is given explicitly, it may not be the case that teachers have the option to withdraw, thereby raising some doubt about the value of such documents.

Degrees of Access

Having gained access to mathematics classrooms, varying degrees of teacher access will be achieved. In part, the variation is related to the ways in which teachers are selected for the research. This can range from full participation to peripheral participation, or even subverted exclusion. The degrees of access can also be influenced by, among other things, teachers' familiarity with research processes and commitment to professional development. Of particular relevance to mathematics classrooms is the degree of confidence teachers have in their content knowledge and pedagogical knowledge. Teachers who are confident in these areas are more likely to welcome a researcher than their colleagues who do not possess such confidence.

Rapport

Research often commences with tenuous relationships between the researcher and the teachers. A goal for the researcher is that over time, rapport with the teachers will develop, and that the research will progress in a way that will be beneficial to all parties. However, building rapport with the people involved in a research project is a long-winded process, and does not always come to fruition. Where rapport does develop, access to a wide variety and quality of information can be achieved. Conversely, a lack of rapport with the participants and their disinterest in the project raises a number of issues. It is necessary to develop good rapport to gain and maintain access to information, and so its absence hinders the degree and type of information and collaboration.

Where there are limited time frames, as is often the case in contracted research projects or postgraduate studies, time is at a premium, so there is often a sense of having to work within the constraints imposed by the context of the study. A contracted time frame also impacts on the development of rapport. Glesne and Peshkin (1992) argued this when they stated:

> If you are around long enough, you can verify that the self that you are projecting is an enduring self: You have said that you will maintain anonymity of respondents and you *always* do, and you have said that you have not come to find fault and you *never* do. Time allows you to substantiate that you will keep the promises that you made when you were negotiating access, and that you will remain the person you have been showing yourself to be. (p. 97)

Compounding the time constraint are the often lengthy negotiation procedures to gain access to the schools; thus the researcher does not have time available to spend negotiating access to another site and recommencing the research. This can be further compounded when there are limited sites that should be part of the research profile.

Obstacles to developing rapport include the imposition of research; the distribution of power between the researcher/academic and the teachers; and the manner in which researchers present themselves in terms of dress, speech, and behavior.

By contrast, where rapport develops, the process of research is more likely to be enjoyable, access to more information is practicable, and a reflexivity between the researcher and the participants is made possible. In the ideal situation, participation, rapport, and collaboration make for the development of a very rich project. However, such an ideal may be very elusive and, as such, it is often necessary to work within the constraints of the project. The disinterest and subtle forms of resistance evoked where such ideals are not met may not call for massive changes to the original research proposal, but it is likely that some modifications may be necessary if the project is to progress at an acceptable level. Negotiation between the supervisor and the student is critical in developing and maintaining a worthwhile project under such constraints.

COLLECTING ETHNOGRAPHIC DATA: FIELD NOTES AND VIDEOTAPE

The presence of an intruder writing copious notes may be seen as threatening by both the teacher and students and consequently affecting the naturalness of the setting. Taking the role of a participant observer suggests that a possible compromise in the quality and quantity of field notes is necessary because the researcher would not be able to simply sit, observe, and record to the degree needed for a project. A solution to this problem is the use of a video camera. It is possible for one to take on the role of participant observer while the video camera assumes the primary role of note taker, allowing the observer to take field notes to supplement the video data. A spin-off of this approach is that the tapes can be reviewed for a more fine-grained analysis of classroom practice at any time. The use of the video camera essentially provides an extra pair of eyes in the classroom, eyes that are able to observe, and record, in far greater detail than is otherwise possible. Events that can be missed in manual observation of the classroom will be recorded permanently on tape and noticed when the tapes are reviewed. This approach also provides an excellent means of examining closely classroom discourse in order to look at the ways in which students are responding to classroom practice. This method of collecting classroom data has been undertaken and justified by a number of researchers (such as Mehan, 1982, 1992a, 1992b; Schratz & Mehan, 1993) and its use is supported by Shratz and Mehan (1993), who wrote:

> Analyzing the micro-world of classroom discourse enables the researcher to examine more critically the factors that explain school performance, such as social class, heredity, ethnicity on the macro level of society. Thus video recording becomes a political tool in disclosing social injustice of educational practice. (p. 4)

Repeatedly viewing the tapes allows the researcher to "see and hear a different version of social life than is otherwise possible" (Mehan, 1992b).

Using video as a resource for data collection enables richer data to be collected. This can be a substantial issue because although access may be granted to classrooms, it may be only token access. With this problem, it is imperative to gather as much data as possible in the least obtrusive and by the most efficient means. Video recording caters for this contracted time frame and detailed analysis.

There are, however, problems associated with the use of video cameras. The extra pair of eyes is a form or surveillance that must be considered carefully before its introduction. After a while, students begin to take the camera for granted (Mehan, 1992b), and so forget its presence, with the result that it may reveal behaviors that are seen as unacceptable in the mathematics classroom. In one instance (see Zevenbergen, 1995; Zevenbergen, Cockayne, & Cherry, 1992), students displayed cunning behavior to avoid the set work. As the teacher roamed the classroom, they were off task unless the teacher was in close proximity, when one would take the lead and ask a question related to a task. At the end of the lesson, the group shared their answers so that if they were called on to offer an answer to one of the problems, they could respond. The strategies were highly developed and provided an excellent means for the students to avoid participating in the mathematics activities, although their efforts also had the potential for excluding them from the learning of mathematics. Access to this type of behavior would not have been possible without camera surveillance. Hence it raises ethical concerns about the intrusiveness of the camera and what is to be done as a consequence of any observation. Is the researcher morally obliged to inform the teacher about this class behavior so that this cohort of students will not be excluded from gaining access to mathematical knowledge? Is the classroom environment organized in such a way that the cohort is not interested in learning mathematics, and if this is the case, what are the options for the researcher?

ANALYZING AND REPRESENTING DATA

Having collected the data, the researcher begins the task of analyzing what has been collected. Some of the analysis of the data begins shortly after the research commences. Data from field notes will be analyzed to look for patterns and relationships. In this case, field notes will incorporate both observations and interview data. Patterns in thoughts and behaviors become the focus, and as vague patterns begin to appear from the copious amounts of data generated, the researcher continues to compare these patterns with the new data. Patterns will be sought in the various techniques used for collecting the data (that is, interviews and observations), as well as in the responses and stimuli noted in the field notes, transcripts, and so forth. Similarities and exceptions are sought. For example, in trying to develop a description of a constructivist classroom, similarities in teachers' and students' descriptions of pedagogy, good practice, and theories of learning will provide evidence of what constitutes practice in this context. Differences in descriptions will also provide key evidence, so that although nonconstructivist classrooms may possess similarities with a constructivist classroom, the differences between the two contexts will indicate the key characteristics of the lived experiences for teachers and students in constructivist classrooms. Similarly, differences between and within cohorts at the one site will indicate areas for further inquiry and clarification. Key events also become a touchstone for analysis. Events such as the Friday test or the textbook activity provide a rich source of evidence of the hidden dimensions of social life in the mathematics classroom. Questions such as, "Who will have access to the LEGO blocks?" or "Who will have first turn on the new computer software?" show important aspects of social dynamics of the classroom. As analyses begin to take some shape, sharing drafts with participants and other colleagues can improve the accuracy of the descriptions (Fetterman, 1989).

The researcher is able to coordinate the perspectives of teachers and students so that they tie in with the aims of the research. In selecting some data and omitting others, the researcher must make choices about which are relevant to the overall aims of the research, and which substantiate the claims being made. Although much data is collected, only a small portion is used in the final product, and decisions have to be made as to what is to be included and discarded, and how that which remains will be represented. Many neophyte researcher face great dilemmas and angst about the inclusion of some data and the rejection of others. As such, guidance and support in this process is critical.

This means that the researcher is in control of what is used and what is to be rejected. Hence, one of the major dilemmas facing the researcher with analyses and writing relates to the representation of the participants. The problems associated with representation are perennial, as exemplified by Schratz and Mehan's (1993) comment that there is a "dilemma of paying attention to the personal voices from the field and at the same time analyzing them from an external perspective" (p. 4). The incorporation of interview data permits a wealth of valuable insights into the construction of meaning, but ultimately it is the researcher's decision as to what will be included and omitted, and in this process some voices are made redundant. In writing the ethnography, it is vital that the voice of the participants be heard and represented, rather than being subjugated to the voice of the researcher. This reinforces an earlier point about the need to circulate drafts of work to ensure accuracy in the report.

GUIDED CONSIDERATIONS

Research inevitably raises considerable concerns about the collection of data, the analyses of that data, and the writing of the reports. Many of the issues that are discussed in the remainder of this chapter deal with critical decisions throughout the research process. As the neophyte researcher undertakes various phases of ethnographic research, there are many such decisions, and some should be made in consultation with an experienced researcher. First and foremost is ethical approval to undertake the research. Individual universities will have ethics committees in various forms, their task being to deal with research ethics. It is essential that any research involving the study of (or experimentation) on people gain the approval of such a committee. Researchers must to seek out and comply with their university's regulations and procedures. For many, formal approval is a sanction to commence the research.

At a less formal level, there are many concerns about the ethics of research that do not appear in the reports of the research. Often the experience of discussing ethical concerns related to the research process endangers the researcher's credibility. A more critical concern is for the inclusion of ethics into a thesis that is to undergo examination. Exposing too many of the contentious decisions and often unresolved conflicts made during the research process may open the student to harsh criticism and the risk of failure. Hence, ethics is often a neglected area of the research report process, a point reiterated by Burgess (1989). Discussion about ethical concerns is often omitted from writings on research, so that discussion of such issues, problems, and dilemmas is conspicuously absent from debate.

Relationship Between Observer and Observed

A tension that exists within ethnographic research is the relationship between the observer and the observed. Coming into a classroom where the researcher is not as a member of that group, but rather is a guest may position him or her in ways that make the notion of ethnographer and participant in the field a misnomer. The varying degrees of access discussed in the previous sections influence the relationships, information, and outcomes of the project, so it is necessary to question the relationships and their inherent distribution of power.

In spite of intentions of being democratic and collaborative, the researcher enters the fieldwork in a position that is privileged and authoritative. (Whether this is justified or not is another issue.) Ultimately, the researcher has power over what will be observed; what will be asked in the interviews; how the observations, data, or both will be used; who will gain most from the research; and what discourses will be used to frame the research, observations, and data. In most cases, the researcher adopts a position of a person doing research on, or with, the researched. Traditional approaches to research reinforce this perception of the expert entering the research site and collecting data on the subjects. More collaborative projects, such as those informed by collaborative action research principles (Kemmis & McTaggart, 1990), are shifting the focus of these definitions, but this shift requires substantive efforts on the behalf of all participants. In discussing this aspect of the research project, it is critical that the various perspectives of research and how these perspectives address both the problems and the solutions to issues of power be considered.

It is imperative to recognize the power that the researcher holds and to ensure that the rights of the participants are protected as much as possible. It is extremely easy for the rights of the participants to be overridden in the name of completing the research, particularly when there are credentials to be gained by the researcher. This dilemma poses serious ethical issues. Does the researcher have the rights, responsibility, or both to continue the research under circumstances like these? How can an informed and fair decision be made to continue the research? If the decision is made to continue, how can it be made fair for the teachers?

Because it is part of the academic culture for the researchers and postgraduate students to produce some formal written report or thesis, the selection of aspects of the data is ultimately determined by the context from which the research originated. Where there is a collaborative, reciprocal research context, there is every likelihood that a very full account of the research question can be developed. However, where credentials and careers are involved, it is highly probable that someone will be in a position to rule and control the research in ways that will render the influence of a partner in the project marginal (hard as he or she may try to do otherwise).

Deception

Much of the ethnographic literature advises that the true purpose of the research be withheld from the participants because such knowledge can flaw the data. For example, if the participants are aware that the focus of the study is on differences in gendered interactions in the mathematics classroom, teachers may change their usual patterns of interacting with the students. This gives the researcher substantially different data than if the research topic had not been known.

Negotiating access to classrooms often presents a dilemma as to whether or not aspects of the research should be withheld. For example, where there is a problem with the teaching/learning of mathematics that may be endemic to a system, (such as the nonrandom success of some social and cultural groups), it may be necessary to withhold some aspects of the research from teachers, principals, or both in order to gain access to key information. Revealing this aspect of the research may jeopardize access to the school and classrooms by positioning the schools and teachers in opposition to the study. Conducting research under these conditions seems to be a form of deception, but such actions are often legitimate because the outcomes of the research process can never be known at the commencement of the project.

In the initial stages of the research, revealing the focus may deny being granted access to the schools and, as a consequence, important areas of research in mathematics may not eventuate. For example, the processes through which hegemony is realized in and through mathematics would need some form of deception in order to be successful. As the research progresses, researchers become better informed, more comfortable about the nature of the research and classroom practice, develop rapport with the teachers and are in a better position to discuss controversial aspects of the research with the teachers. This is the case particularly when researchers share drafts of their work with the teachers/schools.

Burgess (1989) offered a suggestion whereby, through his own research, he would advise schools "that research would be taking place, but it was not possible to specify exactly what data would be collected or how it would be used" (p. 65). This uncertainty about the firmness of the research problem is echoed by Glesne and Peshkin (1992). Further to this, Punch (1986) suggested that fieldwork "often has to be interactionally 'deceitful' in order to survive and succeed" (p. 71).

One way around the problem of deception is through the use of "global questions" (Spradley, 1979). Because the outcomes of the project are not known at the start of the project, using questions such as "how students make meaning in mathematics" can alleviate some of the angst associated with this issue. The open-ended nature of such a statement allows space to include the more traditional approaches to understanding classroom practices, while creating space for incorporating the sociopolitical dimensions to meaning making. The problem statement is in a discourse that is familiar to the teaching profession but would permit the incorporation of the sociopolitical dimension if this eventuated.

Protecting the Rights of the Researched

Having gained access to classrooms, and commenced the research process, it is essential that the participants have the right to be protected. This can be achieved through a confidentiality clause. Initially, and perhaps most important, participants should feel safe about revealing aspects of school life to a researcher. In essence, this means that there should be no chance of (negative) repercussions for giving information. Apart from the collection of classroom data, it is often in the context of incidental or informal discussions with participants that particularly informative and potentially contentious information is given. It is not uncommon for corridor conversations to reveal aspects of curriculum organization, teaching arrangements, and so on that impact on the teaching and learning of mathematics. If teachers and students are to feel at ease with the research, then it is important that they also feel that there are no repercussions for giving information. This confidence influences the type, amount, and quality of information that will be divulged to the researcher. Similarly, if teachers are not to feel threatened by the research, it is essential to provide a means by which their identity and sense of self will be protected. Participants have every right to expect that "when they give you permission to observe and interview, you will protect their confidences and preserve their anonymity" (Glesne & Peshkin, 1992, p. 117).

Examining classroom practice in fine detail, the teacher comes under close scrutiny. For example, the researcher may observe teachers teaching mathematical content that is not in syllabus documents; teachers who use a barrage of tests on Fridays; teachers who berate students in the belief that such humiliation will inspire them to work harder; or teachers who send home math sheets for homework each night in spite of directives banning such activities. So that the individual teachers do not take the research as being a critique of themselves, and to protect them from other possible critiques within their own profession, it is necessary to anonymize students, teachers, and schools so that there is minimal risk of recognition. There are instances in which it can be beneficial for teachers or participants in studies to be recognized, but it is essential that the identification of be negotiated, and the long-term consequences of identification be carefully considered.

Negotiation of Release of Report. Through the process of negotiation it becomes possible to clarify points in a final report that may be ambiguous or contentious, as well as extending the researcher's understanding of the classroom milieu. Feeding back data (however these are collected), drafts, transcripts, and debriefing sessions can be seen as processes through which the participants can gain from the research. Teachers (and, to a lesser extent, students), can be asked to pass comments evaluating, clarifying, expanding or justifying, and in this way provide input into the research that gives them a voice in the research as well as allowing for triangulation of data.

As has been noted on a number of occasions, participants should be given drafts of any reports arising from the data to be edited or commented on. This process allows them to comment on the report and through a process of negotiation, changes can be made to accommodate their perspectives. It is one thing to show participants the raw data, but the interpretations of those data can be substantially different among a group. It is feasible that teachers might be in total opposition to the claims the researchers make, which will require considerable negotiation to arrive at some agreement whereby both parties are satisfied with the representation. Resolving the differences that may arise can be problematic for the researcher. Having given the teachers the right to comment on work means that if there is disagreement in the representation, compromises must be made. For the researcher, the compromise may be central to the research. For example, a poststructuralist analysis of classroom interactions may report that the mathematics teacher is using gendered practices that effectively construct females as marginal. The teacher may not agree with this interpretation of the interaction and, in fact, working from a liberal or conservative position, may believe that those actions are, in fact, gender inclusive. Giving the report to the teachers allows a more complete interpretation of the events. When such a position arises and the parties cannot agree on a common interpretation, it is possible for the researcher to retain one interpretation of the events and gave the alternative interpretation in the footnote. In this way, both voices are represented and the contradiction noted without compromizing either participant.

Informed Consent

Informed consent is a vital part of the research process, particularly in terms of ethics. By not being fully informed about the nature of the research, teachers are not be in a position to make an informed decision to participate in or withdraw from the study. Hence it is important to be open about the research and the research process. Although the unresolved dilemma of how much to reveal of the research problem has been identified, it is imperative that the teachers be made fully aware of as many aspects as possible of the research and research process so that they are in a position to make a relatively well-informed decision. When negotiating access, it is essential that teachers (and other participants such as students and parents, where appropriate) be made fully aware of the research process, what the research entails, and the rights and responsibilities of both the researcher and the participants, so that they will be able to make an informed decision whether to participate or withdraw from the project. A "Principle of Procedures" document, outlining the obligations of both the researcher and the teachers who are participating in the study, can be prepared for the teachers to take away and reflect on their role in the research.

Although a worthy ideal, the notion of informed consent has limitations that are beyond the control of the researcher. In the first instance, the issue of deception means the informed consent is in contradiction with the stated aims of being fully informed. Glesne and Peshkin (1992) identified a number of levels of deception. "Full cover" refers to covert studies, in which the participants do not even know that they are the subject of a study. For example, full cover may occur in an ethnographic study of a tertiary mathematics course where the ethnographer is a student in the class and writes the ethnography as a reflective piece. A situation in which the researcher does not explain in full detail the nature of the study (such as through the use of global questions), or does not fully explain the object of the study (but otherwise provides as much information as possible) Glesne and Peshkin refer to as "shallow cover." This practice raises the issue as to whether the participants were able to give informed consent, because information was withheld. Other than the purpose of the study, participants are able to make as informed consent is possible within any research project. Burgess (1985) lent support by arguing that the issue of what constitutes informed consent in an ethnography is contested, because the actual outcomes of the project are static and developing throughout the life of the project.

Where teachers are seconded to the research by their principal, it may be inadvisable for them not to participate, even when given the opportunity to withdraw. It is questionable whether such participation constitutes informed consent given the salient distribution of power.

In an ideal situation, informed consent is an overarching objective of any research project. However, it is something that can at best be expected to protect the rights of the researcher and researched in ways that are negotiable and involve compromise by both parties. In other words, the research should be conducted in a manner that "respects the rights of the individual whose privacy is not invaded and who is not harmed, deceived, betrayed, or exploited" (Burgess, 1989, p. 60). Overall, although informed consent is a goal that is certainly essential to good research, it is very difficult to implement. Glesne and Peshkin (1992) supported this in commenting that, "Although the partial nature of your knowledge does not obviate the propriety of informed consent, it does make implementing it problematic" (p. 121).

Triangulation of Data

In the initial negotiations of access and the principles of procedure, issues of ownership of data and the procedures of their release must be discussed. Such a process is not without risk for the researcher. Part of the responsibility of the researcher is to protect participants from the pitfalls of research. As has often been the case, researchers come into a situation, collect *their* data, return to *their* institution to write up *their* report and do not contact the source for clearance, validation, or whatever. Asking teachers to provide feedback on data or reports enables the researcher to gain access to more information and to triangulate their data. However, there are a number of potential problems in undertaking such a democratic action.

The process of involving teachers in the release of data can result in different responses that are closely linked to the teachers' involvement in the project. For example, teachers who volunteer for the research are more likely to provide feedback and be involved in the consultation process than those teachers who were co-opted. To represent the teachers and schools in ways that they do not see as fair and reasonable cannot be considered ethical. Often there is a lack of response from participants that may be construed as lack of interest or commitment, but other factors impinge on teachers' willingness or ability to provide feedback—time frames, teaching demands, lack of experience in research, different foci from the researcher, and so forth. In the ideal situation, the researcher has a moral obligation to seek verification from all participants as to the validity of the data, and later, the interpretations of those data.

Because of the potential poor turnaround of data and summaries in the early phases of the project, it might be necessary to opt for a more rigid process of negotiating a mutually acceptable deadline for responses to be submitted and, if there is no response, the assumption that the participants agree with the study. Clearly, there are problems with this approach, but, for practical and pragmatic reasons, this option is often the most suitable alternative for fairly meeting the needs of all participants.

Expert

Coming into the classroom situation where the ethnographer is to take on the role of researcher engenders the perception of the researcher being the expert on research. Hammersley and Atkinson (1983) suggested that this is often the case, so that the hosts have gross misinterpretations of the research process in which the researcher is positioned as an expert in the field and expected to offer tenable solutions to classroom problems. This can lead to the researcher being seen to take on the role of an evaluator, which can have profound effects on the access that is granted. This role is in opposition to that of the ethnographer whose task is to observer the culture of the classroom. When the role of researcher is substituted for that of evaluator, teachers may feel that they are under close scrutiny, which invariably is quite threatening. As such, it is important to stress continually to the teachers that they are not the focus of the research, but rather it is the practices inherent in the classroom that are of interest to the researcher. Although this type of rhetoric may have good intentions, there is some doubt as to how successful it is in allaying misconceptions about the nature of the research.

CONCLUSION

The overarching methodology of educational ethnography allows access to the practices of the classroom and the opportunity to critically analyze this setting. It is not anticipated that generalizable statements will arise from an ethnographic project because of its context-boundedness, although it is quite possible that the practices identified at one site may resonate strongly with other sites because of the institutionalization of schooling and classroom practices.

From the preceding discussion, it is clear that there are many critical decisions and moments in undertaking ethnographic research that may jeopardize the project, or influence the outcomes. The process is fraught with decisions that need to be made impulsively, require professional judgment, and are full of ethical and moral dilemmas that can cause the researcher and participants considerable angst. The decisions that are made on the run can have a lasting effect on the outcomes of the project. Apart from recognizing the impact of these decisions, it is imperative that the researcher consider his or her role in the research process.

The issues and problems outlined in the chapter are not unique, and as such should be considered as integral components of ethnographic research. Clearly, when working with teachers in classrooms, it is imperative that the researcher consider the context of the participants. The constraints within which the research is conducted have a powerful influence over the outcomes. Many of these constraints have been discussed in this chapter, but this is certainly not meant to be a comprehensive list. Part of the ethnographic process is to recognize these constraints and build them into the research and reports. Failure to do so limits the claims that can be legitimately made about the research outcomes.

REFERENCES

Burgess, R. G. (Ed.). (1985). *Strategies of educational research.* London: Taylor & Francis.

Burgess, R. G. (1989). Grey areas: Ethical dilemmas in educational ethnography. In R. G. Burgess (Eds.), *The ethics of educational research* (pp. 60–76). London: Falmer.

Eisenhart, M. A. (1988). The ethnographic research tradition and mathematics education research. *Journal for Research in Mathematics Education, 19*(2), 99–114.

Erickson, F. (1973). What makes a school ethnography "ethnographic"? *Council on Anthropology and Education Newsletter, 4*(2), 10–19.

Fetterman, D. M. (1989). *Ethnography: Step by step.* London: Sage.

Glesne, C., & Peshkin, A. (1992). *Becoming qualitative researchers: An introduction.* Melbourne: Longman Cheshire.

Hammersley, M. (1992a). Some reflection on ethnography and validity. *Qualitative Studies in Education, 5*(3), 195–203.

Hammersley, M. (1992b). *What's wrong with ethnography? Methodological explorations.* London: Routledge.

Hammersley, M., & Atkinson, P. (1983). *Ethnography: Principles in practice.* London: Tavistock.

Jackson, P. W. (1990). *Life in classrooms.* New York: Teachers College Press.

Kemmis, S., & McTaggart, R. (1990). *The action research planner.* Geelong, Australia: Deakin University Press.

Kemmis, S., & Robottom, I. (1981). Principles of procedure in curriculum evaluation. *Journal of Curriculum Studies, 13*(2), 151–155.

McLaren, P. (1980). *Cries from the corridor*. Toronto: Methuen.

McLaren, P. (1993). *Schooling as a ritual performance: Towards a political economy of educational symbols and gestures* (2nd ed.). London: Routledge & Kegan Paul.

McLaren, P. (1989). *Life in schools: An introduction to critical pedagogy in the foundations of education*. New York: Longman.

McNeil, P. (1990). *Research methods* (2nd ed.). London: Routledge.

Mehan, H. (1982). The structure of classroom events and their consequences for student performance. In P. G. Glatthorn & A. A. Glatthorn (Eds.), *Children in and out of school: Ethnography and education* (pp. 59–87). Washington, DC: Center for Applied Linguistics.

Mehan, H. (1992a, January). Understanding inequality in schools: The contribution of interpretive studies. *Sociology of Education, 65,* 21–36.

Mehan, H. (1992b). Why I like to look: On the use of videotape as an instrument in educational research. In M. Schratz (Ed.), *Qualitative voices in educational research* (pp. 93–105). New York: Falmer.

Punch, M. (1986). *The politics and ethics of fieldwork*. Beverly Hills, CA: Sage.

Schratz, M., & Mehan, H. (1993). Gulliver travels into a math class: In search of alternative discourse in teaching and learning. *International Journal of Educational Research, 19*(3), 247–264.

Shimahara, N. (1990). Anthroethnography: A methodological consideration. In R. R. Sherman & R. B. Rodman (Eds.), *Qualitative research in education: Focus and methods* (pp. 76–89). London: Falmer.

Spradley, J. (1979). *The ethnographic interview*. New York: Holt, Rinehart & Winston.

Woods, P. (1986). *Inside schools*. London: Routledge & Kegan Paul.

Woods, P. (1988). Educational ethnography in Britain. In R. R. Sherman & R. B. Webb (Eds.), *Qualitative research in education: Focus and methods* (pp. 90–109). London: Falmer.

Zevenbergen, R. (1995). Students' mathematics culture. In B. Atweh & S. Flavel (Eds.), *Galtha: Proceedings of the eighteenth annual conference of the Mathematics Education Research Group of Australasia, Northern Territory University, Darwin, Australia, July 1995* (pp. 557–563). Darwin, Australia: MERGA.

Zevenbergen, R., Cockayne, J., & Cherry, R. (1992). What do we learn in spatial relations: Playing the maths game. In M. Horne (Ed.), *Mathematics: Meeting the challenge* (pp. 160–164). Melbourne: Mathematics Association of Victoria.

3

Quality Criteria for the Genres of Interpretive Research

John S. Schaller
Florida State University

Kenneth Tobin
University of Pennsylvania

THE STUDY OF EXPERIENCE

In the past decade there has been a marked change in the nature of research in science and mathematics education. Specifically, there has been an increasing acceptance of interpretive approaches to research, but many of the criteria for framing and judging the quality of this work have continued to be objectivist oriented. Although these research efforts have expanded beyond the traditional limitations of quantitative reports designed to gather proof of improved curricular strategies (as evidenced by increased student performance), many of these studies still fail to communicate the intricacies of the classroom experience in a credible and compelling manner. Such research texts fall short of conferring meaning and establishing the adequacy of the overall inquiry in their reporting, either because of the limitations of technical writing styles or the absence of criteria for judging the quality of the work. Science and math educators have struggled for some time with the constraints of the jargon-laden and lifeless character of mainstream research products, but few have broken free of the culturally imposed boundaries of the traditional research paradigm. Many hold on to positivist prescriptions to avoid alienation within the common community of learners, possibly because it is familiar, in much the same way as a teacher continues to teach in an expository manner when research suggests otherwise. Yet researchers are mistaken in believing that the use of technical language alone deters professional alienation, and many writers, recognizing this, are beginning to resist writing techniques that encourage the flattening of language and, thus, the impoverishment of the human experience. As science and math educators, we would do well to remember that if the goal of learning is understanding, then the goal of writing should be to create understanding. What we should seek are the various ways of imagining, capturing, and re-creating the multiple realities of the educational experience within the confines of quality research criteria, and what is needed is a radical rethinking of research in science and mathematics education.

An increasingly overt sentiment among science and mathematics educators insists that a heightened aesthetic treatment of educational insights and experiences in case studies could convey a more authentic and dramatically appealing description of educational phenomena. McCorcle (1984) said that the telling of stories is the purpose of a case study and that the narrative could be the study's most compelling attribute. Narrative is a method whereby a story is crafted from events and the experiences of the writer and refers to discourse that attempts to create understanding by telling a story that answers the question, "What is going on here?" In this way, narrative can contribute to the creation of understanding and knowledge in a more inviting manner for the intended audience. Typically, writings with a high caliber of aesthetic appeal embody those that have historically drawn people to the novel, and have been characterized in academic circles as nonscientific and lacking in method. What is being advocated, however, is not a dismissal of careful and deliberate methods of creating and analyzing field texts. Field work typical of good interpretive research is essential for gathering the facts and can and does contribute significantly to the research text. It is the process of interpreting and reconstructing field texts into research texts that is under review, and what is being argued for is the need for a more subjective treatment of factual information.

Research in science and math education is concerned with educational stakeholders and their relations with themselves and their environments and, as such, this type of research is founded on the study of experience. As educational research moves closer to subjectivity, discussions of how to audit and restrain our subjectivity and to account for it within the framework of the human experience are of critical concern. This obsession for accountability, however, mirrors a similar concern of positivist methodology to account for its objectivity. Heshusius (1992) stated that "the idea of subjectivity and bias makes sense only against the backdrop of the possibility of objectivity, which is to say, of knowing as an act of distancing" (p. 10). Rather than a thorough accounting of subjectivity, one should be concerned with describing the act of merging through inquiry, and what is learned from the process. This approach avoids creating a distance to be crossed by either subjective or objective methodologies, and is instead "about active identification with the phenomena one wants to understand" (p. 18). It is within this framework that we can put our concerns about subjectivity and objectivity into perspective, and view them not as methodological constraints, but as indicators of how we understand the participatory nature of our consciousness as we approach the research problem.

As our understanding of the various ways in which we construct knowledge from our experiences has been applied to the conduct of our research in science and mathematics education, there has been considerable change in what is accepted. This change has brought with it problems in terms of acknowledging the shortcomings of some of the new genres of interpretive research as well as agreeing on the standards for judging the quality of our efforts. What are the quality indicators of research undertaken from different genres? What is the relationship between substantive research issues and methods of inquiry that should concern us? What rhetorical methods for reporting what has been learned from research are appropriate for interpretive studies? These questions have particular significance for those engaged directly in the research process and for those in higher education with the responsibility for preparing a new generation of researchers. In this chapter we address these issues with the intention of providing criteria for producing credible and compelling research products and generating meaningful dialogue toward the determination of what constitutes good research in science and mathematics education.

SUBSTANTIVE RESEARCH ISSUES AND THE METHODS USED TO INVESTIGATE THEM

A key issue in conducting research in science and mathematics education is the manner in which researchers frame themselves, the substantive issues of a study, and the associated methods used to investigate them, and reflect on those frames in relation to one another. The extent to which there is coherence (or lack of it) is an important part of the context of research.

Part of the conventional wisdom of research in science and mathematics education is that researchers are advised to think about substantive issues first and not to think about the methods that might be employed in a study until the research questions have been settled. We cautiously reject this notion, not because we want to assign preeminence to method, but to suggest that researchers explore substantive issues in terms of the methods with which they have confidence as being appropriate. The research design should include a dialectical relationship between the methods to be employed and the issues to be addressed. The manner in which this concern is approached depends a great deal on the history of the researcher and what prompted the decision to engage in research. In the dialectical process, the methods employed should interact with issues addressed throughout the design stage so that one is constantly mediated by the other in an emergent process. This dialectical relationship evolves throughout the descriptive, analytical, and interpretive phases of a study, and care is taken to document what happens and the reasons for taking particular courses of action. At any given time an issue might be methodological or substantive, but there always should be an explicit understanding that it makes no sense to view either in isolation from the other, no matter how alluring it might seem to do so. Thus, the research design constantly evolves throughout a planning phase that precedes field work and is emergent in that the methods to be employed will reflect what is learned from an interpretive study and what is hoped to be learned next.

Interpretive research is an umbrella term generally used to describe investigations designed to capture the essence of the participants' experience and may involve a variety of research strategies including ethnography, participant observation, case study, thick description, and others. An interpretive approach to research rejects the notion that the researcher and the research can be detached from the phenomena of a study by acknowledging that the presence of the researcher and the inquiry process itself make a difference to what is learned. Endeavors to construct understandings that take account of the presence of the researcher and the involvement of participants within a sociocultural setting are of critical concern. Diverse approaches to interpretive research are connected by the researcher's intention to investigate the actions and interactions of participants within an educational milieu and to understand those actions and interactions from the perspectives of the participants. Only then can the assertions or declarations of the research be considered capable of sustaining academic scrutiny. We maintain that the assertions of an interpretive study ought to be viable and the warrants for the viability of those claims ought to be explicit.

Throughout the interpretive phase of reporting what was learned in a study, the focus is on making sense of how multiple accounts of what is happening are regarded as viable assertions by those who act and interact within the research setting. This involves efforts to unravel what is happening within a culture and to ascertain why things happen as they do. Although action is a holistic concept, it is convenient to consider four mutually influencing elements: the goals of the individual, the context in which an action occurs, beliefs that are a referent for a given set of behaviors, and the behaviors that occur. For a given set of actions there is a coherence among the four elements; that is, the beliefs that serve as a referent for a behavioral set are dependent on the context, which in turn depends on the goals of the individual. Therefore, to describe and interpret the actions of an individual requires a researcher to understand the goals of the individual, understand how the individual constructs the context in which a given action is to occur, and identify the belief set associated with a putatively viable set of observed behaviors.

A focus on an individual's actions without examining interactions leads to an insufficient account of what is happening and why (Galtung, 1982). Accordingly, the basic unit of analysis in an interpretive study is an interaction of individuals with others in a cultural setting and of individuals within the social institutions that have relevance to that setting. Integral to this process of interpretation is the hermeneutic–dialectical circle in which the process of making sense of what is going on in a particular setting is informed by individuals holding diverse viewpoints. Participants are selected to include all groups with an interest in the matters under investigation and to maintain the diversity inherent in groups. Data are aggregated to preserve diverse viewpoints as well as to identify patterns of action and interaction associated with central tendencies. Value is attached to learning from diverse perspectives, ensuring that a researcher's accounts are regarded as viable by participants in a study, and conducting research in ways that foreground ethical practices by all participants. If care is taken to make sense of events from the perspectives of the actors, then it is possible to describe what is happening and why from those perspectives. Thus, interpretive research ought to describe the experiences and preserve the voices of different stakeholder groups within their respective educational settings.

JUDGING THE QUALITY OF INTERPRETIVE RESEARCH

Having established the need in educational reporting for a more subjective treatment of factual data that effectively communicates the meaning of the substantive issues central to teaching and learning, we now need to prescribe quality standards for conducting research that ensure the viability of the assertions and the overall adequacy of the research findings. This section of the chapter presents an overview of the criteria used to judge the quality of interpretive research and four examples of different genres of interpretive research: teaching and learning science, student stories, critical autobiography, and fictive stories. Each example is critiqued to demonstrate the application of quality criteria to establish evaluative authenticity and literary credibility.

Quality Criteria

The primary expectation of method is to bring research questions and data collection into an evolving relationship with the substantive focus of the inquiry. One of the tensions associated with an interpretive research design that is emergent from the substantive issues is that critical aspects of the study might not have been planned in sufficient detail. This, however, does not have to be viewed as a reporting inadequacy, as careful presentation of evidentiary material can overcome these concerns. Our position is that the assertions from a study need to be viable in the sense that for each assertion there is ample evidence to support it; that efforts have been made to refute all assertions; and that a negative case analysis of discrepant data has been conducted. It is crucial that the researcher deliberately search for adequate evidence that might disconfirm a key assertion or face criticism on the grounds that only evidence that favorably supports a given assertion was sought. Additionally, a researcher may not have been aware of an evolving assertion during fieldwork, and fail to search for disconfirming evidence that could be analyzed as discrepant cases in the hopes of shedding new light on the assertion in question. Negative case analysis of disconfirming evidence also enables the researcher to refine and adjust major assertions through comparison of confounding cases. The patterns and themes that emerge from the data are continually revised to construct assertions of increased relevance in the revised story. Assertions that are found to be congruent with the emergent patterns and themes are then formulated based on the integrity of the supporting data and a comparative critique of the nonsupporting data. The desired result of these efforts is to establish confidence in the viability of the assertions through a rigorous analysis of the available evidence.

Readers ought to have confidence that the claims embedded in the text are supported by evidence from the study, irrespective of the rhetorical style in which the findings have been reported. More and more science and math educators are turning to narrative in their research texts to substantiate and convey the significance of stakeholder experiences, but in many cases is there is inadequate concern for standards of quality for judging the goodness of their work. Erickson (1986) reminded us that narrative in and of itself is not indicative of interpretive research, and narrative techniques that involve writing like crazy yet have no substantive focus or intent do not constitute a research method. Simply reflecting and writing does not ensure that the research will yield, through interpretation, the beliefs and behaviors of the participants In the final analysis, however, the ultimate decisions regarding handling of the narrative and other methods reside with the researcher, who must decide the most compelling and convincing way of telling the story. Methods of inquiry are not ends in themselves, and one must always take precautions to prevent obscuring the actual substance of the story being told in the defense of methodology, a problem Janesick (1994) referred to as *methodolatry*. A competent researcher must find the balance between the desire to present trustworthy findings and the possibility of sacrificing substance for method in the process. Furthermore, throughout the research she or he must develop guidelines for establishing the credibility of the findings that are supportive of the substantive focus of inquiry.

Interpretive research is a holistic method of evaluation that strives to generate research that is both believable and compelling. Although there may be no one best method of collecting and analyzing field texts, there are still conventions for establishing the quality of interpretive research that, on the surface, can be understood as structures of organization imposed by common sense. To substantiate the findings of such research, Guba and Lincoln (1989) developed the authenticity criteria as an alternative to conventional scientific criteria. The authenticity criteria include fairness and ontological, educative, catalytic, and tactical authenticity, and offer an approach for establishing the quality of goodness in constructivist research.

"Fairness" in research is a criterion that refers to the extent to which a stakeholder's constructions of reality and his or her underlying values are solicited and honored within a study. A researcher concerned with fairness in reporting will seek out and communicate the different value-laden constructions of all stakeholders in a balanced and evenhanded way. The extent to which a researcher's own emic constructions are improved through the progressive subjectivity of the research process is referred to as *ontological authenticity*. Ontological authenticity is confirmed when researchers attest that they are learning from the diverse perspectives of the participants and that they can now understand issues that previously eluded them. Whereas ontological authenticity is concerned with an individual's understanding of his or her own experience, *educative authenticity* is concerned to ensure that an individual is able to understand and appreciate the constructions and value systems of others whether agreeing with them or not. Efforts should be made to familiarize stakeholders with the constructions of others and to ensure that they learn from an understanding of these constructions. *Catalytic authenticity* is concerned with the extent that action is prompted on the part of the stakeholders and other participants within the context of the substantive issues central to the research problem. An example of catalytic authenticity would be the implementation of strategies and theories resulting from an interpretive study. *Tactical authenticity* refers to the extent that participants in a study are empowered to act. This criterion is concerned with the participatory nature of the evaluative process and whether all stakeholders have felt that they had a significant role in the process and an opportunity to contribute to the inquiry in a meaningful and consistent manner. The product of the research process, therefore, should be a document that has been mutually shaped through a recursive process of negotiation between the researcher and all other stakeholders. The satisfaction of the authenticity criteria, however, is not imminent, and should be of critical concern to the discriminating researcher, as should other aspects of the research agenda.

For research to be considered of high quality, careful attention to process from the initial contacts for gaining entry to the final editing of the research text is required. Guba and Lincoln (1989) advised against conducting studies from a purely methodological perspective, given the demonstrated inadequacy of traditional, positivistic methods in accounting for the complexities of the human experience. They asserted that only the authenticity criteria offer promise that stakeholder constructions will be collected and faithfully represented and their rights honored. However, Guba and Lincoln did admit that method is a consideration in constructivist inquiry and that method is critical for ensuring that the results are trustworthy.

Methodology is a consideration of particular importance for the novice researcher, as method provides concrete strategies for disciplined research. Therefore, an interpretive study can be designed to be both authentic and credible without undue concern for epistemological conflict by employing, in addition to the techniques suggested for satisfying the authenticity criteria, six methodological procedures to satisfy issues of credibility. They are *prolonged engagement, persistent observation, peer debriefing, negative case analysis, progressive subjectivity*, and *member checks* (Guba & Lincoln, 1989). These procedures are widely recognized by sociologists, anthropologists, and others who engage in field research. They address interpretive research concerns that are parallel to issues of internal validity in positivist studies; hence they are collectively referred to as *parallel criteria*.

Prolonged engagement ensures that the researcher is at the site for sufficient time to become immersed in the culture and make sense of what is happening. Persistent observation allows a researcher to identify issues that have most salience and to study each in depth through the use of an emergent design. Peer debriefing allows a researcher to describe what is happening and postulate why to a disinterested peer, who can then raise questions and suggest alternative theoretical frames to be considered. Negative case analysis is a process of thoroughly examining all discrepant data that do not fit an assertion and making sure they can be explained. Progressive subjectivity involves a close analysis of the evolving constructions of the researcher over time to ascertain whether the subjective constructions of the researcher change as a result of the study and to ensure that the researcher does not see only what she or he wants to see.

Finally, and perhaps most important, the researcher must ensure that data sources are checked by those for whom they have most relevance. Having recorded the descriptions for different stakeholder groups, it is possible to refer those texts back to the groups, providing opportunities to authenticate them and reflect on their content. Through member checks the researcher can also dispel discrepant assumptions by soliciting stakeholder views and reconstructing more accurate renditions of pertinent events through stakeholder voices. Furthermore, an emerging concern of participatory inquiry that can be remedied through member checking is the phenomenon of self-deception, which Reason (1994) referred to as "unaware projection." Unaware projection is the result of anxiety that can emerge from the process of psychoanalysis which then stirs up our psychological defenses. As these internal red flags are raised, we "then project our anxieties onto the world we are supposed to be studying giving rise to a whole variety of self-deceptions in the course of the inquiry" (p. 327). In other words, member checking serves as a safeguard against discrepant assumptions arising from self-deception. From the standpoint of Guba and Lincoln's (1989) authenticity criteria, the sharing of texts with participants for whom they have relevance serves as a member check from the ontological perspective of a researcher who wants to be sure that an account is perceived as authentic. The review of texts allows participants to see their own actions through the eyes of someone else and as such can serve as catalytic, tactical, and educative catalysts for learning and change. Whereas much of a text will include details that are familiar, there might also be aspects of that account that are strange. Thus, transcribed interviews, field notes, vignettes, interpretive memoranda, and draft manuscripts will be given to key participants for member checking to verify the extent to which the constructions of the researcher fit those of the participants.

Given that the dependability of a research text is assessed by the documentation of what was done in the study and examination of the data in relation to the knowledge claims, it is imperative that as efficient measures as possible be exercised for managing the field texts. For this type of evaluation to be thorough and authentic, all data sources should be logged into an archive from which they can be readily retrieved and linked to the assertions and texts of the study. There are many software programs available for the management and analysis of nonnumerical and unstructured qualitative data in text documents. The ease of entering and manipulating text segments through indexing and searching make these programs invaluable tools for the interpretive researcher. In the examples that follow, a software program called NUD•IST (1994) was used extensively for these purposes and contributed significantly to the ease of handling and analyzing voluminous quantities of material.

The vignettes chosen for this chapter illustrate an evolving relationship between the methods used and the selection of substantive research issues of four different genres of interpretive research in science education. A progressively more challenging rhetorical heightening of the narrative is portrayed as the examples progress from participant observation to critical autobiography to the literal creation of virtual texts through the use of fictive methods. At this point, the reader should bear in mind that the examples we offer are illustrative of a select, but limited, assortment of interpretive studies and are by no means representative of all interpretive research genres. However, it is our contention that the examples given are illustrative of specific guidelines that can be universally applied to many of our research endeavors. It is also our hope that the ideas and strategies represented will serve as catalysts for empowering and creating greater understanding among novice researchers. They too can then engage in their own discussions of what contributes to and what detracts from any given research text's ability to produce narrative accounts that provide vicarious experience that is both credible and authentic in that it honors the constructions of all stakeholders.

TEACHING AND LEARNING SCIENCE

Investigations into the teaching and learning of science represent a genre of research that is probably more common in the literature than any other, and is particularly well suited to interpretive research strategies. The focus of inquiry is on the beliefs, metaphors, and actions of teachers and students within the various learning environments that teaching and learning take place, and the findings generally infer some learning or change that has taken place. Research techniques for the collection and handling of data typically involve interviews, observation notes, anecdotal records, and videotaping.

In a series of studies, Tobin and McRobbie explored the chemistry teaching of "Mr. Jacobs," a 20-year veteran teacher in an Australian high school (McRobbie & Tobin, 1995, 1997; Tobin & McRobbie, 1996a, 1996b, in press-a, in press-b). The research was intensive in two respects: first, it involved direct observation of teaching every day for a period of 5 weeks, during which Mr. Jacobs taught concepts associated with oxidation and reduction and electrochemistry. Each lesson was observed by at least three people, and two videotapes were made. One camera focused on the teacher and the other on the students. A transcript was prepared for the oral text from each videotape. During the 5-week period, students and the teachers in the school completed questionnaires and interviews were undertaken to obtain diverse points of view from students, teachers, and administrators.

Second, the study continued for more than 18 months after the initial period in which the classes were observed. During that time, interpretive texts were returned to the participants for member checks and also given to persons similar to those involved in the study for peer debriefing. For example, other students like those who were involved in the study were shown narratives compiled from teacher and student interview data for comments.

Both narrative and vignettes were used to illustrate the substantive foci of the study, which included beliefs, metaphors, and the actions of teachers (McRobbie & Tobin, 1995); investigations of students' and teachers' perceptions of the learning environments (McRobbie & Tobin, 1997); the pervasive effects on teaching and learning of cultural myths (Tobin & McRobbie, 1996a); limited English proficiency and the learning of science (Tobin & McRobbie, 1996b); students' and teachers' beliefs about the nature of science (Tobin & McRobbie, in press-a); and pedagogical content knowledge and the learning of electrochemistry (Tobin & McRobbie, in press-b).

However, despite the careful and methodical attention to detail demonstrated by the prolonged engagement period, persistent observations and peer debriefing mentioned earlier, Mr. Jacobs' inability to fully participate in the study made member checking difficult, if not impossible, in some cases. Although the researchers would have preferred Mr. Jacobs to be a part of the research team, he was unable to comply with their wishes because he was too busy. His decision to minimally participate in the recursive process of negotiating and preparing research texts ultimately diminished the potential of the study. Although the research team clearly learned a great deal, the educative, catalytic, and tactical authenticity of the study were not as great as they otherwise would have been. With hindsight, it would have been preferable to have selected another teacher to participate in the study so that through member checks it could be established that their constructions were honored and faithfully represented, thus maximizing the study's authenticity. Therefore, selection of participants might be contingent on their willingness to participate fully in a study.

Student Stories

"I like Bruner's ideas on narrative. I think I will do my dissertation on students' narratives." Mike was excited as he burst into my office. "What do you want to learn?" I asked. "Mr. Andrews has agreed to let me use his physics class and I have agreed to team teach with him." Mike was enthusiastic about his study and obviously had some good ideas. I did not want to dampen his enthusiasm, but warning bells were ringing in my head. His focus was on methodology and his initial remarks had not mentioned a substantive focus in science education. My mind raced through experiences with other doctoral students who had become involved in projects and had not been able to easily focus on a research agenda.

Mike had an approach to research that appealed as a way of explicating students' insights into both their roles as learners in their physics classes and their goals. He started his study right away. He attended the classes, wrote pages of field notes, and set up regular meetings with several students from the class, during which he interviewed them and taught them physics. Mike then began to construct stories from the interviews. How did he decide what to include in his stories? Because he wanted the stories to reflect the students' voices, he constructed them from the actual words used in interviews. As such, the stories were aggregations of text over time—likely stories based on what Mike heard and determined to be the most salient features of the texts of particular students. During the interval he was interacting with students it seemed as if there were several ways to proceed. He could either capture the stories of students as integrated wholes and use them to illustrate their goals, or he could use their texts, together with other data sources, to identify patterns around which he could weave stories using text spoken by the students during interviews. Mike chose the latter strategy and developed student stories to reflect their viewpoints about the salient aspects of the course. He was making a decision to downplay an emphasis on description and exercise some interpretive freedom in the creation of his stories.

A critical departure between Mike and his major professor was how to reconstruct the stories. The major professor insisted that an intensive analysis of all data sources be undertaken, whereby all text was read and divided into thematic units on the basis of the meanings given them by Mike. Categories were either created a priori or at the moment a classification decision was to be made. As categories were created they were entered into a theoretical tree (NUD•IST, 1994); however, the tree could be reshaped at any time and was the focus for discussion among Mike, a group of peers with whom he interacted, and his major professor. The relationship among categorical themes was tracked diagramatically and reflected an emerging theoretical frame of the study.

Adherence to this procedure provided Mike with increased confidence that the major assertions were consistent with the data, which were then used to emphasize and frame stories for each student. Accordingly, he was able to support any assertion in the stories with data from the study. The themes of his stories were viable assertions for which there were considerable supporting data and vignettes. In addition, for each assertion or theme, a thorough negative case analysis had been conducted. To the extent possible, Mike used the actual words spoken by students, or entries from his field notes to construct the stories. The stories were then given to the students to check their plausibility. At this time changes were suggested so that the stories became a better reflection of what might have been written by the students themselves. The teacher of the physics class, who was a significant stakeholder in the study, was also provided with copies of the students' stories and invited to comment on them.

However, not all had gone according to plan and the substantive focus of the study remained elusive throughout the research process, despite the thorough handling and analysis of the data. From the beginning, Mike's primary interest was with the students' stories, and the key issues related to the teaching and learning of physics tended to be somewhat ephemeral. Inattention to the selection of a substantive focus was reflected in the final writing of the research text, which focused on issues of cheating, gender equity, ethics, and the use of humor and sarcasm. The data sources did not permit a detailed analysis of the manner in which teaching could facilitate the learning of specific physics content. Instead, an overriding concern with obtaining student stories resulted in a deemphasizing of central substantive issues in the teaching and learning of physics.

This interpretive study is an example of establishing credibility and satisfying authenticity criteria, but omitting a substantive focus. As mentioned earlier, the researcher could avoid such misgivings by employing a dialectical relationship between method and the substantive foci that emerge during the initial planning stages of research and evolve throughout the research process. Failure to select one substantive focus can result in a rambling document that lacks contextual coherence because the researcher is scantily addressing multiple issues with little attention to prevailing patterns and themes within each of the issues. Erickson (1986) warned us against this propensity to ramble, because writing like crazy is not in itself an interpretive process. This dilemma is frequently present in the preliminary efforts of most novice research, and is further documented in the following vignette, together with examples of inadequate efforts to authenticate the findings.

Critical Autobiography

David, a masters degree student, decided to make student teaching the focus of his thesis and using narrative method write a critical autobiography. His original student teaching assignment fell through at the last moment and David was assigned to a school selected because of a belief that he would benefit from learning to teach science in a school in which most students were African American and were from homes in which the adults were either in working-class jobs or unemployed. David wrote a thesis that projected his anger at being placed in the school, which he did not regard as conducive for learning to teach science.

David's thesis was a radical departure from the traditional style of writing; so too was his oral defense. The first two chapters of his thesis dealt with his early life in New York and his days in elementary and middle school. He then wrote about his life as a mathematics student (usually unsuccessful), his promise as a musician, and his early employment as a ferry captain. The main chapter was an account of his experience as a student teacher. David was involved in what he considered to be a power struggle with faculty over his placement for student teaching. The text was a gripping account of a dysfunctional school, an account that graphically illustrated his pain and anger at being compelled to learn to teach in an environment that was unsuited to his learning style. David's presentation at the oral defense of his thesis did not include warrants for his assertions, focusing instead on a discussion organized around a set of 10 sketches described as narrative scenes selected for their personal salience.

We accept David's narrative as a component of autobiographical research, but maintain that more is needed to substantiate claims of authenticity in his work. Although the oral and written texts were interesting, the lack of deconstructive commentary raised questions among the academic community. Could we consider this research, given that this work did not meet the quality criteria for interpretive evaluation? Absent from the written and oral texts were explicit interpretive frames against which the coherence of the assertions could be judged. David's assertions were not explicitly connected to claims from other studies and the narrative did not contain clear-cut empirical and theoretical warrants for most of the assertions. It was as if the telling of the story was sufficient to establish its viability.

What was needed was for David to go beyond a descriptive account of events to include reasons for what happened from the perspectives of the participants in the study. Only in a limited way did the oral and written research texts address the authenticity criteria, and the result was to compromise the integrity of the study's findings. Others became aware of David's constructions and could learn from them, and the study itself catalyzed departmental actions to change aspects of the student teaching experience. However, there was no evidence presented to suggest that David's emic constructions changed throughout the study. Had he employed the hermeneutic–dialectical circle in the design of his study he would have approached participants from within critical stakeholder groups to identify a range of stories associated with the situations focused on in the study. Assessment of these stories would have enabled David to present a number of different accounts, each deemed to be viable by stakeholder constructions. Not only would this have enabled him to learn from the differing accounts and the reasons for participants regarding them as viable, but the availability of the accounts would have enhanced the educative authenticity of the study. In addition, a greater number of participants could have learned from the multiple accounts, thereby increasing the catalytic authenticity of the study. Tactical authenticity was limited because stakeholders who willingly would have provided input were excluded by his approach to the study. Finally, in terms of fairness, it could be argued that David's account of what happened was one-sided and did not honor the constructions of all stakeholders by providing an opportunity to present and clarify different perspectives of what happened.

The studies of graduate students and colleagues engaging in critical autobiography, could be enhanced by their considering how the hermeneutic–dialectical circle could be employed in the early stages of the research to identify, serially and contingently, those participants considered to be essential data sources. The ethics of the design could be considered to the extent that the actions of the researcher exhibited practical wisdom in terms of the balance between being fair, caring, courageous, and truthful (Sockett, 1993). Attention should be given to these four ethical considerations if the research is to reach its full potential, even though it is not expected that one study can attempt to do everything.

Finally, the critical autobiographer needs to be conscious of what makes a study critical. Although other aspects of authenticity should always be considered, in this genre of interpretive research ontological authenticity is of greatest significance. From the outset a critical autobiography should plan to deconstruct the texts to foreground the author's understanding of his or her own experience (Schaller, 1995a). Yet autobiographical research can be viewed as more than a critically reflective tool for self-education through interpretive inquiry on oneself. It is an interpretation of socially and culturally negotiated meanings, mediated through the actions and beliefs of the primary stakeholder(s). As such, critical or interpretive autobiography is also a literary vehicle for the dissemination of research on teachers' beliefs and methods for uncovering them.

Critical autobiography always runs the risk of falling victim to academic concerns ranging from rampant subjectivity to self-deception. This is not to say that objectivity is the goal of the autobiographer, but accounting for one's subjectivity, through peer review and member checking, is. Having colleagues or other close acquaintances review the texts for inconsistencies is necessary for the author to avoid being accused of creating unaccountable fictitious renditions for either unconscious or blatant reasons. What about the purposeful and candid use of fictive methods such as composite characterization, scene-by-scene construction, interior monologue, and third-person-subjective point of view? Are there valid research agendas that can benefit from these liturgical methods that serve to rhetorically heighten the narrative and enhance the meaning by conveying a calculated message to the intended audience?

Fictive Stories as Interpretive Research

Description and interpretation are both constructs of other people's constructs, and, as such, introduce a continuum of fiction into any research text. Yet the deliberate use of varying degrees of fictional elements in narrative prose is becoming more widespread in the reporting of interpretive research. For the social scientist, fictive stories represent a powerful method of creating a compelling and vivid retelling of a story that strives for a wider metaphorical and symbolic context than does conventional writing.

The use of pseudonyms for places and people is one example of a fictive method used to address ethical issues of fairness in reporting. Furthermore, in the case study of "Peter" (Tobin, Kahle, & Fraser, 1990), the researchers modified a number of characteristics in the case study's narrative to ensure that it would be difficult to track down the actual identity of the teacher. The belief of the research team was that certain "facts" could be changed without detracting from the authenticity of the research.

A less common example of the use of fictive methods occurred in a study reported by Tippins, Tobin, and Nichols (1995). The paper was an invited contribution to a journal featuring constructivism and the teaching of elementary science. Each author brought to the research effort field notes and interview transcripts from prior studies, extensive experience of teaching science, and a working knowledge of relevant studies and their theoretical frameworks. The team's goal was to create a composite character and a set of likely events that illustrated critical issues associated with teaching and learning science and science teacher education. The authors' knowledge claims in the article were ratified with warrants of extensive experience in the field that helped not only to create a compelling and believable story, but, in a cautious sense, a credible one.

The use of constructivism as a referent for the various roles "Mrs. Halfaday" assumed as a science teacher was established as the substantive focus in this fictitious account. Many of the procedural and authenticity issues that were so critical to the earlier examples of the different genres of interpretive research can, and should, be applied to the use of virtual texts such as this one. Volumes of field texts and other related data from prior studies can be construed and then reconstrued into a composite account of plausible events to illustrate a substantive issue. By doing so, the author provides the reader-as-participant with an ontological perspective on the story in much the same way as a good novel does, by providing the opportunity to vicariously appreciate and comprehend a range of critical issues more effectively than through technical writing strategies.

Similarly, fictive stories provide for the authors the opportunity to contribute to and shape the narrative from their prior experiences, providing greater ontological comprehension of their own views and positions on substantive issues. In the same vein, likely stories such as the Mrs. Halfaday paper also provide readers with the tactical opportunity to be confronted with the constructions of others, which may catalyze and direct future action on their part. The following notes that illustrate the aforementioned criteria are taken from an account of the process of constructing the Mrs. Halfaday paper (Tobin, 1993).

We agreed to set a context of a Grade 3 classroom. The topic was spiders. "Who is the teacher?" my colleagues asked. "It doesn't matter," I commented, anxious to get on with the business of building a portrait of life in that classroom. But it did matter. The teacher needed to be one that we did know because what the classroom was like would depend so much on her. She had to be female to tell the story we wanted to tell. One of the authors,

Deborah, is of Native American heritage and she could help us build a picture of life in that classroom through the eyes of a Native American female teacher. We were making progress. My colleagues were gaining in their enthusiasm for the task. What would be different about this class? What would we choose to describe and what would we choose to ignore? This would be a class in which the teacher was using portfolios as a way to assess what students know but also around which classroom culture would be built. Value would be given to student–student interactions. Gradually we found ourselves looking into a virtual classroom grounded in a composite of real-life experiences. We eavesdropped on students and conversations involving the teacher and students, gaining direct access into their inner thoughts.

"What is her name?" "Mrs. Halfaday," said Deborah, without a moment of thought. "Here," I said, thrusting some typewritten pages toward Deborah. "I asked Mrs. Halfaday to describe her past history just the other day." Deborah accepted a transcribed interview in which a woman described how she became a teacher and how her pedagogy evolved from an objectivist orientation to a practice centered around constructivist principles over the course of her career. Now we were building a composite character, through the deliberate fashioning of character traits and anecdotes drawn from a number of sources into a single representative sketch of constructivist teaching and learning that seemed authentic and believable. Mrs. Halfaday began to live in our minds and the paper quickly took shape. "Let me interview Mrs. Halfaday," I commented as I moved toward a computer on which I constructed a fictional interview with her. Finally, late into the morning, the paper was completed and edited. We had succeeded in our creation. Almost everything we had written was based on our current un-derstanding of constructivism and in many ways the activity was analogous to a literature review of our past research. The resultant narrative was a likely story that would appeal to teachers and teacher educators alike.

We had completed the writing but there was a final important issue to be resolved. There was no methodology included in the paper. "What do we write about our methods?" my colleagues asked. I was not sure, but I thought the paper was complete. "Should we tell them that Mrs. Halfaday is a composite character?" "What does it matter?" I asked. I found myself becoming aggressive on this point. "The paper is authentic and credible and we have used 'actual' data in many parts and our imagination throughout. Our imagination is shaped and constrained by experience. We have been into many classes and Mrs. Halfaday has emerged from those experiences." A methods section did not fit with the narrative method of describing what we had learned from our research in classrooms and the question of whether or not Mrs. Halfaday was real or imagined seemed at the time to be irrelevant. It would be up to the readers to decide whether there was anything in this paper that was pertinent to the settings in which they practiced. That decision would not rest on the fact that Mrs. Halfaday was not a person in an actual world, but a composite character in a virtual text who spoke vicariously to a real audience. What *was* important would be the extent to which readers could project themselves into the images we had created and whether or not, as a result of their reflections, they decided to try some things differently in their classrooms. In effect, the goal of our research had not changed from our previous work in the more traditional interpretive research genres.

To the extent possible, those researchers that create fictive accounts should be explicit about the knowledge claims they are making in the research text and the warrants for those claims. To the reader it should be clear whether a given claim is based on a theoretical perspective and whether the claim involves a fictional retelling of events that have been experienced or imagined. In this genre of research, the theoretical under-pinnings that support the fictive account are most important and ought to be visible either in the fictive account or in the accompanying interpretive account, if included. In the creation of fictive texts it would be especially deceptive not to be explicit regarding the extent to which the text is fictive and to describe the methods employed in the production of the text. Fur-thermore, we believe that failing to disclose the methods of a study is to ignore a fundamental tenet of appropriate research protocol for good inter-pretive research. That is not to say that there is no meaningful value in likely stories in the absence of full methodological disclosure, but that there would be questions as to the quality of the reporting and the integrity as a whole of such "literature" from a research perspective.

REPORTING WHAT WAS LEARNED FROM RESEARCH

A role of the researcher is to report to others what has been learned from a study in a way that convinces them that chosen forms of expression constitute appropriate research texts. Furthermore, the report is usually written as a rhetorical event to persuade readers that what has been learned in a study has potential relevance to their practices. This section explores some of the issues associated with the standards of writing research texts.

The commonly accepted rhetoric for writing research texts in science and mathematics education is scientific. It has its source in the discipline of psychology, which was the first of the human sciences to adopt the scientific method and develop a scientific rhetoric that became widely ac-cepted as a model for research texts. The codification of this rhetoric for writing organized texts in the typical order of title, introduction, method, literature review, results, and discussion is found in the *Publication Manual of the American Psychological Association* (APA, 1994), which has become the style manual of choice. APA style, however, is couched in essentially behaviorist assumptions about process and knowledge and is procedurally inclined to require adherence to prescriptions rather than thinking or venturing beyond the preestablished headings of the manual. Objectivity is emphasized in the passive third person point of view in most works adhering to APA format, and the empirical evidence experimentally contrived from controlled environments is used to support claims of freedom from researcher bias. However, technical writing that is primarily expository and uses objective conventions such as the passive third-person point of view and nominalizations does not guarantee objectivity. Indeed, Dobrin (1985) insisted that "objectification is often the result when objectivity is the goal" (p. 249). If we want to avoid writing conventions that alienate both the author and the reader from the human experience (which is entirely subjective), then we should oppose traditional writing strategies that are purely technical.

In recent years a new cadre of interpretive researchers has drawn from field experiences and reflections and embraced the broader perspective of participatory knowledge by writing research texts in the form of stories (Schaller, 1995b). Narrative is frequently used in the telling of these stories because of its potential to contribute to the creation of understanding and knowledge by seducing the reader into an interactive relationship with the text. The researcher in essence becomes a filter through which personal experience is shaped and given meaning. As we move away from realism to embrace increasingly aesthetic versions of the human experience, we move, not to myth and fantasy, but to a form of relativism that more effectively communicates understanding and meaning. To accomplish this literary objective, the researcher must embrace the fictional element inevitable in all research and try to imagine his or her way to the story to be told through a continuum of fact to fiction. Hellman (1981) characterized this literary movement as a "revolt by the individual against homogenized forms of experience, against monolithic versions of truth" (p. 8). One method we have illustrated (which is not commonly employed to accomplish this goal within a research context) is characterized by the use of fictive methods. It is relevant to note, however, that all forms of interpretive research are literally interpretations of the researcher's constructions of other people's constructions of their own and others' experiences and so on, and as such are thought experiments (Geertz, 1973), evolving as much from the imagination as from the data.

The purpose of fictive writing techniques such as composite characterization, scene-by-scene construction, interior monologue, and third-person subjective point of view is to provide powerful and authentic representations of individuals and the social milieu with psychological depth. Drenched in social realism and describing virtual characters and events rather than actual ones, fictive stories are seen by many as a text constructed from methodical field work and framed within the personal lens of the researcher (Barone, 1988; Hellman, 1981; Hollowell, 1977). This strategy for creating research texts represents an innovative and creative form of ethnography that, like art, strives to find new ways of imitating life. For educational researchers, these techniques allow the research to explore the potential of the hidden world of the classroom and provide the participants' reflections on their own experiences. These insiders' views, supported by careful research, are conveyed in forms that can give greater depth and dimension to the facts.

CONCLUSION

Conventional writing strategies may be more suitable for traditional participant observer research, and are certainly less likely to arouse academic criticism than the use of fictive methods. Yet, regardless of the methods employed, we have suggested in the cases presented in this chapter that the researcher can greatly increase the power and quality of the research findings through careful attention to fairness and the ontological, educative, tactical, and catalytic criteria for establishing the goodness (and hence the authenticity) of interpretive research. It is our position that these authenticity criteria can best be accomplished through the researcher's careful adherence to six procedural steps. Taken together, the satisfaction of the authenticity criteria through prolonged engagement, persistent observation, peer debriefing, negative case analysis, progressive subjectivity, and member checks constitutes the foundation of quality criteria in interpretive research. Careful attention to the quality criteria is essential to ensure that the declarations, or assertions of a study are congruent with the evidence. Furthermore, the assertions of an interpretive study ought to be viable and the warrants for the viability of those claims need to be clearly specified in the research text.

A carefully planned research design should embrace a dialectical relationship between the substantive research issue(s) and the methods employed, so that neither is viewed independently of the other. As a guiding framework, researchers should consistently explored (from the planning phases to the final draft of the research text) the substantive issues, in terms of the methods with which they have comfort and value as being appropriate. Although at first glance this sounds simple enough, it proves to be a conceptual strategy of great difficulty for the novice researcher. Even more difficult to grasp is the understanding that, in the final analysis, the researcher should exercise caution in sacrificing substance for method. On the surface it is clear that traditional research efforts in science and mathematics education were quantitative exercises that rigorously adhered to method; however, it not clear how many of the findings of these efforts contributed solutions to, or greater understanding of, the substantive issues challenging education today.

If our goal as educational researchers is to address the issues that face our schools and effectively communicate the deeper structures of the classroom experience, then we need to seek more powerful representations of those experiences in our research texts. The utilization of creative rhetoric in our writing must match the task at hand, which often beckons us to go beyond the traditional constraints of technical reports and produce research products that engage the reader in the vicarious experience of the text. The idiosyncratic style, supported by the use of fictive techniques, places increased emphasis on interpretation. The claim that this form of rhetoric is a viable solution to the problem of making experience more comprehensible and sharable clearly demands further consideration. If educational researchers are to command a broader audience for the discussion of educational phenomena in the public arena, then they must be willing to take greater risks to achieve a more powerful shaping of their educational insights. Eisner (1985) reminded us that "educational research provides not so much conclusions or recipes for practice as it does analytical models for thinking about practice" (p. 359). If we are to think clearly of the multiple realities of the educational experience in our studies of classroom life, then we must remain open to alternative ways of organizing those experiences. Redefining the practice of writing up our studies from objective technical reports to research texts that are truly a product of quality interpretive research involves risk, but the ends may justify the means if greater understanding is the product.

REFERENCES

American Psychological Association. (1994). *Publication manual of the American Psychological Association* (4th ed.). Washington, DC: Author.

Barone, T. E. (1988). Curriculum platforms and literature. In L. E. Beyer & M. W. Apple (Eds.), *The curriculum: Problems, politics and possibilities* (pp. 140–165). Albany: State University of New York Press.

Dobrin, D. N. (1985). Is technical writing particularly objective? *College English, 47,* 237–251.

Eisner, E. W. (1985). *The educational imagination: On the design and evaluation of school programs.* New York: Macmillan.

Erickson, F. (1986). Qualitative research on teaching. In M. C. Wittrock (Ed.), *Handbook of research on teaching* (3rd ed., pp. 119–161). New York: Macmillan.

Galtung, J. (1982). *The true worlds: A transnational perspective.* New York: The Free Press.

Geertz, C. (1973). *The interpretations of cultures.* New York: Basic Books.

Guba, E. G., & Lincoln, Y. S. (1989). *Fourth generation evaluation.* Beverly Hills, CA: Sage.

Hellman, J. (1981). *Fables of fact: The new journalism as a new fiction.* Urbana: University of Illinois Press.

Heshusius, L. (1992, January). *Methodological concerns around subjectivity: Will we free ourselves from objectivity? Ponderings at a conference*. Keynote address, Qualitative Research in Education Conference, College of Education, University of Georgia, Athens.

Hollowell, J. (1977). *Fact and fiction: The new journalism and the nonfiction novel*. Chapel Hill: University of North Carolina Press.

Janesick, V. J. (1994). The dance of qualitative research design: Metaphor, methodolatry, and meaning. In N. K. Denzin & Y. S. Lincoln (Eds.), *Handbook of qualitative research* (pp. 209–219). Thousand Oaks, CA: Sage Publications.

McCorcle, M. D. (1984). Stories in context: Characteristics of useful case studies for planning and evaluation. *Evaluation and Program Planning: International Journal, 7*(2), 205–208.

McRobbie, C. J., & Tobin, K. (1995). Restraints to reform: The congruence of teacher and student actions in a chemistry classroom. *Journal of Research in Science Teaching, 32*, 373–385.

McRobbie, C., & Tobin, K. (1997). A social constructivist perspective on learning environments. *International Journal of Science Education, 19*, 193–208.

NUD•IST 3.0.5 [Computer software]. (1994). Melbourne, Australia: Qualitative Solutions and Research Pty Ltd.

Reason, P. (1994). Three approaches to participative inquiry. In N. K. Denzin & Y. S. Lincoln (Eds.), *Handbook of qualitative research* (pp. 324–339). Thousand Oaks, CA: Sage.

Schaller, J. S. (1995a, March). *Autobiography as a method to reflect on curriculum development*. Paper presented at the annual meeting of the Southeastern Association of Educators of the Teaching of Science, Pensacola, FL.

Schaller, J. S. (1995b). *Teacher as a learner: Making sense of teaching through autobiographical ethnography*. Unpublished doctoral dissertation, Florida State University, Tallahassee.

Sockett, H. (1993). *The moral base for teacher professionalism*. New York: Teachers College Press.

Tippins, D. J., Tobin, K., & Nichols, S. E. (1995). Constructivism as a referent for elementary science teaching and learning. *Research in Science Education, 25*(2), 135–149.

Tobin, K. (1993). Referents for making sense of science teaching. *International Journal of Science Education, 15*(3), 241–254.

Tobin, K., Kahle, J. B., & Fraser, B. J. (Eds.). (1990). *Windows into science classrooms: Problems associated with higher-level learning*. London: Falmer.

Tobin, K., & McRobbie, C. J. (1996a). Cultural myths as restraints to the enacted science curriculum. *Science Education, 80*, 223–241.

Tobin, K., & McRobbie, C. (1996b). Significance of limited English proficiency and cultural capital to the performance in science of Chinese-Australians. *Journal of Research in Science Teaching, 33*, 265–282.

Tobin, K., & McRobbie, C. (in press-a). Beliefs about the nature of science and the enacted science curriculum. *Science and Education*.

Tobin, K., & McRobbie, C. (in press-b). Perspectives on the adequacy of teacher representations of knowledge of electrochemistry. In J. G. Newsome & N. Lederman (Eds.), *Pedagogical content knowledge and the teaching of science*. Dortrecht, The Netherlands: Kluwer.

4

Using Clinical Interviews in Qualitative Research

John M. Truran
University of Adelaide

Kathleen M. Truran
University of South Australia

As Wiliam indicated in chapter 1, educational research makes a distinction between quantitative and qualitative forms of analysis. Quantitative analysis uses numbers to measure the variables being investigated, and applies standard statistical techniques to interpret the figures obtained. Qualitative analysis interprets spoken or written language, and sometimes other forms of communication, such as drawings or body language. As the limitations of the former have become more apparent, qualitative methods have developed, particularly to assess educational parameters such as comprehension, attitudes, and relational understanding. The two approaches are best seen as complementary, rather than as opposing, methods. In this chapter we discuss one form of qualitative research, the clinical interview, developed by Piaget (1929/1971) as a major investigative tool, and provide guidelines for conducting such interviews effectively.

Students and supervisors often undertake clinical interviews with individuals or with small groups as part of their research. Some researchers use partly nonverbal responses by asking for drawings and their interpretation (Mountford, 1976). Others make generalizations about how people think and how their thinking develops, assess understanding prior to a course of instruction (Hunting & Doig, 1992), or assess the effect of instruction. Typically, a clinical interview involves presenting a set of questions, some prepared, some following from the subject's responses to previous questions. It is this flexibility that makes clinical interviews such a valuable research tool. The responses are usually recorded on either a tape or video recorder, and later transcribed, coded, and interpreted.

Clinical interviews have attracted both praise and criticism (e.g., Opper, 1977; Vuyk, 1981). They have become increasingly popular, partly because of their intrinsic strengths, partly because of the current popularity of the constructivist paradigm, and partly because feminist researchers seeking alternative sources have found them amenable to theoretical interpretations using grounded theory. They are time consuming to interpret and their administration requires special skills—quick reactions, sensitivity to others, and a deep knowledge of relevant subject matter. However, they can provide reliable, valid and useful findings that are otherwise difficult to establish.

EVALUATION OF THE CLINICAL METHOD

Ginsburg (1981) has listed three legitimate uses of the clinical interview in research:

- The discovery of cognitive attitudes.
- The identification of cognitive activities.
- The evaluation of levels of competence.

These uses are comprehensive, but to maximize their value it is important to follow certain procedures, such as those suggested by Pines, Novak, Posner, and Van Kirk (1978), who emphasized that a good clinical interview has questions which are designed "to assess the child's cognitive structure, not to teach him, nor to inform him of its rightness or wrongness." If researchers' aims match these principles then they should consider using clinical interviews. Here is an example of part of an interview (Booth, 1984) with a 14-year-old girl who had been unable to suggest anything for the perimeter of a polygon with four sides of length m and one side of length p. (For brevity, only minimal detail is provided for excerpts from transcripts quoted in this chapter. If the context can be deduced from the text then it is not stated explicitly. Details such as age and gender are stated only if relevant to the point being made. The letter "I" stands for interviewer, "M" is the first letter of the subject's name.)

I: You know how to do it for this shape? (A new [polygon] provided with sides 5, 5, 4, 3, and 2.) Right? What did you do there?
M: Counted all the numbers up.
I: Right. What do you think you'd do here?
M: Can't, it's got no numbers.

I: If there were numbers could you do it?

M: Yes, but not if it's got no numbers. I don't know what *m* means and what *p* is.

I: Suppose I tell you, that *m* just means some number and *p* means a number, but it's a game and you don't know what the numbers are. Could you tell me anything about how you'd find the perimeter, what you'd do to the *m*s and *p* to get the perimeter?

M: I suppose I'd have to measure them or something.

I: And then what?

M: Count them up. (pp. 15–16)

Some might argue that the interviewer was teaching rather than probing. We would argue rather that the response to the penultimate question confirms that M does not conceive that letters can stand for numbers—she denies it even when she is told it.

The flexibility of clinical interviews has led some to object that findings from them are not valid and reliable. It is true that even if the same interviewer merely questions the same child a second time using the same questions, identical responses are unlikely. Each interview constitutes a learning experience to some extent, so different responses are to be expected. Indeed, consistent responses may imply rote memorization, rather than meaningful learning. Reliability and validity are not absolute virtues: they must be assessed in terms of the way the information is used and the nature of the knowledge claims made. If clinical interviews can show thinking not revealed in other ways, then they are of special value (Swanson, Schwartz, Ginsburg, & Kossan, 1981). Conventional questioning has the same problems: Hart (1983) has shown that small changes in the form of a question often produce different responses or methods, and Alarcon (1982) has shown that interviews may produce responses quite different from those obtained using paper-and-pencil tests. The researcher must take these findings into account and seek to ask questions in a variety of ways to establish whether the subject's responses are stable, or idiosyncratic to the specific question being asked.

Skillful questioning and empathy with the child are essential. Children may try to give answers based on their interpretation of what the researcher wants them to say (Donaldson, 1978). The interviewer must "be prepared to set up counter examples which would give a crucial test to the assumption that the student is reasoning in the correct manner" (Collis, 1975, p. 108). Here is an example from one of the best known of Piaget's experiments (Piaget, 1941/1952, p. 59).

Aud (6;7): We're going to play at selling flowers. Here are eight pennies.—(He counted them correctly.) *Eight pennies.*—Each flower costs a penny. How many will you be able to buy?—*Eight.*—(The one for one exchange was made, and the pennies were put in a row while the child kept the flowers in his hand.) Is there the same number of flowers and pennies?—*No. There* (pennies) *there are more.*—Why?—*They're spread out.*—Could we put one flower on each penny?—Yes.—Then is there the same number of both?—*No. There are more there* (pennies) *because they're spread out.* (p. 59)

By demonstrating that the child was aware of the one–one correspondence between the number of flowers and the number of pennies, Piaget could show that such awareness was not a sufficient condition for a fully developed understanding of conservation of number.

Clinical interviews are more effective with articulate students, but children who can pass a verbal test on a topic are highly likely to be able to pass a nonverbal test on the same topic (Davies, 1965). So an interview should at least be able to indicate what a child can do, and can use nonverbal responses as well to provide a richer source of data.

The flexibility of a clinical interview is of special value when research is first being undertaken in a new topic. Such research usually starts with a fact-collecting stage (Romberg, 1983), in which the informal, flexible approach of the clinical interview is particularly valuable, because it may not be clear initially what the best questions to ask are.

Finally, clinical interviews have an advantage in education that is not often mentioned. The parry and thrust of diagnostic questioning is more interesting than detailed numerical analysis. Asking questions is a major classroom activity, so good questions developed by a researcher can have immediate application by any concerned classroom teacher and can allow the clinical researcher's findings to be an influence for good in classrooms. In this chapter we have chosen examples to encourage such links.

THE IMPORTANCE OF AN EDUCATIONAL THEORY

One test of a good detective story is whether the author has provided sufficient clues for the reader to decide, with clearly stated reasons, who committed the crime well before the *dénouement*. If a person rereads a mystery that a first reading failed to solve, they will see where they skated over critical information that did not at the time look to be relevant. They will see how quite simple statements can be interpreted in more than one way, that not everyone tells the truth, and often people do not tell all of the truth. A detective's skill is to keep an open mind and to focus on the area of primary interest—who committed the crime?

Good educational researchers have good detective skills. Novice interviewers will need to choose their focus and be cautious in their interpretations. No interpretation of educational behavior is value free. In clinical interviews, the questions, both prepared and spontaneous, will inevitably reflect the researcher's theories of how children learn and how their learning may be observed by outsiders. The research report may be read by those who hold different theories of learning. Many theories of learning have been developed (Ernest, 1991) and most retain some validity today.

Constructivism is an educational paradigm currently popular in educational circles. It argues that knowledge is actively built up by the learner, rather than being passively received, and that learning is directed to organizing the experiential world, rather than to establishing unattainable absolute truth. Social constructivists emphasize that knowledge is built up within a community and is validated by the culture of that community (von Glaserfeld, 1991, 1995). The following interview (Frid & Malone, 1995, p. 142) was conducted within a social constructivist framework. It was directed toward finding out the extent to which a child used other people for help in solving a school problem:

I: Do you ever ask any of your friends to help you with it?

L: Um. No.

I: Do they ever ask you for help?

L: Not really. They usually just wait for the teacher to tell them.

Researchers who are interested in different aspects of problem solving might ask different questions, such as:

I: Do you have questions which you would like to ask your friends or teachers?

I: Do you read your textbook to get help when you are stuck?

I: Do you try to explain your difficulty to other people?

The first possibility focuses less on the social aspect of problem solving and more on the cognitive aspect of trying to verbalize a difficulty. The second focuses more on the child's perception of what authorities are available to help him or her to solve a problem. The third focuses on a theory of learning which believes that explaining to others can assist understanding. All these questions are just as valid as the ones quoted, but reflect different ways of looking at what can be done to seek assistance with a difficult problem. Researchers do not have an infinite amount of time with their subjects, so their questions tend to reflect the particular theories to which they subscribe.

If the reader is engaged in writing a thesis, then you probably studied a number of educational theories before starting that task. If not, then you should seek immediate advice from your supervisor. Evaluating, selecting, and working within all these theories can be quite daunting for beginning researchers, especially because many researchers exhibit an evangelical fervor for their adopted theory, a fervor often demanding political correctness and sometimes bordering on paranoia. Do not be put off. Just as in physics, wave mechanics and quantum mechanics have both been found to be helpful for interpreting different aspects of motion, so in education it may be more effective to use more than one theory to interpret your data. Of course, the more frameworks you understand well, the better equipped you are to build up a helpful theoretical base. And the better your base is defined, the easier it will be for you to sustain an acceptable interpretation of your data. What is important in your thesis is that the frameworks you have chosen to work within are made absolutely clear; once this is done there should be no problem about your making valid knowledge claims. Here is a summary from a masters thesis (Carr, 1994) of one such fully explicated framework:

> The research method chosen for this thesis relied on skilled observation and listening, a ready initial acceptance of student ideas and further investigation of those thoughts. Collecting data and the social construction of knowledge was made possible by an intervention comprising group activities. Students were confronted with new ideas and during the interviews were requested to justify responses and encouraged to reflect on their ideas. (p. 16)

However, your framework is only a stepping stone on the path toward your real aim—an answer to a well-posed interesting question.

DEFINING A TOPIC

Although your questioning may be unstructured, this does not mean that your research questions will be vague. Rather, they will be keenly focused on your carefully defined topic. We do not discuss here the process of selecting a suitable topic, but we emphasize that with clinical interviews the topic needs to be particularly well defined. Here are two examples of clearly defined statements. Each follows a summary discussion of previous research work and a statement of its author's theoretical framework:

> The focus this time was senior primary children . . . and their questions about number—could questions be elicited from them, what features might such questions have, could they form the basis of useful investigations in mathematics? (Biddulph, 1995, p. 97)

> Hence, questions remain: are concrete representations effective in teaching algebra; if so, which ones and why; what is the effect of processing load in such use? (Boulton-Lewis et al., 1995, pp. 121–122)

You can see how precisely these research questions are defined. Once you have done likewise, you can use Ginsburg's criteria mentioned earlier to determine whether a clinical interview is an appropriate methodology. You are then ready to start to think about the logistics of conducting interviews. Organizing equipment and planning visits to schools will take some time.

ADMINISTRATIVE MATTERS

Some aspects of this section are concerned with obtaining suitable equipment that may need to be bought or borrowed. Consult early with your supervisor about your needs, so that everyone concerned is aware of what money needs to be spent, where it will come from, who will spend what, and who will own the purchased equipment after you have finished with it.

Working Within Schools

The ideal physical environment for your interviews is probably your own room, where the equipment can be set up in the best possible way. Such surroundings will rarely be available and may not be desirable because the environment will be unfamiliar to the child. Most researchers conduct their interviews as field workers in schools, so interviewing in the school environment is the principal focus of this chapter. Chapter 2 on ethnography touches on this matter also.

Schools are busy places and teachers have a wide range of duties. You will almost always find that they will be cooperative, but you must plan your work carefully to minimize the impact of your interviews on school routine. Similarly, you need to make allowance for difficulties fitting into the many vagaries of a school's timetable. The keys to minimizing disruption to you or the school are flexibility and careful, long-term planning.

Your initial approach to the school should cover at least the following matters:

- Your name, address, and contact numbers (phone, fax, and e-mail).
- The title of your project, and a summary of your research questions.
- The reasons why you want to interview children.
- The reasons why you want to interview children from this particular school.
- A clear statement of the type of children you want to interview, how you want to select them, what you want to ask them, how long you want with each child, and whether the interview will be tape- or video-recorded.

- Your institution and supervisor, with his or her contact numbers.
- The award toward which the results of your research will contribute.
- An assurance that your work is not physically, mentally, or emotionally intrusive, that parental permission will be sought, that the child's and school's anonymity will be preserved and, where applicable, that your research is acceptable to your institution's ethics committee.
- Some indication of how your data will be stored and when and how final results will be made available.

Initially you should approach the school principal. In systemic schools, you will probably then need to approach the head office of the system. You may need to apply on standard forms and your application may have to go before an ethics committee. Permission will usually be granted for soundly based proposals that have the support of the principal, but bureaucracy takes time and some committees may not meet often, so be sure that you allow enough time.

Once permission has been granted, make an appointment to visit the school to establish links and discuss your requirements carefully with your contact teachers well before you start work. For example, if you want to study a wide spectrum of children, you may need to dissuade teachers from offering you their more articulate students. At this visit, inspect your interviewing room to check the facilities to find out what extra equipment, such as extension cords or double adapters, will be required.

You will also need to seek parental permission to interview a child. In the letter state briefly who you are, where you come from, and what the interviews will be used for. Indicate the length of each interview, whether it will be audio- or video-recorded, and what will be done with the records. Emphasize that each child's anonymity will be preserved in any published results. You may avoid discussing the subject matter of your investigations in order to avoid priming the children. A tear-off consent form should be printed at the bottom of the letter.

In many schools teachers will be interested in what you are doing. You can repay their hospitality by offering to lead a staff seminar on the subject of your research and by ensuring that at least a summary of your final results is sent to all those who have helped you.

Ethical Issues

A clinical interviewer is privileged. You will spend time with a child, probably alone, and have the freedom to ask that child any question relevant to the research. Every effort should be made not only to uphold this trust, but also to ensure that the trust is seen to be being upheld.

As a visitor to a school, you will probably be subject to local legislative requirements about compulsory reporting of any child whom you have good reason to believe is the victim of abuse. But remember, too, that you are a visitor to the school, and the school authorities may know far more than you do. Consulting first with a senior member of staff about the situation should ensure appropriate action, with minimal disturbance to the child.

Subjects' responses may depend on whether rewards are offered and also on the size of the rewards (Cohen, 1964). If you wish to offer rewards, be very sure beforehand that such a practice is acceptable to all concerned; it is easily open to misinterpretation. You will need to be equally careful when working with potentially controversial materials such as playing cards.

Environment

The ideal interviewing environment is a small room with a glass door to keep out noise but allow passersby to see what you are doing. Such a room will not always be available. Arrange the space you are given so that the child feels comfortable and secure, and so that it is not possible for untoward suggestions to be made about what you are doing in the room. A large, flat table is usually the best working area. Seat the child nearer to the door than you, with each of you at adjacent sides of the table. Children feel more comfortable with something solid like a table leg between you and them.

Conducting an Interview

When a child arrives, introduce yourself and any assistants such as video camera operators. Ask the child's name and show him or her where to sit. Explain briefly what you are going to do. Point out any equipment, such as pencil and paper or calculators, that the child is free to use, and ensure that the child is happy for the interview to be recorded. Allow time for the child to ask you any questions.

Be sure that you know how the school timetable is running, and that you have enough time to complete the interview. If a bell rings during the interview, check that the child is free and willing to stay.

When the interview has finished, turn off any recorders—sometimes children may want to say something "off the record"—and thank the child for cooperating. Explain the importance of not talking to other children about your questions. Check that the child knows where he or she is meant to go to after leaving you.

DEVELOPING YOUR PROTOCOL

All of these practical details are but preliminaries for your fundamental purpose—asking a sequence of questions to elucidate the subject's thinking on a specific matter. This sequence is called a *protocol* and refers here to the outline of a procedure that can never be totally specified in advance.

Writing and Trialing

Research questions are not like the classroom questions that teachers pose:

> Asking questions to which you already know the answer is a very odd linguistic
> activity, almost entirely restricted to classrooms, or at least to teaching situ-
> ations. In other circumstances it would rightly be considered bizarre, except
> as a conversational gambit (where it is not apparent to the person you are
> talking to that you do know the answer). . . . The oddness of this classroom
> activity is highlighted by the fact that many Aboriginal children in Australia
> have great difficulty understanding it when they go to school. In their culture
> it is considered impolite to ask questions, and to ask questions when you
> already know the answer is clearly verging on insanity. (Ainley, 1987, p. 25)

Questions in a clinical interview are designed to elicit information about
a child's understanding; they are designed to elicit information to which the
interviewer does *not* know the answer, though this may not be obvious to
the children. B. Bell, Osborne, and Taylor (1985) gave this example of what
a clinical interview is *not* like:

I: What is steam made of?
S: It is kinda like water?
I: It is water.
S: Yes.

Start by preparing a set of questions that seem to probe the area of
interest and are sufficiently discriminatory to disclose gross misconceptions. Your literature search will probably have indicated good questions;
including some of these will give added strength to your thesis by allowing you
to compare sets of responses. A theoretical analysis of the situation may well
suggest other questions omitted by previous researchers, many of whom tend
not to work from a deep logical framework. Piaget (1929/1971) tried to use
questions "determined, in matter and in form, by the spontaneous questions
actually asked by children of the same age or younger" (p. 5).

Your initial questions may be quite simple. B. Bell (1993) reported an
interview with a group of children that started with the question, "What do
you reckon rust is?" and, as a result of the students' responses, later included such questions as, "What do you mean by that tarnish word?"; "So
is it, is the rust actually something that eats away, or is it something else
that's making the rust?"; and "Oh, so you reckon water make this rust. So
is the rust eating away, or the water?" The complete interview illustrates
very clearly how interaction with children helps a skilled questioner to ask
the sorts of questions that are likely to bring out the children's ideas.

Your language should be precise, unambiguous, but clear to the child. For example, using the word "die" as the singular of "dice" often confuses children, so it is better here to sacrifice precision for comprehension. Avoid using cue words, especially if you want to see whether children have spontaneous access to an idea. For example, the question "Do you think six *is* the hardest number to get when you toss a die?" emphasizes negative aspects, suggests that there is a hardest number, and focuses on "six." Much to be preferred is, "When you toss a die, is one number harder to get than others, or are they all the same?" Even this question still emphasizes "hardness," and this may be significant, so it would be wise to ask a second question using "easier" to check whether the child's responses are stable. Try to anticipate possible answers to your questions, and prepare a set of possible follow-up questions. Trial this draft protocol on your supervisor and other adult friends.

Once you have what you see as a good draft, test it several times before your major set of interviews. During these tests you will develop your own interviewing style, modify your protocol, and learn how to discourage children from trying to read your body language for an indication of whether they are giving you "right" answers. You will find out whether your protocol contains enough basic questions, or whether, as is often the case, you have assumed too much about where the children are. You will also discover how much you can do before the children become tired or bored. Start your trials with children you know socially, and then with friends' children whom you don't know. Finally, try out your protocol in a real school, preferably not the one where you will be doing your main work, and one that can allow you to meet children from a wide range of cultural backgrounds. Even if you are not using videorecorders in your main project, make a videotape of some of your interviews to help you develop a good style.

You will soon learn how ambiguous language is, and how careful you need to be in using it. Words may have quite distinct mathematical and common meanings (Hughes, 1986):

> I can recall very well the day when Sally, my 7-year-old stepdaughter, came home from school and showed me her two attempts to answer the subtraction problem "What is the difference between 11 and 6?" Her first answer had been "11 has two numbers," but this had been marked wrong. Her second attempt was "6 is curly," but this had also been treated as incorrect. (p. 43)

Sometimes children will apply meanings to words that are quite different from those which adults apply. Consider these responses from an able 12-year-old boy asked a question about the number of heads obtained when tossing 12 coins simultaneously and asked to express his answer by ticking one box out of several describing possible outcomes, such as various combinations of heads and tails as well as "All have the same chance:"

I: What is the answer?

D: All have the same chance.

I: What does that mean?

D: Can vary a lot.

I: Will any [faces] occur more often than others?

D: Yes, 5–7, 6–6, 7–5 more than 2–10.

I: Which one most?

D: Those three about the same.

I: And 8–4?

D: About the same.

I: And 9–3?

D: A bit less.

I: And 2–10?

D: Very unlikely.

I: Which answer would you pick then?

D: All have the same chance. (Green, 1983, pp. 549–550)

This is not a response we would have expected, and it took a lot of probing to find out what the boy really meant. The probing was probably not quite successful, but the questions were excellent. They probed without providing any hints about what a "correct" answer might be, and allowed the boy to stay with his initial response.

Sometimes the response you get will be bizarre. The following interview (K. Truran, 1995) is part of a discussion that related to "J"'s belief about luck:

J: Number 12 never comes up. It would never come up unless you are lucky.

I: Has luck got anything to do with this dice?

J: No . . . um, whenever you roll it, um . . . you just, . . . get the number that comes up and if it's not the right one it's bad luck.

I: So there is luck!

J: Not really. Just a little bit. Not that much.

I: How much luck is "a little bit"?

J: About half an inch (shows by separating her fingers).

In other words, remember that you are working with children who think within different frameworks from you. You must accept their frameworks, and be prepared for the fact that sometimes your interview will not be terribly successful, no matter how skilled you are. But your questions must remain nonauthoritarian, nonleading, and supportive, and must fit well within your educational theory.

These skills take time to refine. Even skilled teachers have found that they are difficult to acquire. It is worth taking the time to develop your skills before starting your major study.

Methods of Recording

No matter how sophisticated your recording techniques, some information is bound to be lost: It is impossible to retain for posterity every nuance of the whole interview. Most interviewers use either a video or audio recorder. Audio recorders effectively record the words used, and some verbal inflections, as well as interjections, giggles, and long silences. They are simple and cheap, and can be small and unobtrusive. Video recorders also record movements and facial expressions. However, if they are controlled by an operator who can focus, for example, on faces rather than hands, then relevant movements or expressions may well be missed. But if they are set permanently to encompass subject, interviewer, and workbench, they may lack clarity. They are more responsive and obtrusive, and require more care to set up and operate, especially when working by yourself. Currently, they are the preferred recording instrument by many researchers, but if you use them you must be sure that you will have the time to analyze all the extra information they provide and that this information will be relevant to your research.

All your equipment must be in first-class order and should be checked every day before going to visit the school, after it has been set up in the room, and every time you return to the room if the material has been left unattended, even if the door has been locked.

Methods of Transcribing

Transcribing data requires careful attention to detail and is slow and tedious. One experienced researcher has found that it takes him one hour of work to transcribe and code one minute of videotape (B. Wollring, personal communication, August 19, 1994). Audiotapes take less work, but not a lot less. Researchers are sometimes tempted to have their transcriptions carried out by clerical assistants, who will have rarely had formal training and will not have been present at the interview, so they will not be able to reflect on all the subtleties of the interview. For these reasons such transcriptions must be second rate. Children's responses are rarely fully organized and it often takes considerable skill to write down what they are saying. Furthermore, the significance of nontextual responses such as voice inflections, giggles, moving around in a chair, and long silences will often not be appreciated by untrained staff.

Your transcriptions will best be made onto a word processor, so that electronic means of analyzing them may be used. Remember to include nonverbal responses in your text where they actually occur. Consistent abbreviations recorded on a special sheet for the more common nonverbal responses will assist later analysis. A trial run with a small representative set of transcripts will help you to design a suitable system.

Use the best equipment you can afford for replaying your tapes. Obviously, a counter is essential. A foot-controlled stop–start mechanism is desirable, and you may need earphones if you share a room. Ensure that you have suitable storage facilities for your tapes and transcripts near your equipment. You will be pulling these in and out of shelves for 12 months or more; it is essential that they are stored logically and accessibly. If using videotapes, arrange the room so that others can watch and discuss the tapes with you.

Label each tape clearly with an easily interpreted code, both on the tape itself and also on its container. Store the containers vertically in a set of clearly labeled file drawers placed so that they are unlikely to be upended. Compile a printed inventory of all the tapes, with a list of the interviews on each side of each tape, their order, their length, and the counter number for the start of each segment. Time spent establishing this system at the beginning of your research will be well repaid later.

ANALYSIS OF SCRIPTS

This section provides only an introduction to the many possible ways of analyzing scripts. Much greater detail on specific approaches is provided in Fielding and Lee (1991), Patton (1990), Strauss and Corbin (1990), and Tesch (1990); see also chap. 5.

There are three basic steps in your analysis—coding, classifying, and summarizing. The whole text, including comments on nonverbal responses, is broken into pieces, the content of each section is described in a standardized form, and similarities between the descriptions are looked for. This is where your detective skills are very important. You must decide where to make the breaks in the text, and what aspects should be described in a way that will maximize the insights gained from the interviews. The better your decisions, the better and easier your analysis will be. The process is difficult and time consuming. Do not expect that you will get it right first time. It is true that much good work, notably that of Piaget, has been done without going through in detail the systematic process described later. An experienced researcher who has read and reflected on the texts in depth is often able to draw conclusions without overtly going through standard procedures. However, beginners will find it easier to work within a formal structure.

Using Computers

Computers can provide you with more flexibility than any other aids, and should speed up your work. But information technology can often create difficulties. Your equipment needs to be good enough and fast enough for its purposes. It must be accessible whenever needed. You will need relevant software, and adequate training in its use. Many software users are not clear what they want of the software when they start, so the trainer needs the ability to encourage users to talk through their needs so that relevant capabilities of the software may be pointed out. Further training is advisable once the user has defined his or her needs more precisely. Sometimes users will need to be told what is possible—word processors can assist the production of a thesis more than most people realize. Most important, you will need prompt access to skilled, sensitive, friendly support when things go wrong. Many institutions are particularly bad in providing support for software. Manuals are rarely available and the knowledge of many members of staff is frequently limited, even if they have the time to share it. You will especially need the sensitive support of your supervisor when you find, as so many students do, that the brick walls built around many information technology departments are totally impregnable.

Methods of Coding Data

Start by examining a representative small number of transcripts to try to find a classification that can describe compactly each situation you have presented to the children, each type of question you have put to them, and each type of response they have given. If you have done your work well, the first two of these groups will not have too many categories, but the number of responses may well be large. You will need to break your text up into "utterances" that will form the units for your classification. Each utterance will be coded with the concepts it conveys and perhaps the nonverbal responses which accompanied it.

Methods of Sorting and Linking Data

Here we discuss five basic approaches for analyzing your coded data. All are similar, but seem to be suited to different temperaments and purposes. All of our examples, of course, only touch briefly on what might be done.

Using Cards. Before the advent of personal computers, researchers had to use file cards to help them sort their data. Each coding, together with its root response, was placed on a separate card which was often color coded. sometimes with colored labels attached at different points on it. The whole set of cards could then be placed on a large, flat surface, usually the floor, and rearranged until patterns began to emerge. The physical disadvantages of such an approach will be obvious to anyone who has children or animals, but there are still researchers who use this method by choice, and it is certainly useful for testing small amounts of data. Its biggest disadvantage is that it is very time consuming to revise your classifications as you come to understand your data better.

Using a Word Processor. Your word processor can be used to do the same type of sorting electronically, using the "index" facility. Index entries corresponding to each of your classifications can be inserted after each segment of text in each document. Once this has been done, an index can rapidly be compiled for one transcript, or for any group of transcripts. An electronic copy of this index may be used to move entries around to look for links between classifications in different transcripts. You will find details on how to do all this in your computer manual.

Alternatively, you can use the "find" facility to locate each example of each classification, and then use "copy and paste" or "move" to gather similar pieces of text together. The larger the document the less effective this method is and it is tedious when working with more than one document. However, it is a useful method for doing exploratory studies, and should be part of your repertoire.

Using a Spreadsheet. An alternative approach is to enter your data on a spreadsheet. The data can be entered in such a way that a "1" indicates the presence of an attribute, a "0" its absence, and no entry indicates that no comment was made. Such an approach requires much care, it does lose some information, and it is difficult to pool results meaningfully from different subjects. However, the ability to rearrange data manually or to sort it automatically by columns or rows can be very valuable for finding out whether different attributes are related.

Using NUD•IST. Alternatively, you can use a specifically designed application. Tesch (1990) summarized many older ones. A popular new one is NUD•IST: Non-Numerical Unstructured Data—Indexing Searching and Theorizing.

NUD•IST is the most flexible of the approaches discussed so far and allows you to change your classifications easily and consistently. It provides a way of defining concepts and testing whether they fit into some hierarchical structure. It is able to incorporate nontextual data such as photographs and children's drawings into its database. It has sufficient flexibility and speed to enable you to undertake "what-if" inquiries to test your own hypotheses about how material fits together. Its major disadvantage is that it requires an enormous amount of work to prepare data for analysis.

Using Concept Map Analysis. NUD•IST generates hierarchical maps. Relational maps are called "concept maps" and illustrate a much wider range of links (Novak, 1990). Such an approach, with its ability to indicate varying strengths of relationships, enables issues that appear to be absolute to be discussed more generally. You need to learn to draw concept maps, and the analysis can be very complicated, but some researchers find the approach to be valuable.

Methods of Summarizing Data

Your research and analysis has been directed to answering your research question. With quantitative data, statistical analyses produce fairly compact and precise interpretations of large sets of figures. You must aim for this with qualitative data as well. Here are two examples:

> The results in this study are unequivocal at one level—the students did not use the knowledge taught to them about the concrete representations. . . . The reason for this appears to lie within the processing loads associated with concrete representations. (Boulton-Lewis et al., 1995, p. 125)

> Within the social realm of the two year five classes involved in this study, the process of "negotiation" of meaning was such that the conjecturing, criticizing, explaining, testing and refining of ideas and procedures was primarily the responsibility of the teacher. (Frid & Malone, 1995, p. 145)

Such compact, precise conclusions are good models for the end product of your clinical interviews. Being clear about what your knowledge claim is will make it much easier to select supporting examples from the mass of data that you have accumulated. Introduce each piece briefly, and comment on it in detail after the reader has had time to examine it. Try to provide both examples and counterexamples to illustrate points that you want to make. It is always hard for a reader of qualitative reports to be sure that representative samples of the examples supporting and opposing a knowledge claim have been quoted. Your case will be the stronger if you can provide other ways of supporting your claims as well.

Using Both Qualitative and Quantitative Methods

This chapter started with a dichotomous classification of research as either quantitative or qualitative. Ideally, the two should be seen as complementary. For example, you might include statements such as:

Of the 45 students interviewed, 43 considered that grass was alive, using state-ments like [here give an extract]. One of the other two (S) considered that grass was not human and was therefore not alive, while the other (T) consid-ered that it was not alive because it did not eat. On further questioning, S changed his opinion, saying [here give an extract].

Such an approach strengthens your case without losing the strengths of the interview method.

Some of your data may be amenable to formal quantitative analysis, usually using nonparametric methods. These are described in standard works (e.g., Daniel, 1990; Siegel, 1956). The process of supporting a knowl-edge claim by more than one method is known as "triangulation" and can add significantly to the strength of your report.

PRESENTATION OF RESULTS: SPECIAL ASPECTS OF PRESENTING CLINICAL RESULTS

Many aspects of presenting results are discussed in other chapters; we deal here with issues relating specifically to clinical interviews.

Submitting Basic Raw Data With Your Thesis

Traditionally, research results have been prepared as prose, perhaps sup-ported by tables and illustrations, and presented entirely in printed form. The very rich basic data from qualitative research cannot fit into such a form, so it is not possible to check an author's assertions against the basic data. All this has now changed. Results of qualitative research can now be easily attached to the thesis using any or all of floppy disks, microfiches, audiotapes, videotapes, and CD-ROMs.

Your thesis will still be written traditionally, because this is a highly efficient way of communicating. But you can refer to each set of data in appendices that contain an annotated summary of the data so that a reader can decide what he or she wants to look at, and be able to find it easily. Include the technical specifications of the material and its reading equip-ment needed to read the material. When your examiners are being chosen, inform your university that they will need to have access to such equipment.

Transcripts may be submitted either on microfiche or on floppy disks set into the back cover of your thesis. Microfiche is simpler. It is cheap, compact, permanent and, because it is nonelectronic, requires only simple equipment for reading. Equipment for making hard copies is fairly widely available, and it is not expensive to copy a few relevant pages. Floppy disks are also cheap and compact and enable critical analysis of your data. How-ever, it is easy for the data to be lost and they require a computer with a compatible operating system to interpret them. Computers and operating systems come and go. A copy of the operating system should also form part of your submission, with its specifications printed in the relevant appendix.

Seriously consider making several microfiche copies of all of your thesis and supplementary material before the thesis is bound to provide you with a portable form of your work that may be lent to others or taken with you if you travel. Indeed, some universities insist on microfiches being made, and only provide access to theses in this form.

The problem with submitting original tapes is that they are bulky and need occasional rewinding. However, if your argument rests strongly on nonverbal responses, such as intonation or body language, then you should provide some examples in tape-recorded form. You will need to check your university's requirements about submitting such data. Allow enough time for it to develop requirements if it does not have them.

In the near future, CD-ROMs will provide a more reliable way of storing both text and kinetic data compactly and permanently in a way that is easily accessible. At the moment recordable CD-ROMs are relatively expensive, and require fairly advanced computers, but this will change quickly.

You may want some excerpts from this data to form an integral part of your submission, especially to illustrate important nonverbal features of the interviews. Make sure that the importance of these excerpts to your argument justifies the disruption the reader will experience in locating them. Thus use only such excerpts as cannot be simply summarized in words without losing important information, and make quite sure that the relevance of each is clearly spelled out in the text. Be sure, too, that the links between text and excerpts are very clear; your readers will want to read, not to be distracted by technical difficulties, and they may not be reading your thesis from start to finish. Given that counters for tape and video players differ from brand to brand, it would be wise to use a nonerasable CD-ROM with clearly defined tracks for such crucial data.

Finally, you need to think seriously about how your thesis will be catalogued and summarized, particularly at a time when such supplements are still relatively rare. At the foot of your title page, place a statement such as "Transcripts from 107 interviews are appended to this thesis on floppy disks using Microsoft Word 5 configured for Apple Macintosh computer." Make a similar statement in your abstract. This should ensure that the information is included in library catalogs and publications of abstracting services, both of which are important ways of making your work known.

Presentation in Written Form for a Thesis

Many aspects of this were discussed earlier under "Methods of Summarizing Data." Remember that you will need to include more background details than have been presented here. At the very least, each excerpt should be accompanied by a pseudonym, and the age and gender of the subject. Include textual records of nonverbal responses and be meticulous about indicating where you have omitted part of the record. You may need to describe the context of the excerpt as well.

The index is an important, but often neglected, part of any thesis. Even if you do not use the index facility for sorting your data, it will be worthwhile spending time building a good index for your thesis; readers will then be able to follow their own trains of thought as well as yours. A good book on indexing will help you to establish appropriate references for the ideas you discuss. For clinical interviews it is also worth indexing references to each subject you have quoted. This enables, for example, a reader to put together all responses by one subject and assess whether the subject is behaving consistently. If you group all the references to excerpts together under some general heading such as "Quotations Listed by Subject," a reader can see quickly whether your quotations have been selected from most of your subjects or restricted to a small number of cases. You could also index references under other headings such as "Quotations Listed by Year Level," "Quotations Listed by Gender and Year Level," or "Quotations Listed by Experimental Situation."

Presentation in Written Form for Journals and Conferences

Many of the skills for preparing journal or conference papers are similar to those discussed previously. But journal editors and conference organizers usually put strict limits on the length of your paper. Because both are important forms of making your work known, you will have to work within the constraints set.

It is simply not possible to lift a section from your thesis and convert it rapidly into a paper or an address. No one likes to let go of all the subtleties and nuances they have managed to elucidate over many years of hard work, but you must. And you must do so without losing the special value of your form of research. Focus on the smallest topic you can manage so that you have room to support your argument with well-chosen excerpts that not only indicate what children are thinking, but also show that it was your skill as an interviewer that allowed so much to be found out.

Preservation of Raw Data

Finally, data gathered and referred to in a thesis should always be freely available to other workers for checking and possible reinterpretation. One of us has visited the room containing Piaget's original transcripts, all reasonably well ordered, and, within 30 minutes, has located the desired material. Furthermore, access to the material was free and unfettered. Once your thesis has been accepted, you have a responsibility to do the same.

Initially, you will keep your collated data with you, because you will continue to refer to them. Arrange the material in the way that you have listed in the thesis. Tapes should be stored vertically, and rewound at regular intervals.

In due course you will find that you are no longer referring to your base data, and are ready to submit it to an official archival source, probably your university library. It may be possible to transfer the material into some more compact electronic form that was not available cheaply when your thesis was prepared. In any case, make sure that the material is properly listed and labeled, so that the cataloging process will be easy.

CONCLUSION

No one chapter on this topic can possible be comprehensive. We have presented one way of looking at clinical interviews. There are other works that, we believe, will be of help to students and supervisors. Some have already been mentioned briefly in the text; others, such as Allen and Skinner (1991), J. Bell (1992), and B. Bell et al. (1985) have covered similar ground but in different ways and with different references. Good interviewing is an art as well as a science, and must be practiced to be developed. As you develop your skills you will be rewarded by being allowed to enter into children's minds and watch how they struggle to interpret the world around them. The following example (J. Truran, 1994) shows a Grade 10 girl struggling to articulate her understanding of symmetry and succeeding extraordinarily well. It was a privilege to be present at that moment:

I: When you throw a dice are some numbers easier to get than others?
S: Not really, there's a sixth chance, you have, when you throw it, no. No.
I: No?
S: No.
I: Why not?
S: Because it depends on the way that you throw it. Just because you throw it one way doesn't mean you could get a six. This is hard to explain. You're not going to get the same, no number is easier because they're all on a plane face and it kind of depends on how much it rolls or how much you shake it and the way it falls depending what side you get. So no side's easier because they're all the same, except they've got different dots on them.

ACKNOWLEDGMENTS

Professor Jacques Voneche, Les Archives Jean Piaget, Geneva, allowed us to examine the original manuscripts of Piaget and Inhelder. Dr. Berndt Wollring, University of Münster, demonstrated the meticulous organization of his vast store of data. We thank the University of Adelaide for providing financial support for these visits.

REFERENCES

Ainley, J. (1987). Telling questions. *Mathematics Teaching, 118*, 24–26.

Alarcon, J. (1982). *L'Appréhension des situations probabilistes chez des élèves de 12–14 ans: résultats d'une enquête proposée à des élèves de 4ème et de 5ème* [Understanding of situations by students aged 12–14: Results of an investigation with Year 4 and 5 students]. Unpublished doctoral thesis, Louis Pasteur University of Strasbourg.

Allen, G., & Skinner, C. (Eds.). (1991). *Handbook for research students in the social sciences*. London: Falmer.

Bell, B. (1993). *Taking into account students' thinking: A teacher development guide*. Hamilton, New Zealand: Centre for Science and Mathematics Education Research, University of Waikato.

Bell, B., Osborne, R., & Tasker, R. (1985). Finding out what children think. In R. Osborne & P. Freyberg (Eds.), *Learning in science: The implications of children's science* (pp. 151–165). Auckland, New Zealand: Heinemann.

Bell, J. (1992). *Doing your research project: A guide for first-time researchers in education and social science*. Milton Keynes, Buckinghamshire, England: Open University Press.

Biddulph, F. (1995). Children's questions about number. In B. Atweh & S. Flavel (Eds.), *Galtha: Proceedings of the eighteenth annual conference of the Mathematics Education Research Group of Australasia, Northern Territory University, Darwin, Australia, July 1995* (pp. 95–101). Darwin, Northern Territory, Australia: MERGA.

Booth, L. R. (1984). *Algebra: Children's strategies and errors*. Windsor, Berkshire, England: NFER-Nelson.

Boulton-Lewis, G., Cooper, T., Atweh, B., Pillay, H., Wilss, L., & Mutch, S. (1995). Children's questions about number. In B. Atweh & S. Flavel (Eds.), *Galtha: Proceedings of the eighteenth annual conference of the Mathematics Education Research Group of Australasia, Northern Territory University, Darwin, Australia, July 1995* (pp. 121–127). Darwin, Northern Territory, Australia: MERGA.

Carr, J. A. (1994). *Student ideas on averages and dispersion: A qualitative study involving year seven and eight students*. Unpublished master's thesis, University of Waikato, New Zealand.

Cohen, J. (1964). *Behaviour in uncertainty*. London: George Allen & Unwin.

Collis, K. F. (1975). *A study of concrete and formal operations in school mathematics: A Piagetian viewpoint* (ACER Research Series, No. 95). Hawthorn, Victoria: Australian Council for Educational Research.

Daniel, W. W. (1990). *Applied non-parametric statistics*. Boston: PWS-KENT.

Davies, C. M. (1965). Development of the probability concept in children. *Child Development, 26*, 779–788.

Donaldson, M. (1978). *Children's minds*. London: Croom Helm.

Ernest, P. (1991). *The philosophy of mathematics education*. London: Falmer.

Fielding, R., & Lee, R. (1991). *Using computers in qualitative research*. London: Sage.

Frid, S., & Malone, J. (1995). Negotiation of meaning in mathematics classrooms: A study of two year 5 classes. *Mathematics Education Research Journal, 7*(2), 132–147.

Ginsburg, H. (1981). The clinical interview in psychological research on mathematical thinking: Aims, rationales, techniques. *For the Learning of Mathematics, 1*(3), 4–11.

Green, D. R. (1983). From thumbtacks to inference. *School Science and Mathematics, 83*(7), 541–551.

Hart, K. M. (Ed.). (1983). *Children's understanding of mathematics: 11–16.* London: John Murray.

Hughes, M. (1986). *Children and number.* Oxford, England: Basil Blackwell.

Hunting, R., & Doig, B. (1992). The development of a clinical tool for initial assessment of a student's mathematics learning. In M. Stephens & J. Izard (Eds.), *Reshaping assessment practices: Assessment in the mathematical sciences under challenge. Proceedings from the First National Conference on Assessment in the Mathematical Sciences, Geelong, Victoria, 20–24 November 1991* (pp. 201–217). Hawthorn, Victoria: Australian Council for Educational Research.

Mountford, C. P. (1976). *Nomads of the Australian desert* (pp. 94–116). Adelaide, South Australia: Rigby.

Novak, J. D. (1990). Concept maps and vee diagrams: Two metacognitive tools to facilitate meaningful learning. *Instructional Science, 19,* 29–52.

Opper, S. (1977). Piaget's clinical method. *Journal of Children's Mathematical Behaviour, 1,* 90–107.

Patton, M. Q. (1990). *Qualitative evaluation and research methods.* London: Sage.

Piaget, J. (1971). *The child's conception of the world* (pp. 2–10). London: Routledge & Kegan Paul. (Original work published 1929)

Piaget, J. (1952). *La genèse du nombre chez l'enfant* [The child's conception of numbers] (C. Gattegno & F. M. Hodgson, Trans.). London: Routledge & Kegan Paul. (Original work published 1941)

Pines, A. L., Novak, J. D., Posner, G. J., & Van Kirk, J. (1978). *The clinical interview: A method for evaluating cognitive structure* (Curriculum Series Research Rep. No. 6). Ithaca, NY: Department of Education, Cornell University.

Romberg, T. A. (1983). Toward "Normal Science" in some mathematics education research. *Zentralblatt für Didaktik der Mathematik* [International Reviews on Mathematical Education], *15*(2), 89–92.

Siegel, S. (1956). *Nonparametric statistics for the behavioral sciences.* New York: McGraw-Hill.

Strauss, A., & Corbin, J. (1990). *Basics of qualitative research: Grounded theory procedures and techniques.* Newbury Park, CA: Sage.

Swanson, D., Schwartz, R., Ginsburg, H., & Kossan, N. (1981). The clinical interview: Validity, reliability and diagnosis. *For the Learning of Mathematics, 2*(2), 31–38.

Tesch, R. (1990). *Qualitative research: Analysis types and software tools.* New York: Falmer.

Truran, J. (1994). Children's understanding of symmetry. In D. Green (Ed.), *Teaching statistics at its best* (pp. 49–51). Sheffield, South Yorkshire, England: Teaching Statistics Trust.

Truran, K. M. (1995). Animism: a view of probability behaviour. In B. Atweh & S. Flavel (Eds.), *Galtha: Proceedings of the eighteenth annual conference of the Mathematics Education Research Group of Australasia, Northern Territory University, Darwin, Australia, July 1995* (pp. 537–541). Darwin, Northern Territory, Australia: MERGA.

von Glaserfeld, E. (Ed.). (1991). *Radical constructivism in mathematics education.* Dordrecht, The Netherlands: Kluwer.

von Glaserfeld, E. (Ed.). (1995). *Radical constructivism: A way of knowing and learning.* London: Falmer.

Vuyk, R. (1981). *Overview and critique of Piaget's genetic epistemology.* London: Academic Press.

5

Classroom Interactions: Using Interactional Sociolinguistics to Make Sense of Recorded Classroom Talk

Robert E. Bleicher
Queensland University of Technology, Brisbane

There is an emergent field of educational research that views classrooms and other learning situations as cultures, and teaching/learning processes as being social/communicative in nature (for example, Bloome, 1989; Cochran, 1991; Corsaro, 1985; Santa Barbara Classroom Discourse Group 1993; Weade, 1987). Collins and Green (1992) expressed the essence of this viewpoint:

> As the members of this group (a culture) engage each other in the everyday events of classroom life, they develop common knowledge (Edwards & Mercer, 1987) and patterned ways of living together (Green, 1983). The patterns that are constructed include ways of (1) *perceiving* the actions, objects and social practices of others in the group; (2) *acting and interacting* with others across time and events of everyday life in this classroom; (3) *interpreting* the actions of members of the class and artifacts of the group; and (4) *evaluating* what is accomplished within and across the everyday events of classroom life of the group. (p. 6)

Viewed in this way, every classroom is a setting in which a social group constructs and reconstructs a "class culture" within a "schooling culture." Teaching and learning, therefore, are viewed as social-communicative processes that must be explored within the situations of class life in which they occur.

The following are examples of the types of research questions that can be examined from an interactional sociolinguistic perspective:

- What counts as science (or mathematics, reading, history, etc.), learning science (or mathematics, etc.), and teaching science (or mathematics, etc.) to participants?
- How do teachers and students make sense of the activities and ways in which they interact in the classroom?
- How do the patterns of the everyday life in classrooms constrain or support opportunities for students to learn?
- How are power, gender, ethnicity, and social background mediated through classroom discourse?

THEORETICAL CONSTRUCTS

The first part of this chapter presents a necessarily brief summary of the key theoretical constructs that help define interactional sociolinguistics. Eighteen theoretical constructs are presented under two major groups: *Classrooms as settings for cultures* and *Communication in social groups*. Although the actual interrelationships between these constructs are more complicated than can be shown on simple diagrams, Figs. 5.1a and b presents them and suggests some relationships.

Classrooms as Settings for Cultures

Classroom as Setting, Class as Social Group

The classroom is conceived as a particular place in which a social group of people (the "class," composed of one or more persons called "teachers," and other people called "students") can come together and affiliate over time. Viewed in this way, the classroom is not limited to the traditional mental image of a room with desks and four walls in a place called school, but could be a laboratory or outdoor setting as well (a rain forest can be a classroom, if used as an educational place to meet and affiliate for a class). This view of classroom is equivalent to what Spradley (1980) called the "place," and the class would be called the "actors" in his terminology.

It can be argued that the group of people called the class is not immediately a social group, but develops into such a group over time (assuming no prior history of the group). As they affiliate, members of the class develop particular interactional patterns and ways of accomplishing tasks to achieve both externally imposed curriculum goals and internal group aims and purposes. A particular class will develop its own unique goals and ways of getting life accomplished; this is what is meant by "class culture."

Three additional constructs, derived from the discipline of cultural anthropology (Erickson, 1986), are essential in describing different aspects of

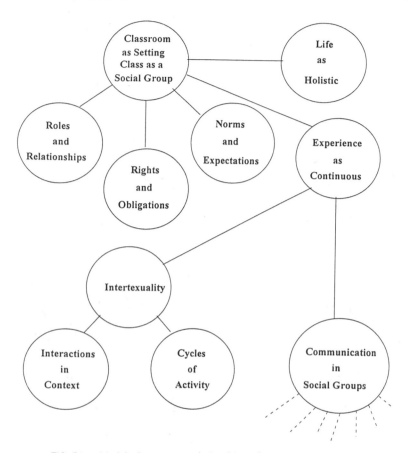

FIG. 5.1a. Model of construct relationships, classroom as settings.

what it means to be a member of a social group: roles and relationships, rights and obligations, and norms and expectations.

Roles and Relationships

Role is not a part of a person's physical, mental, or emotional makeup; that is, it is not internal to the person. Role is part of that fourth dimension of being human, a person's social aspect; as such, it is external to the person inasmuch as it is ascribed by others or institutions to that person. Traditional roles involved in educational settings include principal, student, teacher, teacher's aide, and so forth. Such roles are static, are not much more than mere labels, and, therefore, are not useful for understanding the dynamics of group membership. To understand the culture of the class, it is necessary to get beyond role labels, which mask the complex processes of role construction that go on in social groups.

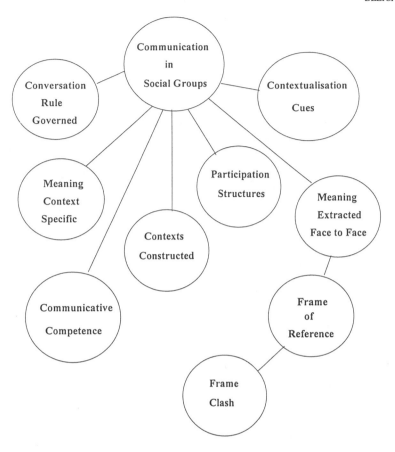

FIG. 5.1b. Model of construct relationships—communication in social group.

Roles, and interrole relationships ("relationships") are not prescribed labels, but in social reality are constructed within a particular social group. Class members assume a variety of roles and engage in a complex set of relationships that changes moment by moment over time. For example, Collins and Green (1992) reported at least four different categories of roles assumed by class members that were socially constructed over time during the school day.

Rights and Obligations

Related to the notion of roles and relationships are those of rights and obligations. People acting in community develop a complex system of rights and obligations. Rights are group sanctions governing the possession and use of certain artifacts, engagement in certain activities, and participation in particular types and styles of social interaction. Linked to these rights are obligations, which are responsibilities that go along with the socially sanctioned rights.

Norms and Expectations

The third aspect of group membership is that it is not arbitrary and without order. "Normal expected ways of acting" are the socially negotiated standards for appropriate social interaction. The norms of acting in a social group are not rigid and they do not cause actions to occur. Norms provide a framework within which people act. A person can choose to modify, follow, or totally disregard a norm.

Nevertheless, acting against a norm can bring repercussions from others. In other words, norms do not have to dictate exactly what goes on in daily social interactions. They are there as known guidelines, and acting beyond them will have consequences for the actor.

Life as Holistic

Collins and Green (1992) described this concept succinctly:

Holism refers to the "seamless" nature of everyday life and to the part–whole relationship among the events of everyday life. Life is not viewed as a series of discrete bits but as a continuous ebb and flow of activity in which some events are recurrent, others are closely related or overlapping, and still others are separate. (p. 12)

They go on to explain the historical perspective of the social group. As classroom events go on over time, some build on others, whereas yet others are once-only occurrences. From these events, a social history is built up for the group that includes a past and a future as well as the present.

The view over time is that class does not finish at the end of a particular period or day. The class reconvenes the next day or week, building on its social history of shared events. Thus, members of the group develop a holistic feeling for life in the group, and the activities of the group have a historical dynamic that fills the gaps between group meetings.

Experience as Continuous

This conceptualizes what the interrelated nature of events is that allows life to become holistic for group members, and how their engaging in daily interactions over time can promote or constrain learning. To understand this construct, it is necessary to introduce three related constructs: interactions in context, cycles of activity, and intertexuality.

Interactions in Context

This construct defines the social situation in which an event takes place. The event is examined within the context of the culture of a particular social group, focusing on which actors are participating, the content of their communicative acts, the manner in which they interact, the roles and relationships among the participants, the perceived purposes of the event, and the perception that the event is a brief of segment of a larger event.

Concentrating on only one event in the life world of the social group puts historical blinders on our analysis of why a particular event is taking place, how it is related to other aspects of social life, how representative it is of life in that social world, and its consequences on future events. In other words, information about what happened before and what happens after any particular event is needed to fully understand an event from a historical perspective. Such longitudinal tracking of events is encompassed by the next construct, cycles of activity.

Cycles of Activity

This is the notion of tracking a series of events over time that accomplish a particular purpose or define a particular topic. It is possible for one single event to also be a cycle of activity, but in educational settings it is more usual to find several events tying together to accomplish some purpose or develop a complete topic of learning. Once a cycle of activity has been identified, the events or lessons that compose it can be better understood in terms of the reason for its happening, its consequences to group members, and its representativeness of life in that social group.

Intertexuality

The third construct that helps frame a way of looking at the accomplishment of continuity of experience is intertextuality. It is explained by Bloome (1989):

> Whenever people engage in a language event, whether it is a conversation, the reading of a book, diary writing, etc., they are engaged in intertextuality. Various conversational and written texts are being juxtaposed. Intertextuality can occur at many levels and in many ways.
>
> Juxtaposing texts, at whatever level, is not in itself sufficient for intertextuality. Intertextuality is a social construction. The juxtaposition must be interactionally recognized, acknowledged, and have social significance. In classrooms, teachers and students are continuously constructing intertextual relationships. The set of intertextual relationships they construct can be viewed as constituting a cultural ideology, a system for assigning meaning and

significance to what is said and done and for socially defining participants. (pp. 1–2)

Intertextuality essentially identifies larger segments of classroom life that tie together different cycles of activity to develop larger themes.

These three constructs (context of interaction, cycles of activity, and intertextuality) deal with structural and curricular aspects of continuity of experience. Another important, and more subtle, aspect of continuity of experience is the establishment of communication systems in a social group over time.

Communication in Social Groups

Conversation Is Rule Governed

This is the notion that there are rules for conversational participation and engagement in discourse that are culturally specific. These rules include turn-taking structures, repair structures, adjacency pairs, politeness conventions, pause structures, appropriate use of registers and code switching, and demonstrating group affiliation. Rule governance does not imply a rigid system of conversational practice, simply that expectations for how conversation should happen exist culturally, and that these expectations provide guidelines for how participants engage in discourse.

Contexts as Constructed

This is the notion that people both co-construct conversation and its contexts by holding one another accountable for following the conversation through such techniques as head nodding, eye gaze, and verbal feedback mechanisms. There are three very important related constructs: contextualization cues, participation structure, and communicative competence.

Contextualization Cues

This was originally a concept developed by Gumperz (1984). The importance of these contextualization cues is that they are central to the social construction of meaning in everyday conversational acts. Examples of exactly what these contexualization cues are and how they operate in discourse are illustrated here in the methodology section, under the heading "Making Sense of Talk." See Bleicher (1994) for a fuller explanation of contextualization cue analysis in science and mathematics education research.

Participation Structures

Participation structures meet the demands for certain types of perform-ance and the range of rights and obligations across different activities. Identification and examination of participant structures is central to the work of Philips (1972). From a careful ethnographic study of the Warm Springs Indian Reservation, she made visible a fascinating system of rights and obligations governing speaking and turn-taking organization that were context specific, a different system operating inside the school and at home. The presence of an Anglo-Saxon teacher and a mixture of Anglo-Saxon and Indian students set up a cross-cultural participation structure in the school.

Communicative Competence

This term was originally coined by Gumperz and Hymes (1972). It refers to a person's ability to know how, with whom, and when to engage in appropriate conversation. It encompasses much more than a command of the lexical and grammatical rules of a language and includes a wide range of interactional skills and cultural knowledge about appropriate engagement in social discourse within a particular speech community.

Meaning as Context Specific

What a speech act means is considered to depend on how it is said, what speech acts preceded it, and what follows it. The basic idea is that people can derive meaning from a speech act only if they have access to the verbal and nonverbal speech acts surrounding it, as well as to the cultural knowl-edge needed to understand the utterance itself.

Meaning Is Extracted From Face-to-Face Interactions

This construct deals with how a person makes sense of face-to-face dis-course. It is concerned with the cognitive demands on one to constantly process all the contextualization cues in order to make inferences as to the meaning of various messages. This idea is very important to understanding teaching/learning processes. Related to this concept is that of frame of reference.

Frame of Reference

This is the notion that people bring a set of cognitive, social, and cultural resources with them in face-to-face interactions. How they make sense of these interactions will be affected by these resources. From participating in many interactions a person will develop a set of expectations for what kind of actions may occur. This set of expectations is called a *frame of reference*.

Obviously, a person will have a different frame of reference for different types of interactions. Also, these frames of reference are subject to change as a person picks up new cues in face-to-face interactions that modify expectations. This construct is related to that of mindframes, used in cognitive science research.

Frame Clash

Simply put, a frame clash refers to the situation in which two participants hold two different frames of reference for the same social situation. Each acts in an unexpected way from the other's point of view. Frame clashes make participants immediately aware of their own actions. An impediment to everyday automatic activity makes the author aware of this activity. Frames of reference tend to make conversation flow smoothly for participants sharing common frames, to the point that they are often unaware of those frames. A frame clash makes the invisible suddenly visible to all participants, and even outside observers.

The nine constructs described earlier are some of the important ideas that underpin the communicative processes constructed in social groups that create a sense of continuity of experience for participants.

Constructs are not static givens. They were originally created by human agents, and are subject to change by the same. It is not surprising, therefore, that some of them will probably disappear from active research use, and new ones will be created in their wake. The names given to represent conceptualizations are not the important concern; rather, the values implicit in the human endeavor of constructing the kernel of the notion need to be brought to the forefront when exchanging points of view in communities of researchers.

METHODOLOGY

An "alloy" of classroom ethnography, ethnography of schooling, and sociolinguistic discourse analysis of the communicative patterns within the classroom is the methodology employed to answer research questions from an interactional sociolinguistic perspective. This second part of this chapter presents data collection and analysis methods in some detail in order to give a feeling of just what kind of work is involved in preparing recorded classroom talk for analysis within this perspective.

Data Collection

Ethnography employs all the usual methods of anthropology, such as participant observation, artifact collection, and ethnographic interviewing to collect data (see chapter 2 by Zevenbergen in this volume). Interactional sociolinguistics employs all of these, but concentrates on direct observation and videorecording of naturalistic learning situations to lead to more detailed discourse analysis. Examples of approaches to analysing ethnographic field notes and discourse are discussed next.

Analyses

Making Sense of Ethnographic Field Notes

A domain analysis (Spradley, 1980) can be applied to field notes. Domain analysis is one way of starting to discover patterns in the data. It is a means of obtaining an early picture of the broad cultural scene in the study situation and guiding the researcher to move from broad entry questions to more focused questions.

Figure 5.2 illustrates the terminology of domain analysis. It gives an example of a *cover term*, an *included term*, and a *semantic relationship*. In the figure, cover term is a category or label, in this case *laboratory equipment*. The atomic force microscope is the included term, in this case a specific piece of equipment found in the laboratory. The semantic relationship here is the linking that makes the appropriate connection between the included term and the cover term. Other semantic relationships include *is used for*, *is the cause of*, *is part of*, and so forth.

A taxonomy is a way of examining relationships between domains. Forming a taxonomy is exactly like forming a domain, only on a larger scale. A taxonomy will include many domains. The technique for doing this analysis involves gathering several domain analyses together and looking for relationships among them. A taxonomic analysis starts to give insights into possible ways people make meaning of their lifeworld. How things are organized is part of the way in which cultural meaning is developed.

These are two systematic ways of dealing with ethnographic data. They form the basis for the first level of analysis applied to the data in order to begin the process of finding social and cultural patterns in the daily interactions of participants.

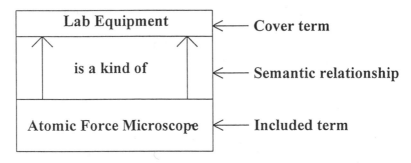

FIG. 5.2. Domain analysis.

Ethnographic methodology eventually identifies crucial instructional events that take place in the study site. Discourse analysis is next applied to these events in order to examine how learning is constrained or supported.

Making Sense of Talk: Three Stages
of Discourse Analysis

The unit of analysis is the message unit, defined as "the minimal unit of conversational meaning on the part of the speaker" (Green, Harker, & Golden, 1987, p. 52). Message units are identified by characterizing the contextualization cues that occur in verbal discourse and are determined by analysis. An example will help clarify what contextualization cues are.

A section of a transcript from classroom talk appears below. "Sally" is teaching a unit on probability to Grade 12 students in a mathematics class. This section comes from the first ten minutes of class time, in which she is defining important terms. Sally is standing to the left of a chalkboard, looking down at some notes she previously placed there. She is supporting her lesson with a graph on the chalkboard that has the words "probability curve" written under it.

Line 1:   and uhm (1.0 second pause)

Line 2:   the probability curve

Line 3:   is just the probability of

Line 4:   (Sally points to the words probability curve, on the chalk-
           board with a piece of chalk she is holding in her right hand)

Line 5:   of what is the chance that

Line 6:   uh (1.5 second pause)

Line 7:   that a certain number

Each line in the transcript represents one message unit. Following are the contextualization cues line for line:

- In Line 1, "uhm" was drawn out to sound like "uhmmmm," with a noticeable one-second pause afterward. This is a common contextualization cue employed by speakers as a way of preparing to launch into a section of explanation. It is often accompanied by a change in the direction of eye contact or other nonverbal activity; in this case, Sally took a quick glance at the class.
- In Line 2, "curve" is spoken at a lower volume than the two words before it, with a marked rise in voice pitch. This has the effect of

dramatizing the whole line, perhaps signaling to the audience that an important definition is to follow (which it does).

- In Line 3, "probability" is spoken at a much slower speed than previous words and "of" is drawn out to sound like "uhvvvv." This kind of slowing down often signals an impending change in body posturing toward the audience; in this case, it is followed by a nonverbal speaker activity.
- In Line 4, Sally reinforces the content of the previous line by pointing to the visual aid.
- In Line 5, "of" continues the thought from Line 3 until "that" is said with unusual emphasis and a noticeably sudden voice cut off.
- In Line 6, "uh" is followed by a 2-second pause, a similar cue to that in Line 2; in this case, it is followed by Sally glancing up at the audience and then preparing to write on the chalkboard.
- In Line 7, the "that" from Line 4 is repeated as if to continue with the topic and "number" is followed by a pause in which Sally begins writing on the chalkboard.

This example illustrates just a few of the broad range of contexualization cues possible in human discourse. Marked changes in tone of voice, special emphasis on a particular word, sudden rises or falls in pitch, unusually placed or prolonged pauses, change in register, formality of form of address, change in dialect by insertion of a dialectic or foreign language word or phrase in the flow of talk, or various nonverbal actions (such as nods, winks, hand motions, change in body posture, and change in eye contact) are all possible contextualization cues that can be employed by speakers to signal that a message has been sent in the discourse between people. Such cues can be identified with a high degree of reliability by researchers, but some hours of training are necessary in order to learn to identify them. Also, contexualization cues are, by their very nature, culturally specific and are part of the reason why there are often communication misunderstandings between speakers from different ethnic backgrounds, above and beyond translation problems between two different languages. Analysis of contextualization cues provides a basis for understanding how students are making sense of teacher explanations.

The next section describes the methodological stages employed to transform the real-time classroom talk into a textual research document that facilitates examination of contextualization cues. This section will be presented in a step-by-step, "how to do it" style which will allow readers to try out the methodology on some of their own data to see how it works. The bottom line is how effective the final analytic product can be in helping to sort out the masses of collected data in a way that leads to defensible interpretations.

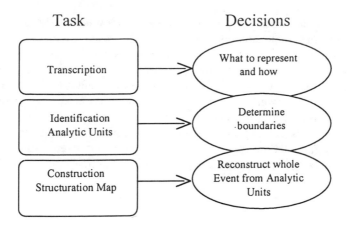

FIG. 5.3. Stages of discourse analysis.

There are three main tasks for the researcher in the discourse analysis: *transcription, identification of analytic units,* and *construction of structuration maps.* Each task requires a particular decision by the researcher. Figure 5.3 shows the overall flow chart of stages used in the discourse analysis.

The goal of discourse analytic methods is to develop a description of the message-by-message socio-communicative signaling between participants; reconstruct how this supported or constrained the accomplishment of larger events (e.g., the teacher explaining how to do a particular mathematics problem on the chalkboard, or a student asking a question); and interpret patterns of socio-communicative acts across events, time, and sites.

Following is a description of methods used to develop transcripts, identify analytic units, and construct structuration maps.

Stage One: Transcript Construction—What to Represent and How?
There are some theoretical considerations implicit in the use of transcripts as sources of data for education research (Ochs, 1979). How talk is represented in transcripts is selective and reflects researchers' decisions and biases in terms of what gets emphasized.

The transcription methodology follows the suggestions of Gumperz and Berenz (1990), employing identification of contextualization cues as one method of breaking conversational data into analyzable interaction units. The subsequent analysis of the transcript is then carried out from an interactional sociolinguistic perspective, employing techniques developed by Green and Wallat (1981). Analysis makes visible unfolding patterns of interaction, and larger cycles of activity that carry across situation and time (Green & Meyer, 1991).

There are three levels of product involved in the construction of a transcript: rough, nonverbal inclusion, and table.

Rough transcriptions are prepared from videotapes. The method employed is to first make an audiotape directly from the original videotape, so that the transcription process can be aided by the use of a transcription machine. This method leaves the operator's hands free to enter the words and sounds being heard directly into a computer database. Transcription is not a straightforward, simple process, and a great deal of patience is involved in relistening to segments sometimes as many as 10 times. The average for transcribing materials is about 6 hours of transcribing time per hour of original videotape. The database obtained from this process is referred to as the "rough transcript," and an example is illustrated below (T = teacher, Y = student).

T: That's a good one that's this one?

Y: Yeah that's the one exactly right

T: Except there's nothing on the bottom
        though

Y: Uh yeah we're missing the heater

Message units are indicated on the printed transcript with slash mark separators (use a pencil, as subsequent reviews of segments sometimes change the original boundary decision). Decisions about where to mark a message unit boundary are made post hoc and include consideration of such features as changes in intonation, pitch, or speed; stress; and significant pauses. Usually, message unit boundaries are marked by more than one of the aforementioned; redundancy in use the of contextualization cues has been noted by Gumperz (1986) as occurring commonly in human communication.

Next appears a short example of the previously discussed rough transcript, broken into the message units, to create a first-draft message unit transcript. The computer file first-draft message unit transcript is opened

T: That's a good one
        that's this one?

Y: Yeah
        that's the one
        exactly right

T: Except there's nothing on the bottom
        though

Y: Uh yeah
        we're missing the heater

on screen and the videotape reviewed as necessary to check the accuracy of verbals, nonverbals, and message units—the second level of product from the construction of a transcript. At this stage, more attention is paid to the timing of pauses and to the timing placement of nonverbals within the context of the verbal text. This can be problematic, as nonverbals do not always coincide with the decision to define a message unit boundary; a nonverbal will sometimes occur in the middle of a message unit.

The technique of inserting a superscript number ([1]) at the point in the text where the nonverbal occurs and then inserting the parenthesized non-verbal at the end of the message unit line is used. The next script illustrates

T:	that's[1] a good one	[1](Tony now looking at the that's this one? schematic as well)
Y:	yeah that's the one exactly right	
T:	except there's nothing[2] on the bottom though	[2](Tony notices that the schematic on the bottom though differs from the actual pump)
Y:	uh yeah we're missing the heater	

this point. Once this process is completed, the computer document is saved as a message unit transcript in the computer database, then reformatted into a table (p. 100).

The third level of transcript constuction—the table—allows the viewer to "keep up" with the real-time videotape interaction. Watching the video without it results in a frustrated attempt to analyze what is taking place. Things happen too quickly, and prior sequences are hard to remember in vivid detail as the current ones are presenting themselves. The script allows for a sense of knowing where things are going, as well as a quick reference for past events, while keeping one's place in the present. Watching events again and again gives a sense of how dense interactions are, how much really goes on, and how little one can consciously process at the moment of happening. Even freezing the ethnographic present on videotape, along with the script, by no means pretends to capture it all. Constant reviewing of material makes the observer keenly aware that even more microsubtleties of human interaction can be captured given the time and interest to do so.

Message unit "squares" are inserted into one of the columns on the table, one for each unit. They are simply a "flag" for the researcher's use (see p. 101). Notice that the number of columns is now five, line numbers have been

	Verbals	Non-Verbals		
T:	that's[1] a good one	[1]Tony now looking at the schematic as well.		
	that's this one?			
Y:	yeah			
	that's the one			
	exactly right			
T:	except there's nothing[2] on the bottom though	[2]Tony notices that the schematic differs from the pump		
Y:	uh yeah			
	we're missing the heater			

added in the first column for reference purposes, and that each square represents one message unit. This facilitates the next level in the discourse analysis. Each message unit is analyzed for its relationship to the next message unit below to ascertain if there is any discourse link that ties them together as a larger unit of communication. The use of squares makes the final analytic document easier to read and interpret.

Stage Two: Identification of Analytic Units—Determining Boundaries.
With this revised table at hand, the relevant segments of the audiovideos and videotapes are reviewed several times. The manner in which a speaker delivers a message unit can suggest (by intonation, pitch, etc.) that the next message unit is tied to it. Such tied message units are referred to as "interaction units" and represent the next larger analytic unit based on the message unit. They can be composed of one or a series of message units. Determining the boundaries between these interaction units is a major decision for the researcher in Stage 2.

Sequence units are not determined by the contextualization cues as are message units and, to some extent, interaction units. They are determined by the content or topic of conversation. A shift in the general topic being discussed would indicate the boundary between sequence units.

Line		Verbals	Non-verbals	Message Units
007	T:	that's[1] a good one	[1]Tony now looking at the schematic as well.	☐
008		that's this one?		☐
009	Y:	yeah		☐
010		that's the one		☐
011		exactly right		☐
012	T:	except there's nothing[1] on the bottom though	[1]Tony notices that the schematic differs from the actual pump	☐
013	Y:	uh yeah		☐
014		we're missing the heater		☐

Sequence units are linked together to form phases. Phases are complete parts of an instructional event in terms of their purpose and content; they are thematically tied. Particular kinds of instructional work are accomplished in a phase, and the various phases in an instructional event will form the whole "lesson."

The table is now updated, indicating where the interaction, sequence, and phase units begin and end in table columns designated for the purpose This revised computer file is referred to as the "script."

The tapes are again reviewed with the script in hand to note any other analytic features of the interaction that inform the specific question at hand. Message unit length depends on the actions of participants in the conversation or the ways in which their actions show that they are working with the messages, not on researcher categories. There is, however, clear guidance in the analytic procedure supported by the script, which is a systematic research tool characterizing where in a conversation between a teacher and learner opportunities to gain insights are enhanced or constrained.

Stage Three: Structuration Maps—Reconstruction of Whole From Units. The researcher now revisits original questions that began the data collection and analysis processes. Features of the interactions that (a) can be clearly demonstrated through the message-by-message description of social interaction, and (b) help to answer these questions are now noted in the free columns of the script. Theoretical and methodological notes are also entered directly, in writing, onto the script. This is where the art of this research methodology comes into play. Success in the analytic process depends heavily on having the energy to persevere in visiting and revisiting the original tapes and in pursuing intuitive and descriptive interpretations of emerging patterns in the data. This is also at the heart of the interactive–responsive nature of the ethnographic analytic process: Questions drive analysis—new analysis reframes questions. The result, at any point in his research cycle, is more and more focused questions, which can be addressed more explicitly by the data at hand.

These maps provide a visual representation of the sequential structure of the talk. They allow the researcher to "zoom out" from verbal interactions between speakers in order to obtain an overall structural picture of how the content "flows." With such maps at hand, the reviewing of audio- and videotapes allows the researcher to conceptualize the interaction within the larger framework.

From these descriptive representations, it is possible to construct supportable interpretations about how communicative acts in a particular learning situation are linked to prior events that have either constrained or supported opportunities for learning. The three-stage discourse analysis model presented in this chapter provides the basis for informing the questions in a study. Although further analyses can always be carried out, the interpretations made possible by these procedures are adequate to support inferences about how learning is supported or constrained as a consequence of socio-communicative interactions in a classroom or other site of learning. The reader is expecially encouraged to read the study by Corsaro (1985), which has been published as a small, very readable book. This is an exemplar of classic interactional sociolinguistic research—it is a study of children in a preschool setting learning to be students and interact with other children. For the latest research being carried out in the field, see readings by Bleicher (1993, 1994), Green and Harker (1988), and the Santa Barbara Classroom Discourse Group (1993).

CONCLUSION

As interpretations begin to be constructed by the researcher, they should be shared with the teacher and students in the study to determine if they make sense to participants. This is what Guba and Lincoln (1989) referred to as "member checks." It is a way of confirming that the researcher is obtaining a fair representation of how participants feel they are making sense of various classroom activities. It is a method of trying to get the participant's point of view about things. Triangulation of the discourse analysis with other data sources, such as field notes and ethnographic interviews, is another important aspect of an interactional sociolinguistic study. Never forget that the researcher should have a good sense of what is going on in the classroom before submitting a particular segment of classroom talk to the more fine-grained discourse analysis. Always keep in mind the purpose of doing the analysis and the theoretical assumptions underpinning this perspective.

REFERENCES

Bleicher, R. (1993). *Learning science in the workplace: Ethnographic accounts of high school students as apprentices in university research laboratories*. Unpublished doctoral dissertation, University of California, Santa Barbara.

Bleicher, R. (1994). High school students presenting science: An interactional sociolinguistic analysis. *Journal of Research in Science Teaching, 31*, 697–719.

Bloome, D. (1989). *Classrooms and literacy*. Norwood, NJ: Ablex.

Cochran, J. P. (1991, April). *The schooling of science: An ethnographic study of college organic chemistry*. Paper presented at the annual meeting of the American Educational Research Association, Chicago, IL.

Collins, E., & Green, J. (1992). Learning in classroom settings: Making and breaking. In H. Marshall (Ed.), *Redefining learning: Roots of educational restructuring* (pp. 31–42). Norwood, NJ: Ablex.

Corsaro, W. (1985). *Friendship and peer culture in the early years*. Norwood, NJ: Ablex.

Erickson, F. (1986). Qualitative methods in research on teaching. In M. Wittrock (Ed.), *Handbook of research on teaching* (3rd ed., pp. 119–161). New York: Macmillan.

Green, J. (1983). Research on teaching as a linguistic process: A state of the art. In E. Gordon (Ed.), *Review of research in education* (Vol. 10, pp. 151–252). Washington, DC: American Educational Research Association.

Green, J., & Harker, J. (1988). *Multiple perspective analysis of classroom discourse*. Norwood, NJ: Ablex.

Green, J., Harker, J., & Golden, J. (1987). Lesson construction: Differing views. In G. W. Nobilt & W. T. Pink (Eds.), *Schooling in social context: Qualitative studies* (pp. 46–77). Norwood, NJ: Ablex.

Green, J., & Meyer, L. (1991). The embeddedness of reading in classroom life. In C. Baker & A. Luke (Eds.), *Toward a critical sociology of reading pedagogy* (pp. 16–22). Amsterdam: John Benjamins.

Green, J., & Wallat, C. (1981). Mapping instructional conversations. In J. Green & C. Wallat (Eds.), *Ethnography and language in educational settings* (pp. 161–205). Norwood, NJ: Ablex.

Guba, E., & Lincoln, Y. (1989). *Fourth generation evaluation*. Beverly Hills, CA: Sage.

Gumperz, J. (1984). *Discourse strategies*. London: Cambridge University Press.

Gumperz, J. (1986). Interactional sociolinguistics in the study of school. In J. Cook-Gumperz (Ed.), *The social construction of literacy* (pp. 45–68). Cambridge, England: Cambridge University Press.

Gumperz, J. J., & Berenz, N. (1990). Transcribing conversational exchanges. In J. Edwards & M. Lampert (Eds.), *Talking language* (pp. 117–135). Hillsdale, NJ: Lawrence Erlbaum Associates.

Gumperz, J., & Hymes, D. (Ed.). (1972). *Directions in social linguistics: The ethnography of communication.* New York: Holt, Rinehart & Winston.

Ochs, E. (1979). Transcription theory. In E. Ochs & B. Schieffelin (Eds.), *Developmental pragmatics* (pp. 87–97). New York: Academic Press.

Philips, S. (1972). Participant structures and communicative competence: Warm Springs children in community and classroom. In C. Cazden, D. Hymes, & V. John (Eds.), *Functions of language in the classroom* (pp. 51–62). New York: Teachers College Press.

Santa Barbara Classroom Discourse Group. (1993). Santa Barbara Classroom Discourse Group [Special issue]. *Linguistics and Education, 5*(3, 4).

Spradley, J. (1980). *Participant observation.* New York: Holt, Rinehart & Winston.

Weade, R. (1987). Curriculum 'n' instruction: The construction of meaning. *Theory Into Practice, 26*, 15–25.

6

Critical Reflections on a Problematic Student–Supervisor Relationship

Peter Charles Taylor
Vaille Dawson
National Key Centre for School Science and Mathematics
Curtin University of Technology, Perth, Western Australia

In identifying mythical elements in our own cultural or professional assumptions, we threaten our ethnocentric self-confidence. We discover a psychic dimension which recognises the power of myth and unconscious desire as forces, not only in history, but in shaping our own lives. We open up a history which . . . pivots on the active relationship between past and present, subjective and objective, poetic and political.
—Samuel & Thompson (1990, p. 5)

Three years ago, we completed a student–supervisor relationship that, on the surface, appeared to have been very successful. Peter's supervision of Vaille's research study had culminated in her being awarded a masters degree with distinction and an Australian Postgraduate Award to study for a doctorate. However, because of our mutual professional concern with ensuring that relations between teachers and students are not disempowering of students (or, for that matter, of teachers), we believe that it is essential to judge success not only in terms of the achievement of predetermined academic goals but also by taking into account the quality of the day-to-day student–teacher relationship. By presenting this account of our joint inquiry into the rough-and-tumble of our own relationship, we hope to convince the reader of the importance of the supervisor and student adopting collaboratively a critical perspective and examining deeply hidden beliefs that can reinforce cultural stereotypes and sustain relations of domination.

The way in which we have chosen to render this critical account of our student–supervisor relationship is somewhat unusual for the field of mathematics and science education. Within our joint account, which represents our present standpoint and frames the chapter, our authorial voices can be heard speaking sometimes individually and sometimes collectively. Elsewhere, our "historical" selves of three years ago are represented by our individual voices speaking independently. Because we wish to emphasize the conceptual distance between our past and present perspectives, a distance born of considerable critical self-reflection and reciprocal negotiation, we have chosen pseudonyms (i.e., "Joanne," "Philip") when we give voice to our earlier selves, particularly in the section in which we discuss the conflicts of interest that occurred between us during our student–supervisor relationship. This writing approach is familiar to historians and cultural anthropologists, for whom "narrative form" and "autobiography" are commonplace research methods and modes of representation recognized for their power to convey personal experiences (Bruner, 1990; Clandinin & Connelly, 1994; Geertz, 1983; Samuel & Thompson, 1990).

We conducted our inquiry as an interpretive research study (Erickson, 1986), the starting point of which was a critical event in our student–supervisor relationship. Initially, we wrote separate interpretive accounts of the way we experienced our relationship, accounts that we shared with each other, presented at conferences, and submitted to colleagues and friends (Dawson, 1996; Taylor, 1994, 1995). As we reflected on the critical commentary that poured in our direction (some thought our writings too personal, too emotional, too naive, too partial), our understandings deepened. Our readings of feminist literature encouraged us to continue with our learning. Research by Belenky, Clinchy, Goldberger, and Tarule (1986) on women's ways of knowing helped Vaille to understand better the nature of the emotional struggle to transform her own epistemology. An article written by Ellsworth (1992), in which she explored the repressive myths of her own supposedly critical pedagogy, was a turning point in Peter's understanding of his own epistemology. Habermas' "theory of communicative action" (Pusey, 1987) and Noddings' (1984) book on caring and ethics took us forward, beyond critique, into a space of new horizons containing compelling possibilities for developing rich communicative relationships. In doing this, we were motivated to learn how to improve our own future research relationship and to tease out possible significances for other supervisors and students who might hold similar research interests.

But what of the epistemology that shaped our inquiry? We had combined key elements of von Glasersfeld's (1990, 1993) "radical constructivism" and Habermas' theory of "knowledge and human interests" (McCarthy, 1985; Pusey, 1987) to form a "critical constructivist" perspective (Dawson, 1994; Taylor, 1996). From this perspective, our knowledge (including scientific and mathematical knowledge) is a human construct, rather than an objective entity, and we gauge its viability (or usefulness) by seeing how well it helps us to understand and predict aspects of both our physical and social environments.

In this account of our student–supervisor relationship, we reveal the shortcomings of our critical constructivist epistemology, particularly the way that a strong emphasis on the "emancipatory" goal of student empowerment seemed to "backfire." Rather than abandon this epistemology, however, we have learned how it can be strengthened. Our inquiry has led us to the realization that the emancipatory goal is not an end in its own right; rather, it should serve the "practical" goal of establishing a rich communicative relationship between the research supervisor and research student. Ironically it was this realization that subsequently enabled us to develop a communicative relationship of such richness that we were able to pursue our critical self-reflective inquiry in a climate of mutual trust and respect.

THE RESEARCH STUDENT

At the beginning of 1994, I was about to commence my third year as a teacher of high school science and my final year as a postgraduate student enrolled part-time in a master's degree program at Curtin University. At school, I had been teaching a course on bioethics that I had responsibility for designing, teaching and assessing. In this 10-week course I aimed to enable students to understand the way medical science practices are governed by human values, particularly ethical values, and to become more aware of their own valued beliefs and ethical standards. However, the resource materials that I had been using in class were designed to convey factual information, rather than to enable students to explore their own personal experiences about issues that they insisted on raising in class. As I was drawn deeper into responding to students' passionate appeals and queries, I began to reconsider my somewhat didactic approach to teaching.

During my studies at Curtin in the previous year, I had become familiar with contemporary learning theories that argued for teaching approaches that empowered students to take responsibility for their own learning. Chief among these were "constructivist" theories of knowledge (Bodner, 1986; Driver, 1990; von Glasersfeld, 1989) and the "emancipatory" goal of reflecting self-critically on curriculum-related assumptions and hidden beliefs that governed teachers' and students' classroom roles (Grundy, 1987). I also had become attracted to action research (Kemmis & McTaggert, 1988), an approach that enables the teacher to adopt the role of researcher and investigate ways of improving his or her own teaching practice.

In Peter's courses on learning and curriculum studies, I had experienced first-hand the joys and frustrations of becoming an empowered learner. I was "forced" to accept responsibility for my own learning by participating in the design of learning activities, examining critically my valued beliefs about learning, negotiating newly valued understandings with fellow students, being subjected to peer assessment, and presenting evidence of my own learning in a portfolio. As a result, I came to realize that my bioethics course had similar student empowerment goals, although I had not expressed them previously in these terms.

With only the research component of the course remaining, I was keen to investigate how my developing ideas about learning might enable me to empower my own students. I decided to undertake an "emancipatory action research" study of my Grade 10 bioethics classes. I planned to introduce innovative teaching strategies based on a constructivist epistemology that would engage students in reflecting critically on their own ethical beliefs and personal experiences, negotiating new meanings and understandings in small-group problem-solving activities and whole class discussions, and participating with me and their peers in the design of their own learning activities. However, I did not intend to abandon entirely my former teaching approach, because I recognized an important role for me in continuing to present new information, pose challenging ethical dilemmas, and stimulate students' own inquiries.

At the beginning of 1994, I approached Peter and invited him to supervise my research study. My previous experience of supervisors was that often they were aloof, busy, disinterested (unless it could be published), and authoritarian. With some trepidation, I sought Peter's assurance that his perspective on the value of empowering students would extend to our student–supervisor relationship, and was very pleased that he gave me this undertaking.

THE RESEARCH SUPERVISOR

Prior to supervising Vaille's research study, I had been exploring collaboratively with school teachers the feasibility of creating constructivist learning environments in their high school mathematics classrooms (Taylor, 1992, 1993; Taylor, Fraser, & White, 1994). This research had led me to understand that, notwithstanding teachers' reform-minded zeal, the transformation of teacher-centered classrooms into learning environments that give priority to students' self-determination and conceptual development can be highly problematic.

By developing an epistemological perspective—"critical constructivism"— shaped by ideas drawn from radical constructivism (von Glasersfeld, 1990, 1993), cultural anthropology (Britzman, 1991; Geertz, 1973; Samuel & Thompson, 1990), critical theory (Giroux, 1981; Grundy, 1987; McCarthy,

1985), and the philosophy of science and mathematics (Davis & Hersch, 1986; Ernest, 1991; Kuhn, 1962; Toulmin, 1972), I had come to understand how well-established cultural forces designed to maintain the existing social order can work in concert to neutralize winds of change.

My research illustrated how powerful cultural "myths," or deep-seated sets of valued normative beliefs, are communicated unknowingly in the daily discourses of teachers and students (Milne & Taylor, 1995; Taylor, 1996). Such discourses interweave into an apparently seamless tapestry the official language of the discipline (i.e., science, mathematics) with a powerful language of socialization. The invisibility of myth (rooted in the collective unconscious) strengthens its pervasiveness and can cause teachers to abandon their seemingly "unnatural" reform ideals, especially when they threaten the existing social order of their institution. In school science and mathematics, the repressive myths of "hard control" and "cold reason" can combine to create a powerful illusion that teacher control, symbolic deductive logic, and objective knowledge are natural ways of understanding the role of teachers, the act of thinking, and the status of knowledge, respectively.

Because of my interest in empowering teachers to contest the legitimacy of repressive myths that govern their teaching, I have a commitment to modeling this transformative practice in my own teaching. One of the main ways that I endeavor to do this is by creating a classroom environment based on the emancipatory goal of enabling students to reflect critically on their deep-seated beliefs about what it means, in practice, for them to become empowered learners. Two important emancipatory conditions are freedom from external constraints (such as the self-serving coercion and manipulation exerted by others) and from internal constraints (such as our own distorted or "false" consciousness). In the teaching that Vaille had experienced in my classes, I had construed empowered learning largely in terms of the emancipatory goal of a critical self-reflective awareness of the cultural myths that govern students' images of themselves as learners. In the previous section, Vaille describes briefly some of my teaching strategies.

I was delighted by Vaille's request that I supervise her action research study, a study that offered the prospect of extending emancipatory learning goals into school science. Because we both valued the idea of student empowerment, it seemed natural that our student–supervisor relationship be free of the coerciveness that can result from asymmetrical power relations, particularly "deficit" relationships based on the uncontested assumption of teacher as expert and student as novice. At Vaille's behest, I agreed to a student–supervisor relationship based on the principle of equity and saw my role as a consultant rather than a controller or director. Later, however, the following event caused me to reflect critically on my assumptions about the nature of student empowerment and my role as a research supervisor.

A CRITICAL EVENT

The starting point of our inquiry is a critical event that occurred shortly after Vaille's dissertation had been examined successfully in December 1994. Having witnessed Vaille's escalating frustration over the writing of her dissertation, Peter wanted to understand what had gone wrong with their student–supervisor relationship. Why had they not achieved the goal of student empowerment they had agreed on at the beginning of the year?

Peter explained to Vaille that he was seriously intent on improving his own supervisory practice and that he would value any insights that she might care to offer about the extent to which she felt that his attempts to be persuasive, especially in regard to her writing, had been coercive. Vaille replied that, indeed, she had felt very coerced by him on several occasions, and that she would provide him with selected extracts of her personal journal. A "can of worms" had been opened! Perhaps the following extract best summarizes Vaille's feelings on the matter:

> It really is impossible (for you) to be emancipatory and noncoercive. You have all the power. It's the same way with my students. They go through my hoops and I go through yours. (Journal, October 1994)

The evidence from Vaille's journal caused us to construct the following interpretive research question:

Why didn't the critical constructivist pedagogy of our student–supervisor relationship feel empowering?

CONFLICTS OF INTEREST

Many factors are likely to impinge on the success of an emancipatory action research study, especially those associated with the restraining culture of the school (such as countervailing expectations of students, colleagues and administrators). The more that teacher-researchers attempt to transform the culture of their classrooms, the greater the resistance they are likely to experience, especially when they are "going it alone" in solo efforts at pedagogical reform. Such was the case with Vaille's emancipatory action research study. In this chapter, however, we do not focus on the culture of the school as a source of disempowerment. Rather, we focus largely on the student–supervisor relationship that occurred, for the most part, within the precinct of the university.

The following recollection presents our joint account of three areas in which major conflicts of interest seemed to occur in our relationship. When we present here the "historical" perspectives that we held in 1994, perspectives that are recorded in our earlier separate writings, we use pseudonyms ("Joanne," "Philip") and indent the passages. Elsewhere in this section, we frame these historical perspectives with the explanatory and interpretive commentary of our present perspectives.

Theory and Authority

Traditionally, the research student's construction of a theoretical framework for their study is regarded as an essential preliminary step, one that should precede and shape data collection activities. In much research, particularly scientific laboratory-based research, it is customary for students to "slot into" an existing research program and to adopt unquestioningly the extant theoretical framework of the research supervisor. Thus, the student's theoretical framework rests almost entirely on the established authority of the research supervisor.

In emancipatory action research, however, the authority of the teacher-researcher's professional experience is central to the research process. The goal of action research is for teachers to improve their own teaching practice by identifying and solving problems of their own choosing. Although this involves regarding as problematic an aspect of their professional authority, if the teacher-researchers are not to be disempowered then it is important that they have ultimate responsibility for identifying (and therefore owning) whichever aspect of their teaching practice they regard as in need of improvement. Thus, the teacher-researchers' professional authority is foregrounded, within the context of the research study, as uniquely valuable and worthy of respect, yet problematic.

But what of the authority of the supervisor, an authority based on special understandings of educational theory and research? Educational theory affects all aspects of the action research process, especially theory about the doing of research. Research supervisors have an important role in drawing on the authority of their own expertise to enable teacher-researchers to develop knowledge and skills in matters such as determining an appropriate epistemology for the research; articulating feasible research questions; designing sound techniques for generating and analysing data; reporting the research to multiple audiences; and selecting and applying appropriate standards for judging the quality of the research process; but, most important, not at the expense of the teacher-researchers' own professional authority.

Indeed, action research was conceived as a means of facilitating a much closer nexus between educational theory ("out there") and the teacher-researchers' ongoing theorizing about their own teaching practice. One of the most important outcomes of an action research study is the ability of teacher-researchers to theorize, with an enhanced sense of professional authority, about the practicalities of their own teaching practice. However, as the following vignettes from the case of Philip and Joanne illustrate, the research supervisor's role in enhancing the authority of the teacher-researcher can be problematic, especially when the teacher-researcher undergoes a radical transformation in epistemology.

"Philip's" Perspective.

From the outset of our student-supervisor relationship, Joanne requested that I help her to develop a better understanding of constructivism. Although she seemed to be attracted by what she had learned already about constructivism, she had only a tenuous grasp of constructivist theory. She asked me for a clear explanation.

Despite the temptation to do so, I was reluctant simply to "stamp my brand" of critical constructivism on Joanne. Rather, I wanted her to continue constructing her own understanding by discussing with me her ideas as she read the literature and reflected critically on the epistemology that underpinned her own teaching. I recommended further readings, including my own papers, and invited her to meet with me on a weekly basis to discuss the development of her action research study.

In those early weeks, I engaged Joanne in a discourse that, I believed, would enable her to test the viability of her growing understanding of constructivist theory. I attempted to "steer" her toward a sound understanding of the central principles of constructivism (that distinguish it from objectivism) while allowing her the "space" to decide on practical implications for her own teaching. At the time, I believed that this approach would result in Joanne's development of a more meaningful understanding than was possible had I explained (or "transmitted"!) the complexities of my own constructivist perspective.

Indeed, I believed my research supervision practice constituted an actual modeling of a critical constructivist pedagogy. I focused my attention on Joanne's current and developing understandings of constructivist theory, endeavored to negotiate the viability of her emerging ideas, and strove to empower her by respecting her right to make her own pedagogical decisions. I also held firm to the principle that she should not adopt unquestioningly my own theoretical perspective on the basis of its implied authority.

"Joanne's" Perspective.

In the early weeks of planning my action research study, I frequently asked Philip about his views on constructivism as a means of shaping my own emergent ideas. However, he seemed to behave as though constructivism was some mystical secret where the uninitiated must pass through certain "rites of passage" in order to understand. Although I read Philip's papers on constructivism, I could not always understand the language. I didn't want a sanitized version. I wanted a person-to-person view. In my journal I wrote at the time:

> I feel you have such a profound belief in constructivism that we have
> never really discussed its merits. It is taken as a given.
>
> (Journal, November 1994)

By not disclosing his beliefs and, more importantly, his doubts about his
beliefs, I felt that Philip, whom I considered to be an authority on constructivism, was absolutely dedicated to the notion of constructivism. I felt that I
could not raise for discussion my own doubts.

My feelings of disquiet increased as I struggled with my own evolving
thoughts. I conceded the failings of an impersonal objectivist stance when
considering issues. What I could not counter, however, was the free-fall feeling
I encountered when I thought from a constructivist perspective. It was like
stepping off concrete into quicksand.

Whenever I felt threatened, I clambered back onto the firm surface of my
previous "separate knower" way of thinking described by Belenky et al. (1986).
A separate knower is one who suppresses subjectivity in favor of the
impersonal authority of an objectivist view of the world. As a science student
at university and then as a medical research scientist, I had been used to
factual knowledge legitimated by authorities such as textbooks, teachers and
research supervisors. This was a very familiar way of knowing and acting for
me, but it was a way that was being contested by constructivism.

Whereas Philip was being careful to avoid imposing his own epistemology, Joanne was experiencing a growing sense of disempowerment because
she felt that she was expected to adopt a compliant "guess what's in my
mind" role. How can we understand this outcome, which is clearly contrary
to the empowering goals of emancipatory action research ostensibly shared
by both the student and the supervisor?

From a rereading of Habermas, especially his "theory of communicative
action" (Pusey, 1987), the emancipatory goal of empowerment is to create
equality of opportunity for participants in a relationship to achieve the
"practical" goal of a type of ethically sound communication that aims to
achieve reciprocal understanding of intentions, goals, and meaning perspectives. Bakhtin (1981) called this a "dialogical" discourse: that is, communication that aims to create a rich mutual understanding of each other's point
of view or valued beliefs without either party feeling obliged to adopt the
other's position simply because of a power imbalance in the relationship.
Indeed, because a dialogical understanding can embrace opposing or conflicting beliefs, it serves to enhance the "less powerful" participant's sense
of agency as a rational thinker, actor, and communicator.

What we learn from the case of Philip and Joanne is that a dialogical
discourse between a research supervisor and student doesn't happen
merely as a result of avoidance action. The supervisor's attempts not to
engage his student in a "monological" discourse—that is, a discourse that
legitimates only the "more powerful" participant's epistemology—resulted

in what we might call a "null" discourse that prevented both parties from understanding one another's individual perspectives and mutual interests.

Furthermore, in his attempts to foster the student's sense of authority in herself as a teacher-researcher—an authority associated with assuming responsibility for reconstructing both her own epistemology and teaching practice—the research supervisor seems to have lost sight of the importance of developing a supportive relationship and sharing responsibility for what amounted to a radical transformation of the student's epistemology. With his focus on the long-term goal of student empowerment, a mutually shared (but differently constructed) goal, the supervisor overlooked the importance of a "duty of care" toward a student (Noddings, 1984) who would, in the short term, need to draw on his authority as a source of reassurance, an authority legitimated by his professional position within the university and his own research expertise.

Voice and Ownership

The novice research student wishing to undertake an interpretive or qualitative research approach faces three difficult questions, each of which has implications for the epistemological framing of research activities: (a) What form of representation (or genre) should I use when writing my research report? (b) What methods of data generation and analysis should I use? and (c) What standards should I use to judge the quality of my work? Unfortunately, there is no simple answer to these interdependent questions.

Although there is a general preference in the field of interpretive research for a form of writing that evidences the researcher's learning (contrasting with the traditional research epistemology of the researcher as a tester of a priori hypotheses), there is no single best way for the interpretive researcher to represent in writing the results of research. Among the eclectic range of writing genres (and their associated epistemologies) that compete for the researcher's attention—realist, confessional or impressionistic tales (van Maanen, 1988); autobiographical narratives (Bruner, 1986, 1990; Carter, 1993); poetic, imaginative or fictional stories (Barone, 1988; Eisner, 1979; Eisner & Peshkin, 1990)—the common thread is a style of writing that gives voice to the researcher's first-hand experiences in the field, a requirement that legitimates at least partial use of the "active first-person" authorial voice.

The research supervisor is faced with a challenging task of advising the student about not only which genre (or genres) might be appropriate for framing data generation and analyses and for reporting the study, but also which standards might be appropriate for judging the quality of the work. The challenge for the research supervisor, therefore, is to guide the student through a minefield of possibilities. Of course, this is not without its difficulties, as the following conflicting perspectives indicate.

"Philip's" Perspective.

Joanne had opted for a traditional dissertation format, a format she preferred over my suggested alternative format that would reflect the learning journey she had taken during her study. Given the time constraints facing her, I felt comfortable with supporting her decision. She successfully completed the early chapters (Introduction, Literature Review, Methodology) with little apparent discontent, although she had commented on the unusually large number of drafts that I required of her. My response was that this was not unusual for interpretive research studies. I told her about another of my students who recently had written 13 drafts of a results chapter for an MSc thesis!

The penultimate chapter of Joanne's dissertation was to present an account of the results of her action research study, and was to be followed by a concluding chapter that presented a brief summary of the results, together with recommendations for future research. Most of my feedback on successive drafts of the results chapter focused on the adequacy of evidence (mostly qualitative data but also questionnaire results) that Joanne had presented to substantiate the claims she was making about the efficacy of her constructivist teaching innovations.

My judgments of Joanne's writing were based on four key standards that I use in my own interpretive research (Denzin, 1990; Erickson, 1986): (a) each knowledge claim must be warranted by adequate evidence (including deliberately sought disconfirming evidence); (b) criteria for judging the adequacy of evidence must be stated clearly (usually in a methodology chapter); (c) acknowledgment must be made of inadequacies in the evidence; and (d) evidence must be presented in a logically coherent and succinct manner. Based on these standards, I recommended, at times, major restructuring of Joanne's results chapter; at other times, I recommended changes in authorial style, expression, and grammar. Overall, my recommendations were aligned with my goal of enabling Joanne to inject into her writing a well-considered subjectivity and to achieve a high standard of qualitative analysis as sound preparation for subsequent doctoral research. This was a future option that I wanted her to consider seriously. She had achieved outstanding grades in her coursework, and an award of distinction for her dissertation would make her very competitive for a full-time doctoral scholarship. She seemed to have a guarded interest in this prospect.

I wrote my evaluative comments in the margins of Joanne's work in a style that was somewhat terse and critical, and sometimes added an accompanying page of summary and recommendations. During our weekly discussions, however, and depending on how much time I had available, I attempted to be more empathic. However, I sensed Joanne's growing displeasure with my critical commentary on her writing. Although I was familiar with this response from students undertaking interpretive research for the first time, I, too, felt uncomfortable and tried to be reassuring by reminding Joanne that she would benefit from the experience but that the final decision to rewrite rested with her.

From my perspective, the main problem with Joanne's data analysis was its incompleteness. The analysis was presented in accordance with the a priori methodological structure of the study, that is, in terms of the methods used for data collection. Although this is an acceptable first way of analysing interpretive data, and often is accepted by my colleagues as an end in its own right, I see it as the beginning of a more insightful analysis in which themes emerge during the process of analysis—a process that involves successive iterations and gives rise to the construction of "grounded theory" (Glaser & Strauss, 1967) or "interpretive assertions" (Erickson, 1986) that infer a significance extending provisionally beyond the boundaries of the study.

However, when I suggested to Joanne (after numerous drafts of her results chapter) that she consider restructuring her partially completed analysis according to key themes rather than methods of data collection, she refused to agree. Sensing Joanne's frustration, I accepted her results chapter without further change and, a short time later, was pleasantly surprised by the high quality of her final chapter.

"Joanne's" Perspective.

As my master's research project developed, conflict arose over my supervisor's insistence that I adopt his academic style of writing. Initially, when I first submitted chapter drafts to Philip I was both impressed and flattered by his careful attention to detail. However, as this process continued through successive drafts, I became increasingly peeved by what I assumed was his hypercritical attitude. I was accustomed to writing papers based on a plan and one draft followed by some final editing. The problem was that, with each new draft, the work became more my supervisor's than mine. This gradual loss of voice increased my dependence on Philip for feedback as I lost touch with my original arguments. I experienced an increasing sense of powerlessness, as the following extract of my journal reveals:

> When I talk to you about a corrected chapter, you never ask me about where I think the weaknesses are. You always identify them. . . . Having you as a supervisor is a double-edged sword. On the one hand, the attention is good; it shows you think the project is as important as I do; it shows you care. The downside is that you have too much input. I sometimes feel it is your project or that I am a dependent passive assistant.
>
> (Journal, October 1994)

Whereas I merely wanted to complete my master's degree, my perception was that Philip wanted me to produce the perfect document on his terms. Finally, after eight drafts of the results chapter, he suggested I reorganize the chapter based on issues that emerged from the data analysis. I was disconsolate! I had already expended far more time and effort on this chapter than I thought necessary. With each draft, Philip's view had further overlaid mine until I could scarcely understand what I had written. I wrote in my journal:

> There seemed to be an expectation that your wishes would be carried out.... From the middle of the year when I began writing, I had this feeling that I was losing touch with the project. I had the data but my interpretation was constantly overlaid by your more experienced, theory-based view.... You weren't nasty or bossy but I felt trapped into moving down your path.
>
> (Journal, November 1994)

I knew that in order to reorganize the chapter I would have to completely rewrite it. I reached a crisis point and seriously considered discontinuing my studies. On suggesting this to Philip, I was surprised that he was taken aback. I hadn't realized that he had not sensed my irritation. I felt that he had used his power over me in an academic sense to coerce me into doing his bidding. I was afraid that I would fail or not be considered for doctoral studies if I did not follow his directions.

Nevertheless, the reader should not suppose that I was an innocent student with a manipulative supervisor, although on occasion I did feel like a fly trapped in a spider's web. By adopting a cloak of passivity, I had found that it was easier and less emotionally draining to acquiesce and let Philip set the agenda. My sense of powerlessness was such that my thinking returned to that of a "separate knower." I looked to Philip as a source of authority and knowledge. He seemed to know everything. I consciously allowed my drafts to become sloppy. After all, what was the point of agonizing over a word when I knew Philip would rewrite the entire sentence!

At this point, I ceased writing the results chapter, our main source of dissension, and chose instead to write the final chapter. Rather than submit a first draft to Philip, I chose to do several successive drafts by myself, almost to see if I was actually capable of writing. I found that it was not difficult to edit my own work. This chapter represented a final synthesis of my data and I felt that it was cohesive and projected my voice. My dissertation was examined and awarded an "A" grade.

One way of resolving these conflicting perspectives is to argue that the research supervisor's approach was exemplary because the student succeeded in producing a high-quality dissertation. It would follow that the painfulness of the student's writing experience was an unfortunate but "necessary evil." However, from the perspective of Habermas' "theory of communicative action" (Pusey, 1987), a guiding ethic of the end justifying the means is unacceptable, especially when it dominates and distorts a communicative relationship. Although the supervisor's goal of maximizing the student's opportunities to undertake future doctoral study was laudable and ultimately might have been empowering of the student, the means of achieving this goal had the opposite effect of disempowering the student by dispossessing her of ownership of her research and by silencing her voice in her writing.

This case helps us to understand that the emancipatory goal of empowerment is not an end in itself. Rather, it serves as a means of developing human relationships that can give expression to the "communicative" goal of rich mutual understanding based on an ethic of reciprocal care and concern of a kind advocated by Noddings (1984). When the goal of empowerment is divorced from the goal of a communicative relationship, then empowerment is in danger of becoming distorted and serving the technical goal of control and, perhaps unwittingly, aiding and abetting the practice of coercive manipulation. This seems to be what happened in the case of Philip and Joanne.

Despite Philip's apparently good intentions toward Joanne, his long-term goal of student empowerment was divorced from the short-term goal of developing a communicative relationship with Joanne, a relationship that might have dissolved some of the stresses associated with her high-risk activity of transforming radically her own epistemology and teaching practice. Rather than enabling Joanne to set feasible short-term goals for her writing (as well as encouraging her to consider optional long-term goals) and to develop a set of standards with which to judge the quality of her own research work, for the most part Philip maintained ownership and control over these standards and endeavored to "steer" Joanne toward a goal that, at the time, was largely of his own choosing and unbeknown to her.

Collaboration and Multiple Agendas

When a teacher adopts the role of a teacher-researcher and undertakes an action research study, her agenda is relatively straightforward: to improve the quality of her teaching practice. When the teacher-researcher also is a student in a program of postgraduate study, her agenda can become significantly more complex. Now, her action research has the additional goal of gaining credit toward a higher degree. When we consider yet another role for the teacher—"collaborative researcher"—then the number of coincidental agendas suddenly increases by another order of magnitude.

Collaborative action research between a teacher-researcher and an "outside" researcher has been recognized as fruitful for involving teachers in a process of pedagogical reform and for generating rich insights into the constraints on the reform process (Kyle & McCutcheon, 1984; Saphier, 1982; Shymansky & Kyle, 1991; Watt & Watt, 1982). Here, the research supervisor also has multiple agendas, including supervising the research student and conducting research activity in the teacher's classroom. Not surprisingly, perhaps, the student–supervisor relationship can become somewhat strained as multiple agendas are pursued and conflicts of interest arise. Consider the following vignettes that highlight the conflicting perspectives and goals of Joanne and Philip as they pursued their multiple teaching and research agendas.

"Philip's" Perspective.

For some time prior to the commencement of Joanne's action research study, I had been developing a questionnaire to assist teacher-researchers undertaking constructivist teaching reforms to monitor students' perceptions of their classroom learning environments (Taylor et al., 1994). I wished to trial it in a school science classroom in which teaching was being transformed, at least partially, from a critical constructivist perspective.

Joanne's emancipatory action research study offered an unrivaled opportunity to trial the questionnaire, which comprised scales that seemed pertinent to Joanne's stated teaching goals of stimulating students' small-group work, devolving control of students' classroom learning activities, encouraging students to exercise a critical voice about the quality of their learning, and linking students' classroom learning with their out-of-school experiences. I asked Joanne to consider helping me with the trialing of the questionnaire. She agreed willingly to administer the questionnaire in several of her classes. With her consent, I visited her classes to observe students' learning activities and, later, she assisted me to organize volunteer students for interviews. For her research assistance, Joanne received airfare to attend a national science education conference, where she presented a paper on her own teacher-researcher activities.

Around the time that Joanne was writing the results chapter of her dissertation, I invited her to read my analysis of interview transcripts and questionnaire results. The account combined whole-class analyses with profiles of eight students selected according to their different responses to Joanne's teaching. In accordance with a guarantee of confidentiality that I had given students prior to the interviews, I had allocated pseudonyms.

In my role as supervisor of Joanne's action research study, I felt morally obliged to assist her in gaining the most from the professional development process that lay at the heart of her research. It seemed to me that my own research report could contribute to her deepening understanding of the nature of her recent teaching innovations and their influence on her students' learning. I wanted to help her to continue moving forward in her professional development by realizing that she, too, was morally obliged to continue asking herself difficult questions that would compel her to seek evidence of the need for continuous improvement in her teaching; questions such as: Have my teaching innovations contributed to the hostility displayed by "troublesome" students? To what extent might I have imposed unjustly my requirements for students to adopt radically new learning roles? What are the inviolable "rights" of students in relation to "experimental" teaching?

I felt that my research report would serve to stimulate Joanne's critical thinking about her own partially completed analyses, particularly in relation to the need to account for disconfirming evidence and to qualify her somewhat ambitious claims about the efficacy of her teaching innovations. In wanting to share my draft research report with Joanne, I was motivated also by a need to enrich the quality of my own research analyses that made claims about the usefulness of the questionnaire. One way that I might have worked toward achieving this goal was by incorporating into my analyses aspects of Joanne's perspective on her students' learning practices.

To my surprise, however, Joanne refused the invitation to read my research report. She stated adamantly that, because I had given guarantees to the students to preserve their anonymity and because of the small number of students involved in the interviews, including two of four "troublesome" students, it would be unethical for her to read accounts that she was likely to recognize.

I had mixed feelings about Joanne's response. On the one hand, I understood her viewpoint and appreciated that an ethical dilemma did indeed exist. On the other hand, I regretted having made a "watertight" guarantee to the students that now seemed to be working against the interests of both Joanne and me, interests that seemed to transcend us and have a broader educational significance.

I argued somewhat forcefully with Joanne (as one might with a peer) that I could resolve this ethical dilemma by revisiting the students, showing them my analyses, and seeking their permission for me to share them with her. I was quite certain that the students would not find the analyses objectionable and that I could readily persuade them to agree with my proposal to share them with their teacher. If students did object, then I was willing to respect their opinion and act accordingly. Joanne refused, however, to allow me to approach the students. Bearing in mind the strength of her feelings, I accepted her decision and put the matter aside.

"Joanne's" Perspective.

Early in our student–supervisor relationship, Philip asked me if I would be willing to trial a questionnaire that he had developed. I was happy to do so. I saw the questionnaire as serving his research interests rather than mine. I had ample data from my own questionnaires and student interviews.

Before commencing my study, I had sought permission from the students, their parents, the school principal, and my head of department to collect data from my students. I had been careful to assure everyone that all data were to be treated as confidential. I reassured the students that none of the data would be used to influence my assessment of them in the bioethics unit. It was a straightforward matter, therefore, to administer Philip's questionnaire under the same conditions as my own.

When he then told me that he needed to interview some students about their responses to the questionnaire I was rather surprised. I worried about whether I had to obtain further permission from the school. This I did by asking my head of department. When organizing students to be interviewed, I reassured them (especially the troublesome ones) that their interviews were totally confidential. I knew that would help Philip to obtain maximum data. Because they would see him as a neutral person, he would have no power over them, in a school sense.

While I was writing my results chapter, Philip asked me to read his research report that contained data from the student interviews. After considering his request, which might have been useful to my own writing, I refused. I felt that I could not possibly betray a student's confidentiality, no matter how much it might benefit my research. Teaching the course on bioethics had heightened my sense of personal responsibility for my students' moral well-being. When Philip suggested that he could go back and get students' permission I had an image of them being pressured into an agreement the implications of which they might not fully understand. They would have been disempowered without even knowing it had happened. I believed that this was an ethically incorrect way of conducting research, and wrote in my journal:

> I was and still am going through a moral stage in relation to educational research. I guess I am ultrasensitive to the collection and use of data. (Some of this relates to my medical research background. We often collected specimens for unauthorized tests.) Students are not pawns and I don't believe they can give consent freely as they are unaware of the consequences.

> (Journal, November 1994)

It seems sensible to suggest that the easiest way of avoiding this type of conflict between a research supervisor and research student is to deny the supervisor the right to have a collaborative research agenda that implicates the student. Perhaps collaborative research unduly complicates the student–supervisor relationship, especially when the student is undertaking a personally challenging emancipatory action research study and is in need of the unqualified and unambiguous support of her supervisor. It could be argued that Philip's research agenda compromised the neutrality of his supervisory role and disabled him from adopting a disinterested and non-judgmental perspective from which to advise Joanne as she struggled with the emotional intensity of running against the "grain" of the school's established culture.

On the other hand, it could be argued that, in the context of a student's emancipatory action research study, the supervisor's collaborative research agenda per se is not necessarily problematic. Rather, the problem of conflicting interests might have a more profound and beguiling source—the culture of education—especially its self-propagating myths. What repressive cultural myths might Philip and Joanne have been perpetuating unknowingly in the mutual enactment of their interdependent social roles of research student and research supervisor, myths that distorted their relationship and contributed to a perception of conflicting interests and unethical actions?

This question is one of the hallmarks of critical self-reflective thinking associated with the goal of emancipation. The writings of critical feminist scholars such as Lather (1986) and Ellsworth (1992) helped us to answer the question. They argued that the repressive myth of "rationalism"—a narrow framework for action that celebrates the logic and control of the expert while ignoring others' needs and emotions—has a major role in derailing emancipatory reforms in education by perpetuating relations of domination. In science and mathematics education, the myth of rationalism has been criticized severely for celebrating "cold" reason and "hard" control while delegitimating the important role of feelings, values, and emotionality in establishing and maintaining communicative relationships between teacher and students (Pintrich, Marx, & Boyle, 1993; Taylor, 1996).

Looking through this conceptual "lens" helps us to understand how the rationalism of Philip's concern for his own research agenda cast a cold shadow over his relationship with Joanne. The preeminence that he attached to the methodological rigor of his own research led him to make successive "well-reasoned" requests of Joanne in a way that failed to acknowledge or preempt her growing concerns and doubts about his intentions, and that did little to foster her trust in him or a perception that he cared about her. Rather, he tended to take for granted the assumption that the authority of his requests to survey Joanne's students and observe their classroom activities was sufficiently well-warranted (within his own research framework) that she would need no other form of assurance about the legitimacy of his planned activities. In the absence of a rich communicative relationship, Philip tended to overlook Joanne's duty of care toward her own students (a sense of duty that had been heightened by her teaching concern with ethics) and to gloss over his duty of care toward her, his own student.

Instead of disclosing the extent of his research agenda at the outset and inviting Joanne's critical commentary as a full collaborator, Philip chose, somewhat naively, to announce his research needs almost as they arose, thereby catching her by surprise and reinforcing her perception of the independence of their individual research activities. This independence became a gulf when Philip proffered his own research report and then offered to obtain the consent of Joanne's students for her reading of it. A rich communicative relationship could have legitimated a critical and empathic examination of Joanne's concerns. In its absence, the perspectival nature of the issue of appropriate research ethics was clouded by feelings of distrust and a perceived lack of care and concern.

The myth of rationalism also has explanatory power in relation to the other major conflicts of interest that we have discussed already. During Joanne's initial struggle to understand her supervisor's constructivist perspective, Philip maintained a powerful commitment to his rationalist goal of autonomous student reasoning. However, the authority of his commitment remained unexamined and unquestioned in the absence of a dialogical discourse with his student and, consequently, overshadowed the authenticity of her communicative needs. Thus, the cold reason of Philip's strongly idealized (perhaps ideological?) commitment displaced a duty of care that might have better supported Joanne in her emotional struggle to challenge the authority of her own experiences as a teacher, student, and researcher while she transformed her own epistemology and tested its viability in her teaching.

In relation to supervising Joanne's research writing, Philip's unwavering commitment to his own set of academic standards for quality writing (bolstered by his long-term "empowering" goal of preparing Joanne for subsequent doctoral research) served to justify his silencing of Joanne's "voice," an experience that she described in terms of feeling an increasing loss of ownership of her work. The hard control of Philip's unyielding grasp of his own theoretically justified standards displaced his sense of moral accountability for Joanne's agency as a thinker and writer, and failed to enable him to address the root cause of her emotional distress. In the absence of a rich communicative relationship in which all knowledge claims are open to critical examination, including the question of appropriate standards, the supervisor and student defaulted to a traditional relationship in which the choice of standards was controlled by the authority of the "expert."

Looking through the conceptual lens of the myth of rationalism provides an insightful view of the three major conflicts of interest that we have discussed here and helps us to understand the extent to which Philip's power and control as research supervisor might have prevailed unfairly (albeit unwittingly) over Joanne's teacher–researcher–student role.

AVOIDING RELATIONS OF DOMINATION

It was a critical event that sparked our inquiry and caused us to examine the hijacking of our intentions for an equitable partnership that we had agreed on at the outset of our student–supervisor relationship. As a result of our inquiry, we are confident that we understand better how Joanne came to feel disempowered and we are confident that we can recommend ways of preventing similar relationships from being caught up in the paradox described by the feminist scholar, Patti Lather (1986):

> How to maximize the researcher's mediation between people's self-understandings (in light of the need for ideology critique) and transformative social action without becoming impositional. . . . This is the central paradox of critical theory and provides its greatest challenge. (p. 269)

We believe that one of the keys to unlocking this paradox lies in refining the critical constructivist perspective that framed Philip's supervisory role. Our inquiry revealed that, although his supervisory actions were shaped by a perspective that recognized theoretically the importance of both communicative and emancipatory goals, the latter tended to prevail as a referent for his role as supervisor. As a result, the goal of student empowerment was linked too closely with a rationalist approach to emancipation, an approach that eclipsed his perception of a need for an enriched communicative student–supervisor relationship. This proved to be particularly demoralizing of Joanne at critical times during her endeavors to transform the epistemology of her own teaching and to complete related research activities.

In the context of the collaborative type of emancipatory action research in which we coparticipated, we believe that the development of a rich communicative relationship between a research supervisor and research student is essential to the viability, vitality, and quality of the research process. We feel that a research supervisor who wishes to support a student in the high-risk activity of emancipatory action research, and who wishes also to join the student in a collaborative research partnership, should assume responsibility for engaging the student in the explicit development of a communicative relationship regulated by the following set of standards that are applicable equally to both of them:

- An ongoing commitment to an empathic, caring, and trusting relationship that places *emotionality* on an equal footing with reason.

- An ongoing commitment to a *dialogical discourse* that aims at co-constructing mutual and respectful understandings based on standards of reciprocal action such as:
  - Being willing to disclose and examine critically one's goals, interests, valued beliefs, and standards of judgment.
  - Having the right to know and challenge the other's justification for one's actions and judgments.

- An ongoing commitment to ensuring that a *metadiscourse* is readily available for discussing the state of health of the communicative relationship by allowing the (often implicit) rules of the discourse to become the subject of critical discussion.

The reciprocal nature of these standards means that the research supervisor who engages collaboratively with the student in a emancipatory action research study cannot feign value neutrality and mask personal interests behind the traditional standard of objectivity, a standard that seems well-suited to relationships governed by the myth of rationalism. On the other hand, by acknowledging the nature of their stakeholding, supervisors do not earn the right to privilege their own (considerable) authority, particularly in judging the quality of the student's work. Rather, supervisor's have a key responsibility to foster students' own judgment-making capabilities regarding what quality control standards are most appropriate for regulating their own research activities.

We have made these recommendations in the spirit of fostering an equitable relationship between research students and their supervisors, but we feel that it is important that equity not be confused with equality. In the context of a collaborative type of emancipatory action research, equality is inappropriate, because the student and supervisor bring to their educative relationship different types of expertise grounded in the authority of their distinctly different experiences. The principle of equity, however, aims to create a mutually valuable interdependency that eschews relations of domination while fostering an educative relationship of coparticipatory teaching and learning.

ACKNOWLEDGMENTS

We extend our thanks to Stephen Kemmis and Jack Whitehead, who read our earlier papers and encouraged us to co-construct the dialogical discourse of this chapter.

REFERENCES

Bakhtin, M. M. (1981). *The dialogical imagination*. Austin: University of Texas Press.

Barone, T. (1988). Curriculum platforms and literature. In L. E. Beyer & M. W. Apple (Eds.), *The curriculum: Problems, politics, and possibilities* (pp. 119–165). Albany: State University of New York Press.

Belenky, M. F., Clinchy, B. M., Goldberger, N. R., & Tarule, J. M. (1986). *Women's ways of knowing*. New York: Basic Books.

Bodner, G. (1986). Constructivism: A theory of knowledge. *Journal of Chemical Education, 63*(10), 873–878.

Britzman, D. P. (1991). *Practice makes practice: A critical study of learning to teach*. Albany: State University of New York Press.

Bruner, J. (1986). *Actual minds, possible worlds*. Cambridge, MA: Harvard University Press.

Bruner, J. (1990). *Acts of meaning*. Cambridge, MA: Harvard University Press.

Carter, K. (1993). The place of story in the study of teaching and teacher education. *Educational Researcher, 22*, 5–12.

Clandinin, D. J., & Connelly, F. M. (1994). Personal experience methods. In Y. Lincoln & N. Denzin (Eds.), *Handbook of qualitative research* (pp. 413–427). Newbury Park, CA: Sage.

Davis, P. J., & Hersch, R. H. (1986). *Descartes' dream: The world according to mathematics*. Boston: Houghton Mifflin.

Dawson, V. (1994). *The development and implementation of a Year 10 bioethics unit based on a constructivist epistemology*. Unpublished master's thesis, Science and Mathematics Education Centre, Curtin University of Technology, Perth, Western Australia.

Dawson, V. (1996). The r(evolution) of my epistemology: My experience as a postgraduate research student. *Educational Action Research, 4*(3), 363–374.

Denzin, N. K. (1990). Triangulation. In H. J. Walberg & G. D. Haertel (Eds.), *The international encyclopedia of educational evaluation* (pp. 592–594). Elmsford, NY: Pergamon.

Driver, R. (1990, April). *Constructivist approaches to science teaching*. Paper presented at the University of Georgia, Mathematics Education Department, Athens.

Eisner, E. (1979). *The educational imagination*. New York: Macmillan.

Eisner, E., & Peshkin, A. (Eds.). (1990). *Qualitative inquiry in education: The continuing debate*. New York: Teachers College Press.

Ellsworth, E. (1992). Why doesn't this feel empowering? Working through the repressive myths of critical pedagogy. In C. Luke & J. Gore (Eds.), *Feminisms and critical pedagogy* (pp. 90–119). New York: Routledge.

Erickson, F. (1986). Qualitative methods in research on teaching. In M. C. Wittrock (Ed.), *Handbook of research on teaching* (3rd ed., pp. 119–159). New York: Macmillan.

Ernest, P. (1991). *The philosophy of mathematics education*. London: Falmer.

Geertz, C. (1973). *The interpretation of cultures*. New York: Basic Books.

Geertz, C. (1983). *Local knowledge: Further essays in interpretive anthropology*. New York: Basic Books.

Giroux, H. A. (1981). *Ideology, culture, and the processes of schooling*. Philadelphia: Temple University Press.

Glaser, B., & Strauss, A. (1967). *The discovery of grounded theory*. Chicago: Aldine.

Grundy, S. (1987). *Curriculum: Product or praxis?* London: Falmer.

Kemmis, S., & McTaggert, R. (Eds.). (1988). *The action research planner* (3rd ed.). Geelong, Victoria, Australia: Deakin University Press.

Kuhn, T. S. (1962). *The structure of scientific revolutions* (3rd ed.). Chicago: University of Chicago Press.

Kyle, D. W., & McCutcheon, G. (1984). Collaborative research: Development and issues. *Journal of Curriculum Studies, 16*(2), 173–179.

Lather, P. (1986). Research as praxis. *Harvard Educational Review, 56*(3), 257–277.

Milne, C., & Taylor, P. C. (1995). Metaphors as global markers for teachers' beliefs about the nature of science. *Research in Science Education, 25*, 29–39.

McCarthy, T. (1985). *The critical theory of Jurgen Habermas*. Cambridge: Massachusetts Institute of Technology Press.

Noddings, N. (1984). *Caring: A feminine approach to ethics and moral education*. Berkeley: University of California Press.

Pintrich, P. R., Marx, R. W., & Boyle, R. A. (1993). Beyond cold conceptual change: The role of motivational beliefs and classroom contextual factors in the process of conceptual change. *Review of Educational Research, 63*(2), 167–199.

Pusey, M. (1987). *Jurgen Habermas*. London: Ellis Horwood and Tavistock.

Samuel, R., & Thompson, P. (Eds.). (1990). *The myths we live by*. London: Routledge.

Saphier, J. (1982). The knowledge base on teaching: It's here, now! In T. M. Amabile & M. L. Stubbs. (Eds.), *Psychological research in the classroom* (pp. 76–95). Elmsford, NY: Pergamon.

Shymansky, J. A., & Kyle, W. C. (1991). *Establishing a research agenda: The critical issues of science curriculum reform*. Manhattan: The National Association for Research in Science Teaching, Kansas State University.

Taylor, P. C. (1992). *An interpretive study of the role of teacher beliefs in the implementation of constructivist theory in a secondary mathematics classroom*. Unpublished doctoral thesis, Science and Mathematics Education Centre, Curtin University of Technology, Perth, Western Australia.

Taylor, P. C. (1993). Collaborating to reconstruct teaching: The influence of researcher beliefs. In K. Tobin (Ed.), *The practice of constructivism in science education* (pp. 267–297). Washington, DC: American Association for the Advancement of Science.

Taylor, P. C. (1994, December). *Collaborative classroom-based action research: Persuasion or coercion?* Paper presented at the annual conference on Research in Science and Mathematics Education. Burwood, Victoria, Australia: Deakin University.

Taylor, P. C. (1995, April). *Critical interpretive inquiry and educational reform.* Paper presented at the annual meeting of the American Educational Research Association, San Francisco, CA.

Taylor, P. C. (1996). Mythmaking and mythbreaking in the mathematics classroom. *Educational Studies in Mathematics, 31*(1, 2), 151–173.

Taylor, P. C., Fraser, B. J., & White, L. (1994, April). *CLES: An instrument for monitoring the development of constructivist learning environments.* Paper presented at the annual meeting of the American Educational Research Association, Atlanta, GA.

Toulmin, S. (1972). *Human understanding* (Vol. 1). Oxford, England: Clarendon.

van Maanen, J. (1988). *Tales of the field: On writing ethnography.* Chicago: University of Chicago Press.

von Glasersfeld, E. (1989). Cognition, construction of knowledge and teaching. *Synthese, 80,* 121–140.

von Glasersfeld, E. (1990). An exposition of constructivism: Why some like it radical. In R. B. Davis, C. A. Maher, & N. Noddings (Eds.), *Constructivist views on the teaching and learning of mathematics* (Journal of Research in Mathematics Education Monographs No. 4, pp. 19–29). Reston, VA: National Council of Teachers of Mathematics.

von Glasersfeld, E. (1993). Questions and answers about radical constructivism. In K. Tobin (Ed.), *The practice of constructivism in science and mathematics education* (pp. 23–38). Washington, DC: American Association for the Advancement of Science.

Watt, D. H., & Watt, H. (1982). Design criteria for collaborative classroom research. In T. M. Amabile & M. L. Stubbs (Eds.), *Psychological research in the classroom* (pp. 134–143). Elmsford, NY: Pergamon.

7

Higher Degree Supervision: Why It Worked

Gilah C. Leder
Helen J. Forgasz
LaTrobe University, Melbourne

Julie Landvogt
Monash University, Melbourne

Substantial modifications have been made in recent years to Australia's higher educational system, with a unified higher education scheme replacing the binary system that had evolved over time. Amalgamation of existing institutions has led to the formation of large, multicampus universities. Before 1988 there were fewer than 20 universities, whereas now there are almost twice that number. The proportion of Australian students completing secondary school, and the demand for tertiary places—both undergraduate and postgraduate—have increased dramatically. For example, the number of PhD students increased from 7,035 in 1983 (Castles, 1990) to 13,623 in 1992 (Castles, 1995), and has continued to grow since then. The rise has been particularly striking for females, whose enrollment almost tripled from 1,897 in 1990 to 5,123 in 1992 (compared with 5,138 and 8,500 for males in 1983 and 1992, respectively). Thus supervisory resources are being increasingly stretched. However, considerable effort is made to preserve the high standards of doctoral work long associated with Australian universities.

Despite this period of turbulence in the tertiary sector, the requirements for satisfactory completion of a doctoral dissertation (as well as those for a master's-by-research degree) have remained largely unchanged. Although some course work may be prescribed as part of the program, the typical Australian PhD is awarded largely on the basis of the thesis or dissertation. In contrast, the Doctor of Education (EdD) degree requires satisfactory completion of a set number of subjects as well as a (smaller) dissertation.

The high standing commonly accorded to the doctorate, and to research, has also been maintained. Australian universities commonly include *a strong commitment to the conduct of high-quality research* in their management plans, and often rely on the efforts of postgraduate students to boost their research output.

Emphasis on original work, and on a substantial or significant contribution to knowledge, are recurring themes in the regulations governing PhD examinations in Australia as elsewhere. For example:

> The degree of Doctor of Philosophy (PhD) at Monash signifies that the holder . . . has submitted a thesis that the examiners have declared to be a significant contribution to knowledge, and that demonstrates the candidate's capacity to carry out independent research. (Higher Degrees and Scholarships Section, Monash University, 1991, p. 5)

and "Recommendation for the degree [PhD] will be made only after the acceptance of a dissertation, which must be a contribution to knowledge and the result of independent work, expressed in satisfactory form" (Stanford University, quoted in Boyer, 1973, p. 17).

The need for comparability in quality of local degrees with those from overseas institutions has also been made quite explicit: "Examiners are invited to judge a thesis at the highest contemporary standard for European and North American Universities. . . . The candidate must make a substantial contribution to learning" (The Australian National University, quoted in Montgomery, 1980, p. 15).

DOING A PhD

What is involved in not merely starting a PhD but completing a significant and original piece of research and reporting the findings in a well-presented and scholarly manner?

In the apprenticeship-like quality of many supervisor–student relationships, the supervisor's research preferences and prejudices can constrain the scope, perspectives, methodology, and directions of a student's work. According to Thorley and Gregory (1995), students who are dissatisfied with the limits imposed are quite likely to opt out of the process. Other obstacles have also attracted attention. Madsen (1983), for example, has argued that successful completion of a thesis requires students to remain at university until their work is submitted, to become autonomous learners yet heed advice, to read widely without losing the focus of the research question chosen, to limit the scope of the project, to write early enough and in sufficient quantity, and to be prepared to polish and refine that writing—but not indefinitely. These steps assume the support and guidance of a supervisor.

Role of the Supervisor

Despite the increasing diversity of research questions asked in doctoral theses, theoretical frameworks selected, and methodologies used, there is considerable consensus about the supervisor's role. Help is needed in defining the topic, "designing" the project, gathering material, writing up, working through drafts to a final product, selecting examiners, and encouraging dissemination of the completed work through conference papers, journal articles, or a book. Induction into the wider research community can be facilitated through the student's inclusion in the supervisor's established networks. Successful transition from conception to birth of a thesis requires a carefully balanced partnership between research student and supervisor, with rights and responsibilities on both sides beyond those commonly listed in university handbooks. An ideal association based on mutual respect between supervisor and candidate might arguably contain:

- Guidance with the research topic and program. Given the continuing knowledge explosion, this is increasingly challenging. Research has become a huge, multipurpose enterprise.
- Advice on ethical considerations and requirements.
- Direction about the size, scope, and standard of a PhD. Despite the apparent uniformity of standards across universities and disciplines, there are considerable variations in acceptable research procedures and methods of reporting.
- Help for obtaining access to, and if necessary funding for, essential resources (e-mail, photocopying, relevant sources—books as well as colleagues). The increasingly complex technologies available place taxing demands on both supervisor and student.
- Support: personal at times of stress or success, as well as for scholarship or part-time research position applications, opportunities for work, references, and so forth.
- Comments, from the outset, on drafts of work as it develops. Constructive feedback, positive as well as critical, is needed. The now mandatory annual progress report can be used as an early warning of unsatisfactory progress should this be necessary.
- Encouragement for attendance and presentations at conferences. These occasions should also be used to provide introductions to others in the field.
- Honesty about the thesis being ready or not ready for submission.
- Thoughtfulness about the selection of examiners.

These considerations apply to mathematics education as well as to doctoral work in other areas. They are touched upon in chapter 10 also.

Some American universities use the descriptor *mentor* rather than *research adviser* (Mauch & Birch, 1989). And, indeed, the relationship between supervisor and candidate formed over the extended period of the supervision process contains many of the elements also described as part of the mentoring process. Jacobi (1991) compared definitions of mentoring in three different fields: higher education, management, and psychology. Commonly agreed functions included support and encouragement, guidance, facilitating access to resources aɴu opportunities, providing information, protection, sponsorship, stimulating the acquisition of knowledge, and (intentionally or not) being a role model. The essence of the mentor/supervision process has been described as one:

> which requires intense devotion.... concentration and absorption to the exclusion of other things. Generally it involves an intensive, long-term, one-to-one relationship of a sensei (teacher). Above all, it requires persistence—hard work, self discipline, diligence, energy, effort, competence and expertness. (Torrance, 1979, p. ix)

Many higher degree students indicate that they are reasonably satisfied with the quality and effectiveness of the supervision they receive. However, surveys of students' views about postgraduate research supervision (e.g., Johnston & Broda, 1994; Montgomery, 1980; Sloan, 1993; van der Heide, 1994) also reveal that, in reality, the relationship often falls short of the ideal portrayed earlier and is considerably more complex.

Common Complaints

What issues are commonly named by students as presenting difficulties? Ibrahim, McEwen, and Pitblado (1980) cited dissatisfaction with an excessively high standard demanded by the supervisor within the time limits of a PhD candidature, a perception that funds attracted for higher degree students were not spent on them, resentment at being used as a cheap teaching resource in undergraduate courses, dissatisfaction with the supervisor's knowledge about the candidate's topic, and the frequency (or rather the infrequency) of contact. Many of these comments were echoed in the more recent surveys of van der Heide (1994) and Johnston and Broda (1994). They also reported that some students felt marginalized and not part of the faculty, that they received insufficient help with the framing of the research questions and the supervision process or, alternatively, that their supervisor was too prescriptive. Many believed that they had insufficient contact with their supervisor. It also appeared that males were generally more satisfied than females with the supervision process.

The obstacles and experiences of marginalization identified in these surveys seem to be exacerbated for part-time research students, who have to juggle their studies with the pressing demands of other duties. Supervisors in faculties such as education, which attracts many mature-age students often with well-acknowledged expertise in their own field, face the additional challenge of balancing the needs of research novices with the expectations of those who are competent professionals in their own right.

Female higher degree students, it seems, are more likely than their male counterparts to feel overlooked, neglected, and unsupported by staff—particularly in informal settings. Discrepancies in male and female staffing ratios in most universities, especially at senior levels, are well known and may contribute to the greater difficulties experienced by some female doctoral students. In many science and engineering departments, in particular, the opportunities to work with female supervisors remain relatively rare. Jacobi (1991) concluded that cross-sex or cross-race mentorships often experienced problems "ranging from mild to severe" (p. 511). Schroeder and Mynatt (1993) found:

> Women with female major professors perceive their interactions more positively than do those with male professors. Specifically, support was found for the hypotheses of more concern for student welfare and for higher quality interactions when the major professor was female. (p. 568)

It is inappropriate to conclude simplistically that same-sex student–supervisor relationships are necessarily preferable to mixed-sex ones. Yet, in some cases, it may be more difficult to foster the collegiality craved by students with a supervisor of the opposite sex.

Contemporary popular literature (e.g., Garner, 1995; Mamet, 1993) has vividly documented the subtle sexual or power-related issues that can emerge when there is a prolonged relationship between two individuals in an academic setting. One lecturer interviewed by Garner discussed the subtle message conveyed by closing the office door, or leaving it open, during a consultation with a student:

> "I leave it up to the student," he said. If I shut the door, it's a statement of my power. It may seem intimidating.... But if the student shut the door and I opened it, it would be saying, "This is a fraught situation, a fraught relationship." (Garner, 1995, p. 154)

Students should not need to fear sexual harassment in the still male-dominated university environment. Supervisors must not take advantage of their more powerful positions. Work done by students must be owned by them. Contributions to joint projects must be properly acknowledged. Pressure—explicit or implicit—must not be exerted to extract personal favors. But students also can exercise unacceptable power. False reports of inappropriate behavior or demands for unacceptable intimacies have grave repercussions for the staff members involved. Both students and supervisors have a responsibility not to abuse their power. The fear of being misunderstood or misrepresented may be given by a supervisor to justify the often-reported distance between supervisor and student of (most commonly) the opposite sex.

Summary

Much has been written by those concerned with schooling about the impact of the social context in which teaching and learning occur. Similarly, the supervision of higher degrees does not occur in a vacuum. It is naive to ignore institutional customs and hierarchies that mold the power structures in the supervision process. It is also inappropriate to abuse them. And it is not possible either to ignore societal expectations and values against which the words and actions of students as well as supervisors are measured.

It can be argued, somewhat cynically, that the bureaucratic quality assurance emphasis on closer monitoring of the progress and completion rates of higher degree students has ensured that the supervision process is attracting more intense attention from administrators, staff, and students. More optimistically, we might hypothesize that the greater scrutiny has been fueled by increased sensitivity toward students' needs, and recognition of the competing and complex demands on their supervisors.

Supervision issues including and beyond those previously discussed (e.g., Connell, 1985) have already been addressed in this chapter from one perspective. The growing number of part-time and full-time students embarking on doctoral studies is placing considerable pressures on the human resources available for supervision, with some inexperienced personnel being drafted prematurely. The increasingly complex demands of technology and the continuously enlarging knowledge base are further challenges to be faced by supervisors as they advise their students about locating research databases, research design and methodologies, and appropriate standards for a doctoral thesis.

Lack of emotional support and insufficient social interactions between supervisors and students are commonly cited areas of discontent by students. Inevitable tensions and competing expectations are created by perceptions of the supervision process as a period of apprenticeship, an exercise in mentoring, and the opportunity to serve as—or be guided by—a role model. As in any relationship between humans, a satisfactory resolution of difficulties encountered requires not merely institutional support and appropriate guidelines but, most importantly, a willingness by each participant to communicate and discuss issues of concern. In the following sections, two case studies are used to describe and reflect on the supervision process in more personal terms.

A PERSONAL REFLECTION: HELEN

Background: Snaring a Supervisor

This saga began a year before I enrolled for the PhD at one of Melbourne's universities. I had resigned my full-time teaching job, and a chance opportunity to work in the School of Education became available. Simultaneously I was about to embark on the research component of my master's degree. "Peter,"[1] the lecturer of my final course-work unit, had offered to supervise. Unsure of the consequences of refusing, I accepted. There were no difficulties with the supervision. But for the PhD, I knew with whom I wanted to work. I had taken one of Gilah's courses on gender issues in mathematics learning for my master's degree. By raising a number of unresolved issues in the field, the course had stimulated my curiosity and desire to learn more. I knew of Gilah's international reputation in the field, had read some of her work, valued her expertise, was familiar with her working style, and had learned of her reputation as a supervisor. One day at morning tea, I tentatively broached the subject with her. Over lunch a few days later, I nervously spoke of my vague research ideas about wanting to know what went on in mathematics classrooms that might contribute to some known gender differences. An hour later, readings had been suggested and an appointment scheduled for a fortnight's time. I was to bring a one-page summary of my thoughts. The supervision process had begun. Ineligible to apply for a scholarship (my master's result was not yet official), I enrolled as a part-time PhD student and accepted an offer to work as Gilah's full-time research assistant on a project that was investigating aspects of what went on in mathematics classrooms.

Phase 1: Part-Time Enrollment (8 Months)

During the 2 weeks leading up to the meeting, I read voraciously and sweated over the one-page research outline. On entering Gilah's office, I anxiously handed over "the page." "Tell me what you've been reading," Gilah said. As I spoke, pertinent and probing questions were asked. Several directed my attention to unknown areas of the literature or to details I had glossed over. Guidance for further reading had been provided. Before leaving, the next appointment was made. A fortnight later, my page was returned. Gilah suggested I repeat the exercise for next time. I was not quite sure how to interpret this response. As I left, I looked at the page again. My thinking had shifted as a result of the reading I'd done over the past month and the words no longer reflected my ideas. The page *needed* to be rewritten. The cycle

---

[1]The authors have agreed to identify themselves but have used fictitious names for others involved in their stories.

of fortnightly meetings continued for some time. Looking back over the sequence of one-page summaries, the evolution of my study is clear. The research questions sharpened, and the project became viable.

A few months went by. Reading turned to writing. Writing did not come easily and it took time to adjust to expected standards and to appreciate and welcome criticism. Gilah gave swift and honest feedback. Good work was acknowledged and critical comments were incisive, focused, and constructive. Self-esteem was preserved.

During this period, the student–supervisor relationship began to change. Mutual respect, trust, and friendship were building and my anxiety and the feeling of being on trial slowly dissipated. A certain security accompanied a sense that both my work and I were valued, interesting, and worthwhile. I was also thriving on the autonomy entrusted to me as research assistant. Only later did I realize the extent and value of the experiences derived from that work. Not only did the project serve as a pilot for my own study, but in being invited to coauthor papers and copresent at conferences, I had gained early entry into academe.

After 8 months, the research design for the thesis had taken shape. For some time we had discussed methodological issues. The study would be conducted in two stages. The first, a large-scale survey, would explore the statistical relationship between Grade 7 students' perceptions of a range of classroom environment variables and their attitudes and beliefs about mathematics and themselves as learners of the subject. To understand this relationship better, an intensive study of two Grade 7 mathematics class-rooms, focusing on a small group of individuals in each, would comprise the second part of the project. I was only later to learn of the wisdom of adopting a combined quantitative–qualitative approach. Not only did the data sources complement each other in addressing the research question, but an effective buffer had been set up against the possibility of an examiner holding traditional expectations of what constituted appropriate research methods in mathematics education. Gilah believed that it was not worth jeopardizing the PhD. Gaining the "plumber's certificate," her term for the PhD, was critical. Once having successfully completed this recognized ap-prenticeship as a researcher, she explained, there were far fewer drastic consequences of adopting more adventurous research techniques.

The time came to seek ethical approval and to get appropriate permis-sions from various educational authorities. A few tips and suggestions from Gilah prevented potential pitfalls. The submissions met requirements and approvals were obtained. A few small pilot studies were arranged and con-ducted.

Now eligible, I successfully applied for a full-time postgraduate scholar-ship. My research assistance work was reduced to the hours permitted under scholarship rules. A new phase of supervision began.

Phase 2: Full-Time Year I—A Settled Routine

It was the start of the academic year. Data collection for part one of the study, the large-scale survey, was planned for the early part of the school year. I was concerned about meeting the costs of duplicating the questionnaires. Gilah advised me how to apply for research support. With funds secured, the data gathering commenced. Much time was spent administering questionnaires and preparing the data for computer analysis. Nonetheless, the regular fortnightly meetings continued. Frustrations experienced during the data-gathering phase were shared. Preliminary findings seemed of as much interest to Gilah as to me. Part two of the study, the in-depth observations of two mathematics classrooms, was partially dependent on the outcomes of Part one. I came to meetings with ideas and we discussed the possible consequences on the research design. We decided to put the Part two plans to the test. Two academics with appropriate expertise were asked to respond to a written proposal. A seminar was arranged. The ensuing exchange was fruitful in consolidating the final details of the research design. Disaster struck when one of the two teachers who had agreed to participate in Part two pulled out at the last moment. Gilah and I came up with a list of contacts and a teacher prepared to participate was found.

Encouraged by Gilah, I presented the results of a pilot study at my first Mathematics Education Research Group of Australasia (MERGA) conference. Her strong supporting letter had accompanied a successful application for a travel grant from the School of Education. Gilah also invited me to coauthor several book chapters and conference papers. Toward the end of the year I was invited to write a book about gender issues in mathematics learning, to which I devoted my summer break and holidays. Later I learned that Gilah had suggested my name to the publishers. Much of the work associated with the book laid the foundation for the structure and content of a literature review. Directly and indirectly my thesis had been influenced by these and other cocurricular activities.

Being full-time, it had also been easy to get involved in faculty life: attending seminars, conversing with in-house and visiting academics, getting embroiled in student politics, and sharing experiences with other full-timers. I met many of Gilah's other students. We swapped notes! The year had been enjoyable and intellectually rewarding. Time had passed swiftly.

Phase 3: Highs and Lows—Uncertainty and Disruption

Formal meetings with Gilah became less frequent as preparations for part two of the study firmed. A seminar Gilah arranged for her PhD students with a visiting mathematics education scholar from the United States provided another chance to have the research design examined. I was particularly anxious about the session because the theoretical framework of my study was founded on a model devised by this visitor and I had to defend my views on its shortcomings. I was greatly relieved to hear a reassuring reaction accompanied by several useful suggestions for subsequent data analyses.

Much of the next few months was spent at the two schools gathering data. There was a problem with the video equipment I had been issued. I was very upset by the unsympathetic reactions to my complaints. I could see the study disintegrating. Distraught, I turned to Gilah, who diplomatically intervened and settled the difficulties.

Earlier in the year, Gilah had encouraged me to attend two international conferences at which we would copresent. She suggested avenues for financial assistance and again wrote strong supporting letters. Although insufficient to cover all expenses incurred, the contributions awarded made the trip and conference attendance feasible. We arranged to meet in Europe, where Gilah would spend part of a period of study leave during the second half of the academic year. We planned that I would spend the period of her leave completing the data collection for part two, starting the analyses, and writing up the statistical findings from part one of the study. A temporary supervisor had to be arranged: someone with statistical expertise. Peter, my master's supervisor, was approached and agreed to take me on. His assistance during this period was invaluable. Although not officially "on board," Gilah was still available for crisis consultation.

Not long before Gilah's study leave, we heard that she had been offered a chair at another university. Although genuinely thrilled for her, I also selfishly worried about my own situation, so I deliberated for some time before speaking out. I had decided that I was prepared to transfer my enrollment, for I was convinced that I would not finish the thesis otherwise. Gilah reassured me that she wanted to see through my project. She investigated the options and discovered that established practice allowed her to continue the supervision without a transfer of enrollment. Technically, however, she could not remain my principal supervisor. Peter, my temporary supervisor, agreed to take on the official role.

The overseas trip and conferences had been exciting. Being at the cutting edge of international research in my field and being introduced to and speaking with people whose work was so familiar to me was stimulating. Contacts made were to provide new friendships and unexpected opportunities in the future. A potential examiner was found following an enthusiastic reaction to one of the presentations. Gilah and I also discussed my future and brainstormed ideas for a postdoctoral research fellowship application. A less settled year had ended on a high note.

Phase 4: Data Analyses and Writing Up

Gilah had begun her new job. I came in weekly to do part-time work and to keep her abreast of my progress. My university's facilities for analyzing videotape were inadequate, so the rest of the week was spent at home in front of a TV monitor or at the computer, summarizing the outcomes. The work was tedious. Gilah and Julie, who was also analyzing videotape, maintained my sanity and motivation during this 6-month period. Julie and I met for lunch each Thursday. We laughed over our shared frustrations and delighted in each other's moments of enlightenment.

With all the data analyzed, the project now had to be brought together into a coherent whole. It was left to me to decide the order in which I would organize the thesis and redraft the chapters. I started at the beginning. There were now two supervisors to read my work. As chapters were finished I would send them to Peter, rework them in response to his comments (mainly editorial) and then pass them to Gilah. Both were organized and returned my work within a couple of weeks. Each was known to set other work aside to make time to get the reading done. To save travel time, Gilah suggested I come to her home to drop off and pick up work.

Writing up took 8 months. It was a very lonely time. The total obsession to finish, the encouragement of Gilah and Peter, and the tolerance of my family and friends kept me going. Much earlier, Gilah and I had discussed and agreed on examiners. She had made the necessary informal approaches. A few months into the writing-up phase, Peter made the formal arrangements for examination. When the final draft was ready, Gilah set time aside to read it. Editorial changes, rigorous checking of references, photocopying, and binding took another 2 weeks, and then it was gone.

Two outcomes of Gilah's mentoring followed the submission of my thesis. Six weeks' teaching about research in mathematics education in Australia at an overseas university had arisen from a contact made at one of the international conferences I had attended the previous year. A 3-year postdoctoral research fellowship exploring gender and mathematics learning environment issues at the tertiary level would follow. Three months after submission, the results came through. It was all over.

Reflections

The PhD is a challenging academic endeavor. Today it is an essential prerequisite for a career in academia. Supervision is a key component in meeting the demands of the thesis and finishing.

It is difficult to conceive of a more satisfactory and effective PhD supervision than the one I experienced. It was a privilege to work with and learn from Gilah. A powerful intellect and a talent for teaching were coupled with compassion, wisdom, generosity, diplomacy, patience, and an exceptional capacity to inspire. Mutual respect and trust as well as a genuine bond of friendship were established. Support and advice were freely given. There was an awareness of when guidance was needed and when to let go. Feedback was dependably swift, always honest, constructive, and confidence building. Opportunities to engage in the full range of academic endeavors were presented. No formal requirement was overlooked. We shared a common goal—*my* obtaining a PhD.

No supervision fits the ideal model. The unexpected cannot be predicted and disasters can occur. To maximize the potential for successful completion requires an honest and trusting relationship and mutual commitment of purpose.

A PERSONAL REFLECTION: JULIE

Preliminaries

It all began the day I submitted the thesis for my master's degree. I knocked on Gilah's door with the lightheartedness of one who has nothing more to fear, and before whom a new life stretches, glowing. We chatted of this and that, and then it came. She suggested that I think about starting a PhD. With good management, she said, further study could be successfully combined with raising a young family. I laughed. Neither was on my agenda.

Time passed. The next time I knocked on Gilah's door I came prepared: baby capsule (with baby), diapers, food, rattles, and various kinds of washing paraphernalia. Doing a PhD seemed not such a bad idea after all.

Initiation

My goals were various. I wanted to work on a single project—something linear, focused, difficult, and *quiet*. The thought of returning to the classroom, and thus having chaos at work as well as at home, was nothing short of repulsive. But I did not have—and still do not have—clear academic career goals toward which the PhD is a means. For me, the process was then, and still is, an end in itself. From conversations with other students I know I am not alone in this. The degree serves as an apprenticeship for research, certainly, but it is not only that. In fact this is perhaps not such a bad thing—honoring learning for learning's sake was, after all, one of the original purposes of a university.

One goal I did have, however, was to work with Gilah. I had little idea of what a PhD would involve, but I was there to learn from a person whose work I admired and (more important) whose determination, commitment, and organization I respected.

Early on, the idea for my research project can only be described as very vague. I had a sense that it might have some kind of connection with the difficulties of the teaching task, and also perhaps with the apparent impossibility of explaining these adequately to outsiders. I wondered about the ways in which teachers' own priorities might affect the way they teach. I liked the (now hackneyed) phrase "the making of meaning." And that was about as far as it went.

All of this had little to do with Gilah's areas of expertise in gender, giftedness, and mathematics(!), and she suggested I visit the university and faculty at which I had completed my first degree and where my ideas might more naturally find a home. But it seemed too foreign a place—to them I had no history beyond my undergraduate life, and it was 10 years on, and I was immersed in diapers. I wanted to be recognized as professional. I was convinced that the qualities of a supervisor had more to do with understanding processes and asking questions than with the detail of knowledge in a narrow specialty. "Persuade me" she said, and I was in.

With what certainty one embarks! Then I could say with confidence, as I filled in the forms in triplicate, what my thesis was to be about. It was only 5 years later, as I neared completion, that I could again say with assurance what my project had been.

For a year I read widely. Every 2 or 3 weeks I had an appointment with my supervisor, and before this meeting I was required to send in a couple of pages of comment on what I had read. I return to these writings with some embarrassment now—they are so assured, so blasé—so *ignorant* of what a final project might be. But also they show me something else—something that to me is quite remarkable. They show me that I had traveled a path.

My thesis is narrower, certainly. It is a thesis of the faculty of education, not the faculty of arts. It does not stretch the boundaries of academic writing to their limits, as I once thought it might; it does not explain the essence of life in teaching, which one researcher dismissively told me is "what every PhD student thinks they'll be able to do." But in it there are still the big ideas with which I began: that we are limited by the tools of language; that teaching is awesomely complex, tantalizingly difficult to describe, and hard therefore fully to understand; that for these and other reasons teachers do not always grapple with the demanding issues of content that some outsiders believe they should. That there was a path is due to the guidance of my supervisor.

Helen has written already about these pathways, about the ordering of the task. My timeline was longer, and I have only recently wrestled with the agonies of completion, but the process was similar. We are very different people, however, and the externals of our lives are different. It is on these details, therefore, that I draw.

Issues of Status

From personal experience and from research I was well aware of some of the defining features of a teacher's life—isolation from colleagues, uncertainty about effectiveness, low status in the eyes of the community, and powerlessness within the system. All this applies in neon lights for the graduate student.

How to explain my employment status for the census? "Full-time student—but I used to hold a position of responsibility in a school, and I initiated significant curriculum innovation." What to reply to those who asked if I was working? "Well, actually your taxes pay my wage—I am on a government scholarship." But how could I feel part of the staff room at the university, where the politics were unfamiliar, of dubious relevance, and where, in spite of the occasional acknowledgment, a graduate student remains an outsider?

The supervisor has an important role in helping the graduate student deal with these issues. In my case, regular lunches with Gilah and other students in the student union or staff club were significant, and early in my candidature she took the initiative of introducing me to Helen with whom my work had something in common, but, more important, who would become a partner in the experience. The significance of regular meetings with the supervisor also cannot be overemphasized. Without these in the early stages I would have been unable ever to find a focus. But their importance was greater even than this—for an hour once every few weeks a person of status and ability would spend time talking about my work as if it were something of value and coherence.

These are issues to do with ego and status. They would affect individuals differently, and were probably particularly marked in my case because my pregnancy and small children meant there were aspects of postgraduate life in which I could not take part. But most people in education come to postgraduate work having been professionals for a time in the workforce. The effect of the sudden loss of status should not pass unrecognized.

Issues of Workplace

An academic in a university faculty has meetings to attend, lectures to give, a common room for company, and a room of her own. A postgraduate student has a desk in a shared room, possibly some work as a research assistant, and the transient company of other students.

The issue of location—or dislocation—is a difficult one. The shared room serves to create a sense of collegiality, and provides a partial answer to the identity problem by creating a home. In my case it was of little value—I needed my computer and my books, and my family responsibilities meant that at least half my work had to be done from home at convenient times. So once Gilah had left the university there seemed little point in spending the time and energy carrying materials from one place to another. I could not justify the time for social activities that would make me more a part of the institution. And to write I needed silence. But I was reluctant to give up my desk and office space—my name was on the door.

Issues of Teaching—The Role of the Supervisor

I divide the role of the supervisor into three:

- There are the obvious tasks of analysis, criticism and synthesis, clearly related to the thesis. Included in this category is the ability to suggest directions without dominating, and to guide the student toward appropriate methodologies.
- A good supervisor can see beyond the thesis when a student cannot— toward career options. She can suggest appropriate conferences; offer opportunities for writing and academic teaching; and ensure that students meet lecturers and other academics—if not as equals, at least as juniors with a degree of knowledge.
- The importance of the personal relationship between supervisor and student should not be underestimated, both for the commitment and for the skills it requires. It is a long project, and in many ways it is a shared one. It is inevitable that aspects of personal life will intervene and interfere. In my own case, I have experienced both understanding for a mother of young children and the responsibilities that entails, and a realistic amount of pushing to achieve what is possible within those limitations. To complete a qualification that did not appear vital at the time, this was an essential combination.

. Honest criticism is also crucial. A student working on a long project, without the confirmation of classes and other students engaged in the same work, needs to place trust not only in the supervisor's knowledge and judgment but also in the honesty of her criticism. It is necessary to endure "This is not at all what I had in mind," to experience the elation of "I think that chapter is just about finished, don't you?"

Successful supervision requires a high level of skill both in teaching and in research knowledge; but it also requires a willingness and ability to respond appropriately to the student on a more personal level. The role is more closely allied to that of mentor than to that of university lecturer.

Changes in Supervision

Gilah had a number of short periods of absence for conferences and other commitments, which had little effect beyond creating useful deadlines. However, in my third year, after the main data had been collected but before they had been analyzed, she had a 6-month period of study leave, during which I had what was to be the first of a number of caretaker supervisors.

Looking back on that time now, I think I did not fully recognize either his responsibilities or my own. I had plenty of work to do, and decided that I could proceed pretty much alone. I dropped in on him a couple of times, showed him some of my work, and had some fairly unstructured discussions about how the final study might shape up. I understood his role to be little more than filling in necessary forms until Gilah returned.

Although he was interested in my project, and was knowledgeable about the field in which I was working, the contrast in personal styles was very marked, and I was not always sure what was expected of me. For the allotted time of a temporary supervision, this can make things difficult. Some of his suggestions would have led to different directions to the work—which might have been interesting to consider at an earlier stage but were distracting now. Some of these knocked my confidence—it is hard to remember that there are many paths possible with the same data, and that many of these can be considered right. It is not easy to resist suggestions made by a senior academic, particularly if the relationship has not yet evolved. Issues of power have many shades and dimensions.

Toward the end of this period of absence there was a major development. Gilah was appointed to a chair at another university. I decided to give the whole thing up.

In fact it did not come to this, although I have friends for whom similar events have led to withdrawal. Gilah was more than generous in her assistance, and continued to supervise me for no credit from that time, meeting with me at her own home to save me the considerable journey, and being patient as my completion date was extended. But the move was bumpy, and involved three further supervisors in all.

The particular details of the difficulties are no longer relevant, and were eventually resolved satisfactorily. It is not unusual for supervisors to be unable to see the project through to its completion—a PhD, even done in minimum time, is a long project. But the impact of changes in supervisor should not be underestimated. The whole history of the project has somehow to be transferred. It is a daunting process, demanding both for the student and for the new supervisor.

Issues of Content: Impact of Disciplines

In some ways my case is peculiar; I am a graduate in French and English working within the field of mathematics education. What am I doing here? What difficulties and challenges arise from crossing discipline boundaries?

I came to know Gilah during my master's degree when I took a subject she taught about gifted children. That area became the focus of my master's dissertation, and has been the basis of much of my professional work since, in writing, teaching and now in research. However, it was not the subject of my doctorate, which sought to investigate ways of giving voice to teachers' knowledge. As I have said already, I wanted to work with Gilah because I admired and respected her professional and personal style, and was somewhat in awe of her achievements. Although the precise area of my thesis was not among her own stated research interests, this was not a problem; she suggested reading paths for me to begin on, and those paths created their own byways. In shaping the project we sought ways to combine our different backgrounds. The focus of the study became primary teachers, who teach both mathematics and language; the exploration centered on whether their beliefs about these subjects affect the way they choose to teach, and how the "dailiness" of teaching could be described while at the same time acknowledging the reasons for teachers' actions.

That is not to say that our different discipline backgrounds are without impact, however. In the early stages we had many challenging (for me, at any rate!) discussions about methodology, and even today we would perhaps ask different questions and choose different approaches to pursue the same issue. But this is not a bad thing. Our separate "home disciplines" serve to set in relief the movement toward independence that should be an endpoint of any student–teacher relationship. They mark baselines for debate, and they serve to push me further.

In a concrete sense her guidance broadened my thesis from one that would have contained qualitative data alone to one that used a large-scale questionnaire to provide a canvas against which the rich contextual detail of classroom analysis could be set. The result was a far stronger under-standing of classroom life than would have been possible with either set of data alone; each added breadth and complexity to the other. Although I find the qualitative, storytelling data more interesting and alive than the neat tables of the questionnaire chapter, I am glad to have gained an under-standing of large number data as well; I can speak with people from both sides of the methodology debate, and I hope my thesis has something to say to all of them.

Within faculties of education such boundary crossing is perhaps more common than in other faculties. That is not to say that subject disciplines are of less importance, but that we are bound by a common interest in education. Perhaps the work of teaching mathematics differs in some ways from the work of teaching language, and perhaps it attracts different kinds of minds. If so, that is something worthy of examination, and interdisciplinary work within education faculties should be encouraged. At my university even postgraduate students tended to group along discipline lines; perhaps there should be greater acknowledgment of the interdisciplinary nature of the central questions of teaching and learning. Certainly for me it has been a source of growth.

Endings

Not long ago my family was picnicking at the Botanical Gardens with another family, in which both adults had recently completed their doctorates in other disciplines. It was in the middle of a period of sleepless nights with which no doubt most who have been through the PhD process are familiar. It seemed to me that my data showed nothing, were not interesting, and that the thesis would be ridiculed by anyone who could be bothered reading it. I could talk about it only with difficulty.

My friends laughed. "Sounds like you're on the final straight." There was more than one hiccup to come, but in the main they were right. I liken it to transition in childbirth, the time when it seems that all that can be done has been done, there has been no result, and the best thing to do is to go home and pretend nothing has happened. The reality of course is that there is no turning back, that the most painful part is still to come, but that in most cases there will be a successful birth.

The support that is offered during that time is crucial.

A PERSONAL REFLECTION: GILAH

Helen's and Julie's personal accounts illustrate clearly the rewards to be gained from supervising doctoral students. It is extremely satisfying to work, over an extended period of time, with highly motivated, mature, professionally accomplished and articulate students. However, their stories did not mention the intellectual challenges their developing work presented for me, the references shared that broadened my horizons, the well-presented arguments that tested my assumptions, the pleasant discussions that strayed beyond the thesis topic. It is clear that we traveled the journey together, in a partnership of changing balance. It is also apparent that both Helen and Julie had taken master's subjects that I taught and that we therefore knew each other before the supervision process began. We clearly had compatible views about academic rigor and meeting deadlines. We agreed, initially with varying degrees of conviction, that the traditional methodologies for research in mathematics education might prove inadequate for exploring issues now considered critical for our understanding of factors influencing mathematics learning. We respected and liked each other. We felt confident that our social contacts outside the office would not be misinterpreted. Given these conditions, the odds for achieving and maintaining a successful supervision process were high. In cases where there has been no previous contact or possibility for establishing rapport, early meetings should include opportunities for informal exchange, without losing sight of the academic purpose for which the relationship is being formed.

Both Helen and Julie were full-time PhD students on postgraduate scholarships. Their candidatures virtually coincided. Yet, because of their different reasons for embarking on a PhD, their different home and personal situations, their experiences, and rates of completion, varied considerably. Had they been part-time students, simultaneously engaged in full-time employment, their stories would be different again. It would probably have been more difficult to arrange the extra activities and experiences described by Helen in particular. I would certainly have been more reluctant to involve them in writings away from the thesis. Helen and Julie's reflections confirm the importance of having a sustained full-time period of study (typically set at a minimum of 6 months) at some time during part-time candidature.

The descriptions of their attempts to cope with my absences from the university—on study leave and then to take up another position—are sobering. Although, as Julie writes, short absences often act as useful deadlines, longer periods of study leave require considerable adjustments by students. Especially in smaller departments, suitable temporary supervisors may be difficult to find. Furthermore, the transitory nature of temporary supervision does not seem to warrant the personal investment deemed necessary for longer term relationships. Questions of power again emerge. To what extent should a caretaker supervisor intervene in directions previously agreed?

Even at this period of limited employment opportunities, academics do change institutions. Some retire at short notice. Many students are left to make their own alternative arrangements. Supervision manuals rarely address the issue of needing to find, and adjust to, successive supervisors— perhaps because its satisfactory resolution is so dependent on individual personalities, circumstances, and institutional goodwill and support. All too frequently it is assumed that the choice of supervisor will be made only once during candidature. Anecdotal evidence suggests that changes in supervision occur more often than is generally recognized. Although there is no ready solution to ease the transition, the elements of the ideal association, outlined earlier in the chapter, can again serve as a useful guide to establish new working routines and reciprocal expectations. Mutual respect, adherence by student and supervisor to deadlines set, respectively, for submission and feedback of work, and a commitment to finishing the project are minimum elements of a successful supervision relationship.

For a variety of reasons, some of the students I was supervising were left behind when I moved institutions and were taken over by others. There was mutual regret, irrespective of the ultimate success of these new arrangements. For me it was most unsatisfactory to leave a developing project in midstream. Learning of the difficulties experienced by some former students in making the needed adjustments to working and supervision style, or to a somewhat modified topic, produced feelings of guilt only partly alleviated with time.

A Final Comment

I have always liked teaching. My own master's and PhD experiences whet my appetite for doing more research. Supervising higher degree students not only allows both but also offers opportunities to work over a sustained period of time with self-motivated learners on a topic of mutual interest. A teaching process that thrives on one-to-one consultations, provides regular opportunities to engage in intellectual debates, and offers an impetus to peruse the latest journals and books is one to be cherished. Contributing in some way to the induction of a new researcher is a further privilege. For me, the times set aside for supervision consultations or reading are highlights in a busy week, provide an important balance to ever-increasing administrative demands, and serve as a reassuring reminder that contributing to scholarship remains a critical function of university life.

AUTHOR NOTE

This chapter builds on an earlier discussion on supervision prepared for the 1995 special issue on postgraduate pedagogy of the *Australian Universities Review, 38*(2).

REFERENCES

Boyer, C. J. (1973). *The doctoral dissertation as an information source: A study of scientific information flow*. Metuchen, NJ: Scarecrow Press.

Castles, I. (1990). *Year book Australia 1990*. Canberra: Australian Bureau of Statistics.

Castles, I. (1995). *Year book Australia 1995*. Canberra: Australian Bureau of Statistics.

Connell, R. W. (1985). How to supervise a PhD. *Vestes, 2*, 38–41.

Garner, H. (1995). *The first stone: Some questions about sex and power*. Sydney: Picador.

Higher Degrees and Scholarship Section, Monash University. (1991). *PhD and EdD information handbook*. Clayton, Victoria, Australia: Author.

Ibrahim, E. Z., McEwen, E. M., & Pitblado, R. (1980). Doctoral supervision at Sydney University: Hindrance or help? *Vestes, 23*, 18–22.

Jacobi, M. (1991). Mentoring and undergraduate academic success: A literature review. *Review of Educational Research, 61*(4), 505–532.

Johnston, S., & Broda, J. (1994, November). *Supporting educational researchers of the future*. Paper presented at the annual meeting of Australian Association for Research in Education (AARE), Newcastle, New South Wales, Australia.

Madsen, D. (1983). *Successful dissertations and theses*. San Francisco: Jossey-Bass.

Mamet, D. (1993). *Oleanna* (Royal Court writers series). London: Methuen Drama.

Mauch, J. E., & Birch, J. W. (1989). *Guide to the successful thesis and dissertation*. New York: Marcel Dekker.

Montgomery, A. Y. (1980). The examination of post-graduate theses: A discussion of requirements for post-graduate theses in the department of computer science at Monash University. *Vestes, 23*(1), 14–17.

Schroeder, D. S., & Mynatt, C. R. (1993). Female graduate students' perceptions of their interactions with male and female professors. *Journal of Higher Education, 64*(5), 555–573.

Sloan, M. (1993). The power differential. In *Compass '93* (pp. 40–43). Clayton, Victoria, Australia: Monash University.

Thorley, L., & Gregory, R. (1995). A broader education for research students: Changing the culture. In B. Smith & S. Brown (Eds.), *Research teaching and learning in higher education* (pp. 89–94). London: Kogan Page.

Torrance, E. P. (1979). *The search for satori and creativity*. Buffalo, NY: Creative Education Foundation.

van der Heide, G. (1994, November). *Students and supervision: The views of post graduate research students in education and supervision*. Paper presented at the annual meeting of Australian Association for Research in Education (AARE), Newcastle, New South Wales, Australia.

8

Teacher, Researcher, Collaborator, Student: Multiple Roles and Multiple Dilemmas

Loren White

Curtin University of Technology, Perth, Western Australia

This chapter is about an aspect of PhD student supervision from the student's perspective. As that student, I had worked for several years in the teaching profession before returning to university to reflect on my classroom experiences. The story itself centers on 6 months of collaboration between the supervisor, Peter, a university-based mathematics educator, and the PhD student, myself, the collaborating high school mathematics teacher. The collaborative effort was not directly relevant to my study program but developed from a mutual interest in understanding ways of learning in a classroom. The collaboration proved to be a difficult time for me, more so after the event than during, as I tried to cope with the unanticipated dilemmas of acting out different roles for different masters. The story touches on issues for PhD students, on the role of research, and on assumptions about teaching, research methods, students, and collaborative practice. In particular the dilemma of being both professional teacher and postgraduate student was personified by a power struggle within myself, between the institutions of university and school, and between supervisor and "student." The story is reflective in that 3 years have passed since the collaboration. During this time I have had time to assess the consequences.

BACKGROUND

I have not always worked as a teacher. After my initial mathematics degree, I worked on research and development programs, in administration and industrial relations. Teaching was a late choice and, after 15 years, is still my preferred occupation. This teaching career has been broken by two periods of full-time postgraduate study and work in various universities.

Collaborating with other professionals from other institutions is not new for me. I have teamed with members from the teaching profession, administration, private companies, and universities in programs of change and research prior to this collaboration. The school in this chapter had, a few years earlier, participated in a major collaborative study conducted by an international research team organized through the local university faculty of which Peter, my PhD supervisor, was a member. This project was successful for the researchers and was widely reported nationally and internationally. However, it also changed the practices of the participating teachers, and not all positively. For myself, although I was not involved directly, the project established valuable academic contacts and I enrolled in postgraduate studies at the local university the following year.

THE SUPERVISING CONTEXT

Two years into part-time postgraduate studies, I accepted a 12-month study exchange to "Deep South" University in the United States to complete a master's degree. This exchange also gave me the opportunity to experience and observe PhD programs for the first time. Deep South master's and PhD students often attended the same seminars and worked together on the same research contracts. The PhD students were directed by their supervisors in both their research topic and research team membership. Participation in the research teams was paid work and a form of apprenticeship. There appeared to be much at stake for students and their supervisors, for choosing the right research programs and supervisors was recognized as being critical for future postdoctoral opportunities and academic careers. Likewise, the university faculty was keen to have a solid research team in place in order to maintain a high research profile and continue to attract research grants and consultancy work. Most PhD students appeared to undertake research associated with, and complementary to, current ongoing programs of the faculty.

Acceptance into a research program seemed to me to assume acceptance of the beliefs underpinning that research. Consequently students rarely were seen to question the fundamental assumptions and philosophical stances taken by the supervisors. This is not to imply that there was all harmony and acceptance in the postgraduate program. There was considerable heated debate, sometimes bitter, between students and supervisors over methodologies and explanations of results, research team membership, and editorial efforts on chapters. However, discussion by students about fundamental philosophical assumptions appeared reserved for attacking alternative theories, discussing texts and other faculty research programs.

On returning from the United States, I enrolled part time in the PhD program at the local university to study mathematics education while I returned to full-time mathematics teaching. Peter was chosen to be the mathematics educator on my supervisory team. He was also one of the lecturers in the associated course work program. Over the year I came to know Peter in terms of his philosophy about knowledge and educational theories, particularly during a few rewrites of my candidacy proposal. The choice of research topic was mine, accepted as appropriate by Peter, and was not dependent on any specific research program of the faculty.

The next year I was awarded a scholarship and enrolled as a full-time student who continued with some part-time teaching. Even after a change in research topic, with another 16 proposal rewrites, I felt I could work comfortably with Peter on my research odyssey. I considered the relationship as one between a professional in education based in a school and a professional in education based in a university. With Peter's assistance and the support of the weekly PhD colloquium I was coming to understand the art of research and theorizing in the manner of academics. Working with Peter on other projects outside the scope of the PhD appeared possible and appropriate.

THE COLLABORATION

At this time I was a part-time mathematics teacher at a high school located in a mixed socioeconomic suburb of a large Australian city. I was also conducting my research on students' understanding of mathematics at the same high school but not with students I was teaching.

I often discussed with Peter some of the different ways I proposed to give my students a variety of mathematical experiences, for he was interested in what I was attempting to achieve with a Grade 8 class I taught. It was my desire to introduce mathematical uncertainty into the program by using the science curriculum, which particularly caught his attention. He considered the class, my approach to teaching, and the situation of students working on a large project with uncertain outcomes, an ideal context in which to trial his revised version of a classroom environment survey instrument developed by faculty colleagues at his university. He suggested that we work together to validate this instrument, which had been revised to incorporate a particular theoretical viewpoint. I had not previously worked collaboratively with Peter in the sense of being coresearcher and coauthor as he was now proposing. However, as we were familiar with each other's views about education and learning, I agreed.

Thus I had unwittingly given myself more roles to carry out at school. I was already a mathematics teacher who was also a PhD student researching the understanding of mathematics by students, and a de facto curriculum developer merging science and mathematics. Now I was to be a co-collaborator with a mathematics educator conducting research on classroom environments. At the time I gave no real thought to these multiple roles, as they appeared unexceptional. However, now I am writing about the dilemmas/conflicts in attempting this collaboration with my supervisor.

RATIONALE TO THE STORY

Much of the following narrative on the collaboration was written as part of a paper presented on the revised Classroom Learning Environment Survey instrument (CLES) at an international conference the year following the collaboration. This chapter followed 2 years later.

ME, THE PhD STUDENT RATIONALIZING THE COLLABORATION

In relation to science and mathematics education, there has been much discussion on the theories of constructivism and the possible ways in which constructivist theories can model learning and teaching processes in a classroom (for example, Confrey, 1995; Pateman, 1993; Tobin, 1991). There is recognition of the complexity of attempting to describe within one theory all of the classroom realities with its subjective activity of meaning construction. The need to integrate sociocultural perspectives with the psychological perspectives of radical constructivism has been argued as essential if constructivist theories are to be used to describe such realities (Bauersfeld, 1995). These realities—the personal interpretations of students', teachers', and observers' experiences of classroom events—highlight the fact that within a classroom there are multiple, simultaneously valid descriptions of teaching and learning.

The problem for the observer-researcher attempting to understand learning and teaching in a science or mathematics class using multiple perspectives with a theory such as constructivism is, therefore, whether one has to describe such classes using multiple theoretical frameworks. Or is there possibly a single hybrid theoretical framework that could be created which would more appropriately provide an adequate coherent description (Confrey, 1995; Pateman, 1993)? Or are we left with having the observer-researcher's own interpretive framework being applied in multiple ways? If the researcher is wishing to "apply" a theory such as constructivism to the classroom, then the framework that describes the theory needs also to be able to describe classroom realities. The language framing Constructivism needs to be adequate to describe the class, or at least be one of the multiple descriptive frameworks if the description is to be understood by others. The researcher is left with the problem of constructing the description framework that provides for the perspectives of other observers such as the teacher. In order to attempt such descriptions, researchers have worked in schools; studied classrooms in action; and interviewed and observed teachers and students, even encouraging them to become researchers. Instruments such as classroom learning environment surveys have also been developed to provide a common data/language basis for description and to help the others become literate with researchers.

The desire of many researchers to understand the teaching processes in a science or mathematics class, or to describe such a classroom, has encouraged collaborative research with teachers (Kyle & McCutcheon, 1984). Arising from such endeavors is the recognition that the teacher/researcher is an essential source of description and interpretation of classroom events (Bogdan & Biklen, 1982; Tobin & Imwold, 1993). Thus, a teacher is considered to be well situated to give input into the process of clarification, elaboration, and validation of theories that frame research on learning, teaching, and classrooms. It was with this idea in mind that the collaboration between me and Peter sought the benefits of both researcher and teacher perspectives to confirm the suitability of a classroom environment survey instrument that had been revised to reflect constructivist principles describing some classroom realities.

A recent variation of constructivism that has been proposed by Taylor and Campbell-Williams (1993), among others, sought to bring an ethical concern to describing teaching and learning from a constructivist perspective. This *critical constructivism*, as it is termed, incorporates Habermas' theory of communicative discourse to help unveil ideological interpretive frameworks operating in a classroom that restrict or constrain learning. Central to critical constructivism is the idea that knowledge is informed by cognitive interests, and that ideology and power serve as an invisible interpretive framework for participants in classrooms, constraining and shaping their own and others' perceptions of what constitutes teaching, learning, assessment, and curriculum. To understand the status of such invisible interpretive frameworks (e.g., the dominant beliefs, social mores) and to help provide description of the extent of critical awareness that teachers and students have in the classroom, revision of the Constructivist Learning Environment Survey (CLES) was undertaken (Taylor, Fraser, & White, 1994). Changes to reflect critical constructivist concerns were made in this instrument.

Before this study, I was familiar with constructivism (von Glasersfeld, 1984) and in particular with social and critical constructivism (Ernest, 1991; Taylor & Campbell-Williams, 1993). I was also aware of discussions among constructivist theorists on complementary sociological and psychological approaches to model knowing and learning in science and mathematics education (Bauersfeld, 1995; Confrey, 1993, 1995). I have tried as a teacher to make explicit to students the contingent nature of science and mathematics and some of its sociocultural history; that is, letting students experience knowledge as an ongoing "socially negotiated human construction arising from experience shaped by language and culture" (Ernest, 1991, p. 42). Hence it was easy for me at the time to both support and appreciate Peter's revisionary purpose and the trial of this instrument in my classrooms.

METHODOLOGY AND CONTEXT FOR THE STUDY

The research I conducted with Peter was a case-study approach that also incorporated collaborative methods (Louden, 1991). In this way an ethnomethodology framework provided by me as the teacher-researcher involved in the day-to-day activities that constituted my classroom became a foundation for the research methods (Eisenhart, 1988). Data sources included my reflective journal entries, Peter's observation notes, in-class discussions with students, student work samples, student interviews, and notes from discussions between me and Peter. The data were used to provide interpretations of ongoing classroom events from the perspectives of me, Peter, and the students. The data from my perspective were reported in the form of a narrative or story in an attempt to make explicit my intentions in the context of action and place (Bruner, 1986; Connelly & Clandinin, 1987).

The students in this study were a class of 34 keen, lively Grade 8s new to high school who were deemed capable mathematics students by their primary school teachers. The same students also met in a science class with a science teacher whose views on teaching were similar to mine. Both the science teacher and I were engaged informally in designing and presenting to the Grade 8s a joint science and mathematics theme that provided them with opportunities to speculate, experiment, and argue their theories about the world. Thus some science processes had become part of the curriculum in my mathematics classroom, as did mathematics modeling in the science room. In my classroom, students were able to hypothesize theories and then confirm or disconfirm, using mathematical and scientific modes of reasoning. If the joint venture amalgamating the Grade 8 mathematics and science courses worked out, the science teacher and I would formalize the program for the following year.

A PROBLEM WITH COLLABORATION

Consequently, while at the high school I wore many hats. I was primarily a teacher, busy helping students to model their world mathematically. This teaching was within my goals for the merging of science and mathematics experiences for students in the classroom. I was also a researcher involved in doctoral studies and a collaborator with a science teacher and a mathematics education researcher.

Reflecting later on my multiple roles raised issues in my mind about the expectations of collaborative research to provide an adequate description to better support theories about classrooms, teaching, and learning. Doubts had already entered my mind during the collaboration but I was too involved to make sense of them. Now, thinking of several incidents that occurred while teaching, the rationalizations made by me at the time of my actions, and the written/spoken perceptions of others present during those incidents, has led me to consider the effects of collaborative research on my own teaching and my PhD program. I now question the belief that one can play multiple roles as teacher, collaborator, and researcher and subsequently be able to merge these experiences within an overall theoretical framework to contribute toward a coherent description of teaching, learning, and the classroom.

FOUR CLASSROOM EPISODES

Four classroom episodes are related here in the form of a reflective narrative. These episodes are contextual reconstructions of specific incidents that occurred during the collaboration with Peter and the science teacher. As such they provide evidence in support of the concerns about the collaboration I have raised.

Introduction and Episode I

Working with the science teacher in attempting to integrate mathematics and science for our Grade 8 students had been haphazard during the first semester. Trying to bend the prescribed curriculum to merge its content with appropriate science processes looked straightforward, but was proving difficult in practice. The students wanted to do mathematics in a mathematics classroom and science in the laboratory. I resorted to providing a variety of experiences for students that supported their ongoing science projects while "Jack," the science teacher, dwelled on the mathematics skills where appropriate. For example, for the gravity project and the insect field research, I had the students conduct some of the experiments in my classroom; organize their raw data in tables, graphs, and scattergraphs; calculate various statistics; discuss survey techniques; and consider ratio and proportion. The students were becoming experienced with mathematical tools used in their science. To me, these short occasional mathematical events, although valuable, were not very demonstrative of what mathematics has to offer in organizing thinking processes involved in hypothesizing, testing, inferring, and justifying.

The students were also becoming a little bored with the short activities interspersed with "normal" mathematics. Much of the problem solving of an empirical nature (where students collect data, look for patterns, conjecture, then attempt to disconfirm or justify) was associated with standard ideal mathematical objects such as lines, squares, cubes, spheres, nice numbers, and in the realm of statistics where correlations were potentially unity. I thought that the students were ready for a large-scale challenge that involved a lot of open-ended mathematics and science processes and allowed scope for diverse thinking.

A failed attempt to have students establish empirically a rule for determining the surface area of a sphere (an enthusiastic student passed around the formula that his mother had told him) gave me the impetus to consider a less ideal shape—the egg. I had almost finished planning the "Egg Project," which challenged the students to find a simple way of estimating the surface area of an egg using whatever means they could think of but that were sensible and testable, when a chance remark aroused Peter's interest. I had been helping him to refine the CLES to incorporate critical constructivist principles (see Taylor et al., 1994). Peter was interested in trialing the CLES with a nontraditional class whose students he could also observe and interview to help validate the instrument. We agreed that this Egg Project could be suitable, as many of the CLES variables such as shared control, relevance, uncertainty, and negotiation could be observed.

From that moment on, my planning of the Egg Project and its introduction to the students changed. Peter was working in a tight time frame to have preliminaries on the CLES completed for a conference in 2 months. In addition, he was not able to attend all class sessions I had planned for the project. Although it was not obvious at the time, I began making changes to accommodate Peter, not only in terms of time but also to maximize the benefit of his time in class. I proceeded to organize some sessions to include more whole class interaction, and I became more directive in instructions to the students working toward some end point. As well, I planned other lessons to be solely group work, so that Peter could move around to talk to the students. It was not total reorganization, but rather a subtle variation. On reflection, I think these subtle alterations were also a subconcious act by me to be seen as a teacher in control and a good manager of students. Previous open-ended tasks with this class had sometimes been riotous.

I found I also was conscious of the variables in the CLES. It was difficult to avoid the use of those variables in my discourse in class and not to incorporate them into the lessons intentionally, thereby biasing the validation study. I think I went too far in preventing myself from directly influencing the study. I concentrated more on facilitating the mechanics of data collection, such as measuring the various attributes of the egg, and subsequent data presentation. I also shifted the emphasis to finding a usable formula as well as exploring the question of finding a simple, good way of estimating surface area. I tended to discuss mathematical uncertainty in terms of the difficulty of accurate measurement and the lack of a known formula rather than student creativity and incompleteness. These variations to my original intentions for the Egg Project were noted by Peter at the time, but I was too close to the action to realize their importance.

The students had noticed the changes in my mannerisms in class and my approach to them during these initial lessons, especially when Peter was present. In turn, they tended to react accordingly. Class discussions became less lively and students often stopped their conversations in groups to look busy when approached by me or Peter. The students had been advised of the purpose of Peter's presence in class; however, I feel they resented both the initial intrusion of the study and Peter's presence.

I think this sense of resentment contributed to one of the most embarrassing moments in my teaching career. To explain, I have reconstructed my notes into a vignette, as my originals lack coherence and respectable language. I was a little angry and annoyed with myself at the time:

It was a nightmare. I had reminded them several times and made sure they wrote it in their diaries. "Bring a hard boiled egg for first session Thursday for the Egg Project." Loud and clear. "... and Dr. Peter will be there!" And this happens. Eleven eggs. That's all. Eleven. Not enough to get started. Thirty-four students, 11 eggs, and most groups with none. Panic. The students were already restless. A bus was late and straggling students had delayed a smooth start. An infernal lawn-mowing contractor cutting grass outside was causing me to shout to be heard. I wanted to shout. I was angry and I wanted to explode, but Peter looked (to me) bemused. Suppress the panic. Stall for time. I am a teacher and where is Plan B? Abandon Plan A and, no, skip Plan B and try Plan C. "OK, students get out your homework from last week. The scattergraphs comparing thumbnail area with length and width of the thumb." I feel a sense of control again. Plan B, working out of the textbook, would have been fairer punishment or "revenge," but I was sure Peter would be more interested in this, and it should have been covered last lesson.

Reflecting on Episode 1. Complicating the project was the decision to use it as a context for validating the revised CLES. The circumstances of a limited time frame and observation opportunities could been seen in retrospect to have changed the planned context for the project. Instead of letting the students get themselves organized to define the problem from their perspective, the teacher did it for them. Consequently, the teacher needed to maintain "control" of the project until the students understood what were the problems. Ownership of the project was not clear. The teacher's loyalties

were split and decisions were being made to accommodate all stakeholders—the teacher, the students, the researcher, and the science teacher. Although the researcher was concerned with not interfering with the classroom environment, he was aware that his presence was not neutral. The
teacher, by being well informed and involved in educational research, also
consciously was trying to be the same teacher for the students. Yet this was
not successful. The students were perhaps resentful of the changes to their
established mathematics classroom environment and, for a while, being the
objects of research. Ownership of the project was taken from them before
they had started. The need to feel responsible and contribute was diminished
and consequently eggs were forgotten, crushed in schoolbags, or eaten for
breakfast on the bus.

Episode 2

After several sessions of observation, Peter and I were becoming interested
in the students' struggle to connect or relate two-dimensional paper images
to actual three-dimensional objects—the eggs. The students were now aware
of the need to validate their speculations with some empirical evidence, that
is, actual measures of the egg's surface area. Initial attempts to simply wrap
the egg in 1-mm-square graph paper and count the squares were very
unsatisfactory. The more refined technique of cutting paper into pieces was
not providing the solution, although it was better. The paper would not lie
flat on the egg, but wrinkled and creased and overlapped, making counting
the squares difficult. Some students were trying to cut the paper into strips
with pointed ends, whereas others were looking for alternatives, such as
painting the egg with ink and rolling the egg on the paper. They found rolling
the egg was frustrating and the patterns on the paper confusing. One group
had decided to peel the boiled egg and glue the shell to the graph paper.
They found to get it flat the shell had to be broken into very small pieces.
The uncooperativeness of the egg's curved surface frustrated the students
and led to many inaccurate estimates of the surface area that were easily
challenged by their peers.

   Peter and I regularly discussed such struggles by the students and in this
case thought we should take advantage of the dissonance of two-dimensional modeling of three-dimensional eggs. I planned a lesson to introduce
an analogous situation of representing the world by means of maps. We
thought that with their regular use of maps in other school subjects and
seeing maps in their daily lives, the students might get possible ideas for
their project. The lesson appeared to go well, with the students participating
and appearing to appreciate the pluses and minuses of various types of
representation of the world. I used a globe, a standard wall map (i.e., the
world ironed flat), and a Form-a-Globe net, a version of an equal area
projection. The equal area got the vote for being the most accurate for com-

paring distance and area. I suggested that perhaps such a net might help them to find the surface area of similar objects such as an egg. The students were left to finish with the task to create other nets and to comment on the possible use of such nets for their project. I collected those responses.

The short postlesson debrief with Peter concluded with a view that the lesson provided valuable experience for the students, but we also agreed we should review this conclusion after a few lessons. I had some doubts about whether our intention to raise possibilities to be used in the Egg Project would bear fruit, as my teaching instincts were suggesting otherwise. The students had come into this class after lunchtime jumpy and restless, as if they had moved from climbing trees to climbing walls. In class the students were enthusiastic, but some were more interested in competing with others to put forth their views than with thinking about their responses. I was left to do a lot of the driving. I had felt that the lesson was valuable with respect to maps of the world. As for the Egg Project?

After reading the student responses on the nets and watching their efforts over the next few lessons, I concluded that little had changed. Eggs were eggs and not the world. Only one group had decided to try nets. In the notes I made a few days after the lesson I commented that:

> I had made the connection between world equal area nets and estimating the surface area of eggs. The students still preferred to cut paper and stick it to eggs and complain about it sticking to them more than the egg. . . . Had I stopped thinking about them as students and begun to see them as subjects to try out 'good ideas' with to help them on the project?

Reflecting on Episode 2. My keenness to take advantage of the perceived conceptual dissonance was framed more by my research interest than by me as a teacher. The two-dimensional modeling of three-dimensional shapes became a focus for me in the project, not the students. The lesson was, perhaps, more for the benefit of the collaboration and CLES study, and although entertaining for the students, remained disconnected from eggs. I would do it differently next time and facilitate its weaving into the fabric of the students' emerging project at a moment signaled by the students. I did this with these students with success later after the first round of reports were completed and when the students were given time to revise, rethink, and redo the project. At this later time, equal area nets became one way for many students to flatten eggs.

Episode 3

Peter had invited me to share his seminar presentation on teaching and learning frameworks incorporating constructivism and the uncertainty of mathematics. The seminars are public forums at the local university for researchers in education to inform people of their latest research interests and conclusions. Education researchers, graduate students, teachers, and education administrators make up the audience. My role was to represent a teacher's voice as part of a collaborative team highlighting the uncertainty of mathematics in a classroom. This was a development arising from the study validating the CLES. Peter thought there were interesting aspects to the Egg Project that had the potential to support a social constructivist framework as a viable alternative framework for teaching and learning mathematics.

The Egg Project was still progressing and I had on hand the students' first-time efforts at reporting. I thought about my 30-minute presentation on a teacher's role in facilitating the notion that mathematics is a social construct and how a strategy such as the Egg Project might facilitate this concept as an experience for students. Peter and I discussed our ideas and planned our respective portions of the presentation to complement one another. Peter was to provide the genesis of the framework with its theoretical underpinnings, whereas I was the teacher rationalizing my activities considered to be demonstrative of the framework.

It was a good seminar. Peter did well to present some complex theorizing and I enjoyed the opportunity to talk about my Grade 8 class and the activities taking place. The large audience stayed on until the end of question time and the organizer was pleased. Some people were still asking me questions relating to the seminar months later. The seminar was videotaped and it was by watching this tape that I began to wonder if it was a teacher talking at this seminar.

Reflecting on Episode 3. I have watched the video several times, sometimes with a colleague. I am still not sure where it went. One colleague commented that I had described examples or incidents related to action in a classroom, the evidence to show I was the teacher, but not the language or logic of a teacher. She was alluding to the manner in which I seemed to be able to make all the incidents coherently intertwined with consistent theoretical language. The talk on the Egg Project went from pragmatic incidents, to product description, to a theoretical overview. Little was mentioned about the teaching problems of classroom organization, managing student on-task behavior, assessment, and motivation. Nor were any questions about these aspects of teaching forthcoming from the audience; instead, they were interested in chaos theory—the merging of physics, mathematics, and God— and its consequences for tertiary mathematics curriculum. It made me think that the schoolteacher had gone. But who or what was the replacement?

Episode 4

The debate—"School mathematics is really useful"—was on today. The students had finished the Egg Project weeks ago and had slipped back into the more traditional fare set out in the syllabus. Common tests were just completed satisfactorily and the students wanted some variety. It was a sunny late spring day. I was in a good mood and so were the students.

Peter was coming to school to do some follow-up interviews. The first round of testing the instrument and associated interviews with the students had gone well, with unexpected results. The interviews had drawn our attention to some interesting problems about how students interpret the questions on the instrument with respect to the contexts they imagined to be related. As I had given my word to the students not to hear their taped interviews or read the interview transcripts, I did not know specifically what Peter was wishing to confirm or query with the eight students he wanted to interview again. Peter had said that with a bit of luck he might catch the end of the debate. I was taping the debate for another mathematics education researcher at the local university, so he would not miss hearing it anyway.

The class had had half a lesson in their groups preparing their arguments for and against the proposition that "School mathematics is really useful." The students had organized a further 15 minutes at the beginning of this lesson to brief their respective spokespersons. The debate was to be a whole-class affair, in that each of the speakers had 3 minutes to put his or her case and then 5 minutes to field questions from the audience. I was chairing the debate and refereeing the arguments.

On arrival, the students checked in with me, and being a warm, sunny day, drifted out to sit in their groups on the grass under the trees adjacent to the classroom. This had become fairly standard practice for group work in discussion phase.

This idyllic scenario lasted about 5 minutes. In the midst of a discussion with a few students on the rules of this debate I sensed something was not right with the shouting coming from outside. I reached the doorway in time to meet a group of girls rushing in talking at once.

"Sir, a bird flopping around on the ground."

"It's dying. You've gotta help."

"It's awful, I want to kill 'Jimmy.' "

My presence outside was obviously needed. At one of the furthermost trees I could see that most students had abandoned their groups and were milling around shouting and pushing and shoving in the vicinity of Jimmy and his friend.

In the short but brisk walk to the crowd and bird, I was informed that Jimmy had done something to the bird and that he ought to be hung, drawn, and quartered; a familiar punishment proposed by those who see the chance to eliminate the enemy. Jimmy was the smallest boy in the class—smart, cheeky, a stirrer and part-time show-off. He would spend half his time in class annoying most others, including me, and yet consistently outperform most in assessments. Moreover, he could handle the most difficult puzzles and challenge problems that often attracted a small prize and consequently win more than his fair share—which was zero, according to many of the girls.

The bird was dead, its neck broken. A couple of the students were trying to will it to life by stroking it and shedding a few tears.

"I didn't mean to hit it. I really didn't mean to."

Jimmy was trying to explain against a background chorus of "Oh, yeah, Jimmy" and calls for punishment.

"What did you hit the bird with?"

"A honky nut."

"Did you throw a honky nut, Jimmy?"

"Yes."

"At the bird?"

"No . . . er . . . well sort of . . . I was not really aiming for it . . . I didn't mean to hit it."

"But it did?"

"Yes."

I had him. Throwing a honky nut was a major breach of school rules. The honky nut is a hard, golfball-sized seed pod of the shady eucalyptus in this section of school. They become dangerous missiles when thrown.

"Back to the classroom everybody. Jane, your group will start the debate in two minutes."

The girls most concerned with Jimmy's behavior tagged along with me back to class. One was carrying the dead bird, which she had wrapped loosely in paper secured by an elastic band.

"You're going to kill Jimmy, aren't you sir? You're not going to let him get away with it?"

"No, he will go straight to 'Mr. Walker.' "

This seemed to satisfy them. Mr. Walker or "Dr. Death" as the Grade 8s call him, is loud, fierce, and quick in executing punishment. To bypass the standard multilevel student behavior management system in place at the school signifies the magnitude of the breach of school rules. I sat Jimmy outside the door, settled the students, and commenced the debate and tape recorder.

I wrote a note for Mr. Walker briefly outlining Jimmy's misdemeanor, gave it and the bird to Jimmy, and sent him to Dr. Death. Because I was chairing and there were no other teachers present, I had to forego the normal procedure for major offenses to personally escort Jimmy to the Deputy Principal's office. Jimmy's going seemed to signify that justice was being done and the class settled nicely into the debate.

The debate was just over halfway when there was a noticeable change in attention by students near the doorway and I could hear tense, terse comments being whispered. There was Jimmy, note and bird in hand, at the doorway, pulling faces at the girls. I fronted Jimmy.

"He's not there, sir."

"Then go and find him."

"I've tried, sir."

"Then try again and if no luck wait outside his office."

Jimmy slunk off and I continued with the debate.

We finished on time, but no Peter. I held back the students he wanted to interview and sat them outside. As it happens in these situations, the group included the girls most keen to see Jimmy punished. I organized my next class. Being a Grade 11 group, they were used to working on set tasks without supervision and I was able to commence preparing the "return to class" slips for the students outside.

"Sir, can I go to my next class?"

There was Jimmy, still with note and bird in hand. I yelled to him get back to Mr. Walker's office and wait there until I could join him. Jimmy left and as he passed the waiting Grade 8s said something that achieved immediate angry responses.

"He's going to get away with it, isn't he?" was the greeting I received when I went over to hand out the slips. "He always does."

Peter arrived and I helped him organize interview space in the empty classroom next door. He had decided to interview an extra group of students on top of the eight waiting if it could be arranged. I said it could as I had done this before. I found out from the Grade 8s present where the required students would be in the school, informed my Grade 11 class that I would be gone for a while and proceeded to personally negotiate the release of the extra students from their current classes. It took about 20 minutes, and after spending about 10 minutes with the Grade 11s answering queries, I was now free to finish dealing with Jimmy.

I knocked on Mr. Walker's door. Jimmy was not there, but Mr. Walker had been there all the time. I explained the situation and Mr. Walker was pretty keen to see Jimmy. He was not in his next class either. I went back to my Grade 11s to release them, as lunchtime had arrived. Peter was still interviewing, so I went to the mathematics staffroom to wait for him and eat. There on my desk was a message:

> I was not sure what I was meant to do with Jimmy. He was very upset. I had a chat to him and we buried the bird together. He was still upset so I have taken him home to his mum.
>
> Regards, School Nurse.

I just burst out laughing. I could not believe it. Perhaps I had forgotten to address the note to Mr. Walker or that part had fallen off on the way to his office. But I had temporarily been outplayed.

Peter had left without seeing me. Running late, I presumed. Jimmy did not come to school for a couple of days and the class assumed he had been suspended. When he did return, it was on my day off school in my part-time schedule. His parents came as well and had discussed matters with Mr. Walker. Jimmy's punishment became a short bout of rubbish duty.

Reflecting on Episode 4. As a teacher, it is important to be fair, equitable, and ensure justice is seen to be done. By not dealing with Jimmy as priority one, I had failed on all counts in the eyes of the concerned girls. Jimmy did escape appropriate punishment. Although he become more manageable and cooperative in the classroom, after this episode the girls progressively became disrespectful. I never did regain the lost ground.

This episode is a late consideration. Although I thought about it at the time the other episodes were included in papers for conferences, it did not appear to provide obvious issues for discussion with respect to the collaboration. The incidents described occurred after the completion of the Egg Project and concerned the unfortunate death of a bird. Yet to me, both at the time and now, the incident as described felt to me the most significant example of the dilemma of my roles and my working relationships with Peter.

The collaboration with Peter had, by now, taken on a life of its own. Peter had submitted the trial of the revised classroom instrument as a possible paper for presentation at a major education research conference in the United States as soon as I had agreed to participate. Peter had advised me the week before this episode that the proposal had been accepted as a joint presentation with me as copresenter. Peter and I had also discussed similar proposals for a second U.S. conference, but with me perhaps presenting a paper of my own on the collaborative process. The deadline for this proposal was within the week. I had never presented solo at any major research conference before and the pressure of putting together a significant proposal was great. I think it was at this point that I became less of a teacher at school and thought and acted as some hybrid researcher-collaborator who incidentally taught in a school. I often felt like an observer in my own classroom, conscious of my own notetaking about the objects in action. I stopped making field notes soon after.

INITIAL CONCLUSIONS ON THE COLLABORATION

It is 6 months since the study and the students are now in Grade 9. Reflection now seems to reveal the explanations and gloss over the sense of flying by the seat of one's pants. The attempts to merge science and mathematics seemed to be successful. The students did use a lot of their science experience in the Egg Project and produced some excellent results. Colleagues and the Principal were impressed with what students produced in their final Egg Project reports. The students were able to achieve very high levels of thinking and understanding of mathematical and science processes in problem solving when given the opportunities and time. Five different formulations for surface area were created by the students. On my own and student testing, three of these were of reasonable accuracy (5% confidence) for a range of chicken eggs.

A large-scale, in-class project was necessary for integrating mathematics and science for this class, but there were problems. It was difficult to convince teacher colleagues that assessments were compatible with other classes covering the same curriculum, and that noisy classrooms and mobile students did constitute an effective mathematics learning environment. Older colleagues were not impressed with these precocious students when they were forced to cover the class when I was ill. Nor were the students impressed when they were forced to stay in their seats and be quiet.

The validation of the instrument was a qualified success (Taylor et al., 1994). The students did well on their grading. In the end-of-year written reports on the teachers and the experimental course that were submitted anonymously by students, all but one of them said that they were highly satisfied with the year's mathematical and science experiences as provided in the course. Was there a problem with the conflicting sense of success experienced by the teacher-researcher, the students, and the academic researcher?

CONCLUDING REMARKS

When trying to make sense of the actions taking place in my classroom and subsequently to provide a coherent description for theory, I found myself faced with several issues. These issues seem to occur in the course of considering myself as a teacher-researcher, and author of the episodes in this chapter and of a paper about the collaboration for a conference, and as a coauthor of the resultant research report. I often experienced difficulties in making sense of the reflective notes I wrote on the teaching sessions, the students, and on some of the many discussion I had with Peter. Yet at the same time the incidents recorded in the notes are themselves still are real to me.

First, problems were encountered with the fact that putting the incidents into a coherent description depended on the purposes for making the description and the nature of the imagined readers: for example, was the purpose to tell the story of the project to fellow teachers, to explain the teaching or learning taking place to an audience of education researchers, or to document the collaboration between the teacher-researcher and the academic researcher for administrators or postgraduate students?

Second, there was for me the ethical dilemma that arose because I found that making the choice of a descriptive perspective necessitates prioritizing one's roles. I now realize that many decisions I had made in planning lessons and in the act of teaching depended on the focus taken in collaborative discussions with Peter and on future nonschool activities I had in mind at the time. For example, was it to enhance student learning under the gaze of the CLES, fit into the time frame of the study, or to enhance the collaboration? Decisions were also being made in a context in which multiple goals were expected to be met—not only meeting the needs of students, parents, administrators, and teacher colleagues, but also those of collaborator and researcher. It is comfortable wanting to believe that by just concentrating on the needs of children you will meet the needs of the other stakeholders. However, observers intrude. The ways of deciding what to observe and what to make sense of do change the construct one has of a classroom, and even more so in this case, where the teacher was one of the observers and knew of goals other than those of teaching. There is professional conflict that is often resolved subtly at the expense of the students. Other interests tend to prevail.

Third, to evaluate the success of my attempts to merge science and mathematics involved consideration of whether the endeavors were a teaching success, a research success, or a collaborative research success. That the project was a research success was evidenced by the incidents that revealed that student–student, student–teacher, and student–knowledge negotiation and student empowerment in these interactions were enhanced. These were key factors of the revised CLES instrument. That the project was a collaborative research success was determined by the fact that both collaborators increased our understanding of and respect for each other's roles and related experiences. Publications and conference appearances occurred as a result of the collaboration.

However, it was not clear to what extent the project was a teaching success. There was evidence that although students came to clearly express in written and oral forms their concerns about the uncertainties of the empirical investigations (i.e., science) they undertook, they still believed that a formula must exist which would give the exact surface area of any egg. The students also did not believe they were attempting or doing real mathematics, thwarting in many ways the intention of the project.

Finally, I found that as I took on the multiple roles (as teacher, as researcher, and as collaborator), there was also a sense in which I played a fourth role. However, it was not clear exactly what this fourth role was. To me it appeared to include a merging or "wearing of different hats" simultaneously, but it was also more than this. A metamorphosis had taken place.

Each of the initial roles themselves had changed as a result of me engaging in a role and then describing the role from the perspective of other roles. I found I could not now revert to being the teacher as I was before. Nor was I the same collaborator with the science teacher or researcher on my own PhD project. I had changed, and I was now not sure of my roles.

For example, in making sense of classroom incidents, I was often confronted with "possible" multiple descriptions reflecting the different roles: that of teacher (where the purposes of the lesson, the students' reactions and a description from the teacher's eyes were recorded); that of researcher (reflecting on the teacher–student circumstance and the interaction taking place, putting myself as the subject in the analytic framework of a social constructivist); and that of a collaborator (having discussions of classroom incidents with the observer-academic researcher). Although all these possible descriptions made by me overlap, no one description seems to cover the others. In order to accommodate all the aforementioned possible descriptions into a coherent whole, I found that no single existing theoretical framework such as constructivism or social constructivism was adequate. To arrive at a coherent description, in a sense I had to create my own framework and hence create my own narrative. Do researchers do the same?

I have changed through the process of adopting this "new" perspective arising from these experiences. This change was not necessarily for the better. I had, since the collaboration, continued to subconsciously reassess the experiences of the students more from the ideals of education research theories than from the pragmatics of me being a teacher of students in a school. The students appreciated the shared journey with me, as evidenced from their written reviews of the year's experience in the classroom. But their reports indicated that the students' experiences were at odds with what they expected in the school. Tension grew between myself and my teaching colleagues over the merits of this new way; not animosity but concern about the pressures placed on teachers to change the perception of what is mathematics and yet prepare students for a high school mathematics career path as prescribed by external assessment agencies. The students were certainly not well prepared for Grade 9 mathematics with different teachers and have struggled to maintain their mathematically able status under the onslaught of traditional algebra and assessment procedures that constantly rank mathematical ability. Here was an ethical dilemma that was in part highlighted by my pursuing my technical interest in research and personal philosophical views about learning, rather than having put foremost the technical interests of the students.

I stopped teaching for a year to think about these points. This is not to say that I considered all of this necessarily negative; the concern I had was that I spent less time thinking of these students as people and more so as objects.

When teachers become involved in research programs with academics, there seems to be an understanding in the literature that the teacher will benefit from the experience. If collaboration is involved, the teacher has the chance to be part of the research team and research questions. For me, it is not clear how exactly such multiple roles can enhance the research process. What exactly is this role of this new emerging breed of teacher-researcher? Where do such individuals belong in an education system? What should their responsibilities be in relation to school practices and research practices? To whom and in what form can they efficiently and adequately report their experiences and findings, considering that most publications edit according to criteria related to their audience?

CONCLUDING THE SUPERVISING RELATIONSHIP

After not teaching for a year I went back to full-time teaching at a different school. I still did activities like the Egg Project and the students still said they enjoyed these breaks from doing real mathematics.

As for the collaboration, it was, I guess, a success although Peter and I have not collaborated on anything else since. The paper written about validating the revised classroom environment instrument was presented at the major overseas conference and won an award. However, some of the key questions raised in that paper challenging the ability of such questionnaires to describe classroom environments remain on the back burner of research as the authors are pursuing other interests.

The issue of the potential conflict for participating teachers in the multiple roles of teacher-researcher and collaborator has emerged as a matter of concern in the area of education scholarly comment (see, for example, *Educational Researcher*, April 1995 and November 1995). Many of the issues raised here are, in my view, unresolvable, as the roles and collaborators respond to different authorities, professors, and associated rules in differing contexts. I do not think my collaboration was a success from a teacher's perspective. I feel that the students were disadvantaged from my lack of 100% attention to their purpose for being in class. Yet it was a success research-wise in that another (in theory potentially useful) classroom environment instrument was well validated. Informing papers were written, new ideas on theory were raised, and my educational theoretical knowledge was broadened. As to whether I am a better teacher for the experience, I am not sure.

For me and perhaps other teachers who adopt the role of an academic researcher and collaborator, there arises a question of one's identity. Are we still teachers? Are we informants or agents for academic education reform? Or are we now researchers based in a classroom? Perhaps modern educators do need to be some or all of these. I think the answers to these questions have consequences for education.

This is where the PhD supervisory relationship posed a problem for me. The collaboration helped me understand an important factor in the PhD partnership with the university: the commitment to a career change. The PhD is as much about leaving one career, in this case teaching, to pursue another. I think it has a lot less to do with expanding on one's understanding of what is happening in a classroom or reflecting on one's views of education. It has very little to do with *anything* from a teacher's perspective.

I sensed a strong clash of professions during the collaboration. Peter and I were following our own perspectives, each subconsciously putting our individual professional beliefs first when it came to making sense in the classroom. This was unexceptional until I was placed in a position of "balancing" both, trying to be more than a teacher in the classroom, serving more than one master through trying to (or not to) anticipate action for many others.

The art of theorizing or generalizing is an important practice for academics and plays a major part in the PhD program. To me it is an art form that one practices. Theorizing is an essential skill for an academic, but not necessarily for the teacher. I found having to ground my descriptions in theory meant suppressing many skills or beliefs underpinning my decision making in my teaching practice and what makes sense to me—in particular, some ethical aspects. The art of theorizing involves the stepping back to establish a background to contextualize its foreground. But to me it also means changing people into subjects, and eventually, objects, which is not a practical way of implementing exemplary teaching practice. For me the art of good teaching is respecting your students as people. I think this is the fundamental difference between educational research and teaching-in-practice. Donmoyer has referred to this issue in relation to similar collaborations (see Donmoyer & Yenni-Donmoyer, 1993).

I guess an essential ingredient in the relationship between a PhD student and his or her supervisor is a better understanding of the conflict between submitting oneself to the belief system underpinning research practice at a university and the practice of one's current profession. Essentially one gives up the current profession in undertaking a PhD. The student is learning the new belief system of a very career-oriented establishment. In some respects, the PhD is an "apprenticeship" during which the art of theorizing is an essential skill and must be practiced. To me, a good supervising relationship needs to recognize this point.

REFERENCES

Bauersfeld, H. (1995). The structuring of the structures: Development and function of mathematizing as a social practice. In L. Steffe & J. Gale (Eds.), *Constructivism in education* (pp. 137–158). Hillsdale, NJ: Lawrence Erlbaum Associates.

Bogdan, R., & Biklen, S. (1982). *Qualitative research for education: An introduction to theory and methods.* Boston: Allyn & Bacon.

Bruner, J. (1986). *Actual minds: Possible worlds.* Cambridge, MA: Harvard University Press.

Confrey, J. (1995). How compatible are radical constructivism, social-cultural approaches and social constructivism? In L. Steffe & J. Gale (Eds.), *Constructivism in education* (pp. 185–226). Hillsdale, NJ: Lawrence Erlbaum Associates.

Confrey, J. (1993). Response to the Burton and Tobin/Imwold papers. In J. Malone & P. Taylor (Eds.), *Constructivist interpretations of teaching and learning mathematics* (pp. 35–41). Perth, Western Australia: National Key Centre for School Science and Mathematics.

Connelly, F. M., & Clandinin, D. J. (1987). On narrative method, biography and narrative unities in the study of teaching. *The Journal of Educational Thought, 21*(3), 130–139.

Donmoyer, R., & Yenni-Donmoyer, J. (1993, April). *Role conflicts in collaborative action research.* Paper presented at the annual meeting of the American Educational Research Association, New Orleans, LA.

Eisenhart, M. (1988). The ethnographic research tradition and mathematics education research. *Journal for Research in Mathematics Education, 19*(2), 99–114.

Ernest, P. (1991). *The philosophy of mathematics education.* London: Falmer.

Kyle, D., & McCutcheon, G. (1984). Collaborative research: Development and issues. *Journal of Curriculum Studies, 16*(2), 173–179.

Louden, W. (1991). *Understanding teaching: Continuity and change in teacher's knowledge.* New York: Routledge.

Pateman, N. (1993). Can constructivism underpin a new paradigm in mathematics education? In J. Malone & P. Taylor (Eds.), *Constructivist interpretations of teaching and learning mathematics* (pp. 69–80). Perth, Western Australia: National Key Centre for School Science and Mathematics.

Taylor, P., & Campbell-Williams, M. (1993). Discourse towards balanced rationality in the high school mathematics classroom: Ideas from Habermas's critical theory. In J. Malone & P. Taylor (Eds.), *Constructivist interpretations of teaching and learning mathematics* (pp. 135–148). Perth, Western Australia: National Key Centre for School Science and Mathematics.

Taylor, P., Fraser, B., & White, L. (1994, April). *CLES: An instrument for monitoring the development of constructivist learning environments.* Paper presented at the annual meeting of the American Educational Research Association, New Orleans.

Tobin, K. (1990). Metaphors and images in teaching. *What research says to the science and mathematics teacher* (Vol. 1, No. 5). Perth, Western Australia: National Key Centre for School Science and Mathematics.

Tobin, K. (1991). Learning from interpretive research in science classrooms. In J. Gallagher (Ed.), *Interpretive research in science education* (NARST Monograph No. 4, pp. 197–216).

Tobin, K., & Imwold, D. (1993). The mediational role of constraints in the reform of mathematical curricula. In J. Malone & P. Taylor (Eds.), *Constructivist interpretations of teaching and learning mathematics* (pp. 15–34). Perth, Western Australia: National Key Centre for School Science and Mathematics.

von Glasersfeld, E. (1984). An introduction to radical constructivism. In P. Watzlaqick (Ed.), *The invented reality* (pp. 17–40). New York: Norton.

9

Guiding Collaborative Action Research in Science Education Contexts

Frank E. Crawley

East Carolina University

We are currently witnessing a trend toward offering more field-based pre-service science education courses. At the graduate level, collaborative action research projects can offer an avenue for field-based experiences for students while providing valuable experiences for practicing teachers.

The purpose of this chapter is to describe collaborative action research (CAR) from the perspective of the instructor and students actively engaged in CAR projects. First, however, a brief overview of the state of science education and current reform initiatives, with particular attention to the state of North Carolina, helps to set the background for the CAR projects reported in this chapter.

SCIENCE EDUCATION REFORM

Sweeping changes have been called for in science education at the national and state levels. International comparisons of science achievement test results present a rather dismal picture of the state of science learning in the United States. For example, when scores on separate subject matter tests are compared for students who have studied biology, chemistry, or physics for 2 years, U.S. students rank 13th among 13 countries in biology, 11th among 13 countries in chemistry, and 10th among 14 countries in physics (Jacobson & Doran, 1988), but students with strong backgrounds in physical science and mathematics, the results show, record higher scores in the other sciences. Regrettably, results of tests administered in the United States reveal racial, ethnic, and gender differences in science achievement as early as Grade 3 (Mullis & Jenkins, 1988), when White students exceed the proficiency levels of Black and Hispanic students in their understanding of the nature of science, life science, and physical science. Race and ethnic achievement differences increase as students progress through school, with the greatest disparities in performance noted in physics achievement for Grade 11 students. More encouraging are the initial findings of the Third International Mathematics and Science Study (TIMSS). Grade 8 students in the United States performed above average in science achievement, compared to the 41 nations in the TIMSS assessment, but their standing was stronger in earth science, life science, and environmental issues than in chemistry and physics. Unlike previous international results, no differences in science achievement were detected for boys and girls (U.S. Department of Education, 1996).

In response to low test scores, the National Education Goals Panel (1994) called for sweeping changes in the vision that Americans hold for their schools. In particular, the Goals Panel issued challenges for teacher education, professional development, and mathematics and science education. Goal four of their report offered the following challenge:

> By the year 2000, the Nation's teaching force will have access to programs for continued improvement of their professional skills and the opportunity to acquire the knowledge and skills needed to instruct and prepare all American students for the next century. (p. 13)

In addition, the report establishes a separate goal for school achievement in mathematics and science: "By the year 2000, United States students will be first in the world in mathematics and science achievement" (p. 10).

The *Data Volume for the National Education Goals Report* (National Education Goals Panel, 1994) presented evidence of instructional deficiencies that exist related to the objective "to strengthen science and mathematics education" (p. 83). In Grade 8, for example, less than half of the students report that they "do science experiments," and only one in ten students report that they "use computers." Low achievement test scores are reported to be linked to the inferior quality of science and mathematics education.

A new vision is advocated for science education with publication of the National Research Council's (1996) standards. Their document calls for co-ordinated reform efforts aimed at bringing about major changes in science education in five key areas: (a) the educational system (how the policies and practices outside of the immediate school support high-quality science programs); (b) science programs (how content, teaching, and assessment are coordinated in school practice over a full range of schooling to provide all students with an opportunity to learn science); (c) science content (what all students should know and be able to do as a result of their school learning experiences); (d) teaching standards (what teachers need to understand and do to provide for their students learning experiences that are aligned with content standards); and (e) assessment (essential characteristics of fair and accurate student tests, assessments, or program evaluations that are consistent with the content standards at the individual, school, district, state, and national levels). The content standards set goals for students' understanding of scientific inquiry; basic concepts in the physical, life, and earth/space sciences; technology; science in personal and social perspectives; and the history and nature of science. The teaching standards call for a departure from the model of teaching-as-telling to a model in which science teachers plan inquiry-based science programs for students; guide and facilitate learning; engage in ongoing assessment of teacher and student learning; construct environments that provide time, space, and resources for learning; develop communities of science learners; and actively participate in the ongoing planning and development of the school science program.

In response to calls for reform, two major precollege science curriculum development projects were begun at the national level. The American Association for the Advancement of Science sponsors Project 2061, and the National Science Teachers Association leads the development of Scope, Sequence, and Coordination (SS&C). These two reform projects aim to bring about the radical changes in the content and process of science teaching that are called for by the Goals Panel, and the content of these new programs aligns with the science standards. The standards document and the Project 2061 and SS&C curriculum development projects have greatly influenced reform projects under development at the present time in schools throughout North Carolina.

The vision for science education in North Carolina is one of students (a) using state-of-the-art technology in science instruction; (b) understanding science as inquiry; and (c) understanding contemporary science concepts. The School Technology Commission of the North Carolina Department of Public Instruction (NCDPI) has called for the infusion of technology into high school science education programs in the form of: (a) videodisk and CD-ROM, (b) microcomputer-based laboratories, (c) telecommunications applications, and (d) decision-making groupware (NCDPI, 1994b). Moreover, state-level reform documents set the goal that all high school science students develop: (a) an understanding of the nature of science, (b) the ability to use science process skills, (c) the ability to use science manipulative skills, and (d) a positive attitude toward science (North Carolina Department of Public Instruction, 1994a; this publication is referred to as the Standard Courses of Study—SCOS—by teachers). In addition to common objectives, the SCOS sets the goal of increased understanding of subject-specific science concepts and principles.

As the nature of science education undergoes radical change, it is becoming increasingly clear that the role of the school in our culture, whether we wish it to or not, is also changing rather dramatically. The present situation is not new, and the clarion call to reform has a decades-old and familiar ring. As early as 1953, Corey noted the dilemma that school personnel face as they struggle to keep pace with the ever-changing face of contemporary society:

> If the lives we lead and shall lead are marked by change as they never have been before, education must change too, inevitably.... Our schools cannot keep up with the life they are supposed to sustain and improve unless teachers, pupils, supervisors, administrators, and school parents continuously examine what they are doing. Singly and in groups, they must use their imaginations creatively and constructively to identify the practices that must be changed to meet the needs and demands of modern life, courageously try out those practices that give better promise, and methodically and systematically gather evidence to test their worth. (p. viii)

More recently, Kincheloe (1991) has observed that school reform efforts which envision a return to a romanticized past are misguided and that meaningful change ultimately must engage teachers in the process:

> The only social/educational visions which have gained public attention in the last years ... offer a misleading vision of a return to a romanticized past, a golden era when teachers enforced rules and students learned the basics.... It lays the foundation for educational reform movements that assume that if order can be reestablished, if educational leaders can just lay out what it is that teachers should do and teachers just do it, schools may return to their previous glory.... Teachers understand that something is not right [when their role in reform is ignored].... I attempt to engage teachers with some ideas that may be helpful in their struggle to control their own professional destinies. These ideas revolve around the notion of teachers as researchers. (pp. vii–viii)

Thus two very different people, separated by nearly four decades, issue similar messages. If science education practices are to be transformed, science teachers must bring about these changes. What reform initiatives call for is the radical transformation of the history and culture of school from a "workplace" to a "learning place" (Marshall, 1990). The study of teachers' lives, therefore, offers a window through which to view current moves to restructure, reform, and transform teaching, teachers, and schools.

THE CAR PROCESS

The students participating in the study reported in this chapter were enrolled in a graduate-level CAR course I taught. In describing the CAR process, the chapter draws heavily on the wisdom of the participants, the 21 graduate students and their teacher-collaborators, who were learning about CAR while they were engaged in the process. These projects took place in science education settings from elementary grades through community college.

The overall goal of the CAR course and projects is to explore what Elliott (1991) referred to as "the dialectical process in which the meaning and significance of structures are reconstructed in the historically conditioned consciousness of individuals as they try to make sense of their 'life situations'" (p. 10). At present science teachers in the United States grapple with the implications for their teaching of recent reform initiatives, and many of them see their traditional teaching methods coming under attack. With the advent of the National Science Education Standards (National Research Council, 1996) measures of quality are being set in place for science teaching, content, assessment, and programs as well as the systems that support science education in the schools. Reformers call on teachers to transform their instructional programs in ways that hold promise for dramatically improving students' understanding of science so that the nation can regain its competitive advantage in the international marketplace.

THEORETICAL UNDERPINNINGS OF CAR

Three bodies of research are particularly important to the action research process and thus they formed the information base for the CAR course: (a) life history, (b) action research, and (c) teacher reflection. In the process of collaborating in a classroom setting, it is reasoned, two rather extensive, diverse educational histories, perspectives, and sets of beliefs and values merge rather abruptly: those of the teacher and those of a collaborator. This merger of minds is all the more supportive of the collaborative process if the partners understand the landmark educational events that have helped to shape their present thinking and to construct the classroom ecology. Key concepts in life history, action research, and teacher thinking literatures are visited and revisited throughout the course as participants engage in CAR.

Life History

Life-history research provides rather startling insights into the influence of personal experience as an early learner on the development of teaching practice and suggests ways in which current reform might proceed if it is to be successful. Contrary to traditional literature on teacher socialization, the most formative socializing influences may not be preservice teacher training and early in-service teaching. The study of teachers' biographies reveals that their own experiences as pupils may be as important, if not more so, than early training periods. In his landmark study of the socialization of teachers, Lortie (1975) noted that countless hours spent in classrooms as students and the personal predispositions of prospective teachers constitute the basis of a beginning teachers' thoughts and actions. Socialization into the profession takes place through the observation and internalization of particular models of teaching that teachers experienced early on as students (Goodson, 1992). Unlike doctors and lawyers, who enter professional training relatively ignorant of their professional duties and places of work, teachers know schools, teaching, and learning (Knowles, 1992). Grounded in years of school experience, teachers resist and resent methods of reform that are prescriptive, that elevate theory above practice, and that place the outside reformer above teachers in a vertical, unequal arrangement of authority. What is needed for current reform to succeed, therefore, is to acknowledge teachers as active learners and classroom changes as a learning process (Butt, Raymond, McCue, & Yamagishi, 1992).

The narrative study of lives has been the subject of considerable inquiry in its own right, outside of school reform (Carter, 1993; Clandinin, Davies, Hogan, & Kennard, 1993; Connelly & Clandinin, 1985; Cortazzi, 1993; Hatch & Wisniewski, 1995; Josselson & Lieblich, 1993). By studying oral accounts of personal experience, researchers and practitioners alike gain insights into teachers' personal representations and explanations of experience (Connelly & Clandinin, 1988; Cortazzi, 1993). Like windows to the content and operation of the mind, stories have the power to reveal who individuals are and how they represent their world. Consequently, experiences have little value until they are connected to or fused with stories. Education then takes on a script-like quality, which assures that the events that constitute people's educational experiences are tied together to form a meaningful whole.

Life history, or *story*, has been called a mode of knowing, a form of knowledge that emerges from action (Carter, 1993). It consists of events, characters, and settings arranged in a temporal sequence implying both causality and significance. In the constructive process of "storying," the mind builds models of the causal structure of events and creates the individual's world. It blends these events with its own mix of cultural and individual expectations. To understand teacher thinking, it is necessary to find the story that structures the teacher's model or theory of events, the personal theories implied in spontaneous behaviors with other people (called *theories in use*) and those used to explain behavior (called *espoused theories*; Schön, 1987). "Through story, then, teachers transform knowledge of content into a form that plays itself out in the time and space of classrooms" (Carter, 1993, p. 7). The act of teaching becomes a narrative in action (Connelly & Clandinin, 1985).

Through the construction of life histories, individuals make visible and open for inspection their personal experiences, representations, interpretations, and subjectivities, and in doing so they gain an understanding of the self. Self-understanding is a precondition and concomitant condition to the understanding of others (Pinar, 1988). Through the use of collaborative autobiographies, teachers better understand both their own and others' teaching in a deeply personal way (Clandinin, 1993; Raymond, Butt, & Townsend, 1992).

Action Research

Action research was briefly mentioned in chapter 1. It has been defined as the study of a social situation with a view to improving the quality of action within it (Elliott, 1991). This approach to improved practice recognizes the complexity and the large number of factors present in any situation such as the classroom. Action research is one of two broad strategies used to conduct inquiry into education; the other, more widely used, is called *analytical research*. From its beginnings in 1926, action research has enjoyed limited acceptance by the educational community. It was ridiculed in the publications of the American Educational Research Association following the publication of the *1957 Yearbook of the Association for Supervision and Curriculum Development* (Foshay, 1994). In recent years, however, action research has gained greater acceptance, and three forces seem to be driving this acceptance. First, researchers now question the applicability of quantitative, experimental methods to improve practice in specific educational settings. Second, teachers are dissatisfied with quantitative research, most of which they believe to be impractical. Third, practitioners have gained a prominent voice in determining what is needed in today's classroom.

Collaborative action research involves two or more "practitioners" working to systematically inquire into a "situation of practice" related to teaching, learning, or both (Oja & Smulyan, 1989; Sagor, 1992). This approach to classroom research serves to address the discrepancy between educational theory and educational practice. The union of researcher-practitioner and teacher-practitioner forges mutual understanding and consensus, democratic decision making, and common action (Oja & Smulyan, 1989). When teachers become researchers, they gain the skill to interrogate their own practice, to question their own assumptions, and to understand contextually their own situations (Kincheloe, 1991). To approach the improvement of practice from any perspective other than that of the teacher as researcher sustains what Whitehead called the "traditional view of educational knowledge," namely that:

Educational knowledge is created by researchers in faculties of mathematics, history, philosophy, psychology, chemistry, etc., in institutions of higher education. The alternative ... is that educational knowledge is created by individuals at work as they answer the questions of the form, "How do I live more fully my values in my practice?" (cited in McNiff, 1993, p. ix)

Teachers and researchers bring highly individualistic perspectives, however, to the research process. Sharing their individual perspectives facilitates the development of collaborative relationships built on mutual respect, trust, and complementary interests, and sets the stage for learning. Teachers and researchers come to understand better how reflection initiates action and action triggers reflection, and, in the process, they experience firsthand what has been called the "theory–practice dialectic."

Teacher Reflection

One way in which teachers acquire professional knowledge is through reflection. Schön (1983, 1987) asserted that knowledge-of-action is acquired through two types of reflection: *reflection-on-action* and *reflection-in-action*. When teachers reflect on their actions, they systematically and deliberately think back to classroom events and their responses to them. When reflecting in action, teachers face a situation of practice and suddenly and quite unexpectedly see the event in a new light, see it differently. The teacher's "reality" is transformed rather dramatically from one of less certainty to one of possibility. This flash of insight is called *reframing*. Russell and Munby (1992) asserted that the ways in which teachers frame and reframe their experience, through reflection on and in action, establishes how the situations of practice are set. Problem setting represents the first step in problem solving and thus transformation of the problems of practice in teachers' lived and storied experiences. What makes reframing a particularly important concept, according to Russell and Munby (1991), is that it is an integral part of a cycle in the development of teachers' professional knowledge. When an initial theory in action encounters puzzles or surprises, backtalk stimulates reframing, suggesting new actions that imply a revised theory in action. Thus reframing mediates theory and practice, revealing new meanings in theory, and new strategies for practice. Reframing is an integral part of the spiraling cycles of action that can take place in the CAR process.

The process of reform, it is argued, should be collaborative and participatory. Collaborative action research brings together teachers, researchers, and other stakeholders in the reform process for the purpose of improving practice:

Its goal is to empower teachers to become self-reflective researchers [i.e., teacher-researchers], that is, practitioners who can examine their own practice systematically and critically. Through the process of investigating and reflecting, teachers become more flexible in their thinking, more receptive to new ideas, and more adept at converting a problematic situation into a problem to be resolved. (Shymansky & Kyle, 1992, p. 758)

Once again, as in the reform efforts of nearly four decades ago, the teacher is the key.

THE COLLABORATIVE ACTION RESEARCH COURSE

The CAR course has been taught each fall semester with graduate students enrolled in the course serving as researcher-collaborators. Each of the 21 students and the author-instructor selected a teacher from one of the region's many educational institutions—public schools, colleges, universities, or informal science settings—located in rural eastern North Carolina. The teachers served as teacher-collaborators for the CAR projects. Some students lacked experience and a license to teach; others were licensed science teachers who were employed at the time of the CAR course. Students who lacked licensure and experience collaborated with an experienced person in an educational setting appropriate to their interest, their career goal, or both. Students who were licensed to teach and were teaching at the time of the CAR course collaborated with another teacher, a supervisor in their school, or a nonteaching graduate student. Except for my name, the names of all participants and school settings reported in this chapter are fictitious.

Students enrolled in the three-semester-hour course Research in Science Education during their first semester of graduate study. The objectives of the course are fourfold: to develop a rationale for the role and importance of collaborative action research in forming and sustaining university–school partnerships; to describe potential contributions of practitioner's inquiry for improving teaching and learning, developing teacher leaders, and bringing about and sustaining reform in education; to articulate a vision of teaching and learning based on the community-of-learners and teachers-as-researchers metaphors; and to successfully complete a collaborative action research project in a classroom or other appropriate educational setting.

The CAR course consists of four parts. First, researcher-collaborators interview themselves about their educational life history (Assignment 1) and audiotape, transcribe, and review tapes for dominant themes and personal theories. They then reflect on their current views of science education and seek out connections between these views and their educational histories. Within a week researcher-collaborators meet with their teacher-collaborator, share their educational life history, and then interview the teacher-collaborator during the following week to gain insight into their partner's educational life history. The teacher-collaborator interviews are also audiotaped, transcribed, reviewed for dominant themes and personal theories, and the results are reflected on in collaboration with the teacher (Assignment 2).

For the second part of the course, researcher-collaborators seek out information on the school culture. To do this, they review the results of interviews with the principal, teachers, and students and review the field notes that they record during school visits and attendance at school-wide events. These data aid in gaining insights to the myths, traditions, and climate of the school.

In the third part of the course, researcher- and teacher-collaborators meet to identify a problem of practice that the team wants to resolve (Assignment 3). In some cases, extended conversations are needed to isolate a specific classroom problem or dilemma for which human and physical resources are available. Once the teams agree on a problem, they identify key concepts and researcher-collaborators review the literature for information relevant to the specific problem (Assignment 4). From the literature review, researcher-collaborators identify ideas that they bring to subsequent meetings to assist the collaborating partners in developing a plan of action.

The fourth and final part of the course gets under way with initiation of an action plan, which marks the beginning of the four-step, action research cycle. Researcher-collaborators chronicle meetings with teacher-collaborators, topics of discussion, observations of school and classroom events, and personal reflections (Assignment 5) in the double-entry journal, which later serves as a key data source to review when writing the CAR report:

> On entering the "Research" course, few graduate students know what to expect. Only those enrolled in the fall semester had the benefit of experience gained by graduate students enrolled in the year before. "Sandra" had heard "through the grapevine" about the course and noted, "When I first heard about this class, I was told that it would be helpful but was a lot of work."

Some students knew that the course was titled Research in Science Education and held traditional expectations. Others expected something different. Here are some comments:

> I thought that I would spend the semester researching and writing about a given topic. ("John")

> I had never heard about CAR before. I was excited to find out that it was a qualitative type of research, different from traditional. The reason I was excited is because I dread statistics. I would much rather do a qualitative study. I also favored CAR over traditional research because I felt that action research was useful. I knew that it would directly benefit a teacher and I could see these results. ("Sally")

My first reaction was, "*Why* would I want to learn about CAR?" Within a few classes I realized how much is occurring that I do not know about in the classroom, from K–12 and also college level. It has also made me more aware of problems teachers face everyday in the classroom. ("Lydia")

I didn't know the difference between collaborative research and "traditional" educational research when I came to this class, so I didn't have much of an opinion. . . . I assumed I would be told what I was supposed to do and how and then my project would come together. ("Eleanor")

As can be seen from these comments, no one had ever heard of collaborative action research. After initial readings and discussions, students came to see that CAR was "teacher research" and gained an appreciation for the process as it was useful to the classroom teacher.

In the sections that follow, each course assignment is explained in the order in which it was completed. The sections focus on the experiences reported by one team in particular, that of "John" and "Eleanor," who served as researcher- and teacher-collaborators, respectively, and who were engaged in a CAR project at the time.

Educational Life History—Assignments 1 and 2

The purpose of Assignments 1 (researcher educational life history) and 2 (teacher educational life history) is to identify, describe, and examine past educational events to gain a better understanding of both present and future perspectives on science education. It is completed during the first week of the CAR course, before identifying and visiting a teacher-collaborator during the second week. In writing an educational life history, students and teachers alike uncover everyday experiences in education that have played a major role in shaping their lives, their current perspectives on education, and what gets noticed (or overlooked) in present-day teaching. Three assumptions underpin the two educational life history assignments. First, experience cannot speak for itself (i.e., an "objective" experience, separate from personal perception and interpretation, is nonexistent). Second, raw sensory experience is meaningless; people actively bring meaning to experience. Third, experience is temporal and storied, and our minds act as selective video recorders. As Albert Einstein and Werner Heisenberg understood long ago, what we see is not what we see but what we perceive. The observer is inseparable from that which is observed (Reason, 1994). In completing educational life history projects, participants learn the way they have come to view and understand the world of education.

The researcher educational life history assignment begins with a self-interview, which is recorded on audiotape. This self-interview is completed in about an hour or so of uninterrupted time using questions that have been developed by the instructor and students. The extended, uninterrupted time is recommended so that each person has the opportunity to get caught up in the dialogue with him- or herself. Participants are encouraged to be spontaneous with their responses to questions rather than taking notes or preparing answers to questions beforehand. Rehearsed responses are discouraged in favor of lively, spontaneous comments, to the extent that this is possible with self-interviews. Questions developed are of three types: biographical, school life, and science classroom. Biographical questions seek to initiate conversation, and examples include:

1. What is your name, age, gender, and ethnicity?
2. Where were you born?
3. What was your birthplace like? (city/suburban/rural, high-/low-/middle-class)
4. If you know, tell how your parent(s) named you.
5. Name the different places you have lived up to now.
6. What did your parent(s) do for a living?
7. What was the highest level of education of your parent(s)?

School-life (and science-study) questions are worded in the hermeneutic phenomenological tradition (van Manen, 1990). Each question both seeks to identify the "facts" of schooling (and science study) and to gain the individual's interpretation or perspective on the meaning of the events. These interview questions include:

1. Tell what elementary school was like for you.
2. What was secondary school like for you?
3. From your point of view, what has college been like?
4. Describe any personal events that have had a major impact on your school life.

Science-study questions include:

1. What was the study of science like for you in elementary and secondary schools?
2. Describe what it has been like to study science in college.
3. Talk about a "good day" in a science class or course. What was it like?
4. Talk about a "bad day" in a science class or course. What was it like?
5. Distinguish between a "good science teacher" and a "bad science teacher."
6. Are there people or events that influenced your decision to study science?

Self-interviews are transcribed verbatim and then set aside for a few days before reflecting on them. Next, transcripts are read and landmark events are identified in each person's educational life. These events are summarized in narrative form. Past experience has shown that it is difficult, or even impossible for most first-time storytellers to move directly into a critique of their landmark events without extended discussion. It appears to be necessary to talk more about past educational events before participants begin to analyze these events and seek out their meaning. The narrative summary serves this purpose. For the next part of the life-history assignment, participants identify beliefs about what constitutes good and bad science instruction and explain how they arrived at these beliefs. Finally, they search for connections among landmark events, past experience as a science learner, and present beliefs about good and bad science instruction. By this time, some people are able to adopt a critical perspective on their own beliefs about science teaching, learning, and teachers. For the most part, participants found intense, critical self-examination to be a difficult, if not impossible, task. In pointing out the difficulty of engaging in self-critical analysis, one person commented, "the eye cannot see itself."

John learned much about himself by exploring his educational life history, as did Eleanor. For example, John reports that, after Grade 10, science became "esoteric and confusing," and has this to say:

> I once loved science. That love was squashed. And now I want to make sure that doesn't happen to anyone else. Around the 2nd Grade we studied the solar system, which is what first interested me about science. In the 10th Grade, I fell in love with biology, mainly due to the teaching of Coach Pascal. The study of science in college has been pitiful.... [It] became esoteric and confusing.... I learned [from my self-interview] that science wasn't very effective for me in college, not because I am so stupid, but because it was not taught in a way that was best for me. I want to teach science to others in such a way that they can understand it.

After looking at her educational life history, Eleanor came to see that her experiences as a learner greatly influenced her current views on learning. As a Grade 7 science teacher, Eleanor articulates clearly what her views are on teaching and learning. She puts it this way:

> I believe in the learner "owning" his/her learning and thinking for him/herself. Students get learning for themselves through experience with guidance from the teacher. I remain in control, however, of content and of behavior. I am responsible for covering a particular curriculum, according to state guidelines, so content is not in the hands of the learner.

John and Eleanor provide a glimpse into their views on science teaching and learning. Through the examination of their educational life histories, they both want science teaching to be a meaningful, memorable learning experience for the students they teach.

Students complete Assignment 2, the teacher interview, during the second week of class. They meet with the teacher-collaborators, provide them with a copy of their "researcher educational life history," and set a time to interview teachers for the "teacher educational life history" (Assignment 2). Personal experience for teachers extends beyond solely being science students to life as science teachers. To get at the contribution of personal experiences as a teacher of science to their educational life history, teachers answer four additional questions posed by their researcher-collaborator. These questions include:

1. When you think about the reform taking place in science teaching and learning, what are you concerned about?
2. What, if any, ambiguities, contradictions, or tensions do you feel in your teaching?
3. Share a story or stories about memorable moments in your teaching career.
4. What is the most pressing problem of practice in science teaching that you face in your class at this time that you and I could work on to resolve?

Space permits only a brief mention of the general nature of teachers' responses to the foregoing questions. Generally speaking, teachers' concerns are of two types: *fundamental* and *reform-related*. Fundamental concerns far outnumber reform-related concerns. Fundamental concerns identified by teachers include discipline, lack of student interest and motivation in class, large class enrollment, and insufficient planning time. Reform-related concerns center on accountability, namely what teachers perceive to be the competing demands between content coverage in preparation for state-mandated, end-of-course tests and the reform dictum for less topic coverage in favor of increased student understanding of unifying science concepts and processes, captured in the popular phrase in the United States "less is more." An additional reform-related concern centers on a fundamental conflict in paradigms, namely between teachers' understanding of learning as "received" knowledge and the reformers' perspective of understanding as "constructed" knowledge, with its emphasis on teaching science as critical inquiry.

Problematizing Practice—Assignment 3

The topic of the final teacher interview question, identifying a "pressing problem of practice," serves to initiate further conversations about problematic aspects of teachers' classrooms. For most teams, conversations on this topic take place in the following weeks. Some teams agree on a problem after a few days of discussion. Other teams are not so fortunate. These team members find it particularly difficult to call existing teaching practices into question. Assignment 3 may require several weeks of extended conversations before a problem is identified that researcher- and teacher-collaborators both think appropriate to study. At the conclusion of their interview, Eleanor identified the problem that she wanted John to help her resolve, namely students' scoring low on her science tests. Only after grappling with the problem of low test scores was Eleanor willing to problematize the more fundamental aspects of her teaching. What does it mean to problematize practice?

To problematize practice, researcher- and teacher-collaborators meet to critically reflect on classroom routines and to ask the question, "How did the situation come to be as it is and how might it be changed?" Researchers find it difficult to accept that to problematize practice is to be critical of classroom practices rather than to criticize the teacher, the students, or instruction. They are helped to see, through extended conversation during the CAR course, that situations often arise in which teachers' actions puzzle or interest them or they want to improve or change. To resolve this situation, whatever its origin, teachers must first acknowledge that the classroom stands as a product of its own history, and that their personal theories about science teaching and learning, products of their educational histories, must be contested. To understand the problem, therefore, team members think back over the teachers' personal histories and the histories of the classroom and then think ahead to the transformations that are required to bring about the desired change. To decide what action to take, action-research collaborators must critically examine (or contest) the language, actions, values, and interaction patterns that have come to be routinized. Therefore, all practices must be treated as problematic; "there are no sacred cows," as one team member commented. Teachers' language, actions, values, and interaction patterns, as well as that of students, are part of rather than apart from the history of the classroom and must be considered problematic. To problematize existing practices, researchers come to accept, is not to point the finger of blame; rather, it is to examine the classroom as an existing discourse system, with its unique language, activities, values, and interaction patterns.

Assignment 3 begins with the "Aristotelian Table of Invention" (Kemmis & McTaggart, 1988, p. 91) to arrive at a thematic concern, or problem of practice. Although use of the table is straightforward, the process is neither simple nor are the results trivial. After reading directions on its use some students have commented that the table seems to be rather academic and is unlikely to yield profound insights into the particular context in which the CAR team operates. Experience has shown that the more researchers have visited, observed, and discussed the *commonplaces of teaching* at the school (the teacher, student, subject matter, and milieu) with teachers and students, the more interesting and truly revealing they find it is to use the table.

At least one team, John and Eleanor, gained new insights into Eleanor's teaching after using the table. Both persons initially had selected different collaborating partners, only to have Eleanor's administrator-partner reassigned by the district office, and to have John's teacher decline to participate in a CAR project due to a "lack of time." Following preliminary discussions with John about a problem of practice, Eleanor expressed concern that she was teaching inquiry-based lessons, but, to her regret, Grade 8 students were failing to make connections, as evidenced by failing quiz and test grades. John and Eleanor decided to make use of the Aristotelian Table of Invention. They focused on the theme of inquiry and collaborated to define new questions about its use in Eleanor's middle school physical science classroom. In working through the table, the problem of control emerged. They reported their revelation this way:

> The point of inquiry teaching is giving students control over their learning, therefore giving ownership of the knowledge to the student [a personal belief Eleanor identified in Assignment 1]. It became evident that students [in Eleanor's class] had no control over their learning. . . . This was a very powerful revelation for Eleanor and neither she nor John are sure she would have believed that the true root of her problem was control had she not discovered it herself through the Aristotelian Table.

As a result of using the table, they decided to pursue the problem of restoring ownership of knowledge to students in the inquiry environment of Eleanor's classroom. Eleanor and John decided to enlist students' ideas concerning how they preferred to be taught and how they believed that they learned best.

John and Eleanor were provided a set of guidelines to follow for reporting the results of Assignment 3, Problematizing Practice. These guidelines take the form of questions that serve as points for reflection. Guidelines provided CAR team members for this assignment are as follows:

1. Briefly describe the classroom (teacher, students, grade level, subject, and school).
2. Identify and explain the thematic concern (problem of practice) that was generated by using the Table of Invention.
3. Reflect on the present situation in relation to the thematic concern (or problem). In doing so, consider the following questions:
   - What language is used to describe the participants?
   - What actions, tasks, events have become routinized?

- What is the rationale for doing things as they are presently done? (i.e., Why do things the way they are done?)
- To what extent do the routinized, classroom events reflect the teacher-collaborator's (or researcher-collaborator's) personal theories, beliefs, interpretations, values?
- What persons seem to be the key players in the problem, other than the teacher? (Seriously consider inviting one or more of these persons to join the action research group.)
- What are the self-interests of the key players (including the teacher- and researcher-collaborator)?
- What are the points of conflict and points of consensus among the key players related to the problem? To what extent do all members hold the same concern for the problem?
- What is the nature of the interaction of the collaborating teacher with students?
- What actions (language, activities, interactions) seem to improve the situation? Which ones seem to frustrate the situation?

4. What are the key concepts that emerge from a critical reflection on existing classroom practice? What additional information might help in the identification of a plan of action (i.e., Step 1 of the four steps in the self-reflective action research cycle)?

Theory Informs Practice—Assignment 4

Collaboration is a necessary but not sufficient condition for successful and mutually beneficial CAR teams. True collaboration involves more than establishing trust and rapport. It involves establishing a partnership-of-equals relationship, in which teacher and researcher have specialized knowledge, skills, and abilities to contribute that enable them to take on meaningful roles in resolving classroom problems. Many of the 21 researcher-collaborators who have participated in CAR projects over the past 2 years have lacked classroom teaching experience, and they have worked to complete requirements for teacher licensure while they work toward completion of master's degrees. With completion of the previous assignment, CAR team members have identified key concepts related to the problem of practice targeted for resolution. With completion of Assignment 4, researcher-collaborators gain access to specialized knowledge, information unavailable to most classroom teachers, who lack connectivity with the Internet or computerized document retrieval services. As a result of their search for information, researcher-collaborators are able to recommend courses of action to their teacher counterparts, actions that represent the best wisdom of researchers and practitioners. Teachers depend on university-based graduate students for the specialized knowledge related to their teaching and, in turn, graduate students depend on the practical wisdom, insight, and expertise available from teacher-collaborators, who propose ways of implementing literature-based teaching practices and suggest the forms of evidence to collect to judge the merits of new teaching practices. Much of the success of the 21 teams that participated in the CAR projects can be attributed to establishing this partnership-of-equals form of collaboration.

There is a considerable body of literature that exists on almost any problem pertaining to teaching and learning, Grades K–12, in any subject area. Unfortunately, the problems that arise in teaching are so highly contextualized that they seem inextricable, and, therefore, impossible to resolve through prescriptive measures. On the other hand, reports of traditional experimental research projects offer starting points for reflection and the development of plans of action to resolve classroom problems. What results from this reflection is a hybridized form of theory that is contextualized and ready for use in the teacher's classroom. Transformation of theory thus initiates and feeds the theory–practice dialectic (Carr & Kemmis, 1986).

In summary, to begin Assignment 4, researcher-collaborators revisit the key concepts that emerged from their critical reflection on existing classroom practices with the teacher-collaborators (Assignment 3). These key concepts (or related terms) serve as the starting point for the ERIC review. Researcher-collaborators complete a 6-year search. They identify 25 citations that seem appropriate to their problem of practice and the context for the study and construct annotations of the citations to share with teacher-collaborators.

John and Eleanor searched for information on three topics: teacher control, student control, and classroom control. In a relatively short time they reported that several helpful articles emerged. One in particular proved meaningful to Eleanor and they noted:

> Entries from the teaching journal of a teacher of behavior-disordered students illustrate her inner struggle as she turned away from the traditional philosophy of classroom control, and the progress of her students as they accept responsibility for their behavior and learning.

Another reference contained information on a model for reorganizing the structure of Eleanor's classroom. John and Eleanor talk about this reference in great detail in their report. They described the model this way:

> Group investigation is an organizational approach that allows a class to work actively and collaboratively in small groups and enables students to take an active role in determining their own learning goals and processes. As part of reform and restructuring efforts, the [authors] implemented the Group Investigation model with sophomores.

This reference proved to be quite persuasive, and John and Eleanor took steps to implement the Group Investigation model in Eleanor's class.

Double-Entry Journal—Assignment 5

Researcher-collaborators maintain double-entry journals throughout the CAR course and project. On the right-hand, "knowledge-construction," side of the page, they record notes on the day-to-day classroom activities and events, on discussions with students and the teacher-collaborator, and on ideas to be presented to the teacher-collaborator. On the left-hand, "knowledge-reflection," side, researcher-collaborators record personal reflections on these activities, events, discussions, and ideas. In particular, researcher-collaborators make knowledge construction and reflection entries in the journal as they record:

1. Changing use of language and the development of a more coherent classroom discourse.
2. Changing activities and the development of more coherently described and justified educational practice.
3. Changing social relationships and emerging changes to the organizational structure of the classroom.
4. Changing ways in which the collaborators participate in the CAR project.

Journal entries also serve as one of the primary data sources on the progress of the CAR project. Preparation for effective use of the double-entry journal begins at the start of the semester with activities and discussions punctuated with time for reflective writing. Thereafter, open-ended questions occasionally are posed in class to stimulate critical thinking about one or more aspects of the CAR course and the CAR process. For example, during the time researcher-collaborators are engaged in self- and teacher interviews, they reflect on the importance of past educational experiences in science, and how these experiences help to shape teaching practice. Examples of the questions include:

1. What is the importance of writing your educational life history from your point of view? Of writing your teacher's educational life history?
2. What role does "self-/other knowledge" play in beginning a collaborative action research project?
3. To what extent might self-/other knowledge impact on perceptions of classroom events?

4. How might the limitations of self-/other knowledge be overcome so that classroom events might be reframed or recast to gain a different perspective?

5. Kincheloe (1991) asserted that if self-direction and emancipation are to be attained, we must become aware of hidden values in how and what we come to know. What do you see to be the implications of Kincheloe's assertion for persons engaging in collaborative action research and employing the "human as instrument"?

By the end of the course, the double-entry journal contains a chronicle of the personal and professional changes and transformations of researcher and teacher collaborators.

The journal serves as a diary for CAR team members. Early in the semester students come to accept it as a sounding board on which they record thoughts, feelings, connections, dilemmas, questions, and so on, that come to bear on their CAR project (and the course), and, in a few cases, it offers insights to the problem of practice that CAR team members later explore. A perusal of Eleanor's journal, for example, revealed five separate entries on the knowledge-reflection or left-hand side of the double-entry journal page regarding the problem of control before its identification as the problem that she and John explored for their CAR project. Even prior to completing Assignment 4, John began to reflect on the themes of control and good teaching. He noted in his journal, "Being a good teacher is knowing when to take control of the class and when to give it up." This doesn't mean that John found journaling easy to do. In fact, in a knowledge-reflection entry he reported, "I too, like Eleanor, am having a great deal of trouble with this journal." Unlike John, Eleanor was a prolific reflector and writer and her journal contained numerous and lengthy commentaries on the CAR course and the progress she and John were making toward completion of their project.

COLLABORATIVE ACTION RESEARCH IN ACTION

The collaborative action research strategy makes use of a four-step, spiraling cycle (Elliott, 1991; Oja & Smulyan, 1989; Sagor, 1992) and a fifth, dissemination, step (McKernan, 1994). The basic cycle includes: (a) planning, (b) acting, (c) observing, and (d) reflecting. The addition of another step, (e) dissemination, brings researcher- and teacher-collaborators together to write and disseminate the final report of the results of the CAR project. Several teacher members of CAR teams have presented results of their study to administrators and other teachers at school staff meetings. Primary responsibility for writing the final report, however, rests with the researcher-collaborator, but teachers approve the report before it is submitted.

Making problematic the teachers' existing teaching practices (Assignment 3) is the preliminary step to initiating the action research project. It consists of lengthy observations, meetings and discussions regarding a suitable problem for the researcher- and teacher-collaborators to pursue. Arriving at a problem of practice is a difficult task for some teams, but once team members identify a problem they decide how and what they will do to resolve it. As with problem identification, this, too, is a difficult task. It is in the planning stage of the action research cycle (Step 1) that theory informs practice (Assignment 4) and researchers and teachers consider action alternatives.

The researcher- and teacher-collaborators identify actions that they can initiate within their individual educational settings, that they have (or can readily acquire) the experience and expertise to carry out, and that can be undertaken within the timeframe and constraints of the researchers' and teachers' schedules. With the plan identified (Step 1), implementing the plan becomes the next step.

John and Eleanor serve as a good example. Both team members had difficulty arriving at "control" as the problem they wanted to explore in Eleanor's classroom, even though it appeared as the topic of numerous entries in her journal before Assignment 3. Use of the Aristotelian Table of Invention, however, provided them with new insights, new ways of viewing the classroom, her teaching, and ways she related to students. What Assignment 3 revealed was that her need for control in the classroom undermined her goal to be an "inquiry" teacher, one who gives students control over their learning. Only after completion of Assignment 4 did Eleanor gain the confidence needed to relinquish control and implement a plan of action that she and John identified from their literature search, the Group Investigation model. John and Eleanor permitted students to select collaborative group members and choose how they would complete requirements on the regularly scheduled physical science topic, the history of atomic theory. Two students requested and were granted permission to change group membership after the plan's implementation.

Once a plan is implemented and the project is under way, researchers and teachers collect classroom artifacts, observe students and document their reactions to the changes in classroom practice, and talk with students about the changes. During this data-collection step, collaborators make use of multiple data sources for purposes of triangulation, such as double-entry journals, field notes, observations, student comments, and audio- and video-tapes. Triangulation is a form of validation consistent with conducting naturalistic studies (Lincoln & Guba, 1985) and facilitates development of grounded theory (Strauss & Corbin, 1990).

John and Eleanor used three primary data sources for their CAR project. Both team members maintained double-entry journals, and Eleanor video-

taped her class for 3 days, during which she implemented the Group Investigation model. Student test scores served as the third data source.

The final step in the action research process brings researchers and
teachers together to reflect on the outcomes of their CAR projects. The
collaborators return to the original problem and consider it in light of their
observations. What one group realized was that they needed to refine the
plan (Step 1) before they proceeded with Steps 2–4. For example, "Frank"
and "Annette" sought to improve the motivation of Annette's biology students by gaining greater commitment and interest in learning, particularly
from four males. To do this, they decided to provide all students with
choices as to which topics they would study and how they would study
them. In the process of doing this they noticed improved motivation, but
three of the four targeted boys were creating disorder as they moved back
and forth among their respective groups to confer. To alleviate this problem,
Frank and Annette revised their plan and placed the three boys in the same
group for the next group activity. Thus began the second cycle of Frank and
Annette's action-research project.

John and Eleanor's project required only one action-research cycle. Once
the action plan was implemented and data were collected, they worked at
making sense of the outcomes—an easy task for this team. Eleanor made
the following observations about the outcome of the CAR project with John:

> Test and quiz scores improved dramatically. Even though I have a hard time
> letting them [the students] choose their own groups (and some in some classes
> WON'T work together again), I believe it [the project] was a success.

In the concluding step of the action research projects, the researcher-
and teacher-collaborators construct the final report. Primary responsibility
for the writing task belongs to the graduate student. In consultation with
teacher-collaborators, teams negotiate the common understanding that has
emerged from their efforts. In the process, what appears to be an uncontested outcome of the project to one member of the team may prove to be
problematic to the other member. Considerable time, therefore, is spent in
discussion, reflection, revision, and rewriting. This final step, the dissemination task, concludes with both parties signing a CAR Project cover sheet
to indicate that they concur with the final report, which is then submitted
by the graduate student. At the same time, some teacher collaborators
provide their principal with a copy of the CAR report and thus receive credit
for their work toward completion of individually negotiated professional
development plans.

John and Eleanor expected to be enrolled in a traditional research course,
as can be seen in their comments in the section of their report titled "The

Collaborative Action Research Course." Eleanor summarized the benefits of her partnership with John and the CAR project:

> This CAR project showed me how wrong were my assumptions. The self-examination [that was] required opened my eyes to my own biases and issues which were at the root of my classroom problem. Without discovering this for myself, I would never have been free to give up the control which was needed. Doing it the way we did showed me I can leave them [the students] to their own resources and they won't fail. Those who need the extra help and guidance can get it. Those who don't can DO IT THEMSELVES and "gain ownership."

CONCLUSIONS

Several conclusions result from teaching the Collaborative Action Research course for two fall semesters and supervising CAR projects conducted by 21 graduate students in diverse educational settings. These conclusions serve as starting points for reflection for persons who, like the author, either teach a collaborative action research course, supervise collaborative action research projects, or both. These conclusions must be tempered by an awareness that more than half of the graduate students enrolled in the CAR course lacked a teaching license and were inexperienced teachers. What is more, they lacked supervised practice teaching science in any educational setting. Situations in which researcher- and teacher-collaborators are both experienced teachers may give rise to different patterns of interaction. Whether these interaction patterns alter the nature of the collaborative efforts is unknown.

The 21 teacher- and researcher-collaborator teams grappled with the multiple dialectics inherent in CAR: (a) between *collaboration* as participant or as observer, (b) between *action* for improved understanding or for improved practice, and (c) between *research* that reifies existing practice or transforms it. In particular, in the context of the projects completed during the one-semester graduate course, the following three findings serve to inform persons who supervise CAR projects:

1. Collaboration may prove problematic with teams in which teacher and researcher roles are strictly defined and adhered to, in contrast to situations in which participant and observer roles are more fluid and team members even frequently exchange roles.

Participation and observation engender different perspectives on teaching. By becoming participants, observers gained greater insights into the complexity of teaching, the difficulty in transforming instruction, and the resilience of existing teaching practices to one-shot interventions. Teachers who became observers acquired new perspectives from which to think about existing teaching practices, vantage points rarely, if ever, available to them. By exchanging roles, each person gained time to, as Somekh (1994) has said, "inhabit each other's castles," thereby forming a genuine partnership, one in which both contributing and learning become a single process.

2. Actions undertaken may result in improved understanding of practice, as well as improved practice.

All teams report improved understanding of practice, from the introduction of cooperative groups in a Grade 4 class to the replacement of lecture with guided computer simulations in a community college biology course. Teachers continued to use some part or all of newly introduced classroom practices following completion of the CAR project, and, in two cases, teachers sustained changes in practice beyond the semester of the CAR study. The presence of a willing and supportive colleague appears to be essential to sustaining reformed teaching practices, particularly in environments characterized by traditional, teacher-centered instruction, as were the settings for a few of the CAR projects.

3. CAR projects have the potential to transform existing practices.

Plans developed and implemented in four settings (Eleanor and John are a case in point) appear to have seeded transformations that were self-sustaining. Teachers in these four settings were willing to problematize all aspects of their classroom practice, and this condition seems to be a prerequisite to educational transformation. In other settings, "reformed" practices represented little more than brief perturbations that soon dissipated and existing practices were quickly restored. Closer examination of these projects reveals common features. In some cases, teacher-collaborators "were volunteered" by the school principal. Thus, these participants were somewhat coerced and lacked personal commitment to problematizing and improving on their teaching practice. In other cases, volunteer teachers seemed to be unable, or unwilling, to treat any aspect of their practice as problematic. In situations such as the latter two, researcher-collaborators were permitted to make only cosmetic changes to existing practices, and they developed and implemented the action plan with no assistance provided by the teacher-collaborator.

Action research and collaborative action research present novices with a vastly different perspective on what it means to "do research" in education. Personal experience has shown that graduate students whose educational background and training are steeped in the natural sciences, with its positivist, experimentalist research traditions, are at first handicapped, confused, and even bewildered with the notion of engaging in participatory research of any kind. They expect to do research "on the science teacher" or "on science students," not collaborate with teachers and students to improve instruction. Also, the rage to generalize rather than particularize research outcomes dominates newcomers' thinking. What participants come to learn about collaborative action research was best summarized by Lydia following a few weeks of campus and school meetings when she said:

> Within a few classes I realized how much is occurring that I do not know about in the classroom, from K–12 and also college level. It [collaborative action research] has also made me more aware of problems teachers face every day in the classroom.

REFERENCES

Butt, R., Raymond, D., McCue, G., & Yamagishi, L. (1992). Collaborative autobiography and the teacher's voice. In I. F. Goodson (Ed.), *Studying teachers' lives* (pp. 51–98). New York: Teachers College Press.

Carr, W., & Kemmis, S. (1986). *Becoming critical: Education, knowledge, and action research*. Bristol, PA: Falmer.

Carter, K. (1993). The place of story in the study of teaching and teacher education. *Educational Researcher, 22*, 5–12.

Clandinin, D. J. (1993). Teacher education as narrative inquiry. In D. Clandinin, A. Davies, P. Hogan, & B. Kennard (Eds.), *Learning to teach, teaching to learn* (pp. 1–14). New York: Teachers College Press.

Clandinin, D. J., Davies, A., Hogan, P., & Kennard, B. (Eds.). (1993). *Learning to teach, teaching to learn*. New York: Teachers College Press.

Connelly, F. M., & Clandinin, D. J. (1985). Personal practical knowledge and the modes of knowing: Relevance for teaching and learning. In E. Eisner (Ed.), *Learning and teaching the ways of knowing: 84th yearbook of the National Society for the Study of Education* (pp. 174–198). Chicago: University of Chicago Press.

Connelly, F. M., & Clandinin, D. J. (Eds.). (1988). *Teachers as curriculum planners: Narratives of experience*. New York: Teachers College Press.

Corey, S. M. (1953). *Action research to improve school practices*. New York: Teachers College Press.

Cortazzi, M. (1993). *Narrative analysis*. Bristol, PA: Falmer.

Elliott, J. (1991). *Action research for educational change*. Bristol, PA: Taylor & Francis.

Foshay, A. W. (1994). Action research: An early history in the United States. *Journal of Curriculum and Supervision, 9*, 317–325.

Goodson, I. F. (1992). Studying teachers' lives: An emergent field of inquiry. In I. F. Goodson (Ed.), *Studying teachers' lives* (pp. 1–17). New York: Teachers College Press.

Hatch, J. A., & Wisniewski, R. (Eds.). (1995). *Life history and narrative*. Bristol, PA: Falmer.

Jacobson, W. J., & Doran, R. L. (1988). *Science achievement in the United States and sixteen countries: A report to the public*. New York: Teachers College Press.

Josselson, R., & Lieblich, A. (Eds.). (1993). *The narrative study of lives*. Newbury Park, CA: Sage.

Kemmis, S., & McTaggart, R. (Eds.). (1988). *The action research planner* (3rd ed.). Geelong, Victoria, Australia: Deakin University Press.

Kincheloe, J. L. (1991). *Teachers as researchers: Qualitative inquiry as a path to empowerment.* Bristol, PA: Falmer.

Knowles, J. G. (1992). Models for understanding pre-service and beginning teachers' biographies. In I. F. Goodson (Ed.), *Studying teachers' lives* (pp. 99–152). New York: Teachers College Press.

Lincoln, Y. S., & Guba, E. G. (1985). *Naturalistic inquiry.* Newbury Park, CA: Sage.

Lortie, D. C. (1975). *Schoolteacher.* Chicago: University of Chicago Press.

Marshall, H. H. (1990). Beyond the workplace metaphor: The classroom as a learning setting. *Theory Into Practice, 29*(2), 94–101.

McKernan, J. (1994). Teaching educational action research: A tale of three cities. *Educational Action Research, 2*(1), 95–112.

McNiff, J. (1993). *Teaching as learning: An action research approach.* New York: Routledge.

Mullis, I. V., & Jenkins, L. B. (1988). *The science report card: Elements of risk and recovery.* Princeton, NJ: Educational Testing Service.

National Education Goals Panel. (1994). *Data volume for the national education goals report (Volume one: National data).* Washington, DC: U.S. Government Printing Office.

National Research Council. (1996). *National science education standards.* Washington, DC: The National Academy Press.

North Carolina Department of Public Instruction. (1994a). *North Carolina competency-based curriculum (Teacher handbook): Science, K–12.* Raleigh, NC: Author.

North Carolina Department of Public Instruction. (1994b). *A technology plan for North Carolina public schools.* Raleigh, NC: Author.

Oja, S. N., & Smulyan, L. (1989). *Collaborative action research: A developmental approach.* Bristol, PA: Falmer.

Pinar, W. (1988). Whole, bright, deep with understanding: Issues in qualitative research and autobiographical method. In W. Pinar (Ed.), *Contemporary curriculum discourses* (pp. 134–153). Scottsdale, AZ: Gorsuch Scarisbrick.

Raymond, D., Butt, R., & Townsend, D. (1992). Contexts for teacher development: Insights from teachers' stories. In A. Hargreaves & M. Fullan (Eds.), *Understanding teacher development* (pp. 122–142). New York: Teachers College Press.

Reason, P. (Ed.). (1994). *Participation in human inquiry.* Newbury Park, CA: Sage.

Russell, T., & Munby, H. (1991). Reframing: The role of experience in developing teachers' professional knowledge. In D. A. Schön (Ed.), *The reflective turn: Case studies in an on educational practice* (pp. 164–187). New York: Teachers College Press.

Russell, T., & Munby, H. (1992). *Teachers and teaching: From classroom to reflection.* Bristol, PA: Falmer.

Sagor, R. (1992). *How to conduct collaborative action research.* Alexander, VA: Association for Supervision and Curriculum Development.

Schön, D. A. (1983). *The reflective practitioner: How professionals think in action.* New York: Basic Books.

Schön, D. A. (1987). *Educating the reflective practitioner: Toward a new design for teaching and learning in the professions.* San Francisco: Jossey-Bass.

Shymansky, J. A., & Kyle, W. C. (1992). Establishing a research agenda: Critical issues of science curriculum reform. *Journal of Research in Science Teaching, 29,* 749–778.

Somekh, B. (1994). Inhabiting each other's castles: Towards knowledge and mutual growth in collaboration. *Educational Action Research: An International Journal, 2,* 357–381.

Strauss, A., & Corbin, J. (1990). *Basics of qualitative research: Grounded theory procedures and techniques.* Newbury Park, CA: Sage.

U.S. Department of Education. (1996). *Pursuing excellence.* Washington, DC: U.S. Government Printing Office.

van Manen, M. (1990). *Researching lived experience.* Ithaca: State University of New York Press.

10

On Supervising and Being Supervised at a Distance

John A. Malone
Curtin University of Technology, Perth, Western Australia

The history of postgraduate supervision and research in tertiary institutions worldwide is a relatively short one. Even shorter is its history in the technological institutes and amalgamated teachers colleges that have recently gained university status through restructuring in countries such as the United Kingdom and Australia. The struggle to establish undergraduate courses and to accumulate a core of graduate students at these institutions has been a necessary prerequisite to the recruitment of staff trained in postgraduate supervision, the development of postgraduate programs, and the growth of a research culture. This situation has only come about within the last 10 or so years, and the research culture is still in the early stages of growth in these newer institutions. Because of this situation, fast-growing tertiary departments are now experiencing pressure as the ranks of staff qualified to supervise postgraduate students are stretched to the limit by the numbers of students who are choosing to study beyond the undergraduate level, many of them through the distance education mode because they live in an area remote from their university, or even in a different country.

Despite the short time span of these developments, a considerable amount of literature has been published that addresses the role of the supervisor (Connell, 1985; Johnston, 1995; Mauch & Birch, 1989; Moses, 1984, 1985, 1990; Parry & Hayden, 1994; McCormack, 1994; Zuber-Skerritt, 1992) and the role of the research student (Madsen, 1983; Phillips & Pugh, 1987). Not so much has been written, however, on the special difficulties of being a higher degree student while living at a distance from the university where one is enrolled, nor of the special difficulties experienced by those who supervise such students. The reason for this situation appears to be that the various doctoral thesis models used by universities have never included a provision for research students who are unable to spend the majority of their time on campus and so take advantage of the resources available there—for example, access to the library and the close proximity of their supervisors.

Equal opportunity and equity demands that have become established worldwide in recent times, however, have highlighted the disadvantages that these models impose on off-campus students. The burgeoning number of part-time professional postgraduate students in universities has created a major need for courses that relate to the requirements of these professionals, and this means that traditional forms of regular on-campus study are often impractical (Bolton, 1986; Evans & Green, 1995). Evans (1995) pointed out that the research field in any discipline is arguably where the "cutting-edge" changes occur, a notion that many universities have taken up and one that makes the idea of research conducted in the workplace a proposition that many potential students cannot ignore. The task is to blend the requirements of the degree with the needs or requirements of the workplace. Action research—that self-reflective form of inquiry undertaken by participants in social or educational situations in order to improve their own practices or their understanding of these practices—is one example of a research methodology that has created the opportunity for postgraduate researchers and supervisors to work efficiently together although not in close proximity, and many universities are now developing procedures to accommodate research students living both nationally and internationally distant from their alma mater.

This chapter describes some of the issues involved in conducting and supervising postgraduate research at the master's and doctoral levels, carried out under such distance education conditions. It discusses the craft of supervising and of being supervised at a distance—the skills involved—in a specific sense. The views expressed are based partly on the author's experience, gained from working for 20 years with postgraduate science and mathematics education research students in one of the largest centers catering for these students in the world, and partly from reviewing what other writers have said about these matters.

A discussion of the unique problems faced by distance education students and their supervisors is followed by a section describing a number of strategies used in the National Centre for School Science and Mathematics at Curtin University of Technology in Western Australia because of their proven effectiveness in overcoming those problems. The chapter concludes with a section detailing the expectations of support that both distance education students and supervisors are entitled to have about their department or faculty, and also the institution administration, for it is the support from each of these organizational bodies that is so crucial in resourcing and facilitating the efforts of both students and supervisors. It is the author's belief that supervisors can and should influence student-related policy decisions that these administrative bodies establish by means of drawing attention to any shortcoming affecting their students or themselves.

PROBLEMS FACING SUPERVISORS AND STUDENTS

The numbers of postgraduate students studying by the distance education mode is not insignificant, particularly in Australia. It is now the fastest growing mode of study in higher education in that country (Johnson, 1998). It has been estimated that around 70% of Australia's science and mathematics teachers (among the main reader groups for this book) are employed outside the metropolitan areas of its major cities (Distance Education Centre, personal communication, January 15, 1994)—a situation that is probably not unusual in many other countries. For this particular group in society, and indeed for all nonurban dwellers, this remoteness from the conveniences that large-city living brings means that they have little or no direct access to any form of university studies or, in the case of teachers, professional development opportunities on an ongoing basis. Distance education represents the only means that these groups of potential students have of gaining on-the-job opportunities to improve their qualifications and, in the case of teachers, to upgrade their content knowledge and learn more about teaching their subject. Consequently, the availability of distance education services assumes a very important role in the career plans of these people.

Similar comments can be made for international students (those studying on campus) or overseas students (those studying in their own country) who have selected the program of a university in a country other than their own. They make this decision for any one of a number of reasons—for example, the absence of a suitable local postgraduate program; the quality and reputation of the program at the overseas institution; the quality and reputation of the supervisory staff; the availability of financial support through scholarships; and so on. The university of their choice takes on a responsibility when it enrolls these students on a distance education basis, and the problems which these people experience are, rightly, of considerable concern to both the university and those staff members with whom these students are associated.

The literature suggests that the major causes of dissatisfaction among postgraduate students studying by distance education are the failure of supervisors to advise and guide them in the formation of their research questions, and the unsuitability of the design of their study programs (Brown & Atkins, 1988). Of only slightly lesser importance are matters concerned with the supervisors' failure to ensure that students have adequate preparation for data collection and analysis (Delamont & Eggleston, 1983); failure to facilitate the development of their students' report-writing skills (Brown & Atkins, 1988); and failure to realize that different students require different relationships with their supervisors, ranging from a high level of dependency to a high level of autonomy (Cox, 1988; Schön, 1987). When external students appeared on campus to fulfill the residency requirements of their research program, complaints focused principally on the lack of regular meetings between student and supervisor (Rudd, 1985; Wright & Lodwick, 1989) and the inadequate resources and workspace which the university provided (Barker, Hall, Chung, Low, & Shoebridge, 1995).

Other concerns for overseas students, according to Barker et al. (1995), relate to the lack of information they receive about the assistance that they might expect from their supervisors prior to enrollment, and the slow turn-around of work submitted to supervisors. On the first of these matters, Parry and Hayden (1994) reported that there is widespread concern among supervisors concerning the extent of their involvement in improving the quality of the writing of their overseas students' theses. This was especially so in cases where English was not the students' first language, where students' skills at written expression were lacking, or where students had trouble with the discourse of the discipline. Such information comes from a database that is relatively sparse, because so few tertiary institutions have, so far, taken postgraduate research students whose only physical presence at the institution may be a relatively brief residency, perhaps as short as 6 months (Smawfield, 1989). The National Centre for School Science and Mathematics has gained considerable experience with this mode of study, and its staff members have acquired a sound understanding of the nature of carrying out and supervising research with this little-understood group of students. The following section first explains the approach to distance education adopted by the Centre and then considers some specific problems associated with postgraduate research and supervision which the Centre's staff members have encountered and dealt with. The issues are drawn from each stage of the distance education student's program, from consideration of his or her readiness to undertake research and the supervisor's ability to supervise it, to the final stages of thesis writing.

RESEARCH AND SUPERVISION
AT CURTIN'S NATIONAL CENTRE

Curtin University has been involved in distance education for a considerable time in Western Australia, having commenced this service to its students in 1967. Likewise, staff members in the National Centre have been providing distance education in science and mathematics to postgraduate students since 1978. The Centre has an annual enrollment of around 350 postgraduate students, 80% of whom are Australians. The remainder consist of students from many overseas countries including New Zealand, the United States, Israel, Indonesia, Nigeria, Brunei, Japan, Singapore, Hong Kong, and Malaysia. Most students are practicing science, mathematics, or computing teachers and educators, although a handful are enrolled in allied health fields—for instance, nursing education, occupational therapy, and agricultural education. A considerable amount of expertise in the delivery and maintenance of a distance education program has been built up over the years, and it is appropriate to describe some of the features of the Centre's delivery program that appear to account for its success in training a significant proportion of the largest group of postgraduate students specifically enrolled in science and mathematics education courses in the world.

Before commencing a thesis, students at the National Centre are introduced to coursework units that prepare them for this task if this is considered a necessary prerequisite. These are units of a semester's duration designed to raise their awareness of issues and trends in science and mathematics education; units designed to inform them about how to design a research project, how to conduct research, how to analyze the data they collect and how to write up and report their results. For the distance education student, this information comes mainly through printed materials—a set of guidelines for the conduct of the unit, together with a package of reading materials appropriate for the course, and a schedule of assignments to be submitted for assessment. Resources are not confined to printed materials. Audiotapes and videotapes are used to support the written word, and staff and students use telephone and fax extensively to communicate with one another. Delivery through electronic mail and the internet is growing in use exponentially as facilities become available in the schools and offices where students work.

At this stage in students' programs, the support and feedback provided to them by Centre staff are intensive. Individual staff members are themselves supported in this task by the efforts of a Distance Education Centre at the university that coordinates the dispatch and return of materials and assignments from students to tutors. Staff members strive to achieve a turnaround time for assignments of no longer than a week, and students appreciate this aspect of tutorship and respond to it. Although it is relatively easy to maintain intensive student–tutor communications throughout a single semester unit of coursework, the same is not generally true for the research component of the program where, because of the nature of the task, students must work by themselves for extensive periods with irregular input from their supervisors.

When the coursework component of the program is completed by those students who require it, they are eligible to move into the thesis component and put their newfound knowledge to use. Students who had no need for prerequisite studies would have moved directly into thesis preparation. Very early in the supervisory relationship, the student should be made aware of the expectations and standards of the supervisor, who should also inform the student of the standards to which the thesis or dissertation should conform. It is the supervisor's job to ensure that there are adequate resources available to assist students in gaining access to research facilities and needed materials. Supervisors should have a sound knowledge of the rules and regulations concerning postgraduate study, including courses offered by distance education, the sequence of events, and the deadline dates that will affect the distance education student. In most universities, the supervisor is responsible for ensuring that postgraduate deadlines are followed, and this is the type of information that often makes little impact on off-campus students, so placing a heavy responsibility on supervisors to ensure that this information is clarified for them. Some of the issues that confront both on-campus and off-campus students throughout the thesis preparation phase of their postgraduate studies, and some of the strategies adopted by their National Centre supervisors to assist them, are discussed in the following sections.

Students' Preparedness for Research

This matter assumes enormous importance in the case of distance education students. The existence of appropriate background studies in research methods is crucial if their programs are to commence and run smoothly as they work on their own. The university's own entry requirements for admission into a postgraduate research program indicate the minimum background studies required, but a necessary precursor is also the postgraduates' self-assessed state of preparedness, with a particular focus on their research skills and (in the case of overseas students from non-English-speaking countries) competence in the English language.

Hall (1995) argued that supervisors need training in how to advise their students on the strength of the prerequisite qualifications they possess, and also on their English language competencies, with particular attention being paid to their skills in academic writing. Most universities have a literacy policy and provide research methods courses for on-campus students, but these are not always available to the distance education student. Part of the postgraduate's residency period can be devoted toward offsetting these deficiencies as far as possible in the time available. A minimum prerequisite for postgraduates is that they have completed a project in the recent past that has involved them in identifying a research topic; planning and carrying out the study; analyzing and interpreting the data; drawing conclusions; and writing up the results. It is difficult to imagine students being admitted into a research master's or doctoral program without this experience behind them.

Supervisors also need to consider carefully whether or not they are able to carry out their job effectively before accepting this responsible position. Moses (1985) suggested that there are a number of questions that need answers provided by the supervisor; for example:

> What is my philosophy concerning higher degree studies? Do I feel responsible for all aspects of the students' work and do I need to keep control, or should my students plan and persevere on their own and only come to me for advice? (p. 13)

It is important, too, that supervisors are clear about and can identify the areas and levels of research they can supervise. It is equally important that they be aware of their own strengths and limitations in research methodology and that students be advised if only general assistance can be provided. Consequently, being a supervisor involves a two-way process—for example, openness about one's own and one's student's competence; openness about the standard of student output and one's own input; and openness about the extent that one regards a student as a junior colleague and what this entails. Such matters take on increased significance for the distance education supervisor in a situation in which they may not be discussed face-to-face.

Prerequisite Studies

As mentioned earlier, prerequisite coursework is required of a students if their level of entry does not meet the university's standards of entry to the postgraduate program. Several prerequisite units are available on the Internet at Curtin University, facilitating access to an enormous number of literature resources, as described in the chapters that follow by Squires, and by Rillero and Gallegos. The Internet unit incorporates an interactive discussion group facility that enables students to network with one another and the unit coordinator, share experiences, ask questions of one another and the coordinator, exchange information, and generally support one another in overcoming their isolation.

Choosing a Research Topic

The initial choice of a research topic is perhaps the first issue that will be troublesome for both student and supervisor if each is located in a different part of the country and even more so if they live in different countries. Possible research topics will vary in importance, feasibility, and viability, and the supervisor must ensure that the candidate becomes involved with a significant topic regardless of where the research will be conducted—research that is expected to produce a thesis of merit and, in the case of a PhD, break new ground and make a distinct contribution to knowledge in the area. The study should be straightforward, manageable in terms of the student's occupational situation, and capable of being completed in a reasonable period of time.

For students, it is most important that their research topics should be of interest and motivating to them, and of course, compatible with the research field of their supervisor. Ideally, distance students should be encouraged to find out the research interests of staff and canvass one or more to seek a supervisor. This process can be greatly assisted by the provision of a simple publication that lists staff members and their interests. Many university postgraduate research departments provide such a publication for this purpose, as does the National Centre (1995). Students will be involved with their topic for a considerable period, often working on their own, and nothing can be worse than involvement with a topic in which they become disinterested or find irrelevant as time goes by. Action research—that self-reflective form of inquiry undertaken by participants (teachers, for example) in social or educational situations in order to improve their own practices or their understanding of these practices—is often the best form of inquiry under these circumstances, focused as it can be within the student's own classroom or other workplace, being of immediate interest to the student, and convenient to organize and control.

Planning the Research

The importance of careful planning cannot be overemphasized, particularly for the distance education student. Madsen (1983) identified inadequate collection of data because of poor planning in the handling of the material, and overall lack of time in planning as among the most common causes of on-campus postgraduates' delays in the completion of theses on time, or at all. The risk of this situation occurring among distance education students is far greater unless there are checks in place to ensure that the work schedule that must be planned at the outset of the study is maintained. The supervisor must insist that the postgraduate prepares a comprehensive research proposal covering all aspects of the proposed study.

The need for such a proposal is considered so important at Curtin University that the distant education student is given one full year after enrollment to complete the document before candidacy in the doctoral program is confirmed. During this time, student and supervisor work on the plan and on the preparation of the proposal, which contains six sections: (a) an introduction, in which the student states the background to the perceived problem under study, why it is important, and how the research process will contribute to its solution; (b) the goals or aims of the study, stated in terms of one or more research questions or interrogative sentences that seek the relationship between the research variables; (c) a review of the relevant research and theory, consisting of an integrated statement that provides an explanation of why the authors, theories, and studies cited are important and relevant to the study under consideration; (d) a statement of the methodology to be adopted, including a description of the framework to be employed and the research design; (e) a statement of the significance of the study—how it will contribute to the literature on the subject, how it will break new ground and who will be interested in the results; and (f) a brief bibliography that will form the foundation for the comprehensive list that will constitute part of the final thesis.

Sampling, Data Collection, and Analysis

Sampling and data collection carried out by postgraduate science and mathematics education students often takes place in educational institutions—schools, colleges, or tertiary institutions—in which higher study is encouraged and where it is accepted that staff members become involved in professional development activities. The location of these educational institutions is immaterial, especially if action research is involved, so, as far as data collection is concerned, being an external student is usually of little disadvantage. Although the data collection stage is one in which less student–supervisor interaction is necessary, the supervisor certainly needs to check on sampling methods adopted, and ensure that data are collected in an appropriate form; otherwise, they may be unrepresentative or may be lost or not collected, necessitating the inconvenience and cost of a second, later collection.

It follows that supervisors should assist distance education students in designing their study and encourage them to sample and collect data on-site as much as possible—within their own classroom or locality—so that, in attempting to circumvent the difficulties like those mentioned earlier, other potentially troublesome factors may also be minimized, including the time and distance taken in traveling to research sites and the costs in both time and resources that accompany studies of a geographically widespread nature.

Data Analysis

When it comes to data analysis, most distance education students need a considerable amount of assistance. This is an area of the study program that should be considered and planned before data gathering to ensure that data collected lend themselves to the analysis required. If students cannot arrange to have their data analysis carried out locally, then their supervisors should organize their number crunching and should assist them to interpret their data. The majority of students find the data analysis aspect of their research most daunting and need much encouragement and support. Despite the number of research methods units students may have studied, they are usually eager to seek a second opinion on their findings. Such advice is sometimes beyond the expertise of a student's supervisor, and the advice of an expert will be sought. The supervisor then takes on a facilitator role, ensuring that the student is kept advised of the progress of this activity, and then ensuring that the results can be interpreted by the student.

Backup Supervision

This problem of the remoteness of the distance education student can be alleviated somewhat by the appointment of an associate supervisor who becomes familiar with the student's work and who will be readily available to assist the student on those occasions when the associate's special expertise is needed or when the supervisor is absent. The student should be informed well in advance of any absences and may even have a say in the selection of an associate supervisor. Although this person is usually another staff member, other arrangements can be made. Often a suitably qualified person located in the student's hometown or a nearby town can be appointed. Students themselves may be able to nominate an appropriate person.

Arranging Face-to-Face Contact

The need for postgraduate distance education students to spend time on campus to meet their supervisors face-to-face, to attend to any deficiencies that exist in their preparation, and to meet university residency requirements is clear. Preferably, external students should be on campus at the beginning of their program, during the research proposal stage, during the major data analysis period, and during the final write-up stages. It cannot always work out this way, but it is best to ensure that students realize that being on campus is the best way to ensure access to the literature and to ensure that certain parts of the research are completed most effectively and efficiently. Of course, these residency periods should be planned to coincide with the supervisor's availability too. The student should be encouraged to visit the supervisor at every opportunity that presents itself, no matter how short the duration of the visit and, similarly, the supervisor should make efforts to visit the student if and when he is in the neighborhood. Many universities fund visits by supervisors to their students once or twice a year, or, alternatively, fund students to visit the campus.

Involving Students in the Supervisor's Work

There are two things that supervisors can do that will be of great benefit to their students. In the first case, the action will demonstrate to students the best and worst features of thesis or journal article writing, and in the second, it makes them aware, in the most realistic way possible, of the standard of thesis preparation to which they aspire. These suggestions are based on the assumption that research students will be regarded as the junior colleagues of their supervisors and entitled to share their supervisors' work—"be collaborated with," as Liston (1994) put it.

The suggestion here relates to the practice of supervisors involving their students in some of their academic duties—for example, passing journal articles sent to them for comment or blind review onto one or more of their students to review collaboratively. The student is then expected to prepare a critique of the article that provides the basis for a discussion session when both student and supervisor have completed the task. This discussion need not be face-to-face, but can be conducted by telephone, fax, or e-mail. Supervisor and student can benefit from this activity, as can the author under review, who usually receives feedback of a most comprehensive nature.

A similar strategy can be adopted with theses sent for a supervisor to examine. In this case, the supervisor's student prepares an examiner's report on the thesis and submits it to the supervisor for discussion. Again, all can learn a great deal from this experience. Care must be taken regarding the ethics of these situations—details of the author of the article or the thesis candidate, along with the origins of the thesis, should remain anonymous, in deference to the confidentiality requirements surrounding the article or thesis preparation. Also, supervisor and student must remember that authors are protected by law against unauthorized use of their work, and reviewers and examiners may not quote or cite an author's unpublished work without permission.

These two activities, which involve students being given the privilege of engaging in responsible tasks, knowing that they enjoy their supervisors' confidence in handling the job competently, and sharing with their supervisors and learning from and with them in real situations, can have a significant bonding effect and enhance the rapport between them.

Writing the Thesis

Supervisors invariably feel obliged to correct students' written work, but will be concerned about the extent of such assistance in theses that are meant to represent the candidates' own work. The issue here is whether or not it is only the ideas that constitute students' contribution to knowledge, or both the words and the manner in which they translate those ideas into the written word. This is not a clear-cut issue, and in order to decide how far to go with a student's writing, many supervisors work to the following rules: they will go to great lengths to correct or even rewrite students' material presented at the early postgraduate level (project work, and so on), but they are less obliging at the master's and doctoral levels, preferring to discuss matters of substance with the student, indicating problem areas, unsuitable or inappropriate prose and better phraseology and terminology, then leave it to the student to make the corrections. The idea of having someone else read material before it is submitted is a good one, no matter who is doing the writing—experienced writers do this and it is a must for students.

Turnaround of Submitted Material

Supervisors must be conscious of the need for rapid turnaround of material (project/thesis results and chapter drafts) sent by students to them. Nothing is more frustrating for the external student than to submit work only to have it disappear for a long period without any feedback. This communication is two-way, however. Distance education students should maintain regular contact with their supervisor by mail, telephone, e-mail, or fax. Many supervisors request this communication on a bi- or tri-weekly basis. Students appreciate this commitment as it keeps them focused amidst the pressures of work, family, and other demands on their time. One method of ensuring that this happens is for the supervisor to encourage students to submit regular progress reports. This requirement keeps students on task and means that their work appears regularly before their supervisors for appraisal.

Keeping Students Informed

Unlike distance education students, internal postgraduate research students often meet regularly to report their findings, discuss their data, and present at colloquia. It has been found useful for distance education students to be kept informed of the activities of these meetings, for it serves the purpose of reducing their isolation by communicating findings, news, and research ideas on a regular basis. A short report on the proceedings of the class or colloquium lets them know that they are part of the larger group. In the event that students are able to visit the campus, they should be encouraged to join the colloquia group to meet their colleagues, perhaps report on their work, and generally develop links with their fellow students.

Combating the Isolation

This issue was mentioned earlier, in relation to the discussion group facility available to students studying units via the Internet. Not all distance education students will have the advantage of this resource, hence there is a need to provide these students with alternative safety nets that allow them to discuss the tasks they face with their fellow students and supervisors, so helping them combat the isolation under which they work. Student networking is one such safety net. If the student is made aware of other students working nearby, then a supportive network can be established which can ease the burden of working alone. An introduction to a network of fellow students and scholars in the postgraduate student's area of interest is a powerful source of input and can motivate students to sustain their efforts until the completion of their degree. The availability of e-mail and its bulletin board is of enormous value here and favors those students who have access to this method of communication, for it means that they can interact with each other regardless of where they are located.

Submitting the Thesis

It is the supervisor's responsibility to let the student know when a draft thesis is suitable for examination, to follow through the administrative procedures associated with the examination process, and even to deal with the task of finding and nominating suitable examiners. Most often, distance education students complete their thesis write-up at home. This means that the responsibility for carrying out a number of administrative chores concerning the submission of the completed thesis that a full-time or on-campus student would normally do fall to the supervisor. Although students and supervisors may have no official input into the choice of examiners, they can suggest possible examiners informally, for their knowledge of the scholars and of the literature on the topic place them in an advantageous position to offer such advice. In addition, supervisors should be aware of help lines and counseling services available to all students, and scholarships and other sources of funding available, particularly as they relate to the special needs of distance education students. Financial support for the student may be available from the supervisor's own research funds or contracts and could be used to assist students to attend appropriate conferences to deliver collaboratively prepared papers.

WHAT CAN STUDENTS AND SUPERVISORS EXPECT FROM THEIR INSTITUTION?

Both distance education students and their supervisors are entitled to certain expectations of support from their department or faculty, and also from their institution's administration, for it is the support of each of these bodies that is crucial in resourcing and facilitating the efforts of both student and supervisor. Supervisors have a voice in policy formulation matters and can and should make efforts to influence the decisions related to distance education taken by these administrative bodies. Although many initiatives concerning students are the responsibility of the students' supervisors, clearly many others fall squarely on the university itself.

Moses (1990) has written about "good departmental and institutional practices" that reflect both students' and supervisors' views on the assistance they want and should be able to expect from their university. These practices include, first, financial assistance, which eases the expenses incurred by students moving from undergraduate to graduate study, provides funds for students to attend the university for residency periods, and can enable students to attend conferences, conduct library searches, photocopy work, and undertake extracurricular activities such as fieldwork. Second, they can cover access to child care for those students with young families. Third, they can provide information and regulations about graduate study and employment. Two other points Moses addressed concern the relationship between students and staff and the integration of students into a research culture—their initiation into scholarly communities. Specifically, these points refer to (a) the students' expectations of access to experienced staff who are well qualified to supervise their research and who will serve as role models and mentors, and (b) the provision of a vibrant research environment. These factors are just as important to supervisors (who are influenced in their work by the context in which they teach and carry out research) as they are to the student.

Over the years at the National Centre, distance education students have been asked to suggest improvements in doctoral supervision. Suggestions have focused mainly on the need for better induction—a firsthand introduction to the university and fellow students for new students who may not visit the campus until some time into their program. In this regard, the university should shoulder the overall responsibility by organizing a university-wide induction program for new students which would include information about, say, doctoral regulations and procedures; an introduction to the university's external studies library, and details of the various avenues of contact that may be utilized to initiate and maintain contact with the supervisor and other university personnel. The university should also provide each new student with user-friendly documentation that specifies its regulations and procedures, as well as the roles and expectations of supervisors, associate supervisors, and students. As at many other universities, National Centre full-time students are provided with computing and library facilities, room and office space, technical equipment, a desk, and access to telephone, fax, e-mail, and stationery. Seminars, research group meetings, colloquia, and contact with distinguished visiting speakers and experts are also among the opportunities available to the on-campus student.

For supervisors, the National Centre attempts to ensure that the staff members' supervision loads are not too great for them to do their job well, that they are encouraged to apply for research grants and to conduct their own research programs. They are given financial and other forms of assistance to attend conferences and to publish the results of their research.

Where such privileges exist, the research and supervision environment at the postgraduate center will be conducive to good working relationships between staff and students and between staff and the administration. The experience becomes a positive and encouraging one when student and staff member see one another primarily as colleagues, and only in a secondary sense as mentor and student. The benefits to students and supervisors are many when the administration considers the individuals involved and promotes a caring research culture. In the words of Zuber-Skerritt and Ryan (1994):

> Departments and institutions, as much as supervisors, influence the quality of supervision which academics can give. We need to move away from placing all of the responsibility onto one supervisor to a collaborative system in which input and responsibility are shared, but without detracting from the mentoring opportunities which benefit our research students. (p. 78)

CONCLUSION

Postgraduate study usually becomes a very intense activity, and the task ahead of the postgraduate distance education student engaged in project or thesis work is a particularly onerous one. Similarly, postgraduate supervision at a distance is a very difficult task. The strategies of research and supervision described in this chapter have been developed over a long period of time and have been found to assist large numbers of students working in isolation. They are the tools of supervisors, and their effectiveness depends on how well they are put to use by individual staff members. This in turn influences the degree to which the efforts of the supervisors are received and acted on by the students. The quality of staff and students are key variables in the success of the assistance provided to postgraduate students studying at a distance. Various other assistance strategies are undoubtedly in use in other institutions in which distance education is available, and it is a responsibility of all those engaged in supervision and research to make themselves familiar with efficient and effective ways of carrying out these tasks.

REFERENCES

Barker, J., Hall, J., Chung, A., Low, J., & Shoebridge, A. (1995). *Improving the quality of postgraduate supervision at Curtin University*. Perth, Western Australia: Curtin University of Technology.
Bolton, G. (1986). The opportunity of distance. *Distance Education, 7*(1), 5–22.
Brown, G., & Atkins, M. (1988). *Effective teaching in higher education*. London: Methuen.
Connell, R. (1985). How to supervise a PhD. *The Australian Universities Review, 28*(2), 38–41.

Cox, R. (Ed.). (1988). Postgraduate research training. In *Reviews of literature and data sources: The characteristics of the training process and those undergoing research training* (pp. 37–45). London: Institute of Education.

Delamonte, S., & Eggleston, J. (1983). A necessary isolation? In J. Eggleston & S. Delamont (Eds.), *Supervision of students for research degrees* (pp. 117–145). Birmingham, England: British Educational Research Association.

Evans, T. (1995). Postgraduate research supervision in the emerging "open" universities. *The Australian Universities Review, 38*(2), 23–27.

Evans, T., & Green, B. (1995, November). *Dancing at a distance? Postgraduate studies, "supervision" and distance education.* Paper presented at the 25th Annual National Conference of the Australian Association for Research in Education, Hobart, Tasmania, Australia.

Hall, J. (1995, February). *What counts as a "good" research supervisor: A case study of overseas postgraduates at Curtin University.* Paper presented at the Teaching and Learning Forum, Edith Cowan University, Perth, Western Australia.

Johnson, R. (1998). To wish and to will: Reflections on policy formation and implementation. In T. D. Evans & D. E. Nation (Eds.), *Opening education: Policies and practices from open and distance education.* London: Routledge.

Liston, R. (1994). *Graduate student–supervisor relationships: A review of Canadian university policies and regulations.* Toronto: Canadian Graduate Council.

Mauch, J. E., & Birch, J. W. (1989). *Guide to the successful thesis and dissertation: Conception to publication. A guidebook for students and faculty* (2nd ed.). New York and Basel: Marcel Dekker.

McCormack, C. (1994). *Constructive and supportive postgraduate supervision: A guide for supervisors.* Canberra, Australian Capital Territory: University of Canberra.

Madsen, D. (1983). *Successful dissertations and theses.* San Francisco: Jossey-Bass.

Moses, I. (1984). Supervision of higher degree students. *Higher Education Research and Development, 3*(2), 153–165.

Moses, I. (1985). *Supervising postgraduates.* Kensington, Australia: Higher Education Research and Development Society of Australasia, University of New South Wales.

Moses, I. (1990). *Barriers to women's participation as postgraduate students.* Canberra, Australian Capital Territory: Australian Government Publishing Service.

National Key Centre for School Science and Mathematics. (1995). *Research interests of staff.* Perth, Western Australia: Curtin University of Technology.

Parry, S., & Hayden, M. (1994). *Supervising higher degree research students. An investigation of practices across a range of academic departments.* Canberra, Australian Capital Territory: Department of Employment, Education, and Training.

Phillips, E. M., & Pugh, D. S. (1987). *How to get a PhD: A handbook for students and their supervisors.* Buckinghamshire, England: Open University.

Rudd, E. (1985). *A new look at postgraduate failure.* London: Society for Research in Higher Education.

Schön, D. (1987). *Educating the reflective practitioner.* London: Jossey-Bass.

Smawfield, D. (1989). The supervision of overseas students: A bridge between two cultures. *Supervision in Education, 39*, 51–61.

Wright, J., & Lodwick, R. (1989). The process of the PhD: A case study of the first year of doctoral study. *Research Papers in Education, 4*, 22–56.

Zuber-Skerritt, O. (Ed.). (1992). *Starting research–supervision and training.* Brisbane, Australia: University of Queensland Press.

Zuber-Skerritt, O., & Ryan, Y. (Eds.). (1994). *Quality in postgraduate education.* London: Kogan Page.

11

Legitimate Peripheral Participation in the Training of Researchers in Mathematics and Science Education

Wolff-Michael Roth
University of Victoria

Michelle K. McGinn
Simon Fraser University

Scene 1. The professor, Michael, is interviewing Celia, a Grade 6 student from the class involved in a study on science learning. Two graduate students initially unfamiliar with research in science education, Michelle and Carolyn, sit next to him; a research assistant, Sylvie, films the interview. At first, Michelle and Carolyn follow the interview quietly; later, they begin to ask a few questions themselves. To them, it's a dry run, for, on the next day, they conduct interviews with other students on their own. After Celia has left, the research team of four (Michael, Michelle, Carolyn, and Sylvie) debriefs about important conceptual aspects of physics to be probed in the interviews, about the interview protocol and details, and about details of the artifacts used to stimulate children's talk.

Scene 2. The research team of four comes together in front of Celia's classroom just before Michael begins teaching another lesson. Michael and Michelle provide Carolyn with a few suggestions for the interviews she is to conduct during the lesson with individual children; they suggest that Carolyn take the children into the hallway to reduce the noise level on the audiotape she uses to record the interviews. Michelle and Sylvie check with Michael for details of the lesson that will affect the way they operate the two video cameras.

Scene 3. The four sit around a low table on which there is a flip chart marked in different colored text and a few diagrams. A map of Celia's classroom printed on acetate marked with colored lines also lies there. A video camera records this data analysis session; this record will become a secondary data source.

At the moment, they are clarifying the distinction between two of their theoretical concepts, resources and tool-related practices:

Michelle: And also, as we saw, you don't need the hammer to be able to do it. You can use your liquid paper, your screwdriver, there are ways around.

Carolyn: But see, then, where is that, is that a resource? Or is it?

Michael: No, a resource means it's just the object.

Michelle: The resource is that object.

Carolyn: Great. So that hammer is a resource.

Sylvie: But when you use it.

Michael: But when you are hammering.

Carolyn: It's a tool-related practice.

Scene 4. The four are meeting to discuss the first draft of an article Michael has written based on their data analysis in sessions such as Scene 3. Michelle, Carolyn, and Sylvie have read the draft, and now ask questions for clarification, point out inconsistencies, and ask to check some of the claims against the data sources and against the records. Later, Michael asks Michelle, the more experienced of the two graduate students, to write a specific part of the findings section. Two months later, Michelle, Sylvie, and Michael present their paper during a poster session at a conference for research in science teaching, and subsequently publish it in a journal for research in science education.

These four scenes are autobiographical and come from our research project in a Grade 6 and 7 classroom in which Michael taught a unit on simple machines (cf. McGinn, Roth, Boutonné, & Woszczyna, 1995). In the scenes, two graduate students and a research assistant engage in various aspects of a study alongside an experienced researcher in science education. Rather than trying to implement directives for data collection from a professor sitting in an office, or learning in some haphazard way, the three relative newcomers to research in science education learn central aspects of doing research in practice, at the actual site of the research, and at the elbows from the more experienced researcher. Rather than sending graduate students and research assistants to do "slave labor," the professor considers that the three will learn essential elements of conducting interviews to elicit students' scientific and mathematical understandings only by participating in all aspects of the research. Even among the three, research competence is not equally distributed. Michelle, having participated in various research projects for some time, is, relative to Carolyn, already an old-timer, and assists the latter in learning important aspects of doing research in science and mathematics education. With respect to the transformation of video-based data, Carolyn and Michelle are relative newcomers compared to Sylvie, so that they learn important aspects of transcribing scientific discourse (including verbal and nonverbal aspects and actions) from the latter.

At the same time, Carolyn, a student in the master's program of counseling psychology, teaches the other members of the team about interviewing more generally. Here we see a small community with members who have different levels and areas of expertise. Expertise is heterogeneously distributed; that is, if one were to rank members of the group across areas according to expertise, the rankings would be different. By participating in research together, members learn from each other.

The purpose of this chapter is to outline a conception of learning to do research in science and mathematics education that takes practice as its core theoretical notion. The central locus of a practice is a community of practice. Essential aspects of any practice cannot be acquired by reading books or following verbal instructions at a distance from the actual site of the practice. In communities of practice, newcomers learn much of the craft by participating with old-timers in legitimate and initially peripheral ways. Eventually they become old-timers themselves. Doing independent research in science and mathematics education on their own too early in the process, graduate students would miss important opportunities to be enculturated to the specific practices of doing research in the domain.

In the next section, we expose one of the fundamental problems in learning to do research. We then provide a conceptual framework for understanding educational learning in communities of practice. Subsequently, we provide three examples from our own situation at Simon Fraser University that illustrate the main theoretical issues. Under Discussion and Implications, we outline some of the contradictions and problems with traditional approaches and our own approach to educating graduate students.

EXPOSING THE PROBLEM: DOING CODING

The following advice regarding coding is presented to novices by a widely used textbook of educational and social science research methods:

- Make codes exhaustive of the response range but mutually exclusive so that a given response will always carry the same code.
- Check consistency of coding across coders and over time. Determine the desired coding of certain sheets and slip them in the batch at random intervals to provide a coding audit.
- Provide each coder with a coding manual, and keep all manuals up-to-date as resolutions of coding problems are agreed on. (Krathwohl, 1993, p. 388)

Directions such as these make it seem as if coding is simply a matter of converting instructions or coding categories to the data at hand. These accounts suggest that novices can learn research by following instructions provided by detailed manuals. However, those with experience in coding (Schoenfeld, 1992) and those who research actual coding work (Garfinkel, 1967) paint a different picture. Learning to code cannot be done in general but has to be situated in the domain-specific practices of the relevant community.

Garfinkel (1967) and his colleagues observed coders of actual patient files to answer the question, "By what criteria are an outpatient clinic's applicants selected for treatment?" Their work showed that "coders were assuming knowledge of the very organized ways of the clinic that their coding procedures were intended to produce descriptions of" (p. 20). This knowledge appeared to be necessary to decide what really happened, regardless of whether they had encountered ambiguous file contents. Garfinkel concluded:

> No matter how definitely and elaborately instructions had been written, and despite the fact that strict actuarial coding rules could be formulated for every item, and with which folder contents *could* be mapped into the coding sheet, insofar as the claim had to be advanced that Coding Sheet entries reported real events of the clinic's activities, then in every instance, and for every item, "et cetera," "unless," "let it pass," and "factum valet" accompanied the coder's grasp of the coding instructions as ways of analyzing actual folder contents. (p. 21)

Ad hoc considerations in coding are irremediable and essential features of the act of coding. It makes little sense to treat ad hoc features of the coding work as if they were a nuisance or, from the coders' perspectives, to treat these features as grounds for complaints about the incompleteness of coding instructions.

A quarter century after Garfinkel's work was published, Schoenfeld (1992), who had worked for quite some time from a cognitive science perspective to mathematics education with assumptions not unlike Krathwohl (the author of the research methods text cited earlier), came to conclusions that were remarkably similar to those of Garfinkel. In the context of achieving reliability in coding mathematical problem solving, two or more coders need to see the world in very much the same way. This, however, is not achievable by means of written procedures and specifications. Schoenfeld realized that some experience in coding tapes of mathematical problem solving jointly was necessary to achieve the consensus that produced consistency; that is, written descriptions of the coding method did not suffice to define just how to get the "grain size" of a particular mathematical problem-solving episode. Coders made distinctions on the basis of "feel" rather than on specified, clean objective criteria. Much of the mathematical and analytic knowledge it took to code the tapes in a consistent way was not expressed in the coding protocols, despite the researchers' efforts to make them as explicit as possible. Much of the knowledge it took to code the tapes resided within Schoenfeld's research group. Schoenfeld concluded that this knowledge was not communicable by means of descriptions: "Employing the [coding] method is a matter of skilled practice, probably best learned in apprenticeship. That practice is rationalizeable and its results are defensible after the fact, but is not easily conveyed in a user's manual" (p. 208).

The lower interrater reliabilities observed between different research teams rather than within a team lies in part in the gap that exists between any description and the event so that, for example, researchers who want to replicate an experiment are frequently unable to achieve the correspondence previously achieved by the original investigator between what was actually observed and the intended event for which the observation is treated as evidence (Garfinkel, 1967).

Coding is but one example of the many aspects of research as practice. To be able to do educational research, a graduate student in mathematics and science education may be expected to learn how to design, test, and validate a questionnaire; plan and conduct an open-ended and unstructured interview; collect videotaped episodes from a science laboratory and conduct a discourse analysis; and engage many other aspects of quantitative research, qualitative research, or both. Central to our framework is the idea that the best way of learning to do research is to participate in varied aspects of research with one or more experienced practitioners. Learning is understood as a trajectory from legitimate peripheral to core participation in a community that practices educational research.

CONCEPTUAL FRAMEWORK

Research as Practice

Much recent research in the social sciences has debunked the myth of human activity as a rational pursuit of goals by application of rule-based knowledge, and has suggested that human cognition is fundamentally situated in and distributed across specific social and physical settings (Garfinkel & Wieder, 1992; Lave, 1988; Suchman, 1987). Most human activities are thus better understood in terms of practices. Practices are discursive and physical actions in specific settings. Although tools and many other characteristics of two settings may be the same, they often give rise to distinctly different practices. Thus, carpenters and cabinetmakers use chisels on wood, but they do so in essentially different ways. Conceptual tools such as mathematical formulae equally differ when they are used by engineers or physicists

(Brown, Collins, & Duguid, 1989); and aircraft engineering designs give rise to different discourse practices when used by design engineers, workers on the shop floor, stockroom managers, sales personnel, or general accountants (Henderson, 1991; Star, 1989). Within each of these communities, practices are relatively homogeneous and characterized by the conventions, standards, behaviors, or viewpoints that their members (practitioners) share.

Legitimate Peripheral Participation

There is an accumulating body of research studies on knowing and learning in a variety of scientific domains that supports the claims that essential aspects of any practice cannot be learned through reading or listening to lectures, whether the practice relates to a specific technique in microbiological analysis (K. Jordan & Lynch, 1993), Mayan midwifery (B. Jordan, 1989), detectors in physics research (Traweek, 1988), architectural design (Schön, 1987), or sociological research (Bourdieu, 1992). Rather, these aspects are appropriated (taught) through modes that are thoroughly practical, in the context of ongoing authentic activities in the domain. Lave and Wenger (1991) proposed the notion of legitimate peripheral participation to describe learning that is an "integral part of a generative social practice in the lived-in world" (p. 35). The adjective "legitimate" of this irreducible concept addresses the fact that newcomers participate in the activities of a community rather than being excluded from such activities (for example, high school students do not, in most cases, participate in legitimate ways in the discourses of the sciences they are to learn). The adjective "peripheral" denotes the fact that newcomers do not yet participate fully in the practices that characterize the community; phenomenologically, they participate in the world only partially in the way core members of the community do because newcomers look at the world and act in it in different ways. For example, graduate students, though participating in their advisors' research, are not responsible for the research in all its aspects.

The notion of *legitimate peripheral participation* implies that to really understand how to design and conduct research, students need to have opportunities to experience *how research is actually carried out*; they need to have opportunities to participate in research. Bourdieu (1992) suggested:

> There is no manner of mastering the fundamental principles of a practice—the practice of scientific research is no exception here—than by practicing it along-side a kind of guide or coach who provides assurance and reassurance, who sets an example and who corrects you by putting forth, *in situation*, precepts applied directly to the *particular case* at hand. (p. 221, emphasis in the original)

To learn to write research reports, students have to participate in writing reports with someone who already is very familiar with this practice. Students need to experience all the false starts, wavering, impasses, renunciations, and situated decisions that after the fact, are rationalized and defended on the basis of some rule. However, what rules do not contain are descriptions of why in one situation they might be applied in a way that seems contradictory with their application in another situation.

Bourdieu (1992) further suggested that, to become researchers, graduate students have to break with their intuitive understandings of the world, a break that is facilitated when students participate in the culture of research; that is, educating social science researchers involves something of an "epistemological rupture" (p. 251), a break with viewing the world as students have done before, and a new beginning that includes the bracketing of ordinary preconstructions and common sense to make them a topic for research. This rupture demands something of a *conversion of one's gaze*, and one can say of the teaching of research that it must first give new eyes.

Why Participation?

Much of the knowledge in a community of practice is constituted by mostly unquestioned background assumptions and common sense. This common sense describes the situation that "amongst any given collection of persons organized into anything that can meaningfully be called a collectivity, there will be a corpus of matters which those persons will find 'obvious,' as 'going without saying' and as 'beyond doubt and investigation' " (Sharrock & Anderson, 1991, pp. 63–64). This is common sense, because it is not stated in the form of propositional knowledge, simply because it is so mundane, is unavailable for "transmission," explication, instruction, or inclusion in a textbook. These are the kinds of understandings that newcomers learn by participating with old-timers in the practice. Bourdieu (1990, 1992) talked of "mimesis," a form of "silent pedagogy" as the process by which newcomers come to know the implicit understandings characteristic of old-timers in a community of practice.

EXAMPLES FROM OUR EXPERIENCE

In this section, we describe three situations from our own work that exemplify how graduate students learn research by becoming part of a community and by participating in doing research. We describe how students learn to design research in two graduate courses taught by Michael: Research Designs in Education and The Research Basis of Mathematics Education. Our second example comes from a research support group of which both of us are members and that contains all students supervised by Michael. In the third example, we describe how Michelle increasingly participates in the writing of research articles.

Designing Research

Design is an activity in which indeterminate situations are converted to determinate ones (Schön, 1987); research design in social situations is no different here. Such a change in the ontological status of the situation is brought about through the situated practice of the designer. Beginning with uncertain, ill-defined, complex, and messy situations, designers construct and impose coherence; they structure their setting in such a way that it maintains a coherence with their earlier experiences. This structure provides a horizon of possibilities and constraints. Consequently, designers develop the emergent design situation, reacting to the consequences and implications of earlier moves.

Because designing educational research is a practice, it makes little sense to learn about it in some decontextualized way. Rather, learning to design occurs as students participate in designing and critiquing design, for "research without theory is blind, and theory without research is empty" (Bourdieu & Wacquant, 1992, p. 162). There is a tight interdependence of theory, research design, and the object of study. Thus, research methodology as a subject independent of theory and the object of research makes little sense; it is, in fact, a "scientific absurdity." What students need instead is to engage in the practice of designing research; and there is no better way than designing an authentic research project—their own thesis or a joint project with a faculty member—rather than designing a fake project for the purposes of completing a course:

> The most decisive help that the novice researcher can expect from experience is that which encourages him or her to take into account, in the definition of her project, the real conditions of its realization, that is, the means she has at her disposal (especially in terms of time and of specific competence, given the nature of her social experiences and her training) and the possibilities of access to informants and to information, documents and sources, etc. (Bourdieu, 1992, p. 252)

Here the array of methods used must fit the problem at hand and must constantly be reflected on in situ, at the very moment they are deployed to resolve particular questions.

In two of the courses Michael teaches—Research Designs in Education and The Research Basis of Mathematics Education—students learn to design research in a studio-like atmosphere that shares many similarities with Schön's (1987) architectural design studio. Here students begin to design without knowing the ins and outs of design. Beginning with students' initial and rather tentative ideas, professor and students begin asking clarifying questions to discover the presenting student's interests. In the process, possible research designs begin to emerge. Students are required to read certain textbook chapters, but use the precepts only later, as after-the-fact descriptions of what happens. In a similar way, occasional discussions of published articles are retroactively described in terms of precepts presented in the textbook.

Inevitably, students' interests lead to a variety of questions that, although sounding very similar, have considerably different consequences for the research to be conducted. Take the following example from one of our recent classes:

Ron, a mathematics teacher interested in technology, proposes the following research question for his thesis:

- Does a computer-based graphing program facilitate students' understanding of functions and their transformations?

This question implicitly suggests a comparison with other ways of teaching functions. It leads to comparisons among students who participate in different types of classes. After deciding how to assess understanding, the question calls for a traditional design in which two methods of teaching are compared on the basis of students' achievement. However, in our class conversation which involves several other students and Michael, it becomes clear that this is not something that holds Ron's interest. Michael then proposes a slight change in the question by adding the word "how" in front of Ron's original question:

- How does a computer-based graphing program facilitate students' understanding of functions and their transformations?

In this case, the question asks for information about the processes of constructing understanding and, specifically, about the interactions of student learning and technology. Michael then asks Ron and the other students to think about what kinds of data they will need in order to make claims about the interactions of student learning in the context of computer technology. One of the problems the class considers is how to elicit student sense-making activity in situ rather than asking them a posteriori. As part of this discussion, Michael suggests setting up collaborative groups as part of the research project and asking the high school students to produce and submit a joint product that any one member can present in a whole-class forum, thus encouraging students to engage in interactions so that every member understands. In this way, the class spends about 30 minutes with Ron's proposal, providing him with ample material to refine his design and to present an update about 2 weeks later.

The central activity in these courses is the presentation and analysis of research questions and associated designs. Each student's question and design is presented in a public forum. This has at least two advantages. First, other students can ask clarifying questions, provide their own perspectives, and elaborate the context of the presenting student's work. Second, an important aspect of this setting is the teacher's questions designed to help the student clarify his or her question. In this review/critique, other students learn to critique each other's work. Later in the course, one can observe that students adopt the teacher's form of questioning and interacting with the presenter. Frequently, students justify their critiques by making reference to one or more precedent-setting cases discussed early in the class. By engaging in such group discussions about other students' research proposals, most participants feel that they learn tremendously about critiquing their own research questions and study designs. Frequently, they revise their own questions and proposals before presenting to the class.

Although these research designs courses comprise 60 contact hours, they are certainly not enough to help students develop more than a cursory competence in designing research. However, the high level of interactions between the graduate students (which often continues into the data collection and analysis phases of their thesis research), facilitates their learning along the trajectory of increasing participation and competence. To increase the level of participation in research with others, we created a research support group consisting of all graduate students who have Michael as their advisor. We describe in the following subsection the continuing participation in research practice that characterizes our work in this group.

Creating a Research Support Group

In the summer of 1993, after a seminar-style course on research in mathematics education, we formed a research support group of ourselves and three graduate students working on their MSc theses in mathematics education. The support group has been meeting regularly for 2 to 3 hours about every third Saturday since that time. Although Michelle and the other graduate students each prepared research proposals during the course (and were therefore at similar stages in their academic lives), Michelle had previously written proposals and participated in research. From this perspective, she was already a legitimate peripheral participant in the educational research community.

As its name suggests, we created the research support group to provide a forum in which the students could discuss research issues associated with designing their master's research projects, planning data collection (in one instance even participating in data collection), interpreting the data collected, and writing parts of the thesis. An important outcome of this research support group was that it facilitated the graduate students' transition from their rather structured course work into the largely independent research aspect of their work toward a degree. The following narrative presents some of the typical features of our meetings and exemplifies several theoretical issues related to legitimate peripheral participation and communities of practice:

> To this meeting, Barry brought a copy of an interview with "Jonathan" (a pseudonym), one of his high school mathematics students. Barry was interested in students' views of mathematics, and particularly in the question why some students do not do well in school although they appear to have a great degree of mathematical intuition. He had interviewed Jonathan because his informal observations suggested that the student was very interested in and was highly competent in many mathematical practices including calculus, vector analysis, matrices, and other topics.
>
> We began by reading the interview individually, following our personal preferences for highlighting parts of the interview, using a variety of colors, or writing comments in the margins. Later, someone began to share observations, comments, and interpretations. After the initial exchanges, we (Michelle and Michael) alternated in asking Barry and the others critical questions about specific interpretations, what dis/confirming data were available in the interview at hand, or what additional data were needed to support or reject a tentative interpretation. Our questioning brought out that, at this stage, Barry did not yet have convincing data to show that Jonathan was more competent than his peers in many mathematical practices. After several suggestions, Michael asked Barry whether it was possible to videotape Jonathan while he was working on one of his fractal programs. Michael followed up by asking the group how to set up such a video session so that Jonathan could talk about the mathematics involved in the program and, in this, exhibit his mathematical understandings and provide material evidence thereof. This leds us to talk about the advantages and disadvantages of videotaping (a) a think-aloud programming session, (b) a joint programming session with Jonathan and one of his peers, or (c) a conversation between Jonathan and Barry in which the student explained a previously completed program or some other work in progress. Michelle, who for her own thesis on everyday mathematics had videotaped an elementary teacher doing mathematics while baking cookies, suggested that it would be important to record Jonathan doing mathematics while programming fractals. At this point, two different conversations emerged. Barry continued to pursue with Michelle the implications of her suggestion in his project. Michael talked to Blair and Trish who had recorded, but not yet analyzed, videotapes of students engaged in mathematical activity.
>
> Later, the group shifted its focus to discuss a draft analysis Michelle had written for inclusion in her thesis. After reading the text, Michelle questioned the other participants about the soundness of her interpretations, and how her argument could be strengthened. At the end of the session, Trish asked Michael to meet individually. Barry, who had more questions about how to interview, retreated with Michelle into her office, where they worked out some of the details for further data collection and writing a first draft analysis of the interview with Jonathan to be shared in a future meeting.

This narrative of a typical meeting shows several characteristics of our group that are consistent with the theoretical perspective outlined earlier. We take a decentered view of apprenticeship into a community (Lave & Wenger, 1991), according to which mastery does not reside in an all-knowing professor master but in the organization of the community of knowers of which the master is just one part. In our research support group, the professor's job is not that of an all-knowing information provider. Rather, our activities are characterized by graduate student independence, mutual support, and mentoring by more experienced others. This view moves the focus of learning to do research away from individual accomplishments onto our community's intricate structuring of learning resources. As much as possible, our students acknowledge the influence of others on their work. Such a decentered approach to knowing allows us to maintain the research support group in the absence of the professor. The group, under the mentorship of the most experienced member (here Michelle) continues to function and accept newcomers.

What we had created was a small research community in which members were at different stages of legitimate peripheral participation. Those who had already developed greater competence in the practice of research mentored and provided advice to those with less. Initially, because of her prior participation in research, Michelle quickly became a resource for the other students. Later, Barry and Blair, who were already engaged in their data collection and interpretation, took on supporting roles for those less advanced in their projects. In this way, everyone developed a considerable understanding for what the others were doing, how the research progressed, what possible problems might emerge, and so on.

Collaboration in Reporting

Certainly the most ideal situation for learning how to do research is to participate with a competent researcher in all stages of ongoing research projects. Here, graduate students can appropriate both explicit and tacit aspects of research practices. The four episodes at the beginning of this chapter already provided a description of our practice of introducing graduate students to research in science teaching and learning. These episodes illustrate a form of graduate student education in research that is consistent with a model of learning as a trajectory from legitimate peripheral to core participation in social science research.

The aspect of research that appears to be most difficult to appropriate is that of learning to write papers, chapters, articles for publication, or grant applications. We know both from personal experience and from sociological research (Knorr-Cetina, 1981) that graduate students in the natural sciences frequently learn to write for publication by drafting a manuscript. They submit the draft to their professor, who marks it up to be redone by the student. After many cycles of this process of writing and critiquing, a publishable piece emerges. We take a different approach. Paralleling our on-site work during data collection, students begin with more manageable tasks such as editing, commenting, and critiquing. Later, they take on increasing responsibility for producing manuscript drafts. We proceeded in the same way in writing this chapter. Michelle commented on, critiqued, and suggested additions to Michael's initial draft. To facilitate the integration of texts and to avoid duplication of writing, we use the same word processor and exchange progressive versions of the final document. Any additional text—whether Michelle's comments to the drafts of this chapter, or Michael's comments to draft chapters of her MA thesis—was enclosed in parentheses and flagged by "$$." The following is an example from the first paragraph after the opening vignette, and ultimately led to the present version of this chapter:

> Carolyn is a relative newcomer compared to Sylvie, so that she learns important aspects of transcription from the latter. ($$I wonder if we could also include here that Carolyn a counseling psychology student, teaches us about interviewing or something to highlight her different area of expertise, and that we all learn from each other?) Here, we see a small community with members who have different levels and areas of expertise.

Or Michelle suggested an addition that led to the current version of the previous section regarding her mentorship role in the thesis support group:

> We need to work on the fact that I am taking over the thesis support group next semester. This really highlights the graduate student as mentor aspect. The others stated themselves that I would be capable of doing this, suggesting that they see me in a bit of a mentoring role as well. (personal note, August 14, 1995)

Through such writing and sharing of draft versions, Michelle participates increasingly in writing manuscripts.

DISCUSSION AND IMPLICATIONS

A community is the central location of knowing for any practice; it is a set of relations between people, activities, and the world over time and in interaction with other communities of practice. The community provides interpretive support necessary for making sense of tools, language, mores, heuristics, and other aspects that constitute the community (Lave & Wenger, 1991). An important consideration in the development of a community is its reproduction cycle. In the case of science and mathematics education research, this can be somewhere from 3 to 5 years, depending on the extent of the studies—a longer time period for a student who pursues a PhD degree than for someone in a master's program.

In our view, the notion of legitimate peripheral participation allows us to understand the career path of a researcher in new ways. It is not, for example, on accepting a position as a professor that a person assumes the functions of a member. Most frequently, the future professor has already done independent research and written research articles. However, the notion of legitimate peripheral participation allows us to consider other aspects of professional practice as beginning at an earlier stage than commonly believed. For example, graduate students themselves begin to serve as mentors to other even newer members in the community. Michelle, for example, is well on her way to becoming a core member. She has taught introductory research methods courses, participated in research designs classes, has mentored other graduate students, and is conducting the research support group on her own. She also has participated in a number of different research projects, and conducted her own independent research. If she decides to pursue an academic career, all she will lack is the formal supervision of a new researcher (a graduate thesis).

The Problem of Class or Group Size

The notion of legitimate peripheral participation points out problems in current approaches to teaching graduate students about research, particularly in the number of students a competent old-timer can effectively supervise. Bourdieu (1992) explained in his *Paris Workshop* that the implications of a practice perspective on social science research were dramatic, and incompatible with much of current teaching of "research methodology." If one has to learn a practice alongside a seasoned practitioner—participating in the actual doing of design and research, constructing a questionnaire, reading statistical printouts, interpreting interview transcripts—it is clear that one can supervise only a small number of graduate student research projects (master's or doctoral theses). We experience this contradiction every time we have to teach a course such as Research Designs with a larger group of students. In our experience, group sizes of four to eight members including the professor are ideal for research classes, seminars, and on-site research. However, even more radically, Bourdieu claimed that those who purport to supervise a large number of students do not actually supervise those students. Here we disagree to some extent with Bourdieu. We believe (with Brown et al., 1989; Lave & Wenger, 1991) that the interactions between those who are not yet central members of the community are just as important as those with core members. These interactions constitute an important part of the experience on which later expertise as a researcher is founded. We find it, therefore, of the utmost importance to create a community of practice constituted of members at varying levels of competence. This allows not-yet-core members to do what their mentors do: engage in mentoring by becoming mentors themselves.

Contradiction and Dilemmas

Lave and Wenger (1991) indicated that by granting legitimate peripheral participation to newcomers, a community automatically becomes subject to the continuity–displacement contradiction that provides newcomers with a dilemma. On the one hand, the new researchers need to engage in a practice. To understand and participate in it, they have to adopt current standards of the community in which it exists. On the other hand, they have a stake in the development of the practice so that they can establish their own future identity. This means they have to establish their own ways of doing research, thus transforming the available practices in the research and therefore the entire community.

Thus, within the notions of legitimate peripheral participation and apprenticeship is embedded the danger of cultural reproduction. We find ourselves in a double bind. Bourdieu (1992) noted:

> Without the cultural tools bequeathed in acculturation, a person would be deprived of a mode of adaptation/learning characteristic to humans. But at the same time, acculturation has the danger of simply substituting for the naive doxa of lay common sense the no less naive doxa of scholarly common sense ... which parrots, in technical jargon and under official trappings, the discourse of common sense. (p. 248)

Bourdieu called for continuous vigilance, constant questioning, and methodological mistrust. Lave and Wenger (1991) suggested that with any new individual, new visions and transformation are automatically embedded in cultural reproduction through legitimate peripheral participation. From this derives the peculiar antinomy of research pedagogy. It must enculturate students in ways of using both tested instruments for constructing reality (problematics, concepts, techniques, methods) and at the *same* time, a formidable critical disposition to question ruthlessly those instruments.

ACKNOWLEDGMENTS

This work was made possible in part by Grant 410–93–1127 from the Social Sciences and Humanities Research Council of Canada. We thank Sylvie Boutonné and Carolyn Woszczyna for their help during aspects of this project.

We extend our gratitude to the other members of our initial research support group—Trish O'Brien, Barry Gruntman, and Blair Jadunath—who with us constitute a community.

REFERENCES

Bourdieu, P. (1990). *The logic of practice*. Cambridge, England: Polity Press.

Bourdieu, P. (1992). The Paris workshop. In P. Bourdieu & L. J. D. Wacquant (Eds.), *An invitation to reflexive sociology* (pp. 217–260). Chicago: University of Chicago Press.

Bourdieu, P., & Wacquant, L. J. D. (1992). *An invitation to reflexive sociology*. Chicago: University of Chicago Press.

Brown, J. S., Collins, A., & Duguid, P. (1989). Situated cognition and the culture of learning. *Educational Researcher, 18*(1), 32–42.

Garfinkel, H. (1967). *Studies in ethnomethodology*. Englewood Cliffs, NJ: Prentice-Hall.

Garfinkel, H., & Wieder, D. L. (1992). Two incommensurable, asymmetrically alternate technologies of social analysis. In G. Watson & R. M. Seiler (Eds.), *Text in context: Contributions to ethnomethodology* (pp. 175–206). Newbury Park, CA: Sage.

Henderson, K. (1991). Flexible sketches and inflexible data bases: Visual communication, conscription devices, and boundary objects in design engineering. *Science, Technology & Human Values, 16*, 448–473.

Jordan, B. (1989). Cosmopolitical obstetrics: Some insights from the training of traditional midwives. *Social Science in Medicine, 28*, 925–944.

Jordan, K., & Lynch, M. (1993). The mainstreaming of a molecular biological tool: A case study of a new technique. In G. Button (Ed.), *Technology in working order: Studies of work, interaction, and technology* (pp. 162–178). London: Routledge.

Knorr-Cetina, K. D. (1981). *The manufacture of knowledge: An essay on the constructivist and contextual nature of science*. Oxford, England: Pergamon.

Krathwohl, D. R. (1993). *Methods of educational and social science research: An integrated approach*. New York: Longman.

Lave, J. (1988). *Cognition in practice: Mind, mathematics and culture in everyday life*. Cambridge, England: Cambridge University Press.

Lave, J., & Wenger, E. (1991). *Situated learning: Legitimate peripheral participation*. Cambridge, England: Cambridge University Press.

McGinn, M. K., Roth, W.-M., Boutonné, S., & Woszczyna, C. (1995). The transformation of individual and collective knowledge in elementary science classrooms that are organized as knowledge-building communities. *Research in Science Education, 26*, 163–189.

Schoenfeld, A. (1992). On paradigms and methods: What do you do when the ones you know don't do what you want them to? Issues in the analysis of data in the form of video-tapes. *The Journal of the Learning Sciences, 2*, 179–214.

Schön, D. A. (1987). *Educating the reflective practitioner*. San Francisco: Jossey-Bass.

Sharrock, W., & Anderson, B. (1991). Epistemology: Professional scepticism. In G. Button (Ed.), *Ethnomethodology and the human sciences* (pp. 51–76). Cambridge, England: Cambridge University Press.

Star, S. L. (1989). Layered space, formal representations and long-distance control: The politics of information. *Fundamenta Scientiae, 10*, 125–154.

Suchman, L. A. (1987). *Plans and situated actions: The problem of human–machine communication*. Cambridge, England: Cambridge University Press.

Traweek, S. (1988). *Beamtimes and lifetimes: The world of high energy physicists*. Cambridge, MA: MIT Press.

12

Supervision in a Graduate Center

Andy Begg
Beverley Bell
Vicki Compton
Elizabeth McKinley
University of Waikato, Aotearoa, New Zealand

We believe that the crux of the supervision process is the relationship between the student and supervisor(s). This philosophy underlies the model for supervision that we offer and are continuing to develop at our center. This model makes explicit not only the typical supervision such as one-to-one meetings with supervisors and research methods courses, but also a number of components that are often only implicit. Another reason for developing our center's model was that the number of students needing supervision was increasing without a proportionate increase in staffing. These reasons led us to consider alternative ways of maintaining the quality of the supervision relationship for our students and to develop the following supervision model.

BACKGROUND

The Centre for Science, Mathematics and Technology Education Research was established in 1989 and had grown from a smaller research unit that began in 1981. It is involved in graduate teaching and research in science, mathematics, technology, and computing education, but not in preservice teacher education. Students are mainly midcareer teachers from New Zealand and overseas. Most of them have not had academic research experience but have had considerable teaching experience. While with us, students are studying for master's degrees, postgraduate diplomas, or doctorates, and are involved in research that includes collecting data within New Zealand, in their home countries, or both.

The center has five permanent academic staff, contract researchers, a secretary/administrator, and a number of associate staff who work primarily in the three schools within the university with which we are associated—Education, Science and Technology, and Computing and Mathematical Sciences. The associate staff are involved in teaching and supervising students of the center, carrying out research, participating in seminars, and other center activities. As the core staff is small, associate staff play an important role in the supervision of students.

The core staff and the full-time students are accommodated in a suite of offices which makes the staff accessible to students. Generally students feel free to pop in at any time, over and above regularly scheduled meetings. The close proximity of offices is also conducive to the cross-fertilization of ideas between subject areas. Full-time students share an office with two other students who generally have similar subject interests, backgrounds, and level of study, and this helps build an ethos of peer support. Whether the students have come from a tropical or temperate climate is another important consideration when grouping students in rooms. Full-time students have their own desks and computers; part-time students have access to computers; computer support is available; and other equipment, such as tape recorders and transcribers, is supplied as needed.

The professional background of the students, the small size of the center, and the management style and ethos that the center are developing all combine to provide an environment that is intended to be conducive to staff and student collegiality. However, in saying this we acknowledge that there is a power differential between staff and students inherent in the process of supervision, particularly if the supervisors are involved in thesis examination. Some examples of instances in which the power differential may be noticeable include: overseas students who come from more formal educational situations, or countries where cultural differences influence the relationship status between men and women, or where the supervision is by colleagues in the same institution. In response to this we attempt to develop an environment that supports collegiality by making the supervision process as explicit as possible, by giving space and voice to students, and by negotiating their concerns.

Within the spirit of fostering a collegial graduate culture and a "student–client" focus, the center is concerned with the professional, personal and social development (Bell & Gilbert, 1995) of staff and students within a research environment. As part of this, the center aims to:

- Provide a regular forum for debate, both formal and informal, between staff and students, and with the wider education community. This is achieved by holding regular subject discussion groups, organizing supervision support meetings, hosting a weekly public seminar, and setting up electronic networks.

- Teach a research methodologies course to help with research processes for the student. Students take this course either before they embark on their thesis or while they are doing their research.

- Provide individual time for students with supervisors. This is done on a needs basis through scheduled meetings and by ensuring that students have ready access to staff at other times.

- Provide support during development and learning. The change in focus from being the teacher to being a learner can cause anxiety for teachers who have not been involved in university study for some years. Overseas people have the additional stress of having to adjust to a new culture.

- Help students to prepare for future academic careers. This includes offering assistance and experience with a range of responsibilities; for example, lecturing, and marking, as well as providing opportunities for involvement in day-to-day management matters.

- Encourage students to submit articles for publication in our yearbook and in other publications.

- Build both independent researchers in a community, and a social community of researchers.

With an increasing number of graduate students we found we needed to set up alternative mechanisms to maintain the quality of the relationships in the research supervision process. Following discussions within the center, and consultation with officers from the Higher Education Office of the University of Auckland, we reexamined our supervision procedures. This led to changes such as the introduction of supervision support meetings to more effectively meet the needs of all involved. From staff and student evaluations of this we have already modified, and will continue to develop, the supervision model. Quotes presented have been taken from students' evaluation sheet, and from discussions with staff and students about the supervision model, both in formal group situations and from informal personal communications.

THE SUPERVISION MODEL

There are three core components in the process and all students are expected to participate in them:

1. Regular supervision meetings.

2. Research methods paper.

3. Supervision support meetings.

Four supporting components that are available and in which students are encouraged to participate are:

4. Regular subject seminars.

5. Professional development seminars.

6. Writing in the English language.

7. Networking within and beyond the center.

The first two of the core components are similar to those in most universities, but some details of how they are organized may be different. The third core component, as discussed later, offers a number of advantages over former supervisory practices in the center. The four supporting components occurred in the past to some extent but, recently, we have made them more explicitly part of the supervision process. These components include helping the student with time management, checking progress, discussing ethical difficulties, interfacing between the university and the student about administrative details, and discussing the importance of building and maintaining good relationships between researchers and participants within the local educational community.

Each of the seven components is discussed in more detail in the following.

Regular Supervision Meetings

The prime purpose of supervision meetings is to provide focused student–supervisor professional interactions, ongoing debates on the research topic, and the sharing of relevant papers. The overall response from students regarding this aspect of their supervision has been very positive. The majority considered this time to be important in establishing the theoretical aspects of their work, and they enjoyed the opportunity for entering into theoretical debates with their supervisors.

The choice of supervisor is important and some negotiation occurs before this is decided. The number of supervisors is determined by the skills of the staff and student, and the topic each student undertakes. Typically, master's students have one supervisor, whereas doctoral students have a chief supervisor and a second supervisor, and sometimes a third is added because of his or her specific skills. An overseas adviser is often included in the panel when the student is returning to a home country to collect data.

The meetings with the supervisor(s) for full-time students are usually weekly at first, although they are less frequent later. The frequency of meetings is negotiated between the participants. This is an important feature of the supervisor–student relationship. Students feel that regularity of the meetings needs to be continually negotiated, as it depends on factors such as the stage of their research and the other commitments they have in the wider context. It is important that students know they are entitled to have input into both the frequency of the meetings and into postponing or canceling them. If students are not aware that they can have this input, undue stress may be placed on them by the meetings. For example, one student reflected on how she felt before this aspect of negotiation of meeting was made explicit:

> My supervisor and I initially planned to meet weekly. There were many times that I felt I had nothing I really wanted to discuss, but because we had planned it, I felt I had to go and have something prepared. I was pleased when he went away on sabbatical, as this meant this weekly pressure was not there.

When students have more than one supervisor, regular meetings are held with all people involved. Students can also meet separately with each supervisor to use their strengths at appropriate times in their research.

The students are given a copy of the center's student guidelines, which contain the homework for discussion (Graham & Grant, 1993) that the student and supervisor work through during their first two meetings. The topics in the guidelines are in three categories, each with a number of issues, and some of these are dealt with only briefly by the supervisor and picked up in more detail in the supervision support meetings.

The framework of these guidelines is given here; details are in Appendix A.

1. Supervisor/Student Understandings
   What is a thesis? Meetings; Advice and support; Time frame; Joint supervisors; Other issues.
2. Departmental Expectations and Resources
   Written information; Access to amenities and resources; What expectations does the department have of the student?; Monitoring supervision; Resolving conflict; Other issues.
3. University Requirements
   University guidelines; Thesis assessment; Extensions and deferment; University protocols; Ethics; Other issues.

From the initial discussions, both the student and supervisor/s consider their responsibilities and discuss how the supervision process will proceed. The list of responsibilities shown in Fig. 12.1 is used to facilitate this.

Working through these guidelines emphasizes the reciprocal nature of the relationship and seems to provide an excellent way of establishing a culture in which each participant has the opportunity to discuss fundamental issues that invariably arise during the course of the supervision relation-

Responsibilities of Supervisors and Students

These are guidelines for negotiation about responsibilities in the supervision process. They are not regulations.

Students can expect their chief supervisor to:

- contribute to aspects of supervision in the Centre, and in particular, meetings with students, the research methods seminars and the supervision support meetings.

- meet with them on a frequent and regular basis. For example, it is suggested that meetings be held at least four times a year for part-time students and at least once a month for full-time students. The frequency is something to be negotiated by the supervisor and student.

- initiate discussions on the supervision activities, the guidelines for supervision and the suggested use of record sheets or log books.

- initiate discussions on the ethics of the research and obtain approval from the Human Research Ethics Committee.

- work towards establishing, maintaining and monitoring the supervision relationship and resolve conflict.

- give feedback on the student's written work within two weeks.

- read in the area of the student's research and pass on any relevant articles to them.

- give academic knowledge, advice and feedback about the research being done by them with respect to:
previous and current research on the topic
planning
research design & methodology
data analysis
writing up the research
timelines and progress.

- engage with them in academic debates.

- facilitate, for the student if need be:
academic networking with national and
    international colleagues
presentations of papers at conferences
interactions with Registry staff
access to and use of research equipment
and materials.

Supervisors can expect their students to:

- attend and contribute to all three aspects of supervision in the Centre
– meetings with supervisors, the research methods seminars and the supervision support meetings.

- meet with them on a frequent and regular basis. For example, it is suggested that meetings be held at least four times a year for part-time students and at least once a month for full-time students. The frequency is something to be negotiated by the supervisor and student.

- participate in discussions on the supervision activities, the guidelines for supervision and the suggested use of record sheets or log books.

- take into account the ethics of educational research and help the supervisor(s) obtain approval from the Human Research Ethics Committee.

- work towards establishing, maintaining and monitoring the supervision relationship and resolve conflict.

- provide written work for comment by the supervisor(s) on a regular basis.

- read in the area of research and pass on any key articles to the supervisor(s) to read.

- seek academic knowledge, advice and feedback about the research being undertaken with respect to:
previous and current research in the topic
planning
research design & methodology
data analysis
writing up the research
timelines and progress.

- engage with the supervisor(s) in academic debates.

- undertake:
academic networking with national and
    international colleagues
presentations of papers at conferences
interactions with Registry staff
safe use of research equipment and
materials.

- be responsive to the feedback on the student evaluation form.
- be involved in professional development activities about research supervision.
- initiate negotiations with the student regarding authorship of publications arising from the research.
- ensure support is available from other supervisors and Centre staff, in particular when the chief supervisor is away.

- give feedback to the supervisor(s) on the appropriate student evaluation form.
- if possible, attend any workshops on the supervision process.
- negotiate with the supervisor(s) regarding authorship of publications arising from the research.
- undertake the research as their own work.

FIG. 12.1.

ship. As stated by one student, "It is helpful for the students to know what they can legitimately expect from their supervisors—the guidelines allowed for this."

The setting up of conflict management strategies, at a time when the relationship was normally uncomplicated by any incidents, is considered to be useful. This is not done because conflict is expected, but indicates to students an awareness that differences may occur, and that both parties need to know how such differences might be dealt with and managed before any problems occur. As one student said, "Setting up a framework which both people have agreed to is important in that it serves to make the playing field more level as the rules are overtly negotiated before the game begins."

The use of the recording sheets (see Appendix B) that the students fill in at or after each meeting is considered helpful in that students understand clearly each participant's obligations to be fulfilled before the next meeting. The sheets provide opportunities to continue negotiating the role of each participant, the regularity of meeting times, and generally reflect on how the supervision process is going. For some students, they provide an important time management tool. For example, one student stated, "The sheets we fill out each time were important in that it allows opportunity to clarify each persons responsibilities and also to set goals to be completed before the next meeting."

Research Methods Courses

We require all our students doing research to have previously completed, or be currently enrolled in (or at least auditing), our research methods course or an equivalent one. This course provides a theoretical discussion of a variety of research methodologies and techniques. Many of our students have not been involved in formal research and assistance in exploring the research literature is important if they are to adopt or adapt methodologies and techniques to suit their own particular philosophy and context. As explained by one student:

This course puts in little signposts so I can get a better idea of how things link together—it's structuring the ideas to help me know what methods there are to choose from and why I might choose a particular methodology for a particular purpose.

The course is currently available either during the year with weekly lectures or as a January summer school block course. The sessions fall into six categories:

1. *An introduction*
   What is research? purposes of research, ethics.
2. *Research paradigms*
   Positivist, interpretivist, critical, and postmodernist paradigms.
3. *Methods*
   A range of qualitative and quantitative methods including classroom observations, surveys and questionnaires, individual and group interviews, and the compilation of case studies.
4. *Issues—including how they are incorporated in the three previous items*
   Feminist research, Maori and indigenous issues research, cross-cultural research, teachers as researchers.
5. *Reading and writing up research*
   Research critiques, literature reviews, writing, statistics, writing proposals, publishing.
6. *Collegial support in the area of research and supervision*
   Both students and staff are encouraged to reflect on their own research throughout the course.

This course not only considers research from a theoretical basis; it also provides an opportunity for the discussion of staff and student research that is in the familiar contexts of mathematics, science, and technology education. Most students are involved in classroom research, which usually occurs in complex conditions. Working through these complexities, in the context of this research paper, allows for a high level of authenticity in understanding differences in methodological approaches. Traditionally, mathematics and science education students have started with a positivist view of knowledge and research and this course is influential in helping them develop alternative perspectives.

Supervision Support Meetings

These 2-hour weekly meetings constitute the third core component. They are typically convened by a staff member who is currently involved in doctoral study or who has had recent experience as a student. The staff member manages and plans the initial sessions to anticipate needs such as writing proposals, drafting ethics statements, organizing familiarization activities in the library, and introducing students to the information technologies that may be available in the library and the center. As the year progresses, the focus of the meetings changes to respond to the emerging needs of the students. For example, when a student is preparing a questionnaire or an interview schedule, the draft can be brought to the meeting and discussed. All staff are invited to attend sessions but the expectation is that they will not dominate these meetings. Staff are sometimes explicitly asked by students to attend, or not attend, according to the topic being debated. The sessions are less formal than taught courses and sharing information and experiences is encouraged.

There are three key purposes for these meetings:

1. To provide general supervisory information to students and avoid duplication for supervisors in their regular meetings with students.
2. To provide a forum for the discussion of the supervision process.
3. To provide support, and the opportunity, for students to build up a supportive peer culture.

General Supervisory Information. Teaching and supervising in a group situation allows supervisors to avoid repetition and provides an ongoing opportunity for discussion by students. For example, the time slot can be used to organize group sessions on the use of library facilities and with software packages available in the center. The following comments from students reflect the usefulness of this strategy:

> Library tours are OK, but it was good to go with other people that you could get back to if you missed something—it was more ongoing.

> It was good to talk to "M," as he had actually used the software package, the one available to me and not some other version of it, in his research … I could see if it would do what I wanted as I had a context … and I felt that if I got stuck—he was available to help.

Having a legitimate forum for general inquiries about research and an opportunity to share with a group how things were going were important aspects of these meetings. Simple logistical help regarding different methods of data collection were perceived to be useful, both in terms of problem resolution, and avoidance:

> I was going to be taping students in a classroom, and it was good to hear how other people got around the problems in doing this. Little things were really helpful when planning my research—things which you only get to hear about

by chance discussions like when people are discussing how things went for them.

Typical issues that arise through the supervision support meetings give an indication of the scope of these meetings. These include:

- Introduction session.
- Discussion of the supervision process.
- Discussing and sharing research proposals, refining research questions.
- Discussing ethics approval forms and helping each other fill these in.
- Organizing library tours.
- Organizing workshops for computer applications.
- Organizing visits to schools and entry to schools for research.
- Discussing particular students' questionnaires and interview schedules.
- Practical hints on data collection.
- Discussing timelines, setting priorities, and monitoring progress.
- Structuring a thesis.
- Sharing updates on research.
- Academic anxiety and stress management.
- Occupational overuse syndrome (repetitive strain injury).
- Assessment and evaluation of theses.
- Academic writing: thesis writing, papers, and getting published.
- Role of research in educational policy.
- Preparation of a curriculum vitae and job applications.

Discussion of the Supervision Process. These meetings provide an environment for staff and students to discuss issues related to supervision and doing research. The staff receive informal feedback on supervision that supplements the more formal evaluation process. Students raise general issues regarding supervision. For example, during 1995 a request was made for assistance with the English language by some international students. In addition, new staff members and students who expect to move to an academic position in the future obtain professional development about being a supervisor. As explained by one such staff member:

> As a new staff member the meetings enable me to experience the wide range of issues that affect the students in the center. This helps to enhance my own skills for other aspects of the supervisory process. However, it is important that I am also a student and that I share the problems I have with my own research. The sharing of these problems give some students more courage to

voice their own concerns. In addition, my presence allows an avenue for students to provide anonymous feedback to other staff members.

Provide Peer Support for Students. The role these meetings had in terms of peer support was an important feature mentioned by many students in their formal evaluation of the center's supervision. This included opportunities for informal general discussion, as explained by a student: "Personally I liked these meetings as we can discuss quite broad issues with our peers and have the opportunity to find out what other students are doing."

The center has many international students with specific needs in terms of written and spoken English. The supervision meetings provide opportunities for these students to share the frustration of being in an unfamiliar culture and, for some, having to write in an unfamiliar language. The meetings allowed participants to help and be helped in terms of specific skills, and in feeling more comfortable generally about being in a foreign country: "I am really grateful to the supervision meetings for organizing a group of people—my peers, to help with my English."

The supervision support meetings provide a forum with peer support for a different sort of debate from those that occur at regular supervision meetings. There have been numerous comments from students that having an opportunity to meet without any supervisors allowed some of them to feel more comfortable and able to discuss ideas more freely:

> Because these meetings were run by my peers, I feel they are more relaxed, and this is important for international students in particular. It is important that the meetings provide a free forum for discussion, without any judgment aspect from supervisors.

> It is difficult to forget that they (your supervisors) are there, sometimes you just want to discuss things without feeling like they are watching and judging you ... even though they don't say anything directly—you still think they might be thinking, "this person doesn't know this."

> Sometimes it is nice to just meet with others—that are at a similar place to you. You want to discuss things and work through them—you don't want an "expert" opinion all the time.

Regular Subject Seminars

The first of the supporting components are the regular subject seminars. Two have been time-tabled to date for center people: a mathematics and statistics education seminar series, and a science education reading group. Others in technology and computing education are expected to be convened when the number of students doing research in these areas builds up. These seminar series have regular meetings and the membership is open to staff, associate staff, and students.

The seminars for mathematics and science vary. The mathematics seminars are often student presentations, including updates on progress and discussion of students' papers, as well as recently published papers of interest. The science seminars tend to be a sharing of papers and a discussion of ideas. These seminars provide an opportunity for practice presentations for conferences, for building a community ethos among staff and students, and for participants to be challenged by alternative ideas. This process is particularly important for staff and doctoral students who may be immersed in their own research for long periods of time.

Center's Professional Development Seminars

The center organizes weekly public seminars and these constitute the second supporting component. These seminars provide an opportunity for visitors, staff, and senior students to present their ideas and work in progress. For senior students, it can act as a transition platform for future papers. One valuable aspect of these seminars is that they provide an opportunity for staff and students to interact with ideas from other subject areas within the center and beyond. Recognizing that many of our students will return to their home countries to senior positions within education, it is important that they develop this general overview of education, as well as more detailed knowledge within their specialty area.

Writing in the English Language

The center employs a lecturer from the Teaching and Learning Development Unit for several hours each week to help students with their writing. This was done in response to two characteristics of the students in the center. The first is a significant number of overseas students for whom English is a second, third, or fourth language, and although these students can cope with the academic concepts, some have difficulty expressing their ideas. The second characteristic is that many science, mathematics, technology, and computing graduates have not experienced writing in a discursive manner and, although English is their first language, they can also benefit from this assistance. The provision of this specialist assistance has gone some way to freeing supervisors from having to deal with the mechanics of the students' writing, leaving them more time to discuss ideas.

Networking Within and Beyond the Center

The fourth supporting component and the seventh component of the supervision model is networking. Our intention is that our students should identify with much more than the local network in their field and that they will feel confident to use the international networks to tap into the expertise of others. Networking has three main foci:

1. Starting with peers, students are encouraged to read and critique each other's work, to share ideas and papers, and to view the learning process as a cooperative venture.

2. This interaction is extended to include staff within the center and other members of the education community. Social functions, business meetings, and other university courses and seminars are some of the opportunities for students to broaden their networks. The staff also have a responsibility for suggesting that students organize meetings with others, especially if these other people have expertise that is not available within the center.

3. Through involvement with personal, national, and international e-mail lists, visitors to the center, national and international conferences, and journals, our students are encouraged to extend their networks beyond those that are physically accessible.

SUMMARY

So far, our model for supervision has been extended from the traditional supervision meetings and research methods class to include a third core component—supervision support meetings—and to make more explicit four supporting components: regular subject seminars, weekly public seminars, assistance with writing in the English language, and networking.

The development of this model has been done on the assumptions that:

- Any supervision model needs to be flexible in order to be truly responsive to both the students' and the supervisors' needs.
- Students should be given the opportunity to play an active role in the establishment, development, and maintenance of the supervisory relationship.
- Opportunities need to be provided for students to meet without a staff presence.
- Cultural perspectives need consideration; in particular, working in other countries involves different ethical positions and a consideration of possible different expectations of researchers from bureaucrats and governments.

POSSIBLE FUTURE DEVELOPMENTS

A crucial part of the supervision process is the feedback that is provided formally through evaluation sheets and discussions in the supervision support meetings, and informally within the everyday activities of the center. This is important as it provides a basis for ongoing development of our model and leads to an increased awareness by supervisors of how they and their colleagues are perceived to work. This helps reduce the isolation that is often experienced by supervisors and may give them confidence to try new strategies.

A number of future possibilities are being considered, including:

- Use of overseas advisers when international students are encouraged to go back to their own countries to collect data. This is because the supervisors do not always know the social context of the schools or other settings in which these people are working.
- Provision of more of these components to part-time and off-campus students.
- An extension of supervision at a distance as part of a distance education initiative.

These possibilities are not features of the model at this stage, but the iterative nature of the model itself provides an opportunity to work through them, and we look forward to incorporating appropriate strategies in the future. Chapter 10 provides a number of such strategies for consideration.

CONCLUSION

We consider this model to provide a framework for high-quality, effective supervision and the participants in the process influence the effectiveness of its operation. Supervision is only as good as the relationship developed between students and supervisors.

APPENDIX A
POSTGRADUATE SUPERVISION:
GUIDELINES FOR DISCUSSION

Supervisor/Student Understandings

1. What is a thesis?
   Issues to discuss might include:
   - What does "thesis" mean?
   - What form should a thesis proposal have?
   - What is the appropriate structure of a thesis?
   - What is the appropriate length?
   - What referencing conventions should I follow?
   - What is the difference between a thesis that passes and a first-class one?
   - What are some titles of good thesis examples in this field?
   - What is meant by "originality"?
   - Who owns papers arising during and after thesis supervision?

2. Meetings
   Issues to discuss might include:

   - Frequency and duration of meetings.
   - Access to supervisor outside of scheduled meeting times.
   - Responsibility of initiating meetings (if not scheduled regularly).
   - Protocol for when one person can't make the meeting.

3. Advice and support
   Issues to discuss might include:

   - Development of the research proposal: how much input from supervisor, how will this proceed?
   - Expectations of feedback: how much, how often, in what form, with how much notice?
   - Support with theoretical content, such as resources, contacts: how much can be expected, given the supervisor's knowledge of the area?
   - What other kinds of knowledge are needed, for instance, of the research process, of academic writing, and so forth—what resources does the supervisor know of, how much help can he or she give?
   - Are there relevant personal circumstances that might make the supervision or completion of the thesis difficult, such as student suffering financial hardship or experiencing relationship difficulties or supervisor going on sabbatical, expecting a baby or ... ?

4. Time frame
   Issues to discuss might include:

   - How long should the different stages take to complete?
   - What would be a realistic completion date in view of our separate commitments and departmental policy?

5. Joint supervisors

   - What roles will be taken by each supervisor, for instance, main and secondary, different theoretical inputs?
   - If there is disagreement about methods and so forth between joint supervisors, how is this to be resolved?

6. Other issues relating to supervisor–student understandings?

Departmental Expectations and Resources

1. Written information

   - What departmental handbooks or other documents are relevant for postgraduate students?

2. What access does the student have to:
   - A study place, pigeonhole, and so forth?
   - Tea/coffee facilities?
   - Photocopying, interloan fees, and so forth?
   - Paid work such as tutoring?
   - Computers?
   - Funding/research grants? If available, how do I apply? When are the deadlines? Who can I contact for more information?
   - Support services, such as technical, secretarial?

3. What expectations does the department have of the student?
   - Seminar presentation of thesis in progress?
   - What else?

4. Monitoring supervision, resolving conflict
   - What are the departmental procedures for monitoring the supervision in the event that one of us is not happy with its progress?

5. Other departmental issues?

University Requirements

1. University guidelines
   - What university documents are available on master's-level supervision?

2. Clarification of thesis assessment
   - How is the assessment of the thesis conducted?
   - Who will be the external examiner? When is this decided? Can the student have a say?

3. Extensions and deferment
   - What are the protocols for extensions and deferment?
   - In the event that I need an extension over the summer, or beyond, what will the position be regarding supervision?

4. University protocols
   - What university-level channels are available in the event that one of us is not happy with the progress of the supervision and the department cannot or is inappropriate to resolve this?

5. Ethics

- What ethical issues need to be considered in the research project?
- Do I need to apply for consent from an appropriate university committee?

6. Other university-level issues?

Note. From *Postgraduate Supervision: Guidelines for Discussion*, by A. Graham and B. Grant, 1993, Auckland, New Zealand: Higher Education Research Office, University of Auckland. Copyright 1993 by A. Graham and B. Grant. Adapted with permission.

APPENDIX B
SUPERVISION RECORD

Supervision Record	CSMTER, University of Waikato
Student: _____ Supervisor: _____	
Date: _____ Course: 0781 _____ Topic: _____	
Matters Discussed:	
Matters Decided:	
Student's Tasks:	Confirmed: _____ _____ _____
Supervisor's Tasks:	Next Meeting:

Note. From *Supervision Record*, by R. Barbour, 1992, Hamilton, New Zealand: University of Waikato. Copyright © 1992 by R. Barbour. Adapted with permission.

REFERENCES

Barbour, R. (1992). *Supervision record*. Hamilton, New Zealand: University of Waikato.
Bell, B., & Gilbert, J. (1995). *Teacher development: A model from science education*. London: Falmer.
Graham, A., & Grant, B. (1993). *Postgraduate supervision: Guidelines for discussion*. Auckland, New Zealand: Higher Education Research Office, University of Auckland.

13

Scholarly Writing in Mathematics and Science Education Higher Degree Courses

Tom J. Cooper
Annette R. Baturo
Leonie Harris
Queensland University of Technology

Scholarly writing is easy to recognize but difficult to define. It has a deceptive simplicity that enables the reader to follow the author's arguments from introduction to conclusion without any "jarring" caused by awkward language or structuring. It persuades the reader that the author's conclusions are the only acceptable conclusions to draw. Inherent in scholarly writing is the ability to design and maintain an overarching framework in which pertinent arguments are embedded, the ability to evaluate statements and conclusions in terms of the framework, and the ability to monitor one's work from the reader's perspective. Thus, scholarly writing is a metacognitive process requiring a sound knowledge base of the mechanics of writing (spelling, grammar, sentence and paragraph structure, etc.).

For this chapter, scholarly writing is considered as a social, political, and historical construction, an evolved product of consensus among the community that reads it. The term *scholarly* is used to denote status or value, so that scholarly writing is writing that the community of readers agrees represents an acceptable addition to the community's knowledge. Because of this, different disciplines or communities may have different requirements for writing that they wish to call scholarly.

Our purpose in this chapter is to explore students' difficulties with respect to writing in mathematics and science education dissertations. In doing this, we analyze the scholarly writing in this area in terms of audience (community), purpose, and form.

The obvious audience for such dissertations is the mathematics and science education research community. However, because mathematics and science education research wishes to maintain status and credibility within the wider education and social science research communities and, to a lesser extent, the mathematics and science research communities, the audience has to be considered more widely. Hence, mathematics and science education dissertations have to be acceptable to these wider communities.

The purpose of the dissertation is to introduce the student (the writer) into the research community and currently requires the student to write a scholarly report on a piece of research that has been undertaken to investigate some nontrivial aspect of mathematics and science education. Writing a research paper is one of the most common university writing tasks: an author must locate, read, select, and organize material from different sources to form an original synthesis (Bridgeman & Carlson, 1983; Nelson, 1992). In their present evolved state, most mathematics and science education dissertations would include a clear statement of the objectives, a synopsis of the salient literature, a succinct explanation of the research design, a full account of the results, a discussion in which inferences are drawn from the results and analyzed in terms of the literature provided, and a summary of the findings.

We believe that the form of scholarly writing can be considered at three levels: (a) the macrostructure, that is, the overarching framework which incorporates and integrates the various components of the entire dissertation; (b) the microstructure, which oversees the flow of arguments within each component; and (c) the mechanics (e.g., syntax, style, referencing), that render the dissertation readable. A scholarly writer is therefore expected to have a coherent macrostructure, strong arguments in the microstructure, and excellent mechanics of grammar, syntax, and referencing. From the author's perspective, the construction of a dissertation requires a consideration of the macrostructure before the microstructure, with the mechanics of writing being of secondary consideration. However, from the reader's perspective, this hierarchy is reversed, with the mechanics of writing being of paramount importance in facilitating the reader's comprehension of the micro- and macrostructures.

Although there are very few studies relating to mathematics and science education dissertations in particular, there is a consensus in the literature on general writing that many students in higher degree courses have enormous difficulties with scholarly writing.

WHAT CONSTITUTES SCHOLARLY WRITING?

Turabian (1973) described written communication as that which is "intended to show the student's ability to express ideas—his own and others—clearly, effectively and correctly" (p. 2). Turabian argued that competence is shown in the student's ability to research a specific topic; to select from amassed materials, facts, and ideas that are relevant and pertinent to the topic; and to organize and document the information properly (i.e., the macrostructure), as well as in the ability to present information clearly, logically, and effectively (the microstructure) with respect to grammar, spelling, and punctuation (mechanics). With all this to do, achieving quality in scholarly writing is difficult.

Barrass (1978) listed eight points that, although aimed at scientific writing, are relevant to scholarly writing in general: *explanation, clarity, completeness, impartiality, order, accuracy, objectivity,* and *simplicity.* He argued that scientists should write "direct, straightforward prose, free from jargon and other distracting elaborations" (p. 32) and should take account of: (a) *appropriateness* to the subject, reader, and occasion; (b) *balance,* to show an awareness of all sides of a question and a sense of proportion; (c) *brevity,* which entails the use of no more words than are needed to convey each thought to the reader and the omission of unnecessary detail; (d) *consistency* in the use of numbers, names, abbreviations, symbols, spelling, punctuation, and terms; (e) *control,* which is shown by paying attention to arrangement, presentation, and organization; (f) *interest,* which is to hold the reader's attention; (g) *persuasiveness,* which is to convince the reader of the forceful presentation of evidence; (h) *precision,* which is to support exact definition, and give accurate measurement; (i) *sincerity,* which is to present the writer's persona with the qualities of frankness, honesty, and humility; and (j) *unity,* which is the quality of wholeness and coherence.

Perry (1993) recommended that, in writing their dissertations, students use consistent styles for headings, spaces, quotations, references, and gender-related language. He seemed to be focusing on the consistency and control aspects listed by Barrass (1978).

Murray (1978) claimed that writing was essentially a discovery process, in which writers examined what they wanted to say and how they wanted to say it, a process which consisted of a cycle of composing, reading, considering, revising, and planning (Graves, 1983; Perl, 1979). As Kelly (1989) summarized: "The act of writing has great generative power, both in the sense of creating ideas and creating language to express these ideas" (p. 80). Hence scholarly writing, having a recursive nature, is the end product of considerable revision.

CAUSES AND SOLUTIONS

Freedman (1984) stated that "writing is a mode of learning and, in fact, a mode of knowing that is central to academic enterprise" (p. 98). Yet despite the importance of scholarly writing, there was a general consensus in the literature that this skill was rarely taught in conjunction with higher degree courses (Boice & Johnson, 1984; Greaser, 1979; Reitt, 1980). According to Riggar and Smith (1987), "the facilitation of graduate students' writing efforts through seminars, workshops, classes and even mentoring is a rare commodity in academia" (p. 3).

The lack of instruction in writing skills and strategies is seen by some researchers as the reason for students' poor writing performance. For example, Lewins (1988) argued that students are not being taught to think through the constituent parts of a dissertation to derive a coherent whole. This position is supported by Freedman (1984), who stated that the majority of students seeking help with their writing through the Carleton University Writing Tutorial Service had problems in the category of "pre thinking and thought problems" (p. 82) such as analysis of the assignment, the delimitation of the topic, the determination of the appropriate research strategies and the attempt to find significance and focus in the data amassed. As Nightingale (1988) summarized:

> No longer can teachers in higher education simply condemn a lack of basic skills. Very few students reaching higher education make simple errors which can be corrected by remedial instruction. Rather the complex demands of study at this level may, at times, result in failures to produce correct language which are, in fact, caused by difficulties in dealing with the subject content NOT the lack of knowledge of correct forms. Understanding of content and ability to communicate it skilfully are inextricably intertwined. (p. 278)

With respect to science students' scholarly writing, Barrass (1978) contended that many scientists received no formal training in writing, even though writing is a part of science. Woodford (1967) claimed that lack of examples of scholarly writing in the pertinent literature was another contributing factor to students' writing problems, arguing that articles in scientific journals (including those of the highest standards) were generally poorly written and that some of the worst written articles were by authors who consciously pretended to a "scientific scholarly style." He contended that although readers recognized the writing as pompous, they believed it was their responsibility to grasp the conventions of the writing style in order to understand the author's meaning. Woodford strongly asserted that, as pieces of communication, the articles were "appalling" and, as writing models, exerted a corrupting influence on young scientists' writing, reading, and thinking. This position is supported by Hertzog (1988), who maintained that students believed that the writing in published work, because of its status, should be imitated even when it was poorly constructed and difficult to understand.

However, the literature revealed that well-written journal articles are also a source of students' writing problems. For example, students do not have access to others' work in progress and see only finished products, so they do not realize the number of drafts, revisions, and rewrites which have to go into a finished piece of writing (Becker, 1986; Bridwell, 1980; Graves, 1984; Perl, 1979; Pianko, 1979). Because of this, Becker (1986) contended that many higher degree students feared writing because they would not be able to organize their thoughts and their writing would be chaotic and confusing. They were afraid to let others read their first drafts in case their unfinished work was criticized and ridiculed. In endeavoring to overcome this behavior, Graves (1984) provided students with examples of the first draft as well as the final product of one of his own articles.

Becker (1986), however, found it difficult to convince his students that his behavior in writing a manuscript 8 to 10 times was normal. He postulated that, in undergraduate studies, students became experts at "one-shot term papers" (p. 14), a technique that failed when, as graduate students, they were required to produce longer (and more theoretical, we suspect) papers; that is, the one-draft papers did not reach a high enough standard for the students to feel confident that sharing their writing would not attract ridicule or criticism. Moreover, Becker maintained that the short essays that constituted the written academic tasks of undergraduates focused on topics in which the students had no interest, little knowledge, and no real choice. Hence, these essays were so artificial that any reader "would not choose to read it if he [or she] were not being paid to be an examiner" (p. 86).

PROMOTING SCHOLARLY WRITING

In promoting scholarly writing, the literature revealed that students' beliefs and the consequential effects of these beliefs need to be considered. For example, higher degree students appear to be motivated toward developing scholarly writing techniques because, according to Becker (1986), they believed that their professional futures rested on how peers and superiors judged what they wrote. This was in contrast to undergraduate students, who believed that what was written in one short essay would not affect their lives to a large degree. According to Freedman (1984), "Students begin to write better—and seek help with their writing—at the level of upper division courses, where suddenly they have something important to say, and someone to say it to" (p. 32).

However, students' reactions to comments on their writing were often negative, thus making it more difficult for the supervisor to encourage scholarly writing. Becker (1986) claimed that students were not receptive to revisions because they felt that these highlighted their status as "subordinates in a hierarchical organization" (p. 46). In addition, he discovered that students often had fixed notions of what constituted scholarly writing, thus impeding their ability to perceive their own shortcomings. As an example, Becker cited one of his students who believed that "the way someone writes—the more difficult the writing style—the more intellectual they sound" (p. 29). Becker suggested that this was possibly one reason why scholarly writing was sometimes verbose.

Richards (1986) also argued that graduate students' writing was affected by their beliefs about the "academic and elitist nature of higher-degree courses" (p. 109) and consequently wrote to project a persona acceptable to the academic research community. Thus, she argued, students were reluctant to change what they perceived to be the acceptable elite writing style.

Becker (1986) claimed that criticism did not necessarily encourage students to reflect on their own poor writing. In fact, it could cause adverse reactions. He reported that even scholars often reacted to criticism in one or more of the following ways: (a) by reverting to what Becker called "school talk" (e.g., "Do I have to do such and such because they say so?"); (b) by feeling maligned, like "an artist whose masterwork had been mauled by philistines" (p. 22); or (c) by believing that reviewers were whimsical, without real standards, and prime to making capricious decisions. Becker argued that if scholars (who are enculturated in the demands of the research community) exhibit these reactions, then no less should be expected from students. He also contended that these adverse reactions could be largely overcome if students were shown the variety of ways that writing may be misinterpreted by others.

Becker (1986) also made the point that much professional writing became "privatized": that is, scholars tended to write in isolation. However, he reported that some scholars overcame the problem by developing a reading circle, a group of friends who read their work in progress and helped them to sort out the first draft. Becker argued that such reading and editing circles were based on trust, usually resulted in reciprocal relationships being developed (with members helping each other), and could be of benefit to writers.

Notwithstanding the students' beliefs about scholarly writing and their often adverse reactions to criticism of poor writing, the literature agreed that many problems could be overcome. However, Barrass (1978) contended that the writer must first recognize the possibility of improvement for the desire to improve writing to be fulfilled. He firmly maintained that all written compositions should be treated in the same way, namely, "always think, plan, write and then revise" (p. 37).

There was a mixed reaction in the literature in relation to deficits in the mechanics of writing. Freedman (1984) reported that relatively few of the students involved in the Carleton University Writing Tutorial Service had persistent difficulties with grammar. She claimed that students with weaknesses in grammar often had more serious prethinking and organizational problems and, once the thinking problems were resolved, the grammatical difficulties, especially those related to sentence structure, were resolved as well. To this end, Moses (1992) suggested a comprehensive checklist for students to follow in order to self-check and revise their drafts. She argued that such a checklist would be helpful, as it offered a practical framework on which students could focus their prewriting reading and assess their work. Hubbuch (1989) also suggested a checklist for editing written papers. Sloan (1990), however, was critical of handbooks on writing and style that espoused sternly prescriptive attitudes and expected students to avoid various error types.

CLASSIFYING STUDENT DIFFICULTIES

In their research, which focused on identifying the formal and mechanical errors in college writing, Connors and Lunsford (1988, 1993) noted the lack of research findings in this area, despite the fact that the correction of student papers by teachers and educators is an important part of university life. Their research also found that many students saw teachers as error-obsessed and concerned only with mechanical issues, whereas the teachers' responses clearly showed that they were more concerned about how their students planned and ordered their writing. Their study did not, however, extend to student reactions to the corrections and comments made by teachers.

In an earlier discussion paper, Cooper and Baturo (1993) classified dissertation-writing problems as follows:

1. Errors of *syntax and mechanics*. These included ungrammatical writing; inconsistent and incomplete referencing; bald, unqualified, and unsubstantiated statements; and incomplete placement of references (making it difficult to determine whether statements reflected the literature's perspective or the author's personal perspective).

2. Errors of *style*. These included poor sentence structure (which constricted the flow of meaning within and across sentences), inelegant writing (e.g., omission of small words and connectives, tautologies, value-laden adjectives and adverbs, repetition, long and convoluted sentences), and inappropriate placement of phrases and poor integration of ideas.

3. Errors of *structure*. These included inconsistency across purposes, research design, and conclusions (e.g., confusion between experimental and generative designs, qualitative and quantitative approaches to research, or naturalistic and intervening research techniques or categories); absence of delineation between observations and inferences; and absence of scaffolding in writing (e.g., lack of pre- and postorganizers).

Cooper and Baturo (1993) proposed that syntactical and stylistic deficiencies in students' writing had their roots in the schooling and undergraduate years, whereas structural deficiencies were due to a lack of awareness of the role of logic in planning a dissertation structure.

Lankshear (1994) argued that coherent and consistent lines of argument are essential for scholarly writing. He characterized the claims possible in an argument in four ways: *empirical, conceptual, normative,* and *metaphysical.* Empirical claims deal with "how the world is" and are supported by sensory observations; conceptual claims are about the meaning of terms and are accepted as true or false by argument from definitions; normative claims deal with values (good/bad, etc.) and are based on judgments about quality, propriety, etc.; and metaphysical claims are based on personal beliefs and are therefore unverifiable.

He contended that a valid argument consists of "true" premises or supported premises, followed by reasoning that conformed to the rules of logic. He stressed the need for scholarly writing to clarify concepts, make distinctions, classify and identify categories, and create taxonomies, and he emphasized that such writing needed to be sensitive to a range of perspectives and theories.

CASE STUDIES

Because of our concerns at Queensland University of Technology with mathematics and science education students' dissertation writing, a small study was undertaken to: (a) identify and classify the students' writing problems in terms of mechanics, microstructure, and macrostructure; and (b) develop and document methods to effectively diagnose and remediate these difficulties and errors. Fourteen masters of education students, whose supervisors had identified as having writing problems, participated in the study. English was the first language for 9 of the 14 students but, because research has found that second-language writers exhibit very similar strategies to first-language writers (Cumming, 1989), this chapter does not differentiate between first- and second-language writers.

The students were in a variety of situations with respect to their dissertations, from being in the initial stages to nearly completed, so data were obtained from work in progress. Hence, the final draft of the dissertation was examined in some cases and attention was given to drafts of chapters in other cases. As improvement in writing was the motivation for the study, there was an attempt to remediate students' difficulties identified from analyses of drafts of their dissertations.

A researcher-editor who was not involved in the MEd courses interviewed the students a number of times. In most instances, the students were interviewed individually but, on occasion, the relevant supervisor was present. The interview focused initially on errors identified in the dissertation and later on the individual student's reactions to suggestions for writing improvement. This interview process was essentially ad hoc, being contingent on the errors found and the student's reactions and responses.

The editor's role was to focus on the mechanics and, at times, the microstructure of the dissertations. To this end, the editor read the dissertations with detachment, focusing on mistakes (usually careless and one-off) and errors (recurring mistakes) in the mechanics of structure, style, and grammar. In cases where the meaning was not clear or was ambiguous, the editor asked the student to explain the material. From this explanation, a different way was found of expressing the information.

The students' amended dissertations were then read by the supervisor and other researchers and the student was given advice on content, microstructure, and macrostructure. Where appropriate, the supervisor, the editor, and other researchers discussed each student's progress.

Specific comments, suggestions, and corrections were made on each dissertation and, except for those students who chose to work from written suggestions, discussed with the students, who were at liberty to accept or reject the suggestions. On students' requests, new drafts of the dissertation were read a second time or, in some cases, several times.

Students' errors were categorized in terms of *mechanics* (spelling, grammar, tense, sentence and paragraph construction, and referencing); *microstructure* (maintaining the flow of argument within a small section of the dissertation); and *macrostructure* (the organization and structural consistency of the dissertation). There was no attempt to quantify the errors and mistakes because of the small number of students sampled.

Errors in the Mechanics of Writing

In this study, we have categorized the mechanics of writing as either *general writing* or *scholarly writing* (see Table 13.1). The mechanics of general writing ranged from low-level skills (e.g., spelling, punctuation, tense) to higher level skills (e.g., rules of grammar, sentence structure). These skills can be self-acquired through reference to an appropriate style manual which, for the mathematics and science education students at QUT, is the *Publication Manual of the American Psychological Association* (APA, 3rd ed., 1987).

The mechanics of scholarly writing also include low-level skills (e.g., referencing) and higher level skills (e.g., synthesizing the literature, supporting claims by referencing the appropriate literature). However, these skills are not often stressed at the undergraduate level and consequently require intervention, a task that is normally undertaken by the supervisor. In addition, scholarly writing needs to incorporate an awareness of those skills that are idiomatic to the English language (e.g., the use of prepositions) and skills that are changing as a result of social influences (e.g., sexist or ethnically biased language).

TABLE 13.1
Categorization of Writing Mechanics

General-Writing Mechanics	Scholarly Writing Mechanics
Spelling	Unsubstantiated claims
Use of apostrophe	Synthesis of literature
Hyphenation	Circumlocution
Punctuation	Tautology
Subject/verb agreement	Value-laden words
Tense	Omission of articles
Referencing (punctuation)	Incomplete sentences
Wrong or missing prepositions	Dangling or misplaced modifiers
Inappropriate words	Structural ambiguity
Sexist language	
Ethnically biased language	
Other errors	

Because the errors in the mechanics of general writing were usually entrenched through years of misuse, they were seen as a starting point for individual attention from an expert in the area. These types of errors were the major focus of the individual interviews with the researcher-editor.

For the purposes of analyzing the participating students' dissertations, the mechanics have been categorized as those that are essential for comprehension (*general-writing mechanics*), and those that are required to reach a level of scholarly writing (*scholarly writing mechanics*). Table 13.1 shows how we have differentiated between the various skills that are required for scholarly writing.

General-Writing Mechanical Errors.

1. *Spelling.* Spelling errors were often typographical (e.g., *diversed* for *diversified*), but many that were not (e.g., *comented* for *commented*). With the advent of spelling checks on computers, spelling errors, the omission and misuse of the apostrophe (see Item 2), and the use of hyphens (see Item 3) are not occurring as frequently as they used to. However, a spelling check will not pick up errors such as *casual* when *causal* is meant.

2. *Use of apostrophe.* The misuse (e.g., *all student's intuitive knowledge* instead of *all students' intuitive knowledge*) or lack of use of the apostrophe (e.g., *learners perception* instead of *learner's perception*) were other sources of error for many students. They seemed to be particularly confused when homophones were involved (e.g., its it's; who's whose; there's theirs; they're there). Another use of the apostrophe that appeared to be not known at all was that the possessive " 's" might be required when a noun was followed by a gerund. Therefore, *focused on the student identifying the correct procedure*

should be written as *focused on the student's identifying the correct procedure*, because it was the *identifying* ability not the *student* that was the object of the focus. It would have been less messy to have avoided the gerund altogether and written *focused on the student's ability to identify the correct procedure*.

3. *Hyphenation*. The students were generally unsure as to when to hyphenate. For example, *underachiever* and *socioeconomic* do not require hyphens, but were hyphenated by some students. Prefixes such as "co-" and "non-" caused confusion, possibly because some words beginning with these prefixes are hyphenated and others are not (e.g., *coordinate, cooperate, co-author; nonconformity, non-cooperation*).

In other cases, hyphens were omitted when phrases were used as adjectives (e.g., *one to one correspondence*, instead of *one-to-one correspondence*) or when two words were used as a single descriptor of the related noun (e.g., *low achieving students* instead of *low-achieving students*).

4. *Punctuation*. The conventions for the use of all punctuation are set out in the APA manual.

The *comma* seemed to be the most poorly used punctuation mark. It was often misplaced when used in place of parentheses. For example, *to select from amassed materials, facts, and ideas* is clearer when written as *to select, from amassed materials, facts, and ideas*.

Sometimes a comma was omitted, leaving the reader bewildered as to the meaning of the sentence: for example, *Following success or failure attributions to ability or task difficulty (stable factors) respectively increase or decrease expectancy of future success to a greater extent than attributions to effort or luck (unstable factors)*. It is unclear whether "respectively" refers to "attributions," "stable factors," or "expectancy."

5. *Subject/verb agreement*. Very often, the subject of a sentence did not agree with the verb in number. Examples of this were: *reading and writing was considered; the interview method of data collection have a lot of strength*.

The word *data* was used as both a singular collective noun and as a plural noun in some dissertations. Although both are now acceptable, the onus is on the writer to be consistent in using the word in its singular or plural form.

6. *Tense*. Tense was often inconsistent in the students' writing, both within a sentence (low-level mechanics) and within particular sections (high-level mechanics). For example, when quoting a source within the literature review, it is generally good policy to use past tense (e.g., *Smith (1984) stated mathematics knowledge is* . . .). When talking about something happening later in the dissertation or when theories or models are described, present tense is recommended. An example of inconsistent tense in a sentence is provided:

There are 10 boys and 8 girls in the class who were involved in the exercises, and as all have attended the field location (Sea World) at least once during the past 6 months and twice in the past 12 months, have a high familiarity with the field site. Apart from the mix of tense, this sentence has other problems: for example, the omission of the comma after "and" (required because of the parenthetical nature of the text following). This student had problems with the scholarly writing mechanics as well as the base-writing mechanics. Merely correcting the subject/verb agreement will not overcome the structural inadequacy of this student's writing. One way to improve the scholarliness of the writing would be to write: *The exercises involved 10 boys and 8 girls, each of whom was familiar with the field location, Sea World, having visited the site twice in the past 12 months (with at least one visit during the last 6 months).*

7. *Referencing.* There are two types of situations in which referencing occurs—within the body of the paper and in the bibliography. Although the students are required to use the referencing conventions of the APA (1987), several did not adhere to these conventions. One of the greatest source of errors for students in referencing was the use of the ampersand (&). It is used in the bibliography when authors and editors are listed and used in the body of the paper in parentheses only. Thus, in the body of the paper, *(Austin, and Houson, 1979)* should be *(Austin & Houson, 1979)* and *Austin & Houson, 1979, stated that . . .* should be written as *Austin and Houson (1979) stated that . . .*

Within the body of the paper, students often wrote bald, unsubstantiated statements, a referencing error that is difficult to rectify without guidance by an expert and therefore will be dealt with in the section on good writing mechanics.

8. *Wrong preposition.* In the case studies, the following examples of using the wrong preposition were noted: "limitations for"; "based around"; "existing of"; "fatigued with." This type of error was difficult to eradicate because the wrong usage had usually been long-term and therefore sounded quite natural to the writer. Because of the idiomatic nature of prepositions, they were the source of enormous difficulties for students whose first language was not English.

9. *Inappropriate word.* A word is inappropriate when the meaning does not fit the context and does not express the intended meaning. An example of an inappropriate word is a malapropism, such as *The students exhibited exotic behavior on this task,* when the writer meant that the students displayed *erratic* behavior. Other types of inappropriate word usage often occur as a result of the writer using a new or unfamiliar word (e.g., *a vexed question* instead of *a vexing question*) or through the substitution of a homonym (a similar sounding word), for the intended word (e.g., *Their not learning* instead of *They're not learning*).

10. *Sexist language*. Gender should not be of any significance in academic writing; therefore, writers should try to avoid sexist words, particularly those that patronize or denigrate women. Gender was a particular difficulty for some students who still used *he* to stand for both *he and/or she*. The APA gives very good guidelines for overcoming sexist language.

11. *Other errors*. The previous errors serve only as illustrations of the main types encountered in the writing examined in this study. Other errors exhibited by the cases included:

- The use of acronyms that were not explained in full at the first mention.
- Overuse of the word "that" (resulting in a static, monotonous delivery).
- Omission of prepositions, participles, and articles (e.g., *a, the*).
- The unqualified use of *it, this, that*, and *these*, which need to be qualified by a noun in most cases if the meaning is to be unambiguous.
- The use of capitals where they are not necessary.
- Failing to define specialist terms.
- The misuse of brackets.
- The use of value-laden words.

Scholarly Writing Mechanical Errors.

1. *Unsubstantiated claims*. This was a common practice among the dissertation writers and two types of errors emerged: (a) no reference to the literature to support the claims, and (b) reference to the literature but without making clear what was supported and what was not. An error of each type is provided in the following.

For two thousand years, mathematics has been dominated by an absolutist paradigm that views it as a body of infallible and objective truth, far removed from the affairs and values of humanity. Without substantiation, this statement can only be considered to be the writer's personal opinion. Substantiation is needed to take the statement from the realm of personal opinion to a consensus of expert knowledge.

Many students placed a reference so that it was difficult to determine whether the statements reflected the literature's perspective or the author's personal perspective. For example:

To adults, the equals sign in sentences such as 2 + 4 = 6 is, intuitively, an abstraction of the notion of sameness and, on a more sophisticated level, an equivalence relation. Sentences with no plus sign (e.g., 3 = 3), or more than one plus sign (e.g., 2 + 1 = 2 + 1), do not suggest an action to adults; rather, these sentences are seen to "require a judgment about their truth-value". 6- to 12-year-old students were found to: (a) understand the equals sign in number sentences such as 2 + 4 = as meaning that something had to be done; (b) not see 3 + 2 = 2 + 3 in terms of

sameness, but rather as an action by restating the sentence as 3 + 2 = 5 or 5 = 2
+ 3; (c) not accept the equals sign in sentences without it being preceded with one
or more operation sign; (d) have "an extreme rigidity" about written sentences
and a tendency to perform actions rather than reflect; and (e) not to "change in
their thinking about equity as they get older". (Behr, Erlwanger, & Nichols, 1980)

The position of the reference causes one to attribute the entire paragraph
to the authors cited. However, the lack of a specific page number in the
reference, combined with the lack of indenting, leads the reader to suspect
that perhaps only some of the paragraph could be attributed to the cited
authors. To whom, therefore, should the internal quotations (if that is what
the quotation marks indicate) be attributed—the original authors or the
dissertation writer?

2. *Synthesis of the literature.* Students often made a series of "motherhood"
statements when reviewing the literature, resulting in short, abrupt paragraphs that invariably began with statements such as those shown in the
following. (Space does not permit the inclusion of the entire paragraphs.)
Students need to be taught to organize the literature around the pertinent
arguments, rather than simply providing an historical account presented in
a time sequence:

Work by Lanzetta & [sic] Hanna (1969) showed that . . .
Weiner (1972) expected that . . .
Nicholls (1976) challenged . . .
Sohn (1977) noted that . . .

3. *Incomplete sentences.* Students often do not write complete sentences
(Connors & Lunsford; 1988; Cooper & Baturo, 1993; Sloan, 1990). A sentence
is a group of words expressing a complete thought, so it must have a subject
and a predicate that contains a finite verb. An incomplete sentence leaves
the reader guessing as to what the intended message is. For example: *A*
classroom environment in which diversity can thrive, and where the learners
feel free to express themselves without feeling guilty or dumb announced Beder
(1990). More information is needed to make the meaning of this sentence
clear. A suggestion for improvement is: *According to Beder (1990), what is*
required is a classroom environment in which diversity can thrive and where
learners feel free to express themselves.

Another example of an incomplete sentence is: *The first being relatively*
simple so as to settle the students to help confirm their ability and procedural
level. There is no finite verb in this sentence, only infinite verbs (*to settle,*
to help), hence the reader is unable to distinguish the subject from the
predicate. Perhaps the author mistakenly thought that in this instance "being" was a verb. To correct this problem, the entire sentence needs to be
reconstructed because merely substituting the verb "was" for "being" will

not produce a flowing sentence. The following was suggested: *In order to settle the students, so that their true ability and procedural level could be confirmed, the first task was relatively simple.*

4. *Dangling or misplaced modifier.* A modifier is a word, phrase, or clause that limits specifiers, qualifies, or describes another word. Because English is a language that depends on word order, related words (i.e., the adjectival and adverbial modifiers) must be placed as close as possible to the words that they modify. Misplaced modifiers "are as disconcerting as a pebble that jars one's teeth in a mouthful of plum pudding" (Fowler, 1968, p. 436). They require several attempts to comprehend the meaning or they lead to a misunderstanding of the meaning (Corbett, 1987). Following are examples of difficulties with modifiers.

This model is based on incorporating the common verbal cues present in many percentage application problems, being the words is, of, percent. After much deliberation, the following was suggested as an alternative: *This model incorporates the common verbal cues (is, of, percent present in) that are often given in many percentage application problems.* Note that other aspects of the sentence (e.g., *on incorporating*) also impeded comprehension of the original sentence.

Program planners would seriously question Ausubel's assumptions on the cognitive abilities of our high school students which would enable them to learn mathematics in a purely expository manner. The modifying clause "which would enable . . . manner" is misplaced. In the example, the clause refers to "students" when, in fact, it relates to "abilities." The suggested change was: *Program planners for our high school students would seriously question Ausubel's assumptions concerning the cognitive abilities required for learning mathematics in a purely expository manner.*

5. *Structural ambiguity.* An ambiguous word, phrase, or sentence is one that can be interpreted in two or more ways. The most common sources of ambiguity are inexact reference of pronouns; modifiers that can be misinterpreted; incomplete idioms (e.g., "I liked Alice as well as Bill."); and ambiguous words (Ebbitt & Ebbitt, 1982, pp. 364–365). Some samples of writing that exhibited structural ambiguity are provided here.

Cohen and Manion observe that it may also be used at the other extreme from this project which involves a single teacher. It may be a "sophisticated study of organizational change in industry using a large research team and backed by government sponsors" (pp. 208–209). However, it is essentially . . . In this example, "it" refers to different nouns and is therefore ambiguous and confusing to the reader.

Cobb (1988) argues from a radical constructivist perspective that cultural knowledge in general and mathematics in part can be taken as solid bedrock upon which to anchor analyses of learning and teaching is questioned. Apart from inadequate punctuation, this sentence is flawed in that the reader is unsure whether the meaning of this sentence is: (a) that Cobb supports cultural knowledge as bedrock on which analyses of learning and teaching is based; (b) that Cobb supports cultural knowledge as bedrock on which to anchor analyses of learning, but questions teaching; or (c) that Cobb questions both the learning and teaching.

6. *Circumlocution.* This is the art of using many words when a few would do. Circumlocution often stems from a mistaken belief that verbosity and erudition are synonymous (a point also made by Becker, 1986). Some examples of this from the students' writing are provided here and are followed by the suggested revisions.

The question was then posed as how, (The question then asked how);
In order to respond to the importance, (To respond . . .);
It is this question that is, (The question is).

7. *Tautology.* Fowler (1968) defined a tautology as that which says the same thing, so it could be considered as a special case of circumlocution. He described several forms of tautology but the form that occurred most often in the sample of students' writing was what he called the "abstract appendage" (p. 615). For example, *planning beforehand* is tautological because "planning" means "in advance" or "beforehand"; *a positive added bonus, revert back,* and *linking them together* are other examples. A tautology · is often written without conscious awareness but, when written deliberately, its use appears to stem from a misguided appreciation of what constitutes scholarly writing.

Other tautologies are even more verbose and, as the following example shows, interfere with the flow of the argument: *McLaughlin had done a thorough research on the topic and examined how various researchers' opinions were on self-evaluation.* Because "thorough research" is undertaken with a view to examining the work of other researchers, the sentence is tautological. Replacing "and" with "to" would be an improvement but simpler wording would be preferable as shown by: *McLaughlin began by examining how various researchers conceived of . . .*

Errors in the Microstructure of Writing

A dissertation is a specific writing genre and, like all genres, its conventions and requirements must be maintained throughout the writing. Thus students need to maintain "a sense of audience appropriate for the focus of their study" (Cooper & Baturo, 1993, p. 5) and to maintain a consistent argument within and across paragraphs.

One of the greatest challenges at the microstructure level was to ensure that arguments flowed from one sentence to another and from one paragraph to another. We have already enumerated the many ways in which the flow of argument within a sentence is hindered by poor mechanics of writing. However, there are students whose mechanics are quite good but whose paragraph construction is such that the flow of meaning "within and across paragraphs is constricted" (Cooper & Baturo, 1993, p. 4). Although space does not permit the use of examples of faulty paragraph construction, some of the ways in which this problem can be improved are provided (e.g., connectives and their placement; the appropriate placement of phrases, clauses, and sentences; and convoluted sentences).

Another aspect of microstructure is *consistency* in argument across paragraphs. Inconsistencies were evident in sequencing, relationships, connections, switches in argument claims, and logical development. The absence of such a consistency was the major microstructure difficulty exhibited by the students. It was difficult to identify and repair because inconsistency is a structural fault in an argument and, as such, incorporates logical inadequacies with respect to the content of the dissertation as well as difficulties in generic writing skills.

The *tone* of a dissertation needs to be formal, precise, and succinct but, in the case studies, some students found it difficult to maintain the formal register in their writing, lapsing, at times, into the use of colloquial expressions that were too informal for the genre. Some examples were: *Schoenfeld reckons, Weiner figured, doing sums, pretty realistic*. One student's writing, although exhibiting good writing skills, was marred by a flowery, poetic style that was not in keeping with the genre of a mathematics education dissertation. An example of this writing is shown in the following:

> *However, in relinquishing the certainty of mathematics it may be that we are giving up the false security of the womb. It may be time to give up this protective myth. Perhaps human beings, like all creatures, are born into a world of wonders, an inexhaustible source of delight, which we will never fathom completely. These include the crystal worlds and rich ornate webs which the human imagination weaves in mathematical thought. In these are infinite worlds beyond the infinite, and wondrous long and tight chains of reasoning. But it could be that such imaginings are part of what it means to be human, and not the certain truths we took them to be. Perhaps facing up to uncertainty is the next stage of maturity for the human race. Relinquishing myths of certainty may be the next act of decentration that human development requires.*

The inappropriate tone of the paragraph made it difficult to ascertain what the writer meant within some sentences (e.g., "infinite worlds beyond the infinite") and across the entire paragraph. It certainly does not meet the criterion of succinctness because the writing could be condensed to the following without losing its meaning: *The myth of mathematics is that it is based on certainties. It is time to move forward and challenge this.*

Flow of Argument Within and Across Paragraphs.

1. *Connectives*. In developing a flow of argument, connectives are important, particularly in conceptual claims (Lankshear, 1994). Typical connectives are *because, through*, and *therefore*. The flow of argument can be interrupted if a connective is omitted, wrongly placed, or inappropriate, as it was in many of the dissertations under review.

2. *Placement of phrases, clauses, and sentences*. The flow of meaning within and across sentences can be interrupted by the unnecessary placement of phrases (such as *dangling or misplaced modifiers*), clauses and sentences, as in: *Chouser tested the students using the test as social aspects of science and understanding using "Methods & Procedures of Science: An Examination," the "Watson–Glasem Critical Thinking Appraisal," and "Understanding of Selected Biological Principles: an Examination."* The placement of the phrase "using the test as social aspects of science and understanding" makes the meaning of the sentence unclear, particularly to a nonexpert in the field. Do the titles name the tests used? Were the tests social aspects of science or did the procedures test the social aspects of science? Further, repetition of the connective "using" in such a short space of time was jarring.

3. *Convoluted sentences*. Many students used overly long and convoluted sentences containing awkward phrasing. Some (e.g., the first example provided) can be amended quite easily by partitioning the sentence into smaller sentences:

Chouser (1975) made a comparison of two groups of college students who were subjected to different approaches to teaching biological science, with the control group taught inside of laboratory and an experimental group which was taught by outside activities.

This sentence is overlong and would be improved by partitioning it into smaller sentences, namely: *Chouser (1975) made a comparison of two groups of college students who were subjected to different approaches to teaching biological science. One group (the control group) was taught in the traditional laboratory environment while the other group (the experimental group) was taught in a field environment.*

The following example was fraught with missing information, ambiguity, and convolution:

Tasks 13, 14, and 15 were missing add and subtraction and checked which procedures students use to solve the tasks, to check whether non-canonical sentences were more difficult than canonical sentences, and if the sign changes were difficult. Task 16 was designed to check whether students could handle multicolumn subtraction. The task required students to take larger from smaller and was included to check whether students, when reaching an impasse, would try a smaller example or look at the examples above or possibly recall from memory some device to assist in solving the task.

What actually was the focus of Tasks 13, 14, and 15? Were the tasks *missing add and subtraction* and, if so, what were they? Or were the tasks *missing add[ition] and subtraction [operations]?* Or were the tasks lacking the *missing addend* type of subtraction problems? The use of the conjunction *and* at the end raises questions as to whether this was a different piece of information or whether it was part of the list of things to be checked. The reader needed to scan the subsequent sentences in an effort to determine the sense of the opening sentence and, in this example, remained none the wiser for having done so.

If a paragraph of this nature is an isolated instance in a dissertation, then there is really no problem. Unfortunately, however, this style of writing proliferates in some dissertations, often stemming from the students' view of what constitutes scholarly writing.

Inconsistencies.

1. *Inconsistencies in sequencing.* Some students had difficulties in maintaining coherence between paragraphs. No discernible line of argument was evident across paragraphs in sections of their writing. Sometimes their paragraphs seemed to be random in focus, switching from topic to topic and back again. In one of the case studies, there were major difficulties with microstructure in the review of literature. For example, summaries of the work of researchers were presented one after the other with no apparent relationship between them, and no end in sight (see Item 2 in the section on scholarly writing mechanics). Paragraphs and part paragraphs had to be categorized and reassembled so that similar topics were treated together. A focus for each category was determined to allow paragraphs to be ordered so that a line of argument emerged.

2. *Inconsistencies in relationships.* In a dissertation, there are situations in which subsequent sections should bear a logical relation to each other; that is, the second section has to be built on the first. For instance, the discussion of significance should relate to the purposes, or the posing of an alternative theory or model should take into account the description of the original. Some students did not set up or maintain these relationships. For example, the main purpose of one dissertation was to extend a previous study in the same domain of knowledge. However, when arguing the significance of this purpose, the student failed to emphasize the originality of the study (i.e., the extensions). Instead, the argument for significance referred only to the importance of the domain of knowledge.

3. *Inconsistencies in connections.* To develop an argument, connections may need to be constructed between two sections to allow parallels to be drawn or distinctions emphasized. However, when doing this, some students found it difficult to be consistent within the type of connection being made.

For example, one student used a counterbalanced design in which treatments were switched between groups after the first posttest. In reporting this, the student failed to maintain the distinction between the two treatment effects and the sequence in which the treatments were given.

4. *Switches in argument claim*. Earlier in this chapter, we reviewed the four claims that are possible in an argument (Lankshear, 1994): *empirical*, *conceptual*, *normative*, and *metaphysical*. Each of these claims is supported differently: that is, empirical by observation; conceptual by logical argument; normative by individual or group judgment; and metaphysical by belief (and, consequently, unverifiable). Sometimes writers mix up the claim types and their support method. For example, a student might attempt to support a conceptual claim by recourse to observation or they argue for a normative claim using logic.

5. *Logical development*. An argument is a line of reasoning that links a conclusion to its premise and therefore the laws of logic need to be followed in developing an argument. However, a line of reasoning can proceed directly from premise to conclusion or it can proceed indirectly from the opposite of the conclusion to the opposite of the premise. Sometimes students did not follow these laws, resulting in: (a) failure to join all steps in a line of argument; (b) failure to set up the premise, with the result that the argument is cyclical; or (c) failure to set up the indirect argument correctly either proceeding from the opposite of the premise to the opposite of the conclusions, or by failing to describe the opposite accurately.

The last instance can produce a "straw" argument in which the opposite to what is wanted is defined in a limited way, thus allowing it to be easily knocked down.

Errors in the Macrostructure of Scholarly Writing

Cooper and Baturo (1993) identified purposes, literature, design, results, discussion, and conclusions as the components of a dissertation. An important part of the scholarliness of the writing is the way in which these components are integrated in an overarching framework, or macrostructure. Aspects of macrostructure that students have difficulties with are: quality and clarity of purposes; consistency across components; relationship between components; discrimination between components; and presentation of the dissertation.

1. *Quality and clarity of purposes*. The purposes of a dissertation are the starting point for both writing and reading. They set up the parameters for the literature, the analysis of the results, and the conclusions; they determine the design. It is crucial for the macrostructure that the purposes be clear

and coherent, and that they be worthwhile, a point that was not apparent in some case studies.

The "so what?" test (Huff & Geis, 1984) is an illuminating first test for a dissertation and a test that, in the first instance, some of the students failed. Their initial purposes were so general and inclusive that they did not give any worthwhile direction to the dissertation.

The other test of purposes is clarity. Some students' purposes were so lengthy and so poorly expressed that it was difficult to discern their intentions.

2. *Consistency across components.* Nearly all students, particularly in their first drafts, experienced difficulties in maintaining coherence across the dissertation's major components: purposes, literature, research design, results and analysis, discussion, and conclusions. For example, one student proposed using a quantitative research design (hypothesis testing) to meet generative purposes (to develop an explanation).

In another dissertation, the main purpose was to determine whether young children spontaneously used a particular form of reasoning in given tasks. However, the data collection utilized an interview technique in which the desired reasoning was cued by suggestions from the interviewer. Such a design could not show spontaneous use of the reasoning and therefore could not achieve the dissertation's purposes.

Dissertations in which inconsistencies across components occurred nearly always had other flaws. For example, the main purpose of one dissertation was to validate a multistep developmental model of learning in a particular mathematics domain. However, the design was not the expected quantitative validation. In fact, it was qualitative, involving categorization of children's responses to tasks that were developed from the model. The proposal was that the model would be "validated" if these categories reflected the model's steps. This design was flawed in at least two ways: (a) there was disparity between purposes and design; and (b) the argument was a closed cycle.

3. *Relationship among components.* Within the macrostructure of a dissertation, components build on each other in a logical progression. For instance, the findings of the literature are commonly used to: (a) provide evidence of significance (e.g., the literature shows a gap in understanding at this point); (b) provide models of learning and teaching that are used to analyze data; and (c) provide the theoretical validity for the choice or development of instruments. Obviously, the results form the basis of discussions and conclusions for the dissertation. This is sometimes a major failing of students. For example, one student prepared a literature survey which showed that there were three types of mathematics problems to which problem solvers have to apply their domain knowledge. The student then developed an appropriate quasi-experimental design to compare three methods for teaching this domain of knowledge. However, his pre- and posttests contained only two of the problem types described in his literature and an extra

INTRODUCTION	Purposes, background, and significance
LITERATURE	Survey of pertinent literature and implications for the study
DESIGN	Subject, instruments, procedure, and analyses
DISCUSSION	Discussion of results in light of literature
CONCLUSION	Conclusions, limitations, and implications

FIG. 13.1.   Classical structure of dissertations.

problem type that was not related to his purposes. The test results could not be used with validity to compare the treatments.

4. *Discrimination between components.* At Queensland University of Technology, the basis of writing has been a classical dissertation design similar to that shown in Fig. 13.1. In the MEd course, students are introduced to this framework but, as the case studies revealed, some fail to realize the purpose and interconnectedness of the component parts. To show clearly the macrodevelopment of a dissertation, components need to be discriminated between as well as related to each other. For instance, it is important for the reader to be able to discriminate between the literature and the findings and between the results and inferences. Failure to differentiate between results and inferences was a problem for some students, particularly one student who did not write a separate results section but simply listed inferences. This resulted in his dissertation being unconvincing and its findings inadequate. When he rewrote the dissertation to include a separate results section, many more commonalities than could be seen in his original inferences were revealed.

5. *Presentation of the dissertation.* Given the mechanical nature of this aspect of dissertation writing, it was surprising that most students were unable to construct and maintain a format that would guide the reader through the dissertation. The inconsistencies in levels of headings and the ad hoc use of italics and underlining further complicated the reading of the dissertations, particularly when these flaws were combined with the writing problems described in this chapter. In addition, the lack of pre- and postorganizers within each major component of the dissertation often left the reader bewildered as to why some things were included or where the dissertation was heading.

CONCLUSIONS

Students come to the MEd courses with years of experience in the mechanics of writing, with less experience in developing the microstructure of scholarly writing, and virtually no experience in the macrostructure of dissertations.

It is natural, therefore, to assume that the supervisor's role in dissertation writing would be to focus on the macrostructure, with perhaps some guidance on the microstructure. This was not the case with the students in this study. In line with the findings of Freedman (1984), 11 of the 14 students had difficulties with all three categories (mechanics, microstructure, and macrostructure), which obviated the need for a series of intervention episodes.

Because the general-writing mechanics of the majority of students were so poor and so entrenched, the initial focus of the episodes was in this area. When students' general-writing skills were sufficiently improved to enable comprehension, the focus of the episodes shifted to include microstructure and macrostructure problems, depending on their individual needs. The objectives of the intervention episodes for all three categories were to make the students aware of their errors, to provide basic knowledge of scholarly writing, and to facilitate a process of monitoring that would enable them to take control of their own revisions. The episodes involved the students in a cycle of composing, reading, considering, revising, and planning, as recommended by Graves (1983), Murray (1978), and Perl (1979).

Different approaches were required for fostering awareness, knowledge, and control of the three categories of errors. Mechanical writing difficulties were easy for the editor to identify and to provide suggestions for amendment. However, the habituated nature of most mechanical errors made it difficult for the students to take control of the recognition and amendment processes when they were writing by themselves. On the other hand, the macrostructure of the dissertation required time and experience before awareness and knowledge were developed. The dissertation structure of Fig. 13.1 was used as an overarching framework to enable students to exercise control of the macrostructural development of their dissertation.

The most difficult fault for the students to gain awareness, knowledge, and control of were microstructural. Intervention in this category was extremely time-consuming because the idiosyncratic nature of these types of errors meant that, at times each sentence had to be decoded before the meaning of a paragraph emerged. Once the paragraphs had been decoded, other weaknesses in the logical development of an argument became evident and these, too, needed to be addressed. A further implication of the idiosyncratic nature of these problems was that there was no guarantee that the same errors would not recur. To overcome this, good microstructure writing practices were modeled and contrasted with students' writing. The students were asked to compare the model with their own writing and to imitate the model in their future writing. Particular attention was given to the use of headings as a means of planning and maintaining consistency within both the micro- and macrostructure of the dissertation. This approach did seem to encourage students to become critical writers who were aware of the need to consider their writing from the reader's perspective.

Students became more able to indicate when they were not happy with a sentence construction, even though they might not know how to "fix" it. At this point, progress toward improved writing appeared to accelerate.

Student Responses

Most of the students were pleased to participate in the study, particularly the four students for whom English was a second language. One student expressed surprise at being asked to participate, saying that she had consistently received high marks in her previous studies and at no time had her writing skills been challenged. Some students worked in conjunction with the editor to amend sections that required rewriting, whereas others preferred to work by themselves from the editor's written suggestions. All but three students—"Brian," "Charles," and "Frank"—worked productively with the editor and their supervisors to improve their writing.

Brian was a native English speaker who prided himself on knowing the rules of writing; he felt that his present supervisor had asked the editor to look at his work in order to "nitpick." Brian had had three different supervisors (consecutively, not concurrently), each of whom had worked long and hard with him to produce a final report. However, each supervisor had thought that the quality of the report was rather tenuous and had asked a colleague to review Brian's dissertation before being submitted. On each of these occasions, the reviewer rated the dissertation as unsatisfactory in its current form. Therefore, by the time Brian was admitted to this program of intervention, he had had similar advice from four different academics (two supervisors, two reviewers).

Brian's writing was very basic in style, form, and structure, was flawed by many errors in the basic general mechanics, and made neither coherent nor logically sequenced arguments. Even when the editor explained that the rules he adhered to (e.g., a paragraph could not be longer than 100 words) did not hold, Brian believed this was because the "rules had changed," not that the rules had never been valid. He required a detailed explanation for each suggestion but, once the reason was clear to him, he would act on the advice. Although the mechanics of his writing had improved as a result of the interventions, he still had major micro- and macrostructure problems.

Underlying Brian's writing was the belief that academic writing was elitist and esoteric (Becker, 1986; Richards, 1986) and consequently of little use to the practitioners for whom he thought he was writing. He thus failed to understand the purpose of the dissertation and the audience at whom it should be directed. Other students had similar beliefs initially but were able to adapt their writing to meet the purpose and audience requirements of a dissertation. However, in Brian's case, this has proved to be an almost insurmountable barrier to scholarly writing.

Charles was a bilingual student who, because he felt that he communicated very well in English, was affronted at being asked to meet with the editor. His initial reaction to criticism of his writing was like "an artist whose masterwork had been mauled by philistines" (Becker, 1986, p. 22). He only attended one intervention episode and indicated a lack of interest in attending to the difficulties the editor had identified in his writing.

Frank, another native English speaker, worked happily with the editor on his many mechanical errors and then with his supervisor on the microstructure of his chapters. However, after completing this to the satisfaction of all concerned, he would not accept his supervisor's advice regarding a major macrostructural problem in his dissertation.

At the time of writing this chapter, 13 of the 14 students had completed their dissertation and, of these, only Brian's had not been submitted for examination. His dissertation had been sent to yet another colleague for yet another review and had been, yet again, rejected. Charles and Frank were the only two students to receive a resubmission grade. This provided the stimulus for these two students to become more receptive to the advice that had been given them, a behavior that was in line with Becker's (1986) argument that students need motivation for improvement. Frank quickly corrected all deficiencies and his thesis was then graded satisfactory. Charles took a long time to come to terms with the resubmission grading but lately has begun to show more interest in attending to the earlier advice he had been given and this has resulted in an improvement in his latest drafts.

The students' reactions to suggestions concerning microstructure and macrostructure were sometimes not as positive as their reactions to feedback on mechanics. In other words, the students were more defensive toward the editor, the supervisor, or both when lines of argument were critiqued than when clarity of writing was criticized. In this, they exhibited all three reactions to criticism that were described by Becker (1986): reverting to "school talk," feeling maligned, and believing that reviewers are capricious. Students with the first reaction tended to disengage from the writing process and merely wanted to be told what to do; thus it was difficult to motivate them to think about the micro- and macrostructural aspects of their writing. Students with the other reactions tended, in the long term, to benefit from discussion of their writing if their defences could be circumvented without loss of dignity.

For most students, it was necessary to draw their attention to their responsibilities in the writing process. Several students seemed to think that it was their role to develop the ideas but that it was the supervisor's responsibility to ensure that these ideas were presented in a logical sequence and free of mechanical errors. Thus, in general, the students' reactions to suggestions depended on their beliefs about the correctness of their writing and about the nature of academic writing.

Looking Ahead

Most of the students in this study had major writing weaknesses, indicating that undergraduate science and teacher education courses had not provided the grounding in scholarly writing that should have been expected. Our findings echo those of Barrass (1978) showing that, in 20 years, little has been done to improve the standard of scholarly writing. It is interesting to speculate where students' writing will be in the future.

Technological tools such as spelling and grammar checkers and thesauruses should alleviate many of the difficulties students now have with the mechanics of dissertation writing. We have already noted the positive impact of a spelling checker, and the development of a more sophisticated one than is currently available will probably have a similar effect on the mechanics of general writing. Thus, in the future, the mechanical aspects of writing should no longer need the emphasis they have had in the past. However, there already exist print options that could reduce mechanical errors. For example, most style manuals cover deficiencies in writing, and dictionaries and thesauruses can assist with the appropriate choice of words, yet most students in the study had neither read the manuals adequately nor made good use of dictionaries and thesauruses. However, unless students are made aware of their responsibility in this area, it is possible that the new writing-support software packages will not be used by students and, consequently, the mechanics of writing will continue to require attention.

Hopefully, there will also be computer software that will automatically format references to a requisite style (e.g., Harvard or APA). This should then eradicate one of the most low-level and time-consuming of tasks and one that students seem to leave to their supervisors. However, the students will still need to be aware that accurate and complete referencing is their sole responsibility. As Bruner (1942) stated, an inaccurate or incomplete reference "will stand in print as an annoyance to future investigators and a monument to the writer's carelessness" (p. 68) and will damage the writer's credibility as a careful researcher (APA, 1987).

We foresee a need for continued intervention in the micro- and macrostructures of dissertation, although we are unsure as to how such intervention can be provided effectively in terms of time and results. Nevertheless, we believe that intervention to offset scholarly writing problems is more likely to be successful if it focuses on helping students: (a) become aware of their writing weaknesses; (b) acquire the appropriate knowledge; and (c) take responsibility for monitoring and evaluating their writing.

REFERENCES

American Psychological Association. (1987). *Publication Manual of the American Psychological Association* (3rd ed.). Washington, DC: Author.

Barrass, R. (1978). *Scientists must write*. New York: Wiley.

Becker, H. S. (1986). *Writing for social scientists: How to start and finish your thesis, book, or article.* Chicago: University of Chicago Press.

Boice, R., & Johnson, K. (1984). Perception and practice of writing for publication by faculty at a doctoral-granting university. *Research in Higher Education, 21*(1), 33–43.

Bridgeman, B., & Carlson, S. (1983). Survey of academic writing tasks required of graduate students and undergraduate foreign students. *Written-Communication, 1*(2), 247–280.

Bridwell, L. S. (1980). Revising strategies on twelfth grade students' transactional writing. *Research in the Teaching of English, 14*, 197–222.

Bruner, K. F. (1942). Of psychological writing: Being some valedictory remarks on style. *Journal of Abnormal and Social Psychology, 37*, 52–70.

Connors, R., & Lunsford, A. (1988). Frequency of errors in current college writing, or Ma and Pa Kettle do research. *College Composition and Communication, 39*(4), 395–409.

Connors, R., & Lunsford, A. (1993). Teachers' rhetorical comments on student papers. *College Composition and Communication, 44*(2), 200–223.

Cooper, T., & Baturo, A. (1993, July). Mathematics-education students, writing and higher-degree courses. In M. Carss (Ed.), *Proceedings of the biennial national conference of Mathematics Education Lecturers Association* (pp. 61–68). Brisbane, Australia: University of Queensland.

Corbett, E. P. (1987). *The little English handbook: Choices and conventions* (5th ed.). Glenview, IL: Scott, Foresman.

Cumming, A. (1989). Writing expertise and second-language proficiency. *Language Learning, 39*(1), 81–141.

Ebbitt, W., & Ebbitt, D. (1982). *Writer's guide and index: English* (7th ed.). Glenview, IL: Scott, Foresman.

Fowler, H. W. (1968). *A dictionary of modern English usage* (2nd ed.). Oxford, England: Oxford University Press.

Freedman, A. (1984). The Carleton university writing tutorial service. In L. Young (Ed.), *Carleton papers in applied language studies* (Vol. 1, pp. 15–37). Ottawa, Ontario, Canada: Center for Applied Language Studies, Carleton University.

Graves, D. H. (1983). *Writing: Children and teachers at work.* London: Heinemann.

Graves, D. H. (1984). *A researcher learns to write: Selected articles and monographs.* London: Heinemann.

Greaser, C. U. (1979). Improving the effectiveness of research writing. *Scholarly Publishing, 11*(1), 61–71.

Hertzog, M. (1988). Issues in writing proficiency assessment. Section 1: The government scale. In P. Lowe, Jr. & C. W. Stansfield (Eds.), *Second language proficiency assessment: Current issues* (pp. 77–90). Englewood Cliffs, NJ: Prentice-Hall Regents.

Hubbuch, S. (1989). *Writing research papers across the curriculum* (2nd ed.). Fort Worth, TX: Holt, Rinehart & Winston.

Huff, D., & Geis, I. (1984). *How to lie with statistics.* Harmondsworth, Middlesex, England: Penguin.

Kelly, P. (1989). Theory, research and pedagogy in ESL writing. In C. N. Candlin & T. N. McNamara (Eds.), *Language, learning and community* (pp. 63–79). Sydney: National Centre for English Language Teaching and Research, Macquarie University.

Lankshear, C. (1994, March). *An approach to critique of academic texts.* (Available from A/Prof. Colin Lankshear, School of Language and Literacy Education, Queensland University of Technology, Brisbane, Queensland 4001, Australia)

Lewins, F. (1988). *Writing a thesis: A guide to its nature and organization* (2nd ed.). Canberra, Australian Capital Territory: The Australian National University.

Moses, I. (1992). *Supervising postgraduates (no. 3).* Campbelltown, New South Wales: Higher Education Research and Development Society of Australia.

Murray, D. (1978). Internal revision: A process of discovery. In C. R. Cooper & L. Odell (Eds.), *Research on composing: Points of departure* (pp. 85–103). Urbana, IL: National Council of Teachers of English.

Nelson, J. (1992). *Constructing a research paper: A study of students' goals and approaches* (Tech. Rep. No. 59). Berkeley, CA: Center for the Study of Writing.

Nightingale, P. (1988). Understanding processes and problems in student writing. *Studies in Higher Education, 13*(3), 263–268.

Perl, S. (1979). The composing processes of unskilled college writers. *Research in the Teaching of English, 13*, 317–336.

Perry, C. (1993, May). *A structured approach to presenting PhD theses: Notes for candidates and their supervisors.* (Available from Dr. Chadwick Perry, School of Marketing Advertising and Public Relations, Queensland University of Technology, Brisbane, Queensland 4001, Australia)

Pianko, S. (1979). A description of the composing processes of college freshmen writers. *Research in the Teaching of English, 13*, 5–22.

Reitt, B. B. (1980). The editor turns teacher. *Scholarly Publishing, 11*(3), 256–266.

Richards, P. (1986). Risk. In H. S. Becker (Ed.), *Writing for social scientists: How to start and finish your thesis, book, or article* (pp. 108–120). Chicago: University of Chicago Press.

Riggar, T. F., & Smith, E. R. (1987). *Annotations in academic publishing.* (ERIC Document Reproduction Service No. ED 292 083)

Sloan, G. (1990). Frequency of errors in essays by college freshman and by professional writers. *College Composition and Communication, 41*(3), 299–308.

Turabian, K. L. (1973). *A manual for writers of term papers, theses, and dissertations* (4th ed.). Chicago: University of Chicago Press.

Woodford, F. P. (1967). Sounder thinking through clearer writing. *Science, 156*, 743–745.

14

Writing for Publication

Jack J. Hourcade
Holly Anderson
Boise State University

After our mathematics or science education research project has been completed, it is natural for us to wish to step back and catch our breath for a moment. However, there is still a critical step remaining in our scholarship. We must decide on a vehicle to share our new knowledge with others. There are many ways to disseminate our research results, including submitting project reports and presenting at professional meetings. However, for most of us, the scholarly vehicle of choice remains a professional journal.

Submitting research reports to some agency might mean that only one person will see the results of our work. When we present at a professional meeting the results of our research may reach only one or two dozen of one's colleagues. However, even small academic journals have hundreds of readers, with larger journals having worldwide readerships of over 100,000. Thus, by far the most efficient way to present our research work to the world is through publishing papers in journals.

Besides access to the wider audience, journals provide a rigorous screening function in furthering the knowledge base in mathematics and science education. Most journals reject many more articles than they accept. What this means is that when an article is accepted for publication by a respected journal, it most likely has been reviewed by a panel of experts and found to make an important contribution to the body of knowledge. To help emerging scholars successfully present their mathematics and science education research in journals, in this chapter we will (a) identify a rationale for scholarly writing, (b) list reasons scholars give for not writing, (c) provide an overview of how scholarly journals function, and (d) suggest practical ways of increasing scholarly productivity.

WHY SCHOLARS SHOULD WRITE

After completing a graduate degree, the mathematics or science educator may return to teaching children, or perhaps to a university position. In either case the return to the day-to-day requirements of teaching makes it difficult for many of us to keep in mind the importance of continuing our scholarly writing. However, there are many reasons for doing so.

Professional Sharing and Repayment of Debts

As we generate research and acquire knowledge that contributes to professional competence or advances the field, we have a professional obligation to share that knowledge with colleagues elsewhere. Starting with our undergraduate education, continuing especially through our graduate programs, and even as established scholars, every one of us who has completed an academic degree owes a tremendous debt to those scholars who preceded us. They established and shared with us the knowledge base that we acquired at the undergraduate and graduate levels.

When we complete a graduate degree and then move on to continue teaching at the university level, we have an arguably even higher level of debt. Most of the content and curriculum we present to our students originates, not with us, but with the scholars who preceded us. The only way we can begin to repay this debt is to be as generous in sharing our new knowledge through professional dissemination as were our predecessors. Publishing in scholarly journals is the most efficient way of disseminating our new information to large numbers of our colleagues elsewhere. This in a small way begins repayment of our debt.

Satisfaction of Professional Achievement

For many of us the process of writing itself is inherently difficult. It is not unlike an act of artistic creation, in which the real payoff is not in the work itself, but instead in the creation of a new product. The act of sitting before a blank piece of paper (or a blank computer screen with its maddeningly blinking cursor, reminding us that nothing has been written yet!) is a labor of professional commitment.

Nevertheless, when a manuscript is completed, we gain a sense of professional accomplishment that simply cannot be achieved any other way. When our paper appears in print in a respected journal in mathematics or science education, we can take great pride in the fact that the paper was reviewed by individuals identified as experts in these areas, and was found to be worthy of national or international professional attention. There is something unique in writing, perhaps in the permanence of the product, that yields an unmatched sense of professional accomplishment.

Advocacy for a Position

Another reason we write for publication is that such writing provides the chance for advocacy of a particular theory or belief. By tradition, scientific research purports to be value-free and driven only by the search for objective truths. However, in reality many of us hold dear some particular belief, and we conduct research in the hope of finding that belief supported by the data. Many advances in the knowledge base are directly attributable to individuals who believed in some issue, and then undertook the appropriate research procedures to provide data-based documentation for that position.

Personal Material Benefits

Although less often acknowledged, there are personal benefits in publishing in professional journals. Seeing your name in print, and seeing others cite your work, is personally exciting and fulfilling for many of us. In addition, especially if you choose to devote some time to studying various aspects of a particular question, you can become acknowledged as one of the few "experts" on that issue.

Such acknowledgment can yield additional benefits, including requests to present papers at conferences, and invitations to consult with colleagues in the profession. Also, with a history of success in publishing in journals, doors open for us in other more lucrative avenues of scholarly writing, such as developing instruments or writing books for commercial publishing houses.

For those of us either seeking our first university position or considering a move, the presence of an ongoing scholarly agenda, as documented through journal publications, is a powerful asset. Your record of scholarship is a primary factor that will distinguish your application from others.

Even when not actively looking for such a position, none of us can assume we will always be at a particular institution forever. The reality of the academic marketplace is that, all else being equal, universities will find active scholars to be more valuable and attractive than other candidates. In many ways scholarly publications serve as the currency of the academy. A record of scholarly achievements will enhance your salary and promotion prospects, even if you are not actively seeking employment elsewhere.

Personal Intellectual Benefits

Over and above the material benefits scholarly publishing can provide, professional writing provides fertile ground for substantial intellectual stimulation and growth. There is much truth to Wallace Stegner's saying, "I don't know what I think until I see what I have written." The act of committing your thoughts to paper illuminates and clarifies your present ideas, and can help you to generate fresh insights.

Maintenance of Currency

A maxim in mathematics and science education is that a new graduate degree has a scholarly half-life of approximately 5 years: that is, without active attempts to stay abreast in the field, 5 years after graduation you will be only half as knowledgeable about the current state of the field as you were at graduation. Ten years later, you are only 25% as knowledgeable, and so on.

One way to maintain our currency is to establish and continue an ongoing scholarly agenda. Perhaps the single biggest advantage in doing this is that doing research, and writing up that research for professional dissemination, forces us to read, and read, and read some more. Reading as background to our scholarly work is the most effective way to stay current in mathematics and science education.

Part of the Job

Over the past 30 years, many regional higher education institutions have seen their roles and responsibilities shift substantially. From their origins as teaching-only programs, many have moved toward more comprehensive university functions. Foremost among these new responsibilities has been the generation of new knowledge through research.

In past years, you might have been able to obtain a position in a smaller program where teaching was the only significant professional expectation. However, today it is rare to find a university position in any area, including mathematics and science education, in which clear and significant expectations for scholarly productivity do not exist. Substantial demands for research are universal in higher education today. It is simply part of the job.

The Revitalization of Teaching

Many of us at either the undergraduate or graduate levels have experienced the distinct displeasure of taking a class from a distinguished researcher, only to find that he or she appears to lack even the most rudimentary instructional skills. Such experiences happen often enough for some of us to have concluded that good researchers are not good teachers: that one does one or the other but not both. However, many of us who are active in scholarly activities have found that our research substantially benefits our university classroom instruction. This occurs in several ways.

First, as previously noted, to be successful in publishing in journals, you must be actively reading in the field. This reading forces us to stay current.

Those of us who do not engage in research can easily grow out of touch with the realities of mathematics and science education, lending further credibility to the ivory tower disparagement. Doing research, with the reading background it requires, keeps us from falling into a professional rut.

Second, the new information gathered as a result of our research can be shared with students, especially at the graduate level. When we do this our students have access to new knowledge even before it appears in print.

Finally, in doing research, we will find ourselves more empathetic to our university students and their situations; that is, in doing research, we find that we must search for information in the library, collect references, prepare papers, respond to criticism, revise papers accordingly, and meet deadlines. In short, we must do the same things we ask our students to do.

Love for Our Field

Most of us initially began study in mathematics or science education because of a love of the subject matter. By writing in our field, we can establish a more powerful, and more intimate, relationship with it than is otherwise possible. Simply put, the most intense way for us to learn about and become involved in our field of study is to do research and publish within it.

The Fun of Research

After all the aforementioned, the introduction of a concept such as "fun" in conjunction with research may seem a bit out of place. Yet most of us can readily identify many ways in which research efforts are enjoyable.

To begin with, most of us see ourselves first as students of a discipline. To that end a major drive for us is to learn new information in our field. Almost any effective researcher can speak excitedly about the thrill that occurs when research reveals previously unsuspected relationships, or when new knowledge suddenly surfaces. For successful researchers, the fun of learning never stops.

In addition, many of us find our most effective and enjoyable work is done in collaboration with colleagues. Such arrangements provide several benefits, combining as they do professionalism with social interaction. It is fun and productive to bounce ideas off one another, to see in what unexpected directions a research effort might go as we brainstorm.

WHY DON'T MORE RESEARCHERS WRITE?

In most journals a disproportionately large number of articles are written by only a small number of individuals. Given all the reasons why scholars *should* write, not to mention the importance that publishing in professional journals has for those employed by universities, why don't more of us write for and publish in professional journals?

Some in higher education argue that additional professional writing should be discouraged, because most journals already have more manuscripts submitted to them than they could possibly publish. Others suggest that much of what is presently published is of poor quality, and thus what is needed is *less* professional writing, not more of the same.

However, we would argue that many superior ideas never emerge because our colleagues never get around to committing them to paper. So why don't more of us write for publication? The following are reasons academicians often give for why they do not write and publish more.

Distractions

In education other duties often take time that might otherwise be put into our writing. For example, when we begin at a university we are assigned courses that we may not have taught before. Given the immediacy of instructional demands early in our careers, it is easy for us to justify putting time into teaching instead of scholarly writing. Because teaching has deadlines regularly coming due and scholarly writing does not, what happens is that the teaching gets done, but the scholarship does not.

This is further complicated by the fact that, in teaching, the response to our work is immediate, and usually positive. In scholarly writing, the response is slow, and too often negative.

Timelines

Interestingly, many of us find it easier to prepare and present papers at professional conferences than to write up equivalent papers for possible journal publication. Similarly, most of us teaching at the university level are more successful in preparing university classroom material than in preparing manuscripts for submission to journals.

The likely reason for this is that, for both conferences and classroom instruction, specific deadlines are involved. Most people are able to generate prodigious amounts of energy when deadlines are involved. However, journals instead operate on a "whenever" basis. For too many of us, the "whenever" too easily slips into "never."

Writing Blocks

Some scholars report that the reason they are not writing is due to "writer's block," a vague and ultimately circular argument ("I don't write because I have writer's block." "How do you know you have writer's block?" "Because I can't write." "Why not?" "Because I have writer's block!" and so on . . .).

However, there may be some specific reasons why some of us find it difficult to write.

One of the most challenging situations we can experience is spending weeks or months on a manuscript, sending it off with high hopes to a respected journal, and then having it returned with unusually harsh and caustic criticisms. For example, one of the authors of this chapter labored over a manuscript for months and submitted it to a journal, only to have it rejected. The comments from the reviewers included one that said, "Undergraduates in my classes write better than this!"

Early in your career your ego is still fragile. Criticism, especially when brutal and unkind, is painful. Unfortunately, one way to avoid such pain in the future is simply to avoid further writing efforts. After one or more rejections, putting off subsequent writing attempts becomes easier and easier.

Artificially High Expectations

Many of us discount our writing abilities while maintaining grandiose expectations of the originality and significance of publishable work. We sometimes use the best work of other, more well-established scholars as a benchmark, a minimum criterion level. It is easy to establish goals for ourselves that are so high that they can never be met, thus making any attempt to do so pointless. Once such beliefs are in place, it is easy to persuade ourselves not to write.

Inertia and Momentum

The hardest publication for most of us is the first one. What often happens is that few first, laborious, and difficult-to-complete manuscripts are accepted for publication. With each rejection, subsequent writing attempts become harder and harder, until writing simply is not attempted any longer.

Conversely, most productive writers find that each subsequent publication is easier to achieve than the last. Successful writing begets successful writing; nonwriting begets nonwriting.

Poor Preparation

Surprisingly few graduate programs offer specific instruction for their emerging scholars in writing for publication. What happens instead is that these very specific skills are instead shaped over time through experience, as we become increasingly competent in writing and journal article preparation. Most productive scholars have essentially taught themselves these skills. For others of us, the difficulties and setbacks that are inevitable early in our careers are so overwhelming that the learning curve is halted, and we stop writing.

Inherent Difficulty in Writing

Many of our daily university tasks are mundane, routine, and mechanical: preparing overhead transparencies; entering grades in a gradebook or computer; attending committee meetings; explaining course or university policies to students; and so on. In stark contrast, writing is arguably the most intellectually demanding work we do. In scholarly writing we grapple with complex ideas at the most abstract levels.

In university settings, we are able to express ourselves orally, with students serving as listeners. However, readers of our professional writings are very different from listeners. A different and higher set of standards for clarity of expression comes into play in writing.

In addition, perhaps as a residual effect of grueling sessions while in graduate school, many of us associate writing with marathon work periods and soul-deadening fatigue. Thus writing, difficult to begin with, becomes next to impossible.

Nothing to Say

Many who are not presently engaged in active research efforts will explain their lack of scholarly writing by suggesting they have nothing of value to contribute to colleagues in the field. It is easy to be intimidated and overwhelmed by the quality and quantity of information appearing in journals, concluding that there is nothing else that can be said. However, such a conclusion is flawed.

Even those of us not actively engaged in a research investigation at present can still be reading in the professional literature. Reviews of literature that synthesize present information, draw new inferences, or both are always useful. Many faculty who say they are not doing research at present nevertheless are engaged in the field, and can draw on those experiences and questions in developing scholarly papers. Graduate students are yet another fertile source of ideas for scholarly papers. In short, if you read in the field, you have potential contributions to make.

HOW JOURNALS WORK

In preparing a manuscript for a journal it is useful for us to understand how academic journals operate. On occasion, a journal may invite an author, especially one of great prominence and stature in a particular area of study, to submit an article. Usually, however, manuscripts are submitted by individuals without such an individualized invitation. Thus, most articles in professional journals were not specifically invited as such, but were in essence freelanced.

Unlike popular magazines, few academic journals pay the authors any fees. Journals often use the term "contributors" instead of "authors" to emphasize this very point.

Some journals charge researchers for publishing their articles, usually on a per-page basis, and a few journals also charge a review fee, presumably to discourage frivolous submissions. Unlike so-called "vanity presses" that publish popular literature for a fee, those professional journals that charge authors are not necessarily poor choices. Indeed, many universities will subsidize their faculty members who publish in these journals. However, given that most first-rate journals have no such charges associated with publishing in them, usually a journal that has no charges is preferred.

Types of Journals

Journals may be divided into two types, *refereed* and *nonrefereed*. Refereed or peer-reviewed journals are those in which an editor receives manuscripts submitted for publication, removes any information that might identify the author(s), and then sends out each "anonymous" manuscript to several reviewers. (On occasion, an editor may decide on receipt that a manuscript is so clearly unsuited for the journal that he or she simply returns it to the author, without sending it out for review.)

In nonrefereed journals, the editorial decision to accept or reject is made in-house, either by the editor or by staff at the journal. Because these reviews are made with the authors' names and affiliations known, some degree of editorial objectivity is lost. However, the advantage is that acceptance decisions can be made much more quickly and efficiently than in a refereed process. Usually refereed journals are considered stronger and more prestigious than those that are not.

The Review Process

In refereed journals, the reviewers (often two or three) use a rating instrument developed specifically for that journal's needs in evaluating a manuscript's suitability. The comments and recommendations from these reviewers are then returned to the journal editor, who makes a final determination as to the disposition of the manuscript.

A journal editor has several options. The first is to accept the manuscript as is, with minimal or no changes. In our experience, this is rare. A second option is to accept the manuscript contingent on the author(s) making changes recommended by the editor, reviewers, or both. Although on occasion these changes are negotiable, usually the editor has a clear idea of what the journal's needs are, and how the manuscript should be changed to best meet those needs.

A common third option is for the editor to return the manuscript to the author, asking that certain changes be made to the manuscript and then resubmitted for reconsideration. This is often the case when the reviewers are split over the value of a manuscript, when important information is missing, or when the editor sees much value in some parts of the manuscript while having significant reservations about other sections. In such a case, the author should consider the manuscript to have substantial merit, and consider carefully the recommendation to revise and resubmit. Surprisingly, many authors never follow up at this stage, and so manuscripts that have potentially great worth are never published.

A final option for the editor is to simply decide, after reviewing comments from the reviewers, that the manuscript is either inappropriate or of insufficient quality for the journal. The author is then sent a polite letter thanking him or her for the submission.

Whatever the ultimate editorial decision, usually the letter from the editor explaining this decision will include the comments from the reviewers. These anonymous comment sheets are an invaluable source of objective feedback on the manuscript.

Given the lengthy process outlined here, timelines for refereed journals may stretch on. Typically, an editor of a journal will acknowledge receipt of a submitted manuscript within 2 weeks. At that point the manuscript is sent out to reviewers, who are given 1 to 2 months to review the paper and return comments and recommendations to the editor. Thus it may be several months from the original receipt of a manuscript by the journal to the determination that the paper will or will not be published. Once the article is accepted, another, often longer, period passes before the paper appears in print; 6 to 12 months is not uncommon.

Given these long timelines, sometimes we are tempted to submit a manuscript to two or more different journals simultaneously, thinking that the first journal that decides to publish it will receive it. However, given the substantial investment a refereed journal must make in sending out a paper for review by several reviewers, this practice is considered to be unethical. Before sending a manuscript out for review, many journals require a statement from the submitting author affirming that the paper is not being considered by any other journal.

Acceptance Rates

When we begin submitting our first manuscripts to journals, one of the more discouraging facets of publishing is the discovery of how low the acceptance rates are. Few journals accept even half of the manuscripts they receive.

Many national and international journals have acceptance rates of 10% or less. The lowest acceptance rates are usually found in those journals that are refereed, are the major publications of professional organizations, have the largest circulation sizes, and are the most well established. Conversely, smaller state or regional journals usually feature higher acceptance rates.

Size of readership is not necessarily always associated with acceptance rate and prestige. Some smaller journals emphasize highly specialized and advanced areas of study, and may be at least as rigorous as more general journals with larger readerships.

Publication of the Manuscript

When a revised manuscript finally has been accepted for publication, the author will be notified in a letter from the editor. At that point the editor may make additional requests for changes. The editor will also make an estimate of how long it will be before the paper appears in the journal, often tentatively determining which particular issue the manuscript is slated for. In addition, the author will be asked to sign a copyright waiver assigning copyright privileges for the paper to the journal.

At some point before the manuscript appears the author may be sent galley proofs. These pages display the manuscript as it will look and appear in the journal. This is the last chance for the author to correct factual mistakes, typographical errors, spelling errors, and so on. Usually substantial changes are discouraged at this point.

When the manuscript is published, almost all journals will send the author one or more complimentary issues. Some journals will also send reprints of the manuscript as it appeared in the journal, along with ordering information should additional reprints be needed. Those journals that charge for publication are likely to send large numbers of reprints, presumably to partially compensate the author for the publication charges.

WAYS TO INCREASE SCHOLARLY PRODUCTIVITY

Most productive and successful authors of journal articles have identified a variety of strategies to enhance the chances of success when they submit manuscripts. We have found the following suggestions helpful in becoming more successful in publishing in journals.

Seek Collaborators

Preparing manuscripts is difficult for most of us; doing so in isolation is nearly impossible for many. Few of us are equally skilled at all aspects of research and publication. The process of scholarly inquiry requires generating the initial research idea, undertaking reviews of related literature in the library, conducting the research and collecting the data, carrying out any statistical analyses of the data, writing the research report, and determining the journal to which the paper should be sent. It is inevitable that most of us will be more adept at some of these tasks than others.

It is important for us to identify potential collaborators whose skills complement our own. This allows us to best use our own particular strengths while maintaining a high level of scholarly productivity. In addition, much as with team sports, it is more fun to be able to share both successes and disappointments with others.

There are many ways in which potential collaborators can be found. When first beginning to write it can be useful to identify a more senior colleague in the field, especially at our own university, and offer to work with that individual, perhaps bringing in potential research ideas. Senior faculty members are likely to have had some success in publishing, and can help the emerging scholar with practical suggestions and ideas.

Alternatively, two individuals just beginning careers in research may find their enthusiasm and energy admirable substitutes for experience. By joining professional organizations and attending meetings we can quickly identify others who share our interests. Journal editors also are often willing to pair up potential contributors with others who are working in similar areas. Although initially seeking out potential collaborators can be difficult, it may be easier if we keep in mind that most other scholars are also looking for ways to improve their scholarly abilities and productivity, and thus are likely to welcome our invitation for collaboration.

Even if you choose not to write with colleagues, it can be invaluable to use them as readers of your manuscripts before sending them out. It is important to remember that such review work is usually thankless, in that a careful reader likely will identify problems that you would rather not hear. A reader who hands your paper back shortly saying all looks wonderful is not being very helpful. Instead, it is better to seek out colleagues who will give your paper a critical reading, as it is only through such reactions that writing improves. Constructive suggestions from colleagues usually are easier to accept than harsh impersonal comments from anonymous journal reviewers.

Preparing the Manuscript

Before writing the first word, we must devote some substantial time in preparation. Perhaps the best preparation is simply to *read* on that topic as extensively as possible, paying special attention to recent work. There simply is no other way. To be successful scholarly writers we must read.

Any submitted manuscript will be reviewed by experts in that particular discipline or subdiscipline. They themselves are likely to have recently written on the topic, and will look to see if that work is noted. If important recent works on the topic are unacknowledged, the entire manuscript will be downgraded. Such omissions are one of the most frequent reasons manuscripts are not accepted for publication. The safest way of dealing with this problem is simply to be well read, and to talk to colleagues to help identify important recent work in this area.

Many of us find it useful to begin by preparing a tentative outline of the main points the paper will include. Once this outline is complete, an introduction should be written that identifies for the reader the author's familiarity with contemporary work in the field, shows clearly whatever new ideas or thoughts are being proposed, and notes how the present work ties in with and grows out of more established work.

Most successful authors have found that once an outline is developed and an introduction written, the remainder of the paper can be finished easily. Once these two elements are in place, the work is more than half completed.

Writing Style

Although it occurs first, the title of the paper should actually be written last. This is because it should convey to the reader a clear and concise preview of the paper's content. This cannot be done successfully until that content has been determined.

The introductory paragraph plays an absolutely decisive role in delivering the content of the paper to the reader. It is at this point that the reviewers will make their crucial first impressions, gathering a sense of the paper's overall style as well as its content. Significant problems here will cause reviewers simply to stop reading, having already decided the manuscript should not be accepted.

One of the most critical variables determining the ultimate resolution of a submitted manuscript is its tone and style. Much otherwise useful professional writing is weakened by an overuse of polysyllabic jargon. Certainly there is a need for a professional vocabulary, which serves as a specialty shorthand between writer and reader. However, we must avoid the temptation to work as many big words and complex sentences into a manuscript as possible, hoping to make the paper appear learned. All this does is impair the manuscript's overall readability. A smooth, clear, and unpretentious style is best.

The degree of formality in the writing is increasingly a matter of your own taste. Over the past decade many journals have begun accepting first-person references in the text (for example, saying "We decided that . . ." as opposed to "The authors decided that . . .").

An important stylistic guideline is to write for the readers of the journal, not its editors, that is, instead of wondering what the editors want, you should consider what the *readers* want, and write toward that audience instead.

An unfortunate side effect of writing a graduate thesis or dissertation is that we may tend to include *everything* in our subsequent writing, making our papers bloated, and not as focused as they might be. Although this may not be inappropriate in the limitless boundaries of the graduate thesis, it can serve to mask truly important points in a journal article. It is always better to be concise. Generally most journals prefer manuscripts to be between 10 and 20 pages, in typescript or word-processed output, and double-spaced.

Use of References

The knowledge base in mathematics and science education emerges as the result of many individual research results culminating in a more general conclusion. In a research paper we should display familiarity with the previous research pertinent to the question under study by referencing that material as appropriate. Failure to do so suggests that we either are unfamiliar with the topic or we are sloppy. Neither impression is likely to help our manuscript's chances for publication.

It is especially important that we include recent sources in these references. On seeing a paper dominated by old references, most reviewers will conclude either that (a) this is an old "boomerang" manuscript, sent out to many other journals in the past but always returning unaccepted; or (b) we have been careless and sloppy in our library research work.

The references should be double-checked to make sure that each reference in the text is included in the concluding list of references. Also, basic information in each reference (for example, the spelling of the author's name, the correct date, volume, and issue number) should be checked.

Topics

Perhaps the easiest way to move into scholarly publishing is to identify from your thesis or dissertation those portions that best lend themselves to publication in a journal. Usually what works best in transforming a graduate project into a publishable journal manuscript is (a) a substantial downsizing of the review of research, including only those sources most relevant and recent; (b) the inclusion of only the most important findings; and (c) a concise discussion of the significance of those results.

Although perhaps unfortunate, trends in scholarly study rise and fall just as they do in the world at large. Thus you may find that a paper that would not have been well received at some point in the past would be considered especially timely now.

The timing of the submission can be significant. By being conscientious in our professional reading, we can be aware of which topics are particularly attractive to editors at any time. All things being equal, a paper on a currently hot topic is more likely to be accepted.

It is not uncommon to have a paper turned down simply because the journal has either just accepted or recently published a very similar paper, despite whatever merits your paper has. It actually may be that the earlier paper is not as strong as yours. Consequently we can increase our chances by sending a manuscript to a journal that has not recently published a paper on that particular topic.

There are two philosophies in selecting topics. One holds that the most efficient process is simply to identify one topic, and mine it exhaustively. In concurrently or consecutively preparing several papers all focusing on one topic, we can use essentially the same review of literature, and also piggyback one paper off another. Further, this approaches over time allows us to establish a reputation as experts in a particular area.

Alternatively, many of us find it more rewarding to move from topic to topic. The excitement of a new topic can help us overcome some of the inherent difficulties in scholarly writing.

Know the Journal

Before sending a manuscript out to a journal, perhaps the single most important task for us is to *know the journal*. Almost any journal editor can give example after example of manuscripts submitted that are clearly inappropriate for the journal. In such cases the manuscript is simply returned to the author without even being sent out for review. Such a waste of time and effort can easily be avoided by being knowledgeable about the journal and its readership.

The best way to do this is simply to read several recent issues of the journal to determine its suitability for any given manuscript. Specifically, we should read for content and style, considering such issues as topics, manuscript formats, and typical lengths of articles. Besides this, almost all journals feature a Guidelines for Authors section in each issue that directly identifies the sorts of manuscripts the journal seeks, and outlines the format and style requirements. By reading several issues of a journal and adhering to the journal's guidelines, we significantly enhance our paper's chances of acceptance.

Select the Journal Carefully

An initial and significant obstacle for us is the identification of a journal appropriate for the new manuscript. To help guide the writer in the initial journal selection process, a number of directories to publishing in journals of education are available. These directories poll large numbers of journals in education, soliciting such information as type of review (refereed or nonrefereed), acceptance rate, time required for review, publication guidelines, and so forth. Examples of these directories include *Cabell's Directory of Publishing Opportunities in Education* (1989) and Heward's (1979) *The Writer's Guide to Educational Journals*. These directories are most useful in the initial determination of possible journals to which to submit.

However, journal emphases and guidelines can change rapidly. Thus directories are best used in the initial identification of several possible journals. At that point, current issues of those journals should then be carefully reviewed.

The selection of the journal to which a manuscript will be sent may be the single most important decision we make. Should we find more than one journal for which a manuscript might be appropriate, the decision about which of these to send the manuscript first arises. Several considerations come into play here.

The journal's acceptance rate is always important. The quality of the manuscript should be a prime determinant. If the manuscript is truly one of consequence, with significant results of substantial importance to the field, then we should submit it to one of the more prestigious and rigorous journals in that area.

However, early in our careers we are often better off submitting manuscripts to less rigorous journals. Scathingly critical reviews from the most rigorous journals can depress our interest in further submissions.

Journals published on a state or regional level are often excellent starting points for beginning scholarship. Editors of these journals often experience "empty journal terror." If they have a scarcity of quality manuscripts to offer their readerships, these editors often are more than willing to work extensively with us as prospective contributors, as they have an interest in developing a manuscript so that it might be published in the journal. These editors will sometimes suggest a pairing up of the contributor with another individual who can help rewrite and strengthen the paper to the point where it should be published.

As success and skills are gained at this level, we might raise our sights a bit, aiming for more rigorous journals. Personally we have found it useful to arrange two or three journals in order of their prestige, and then simply begin with a submission to the top-listed journal. We have been pleasantly surprised more than once after sending a manuscript to a rigorous journal, anticipating a rejection while seeking useful suggestions and an editorial critique, and instead finding the manuscript accepted! Even the best journals occasionally have periods in which fewer manuscripts are in the pipeline, and thus acceptance rates will vary a bit from time to time.

One particularly successful colleague of ours has adopted a basic philosophy of scholarly writing in which she concludes that if her manuscript is accepted by the first journal to which it was submitted, she had set her sights too low. Although this attitude might not work for all, there is something to be said for having high expectations for our work.

Besides the journal's acceptance rate, a pragmatic consideration can be the journal's timeline, that is, (a) how long does the journal require before a determination regarding a manuscript is reached, and (b) how long before an accepted paper appears in print? Some of us, especially at universities where we are under time pressures for tenure and promotion, may find ourselves drawn toward journals where decisions are reached quickly. Quick decisions are more likely with nonrefereed journals, where these editorial determinations are made in-house.

We can also review recent past issues to learn the sorts of people who have successfully contributed papers to the journal. For example, some journals specifically emphasize and solicit contributions with a practical orientation from field-based practitioners, whereas others encourage more theoretically oriented pieces, especially from universities and research centers.

Sending Out the Manuscript

After a target journal has been initially identified, a phone call to the journal's editor for a preliminary determination of the suitability of the manuscript can be a good idea. This can save time, because the editor can tell us if the paper sounds clearly appropriate, or inappropriate, for the journal.

Before sending the manuscript to the journal, it should be extensively proofread. Although word processing spelling checkers have proven to be most useful, there is no substitute for having a colleague carefully read the paper. By the time a manuscript is ready for submission we have been working with it so intimately over time that we are simply unable to see problems that a fresh reader will detect immediately.

When sending the manuscript to the journal, it is best to address it to a specific person. The editor's name should be obtained from a recent issue and the manuscript be sent to the journal personally addressed to that person. The manuscript should be accompanied by a one-page cover letter explaining the submission, and noting that the paper has neither been published elsewhere nor is being considered elsewhere. We always keep copies of our papers in case of loss in the mail.

Most journals require that several copies of the manuscript be sent. This is especially true of refereed journals, where three or more reviewers might be asked to review the paper. The specific number of copies required will be listed in the journal's author guidelines. In addition, many journals request a saved copy of the manuscript on computer disk, along with information on the type of computer and word processing program used. This makes it easier for the journal to make minor editorial changes.

Theme Issues

It has been personally useful for us to be aware of the opportunities presented by theme issues of journals; that is, from time to time a journal will devote an entire issue to a particular question in that field. Many editors report that they receive fewer submissions for these theme issues than they would like, so the acceptance rates for these special issues may be higher than usual for the journal.

Additional Suggestions

Get Started. No paper can or will ever be the final word on any subject. However, either consciously or unconsciously, many of us have this sort of expectation of our work. With such an expectation it is impossible to produce work that will reach that level. Thus, instead we simply choose not to write at all. An unspoken but deep-seated obligation to provide "THE TRUTH" can be paralyzing.

It is more helpful for us to instead see each manuscript as simply one statement in an ongoing professional exchange. The blank computer screen is the biggest hurdle. We have found for ourselves that the best way to resolve this is simply to get something—anything—down first. It is much easier to go back, refine, and strengthen already existing material than to try to produce perfection from the start.

Take Advantage of Papers Generated for Other Purposes. Most of us have written papers that were never intended for journals (for example, university course lectures, project reports, presentations at professional meetings, written rationales for new courses, etc.). We can take advantage of these and other writings by using them as starting points, basic structures that then can be expanded into publishable manuscripts. Many successful publishers have adopted a philosophy of never writing anything without an eye toward ultimately publishing it.

Keep a Planning File. As possible ideas or topics for scholarly writing occur to us, we jot them down on bits of paper, and drop them into a folder labeled "Ideas for Manuscripts." Rather than trying to remember the idea for when we have more time, we simply record it and forget it. Later we go back to that folder, sift through the compilation of ideas, select one that seems appealing, and begin work.

Keep a Writing Record. Many successful researchers have found keeping weekly, monthly, or quarterly records of such things as how many manuscript pages were written or how many manuscripts were sent out to journals useful in increasing their scholarly output. One productive colleague of ours simply posts on his wall all letters from editors acknowledging receipt of manuscripts so that he can quickly glance up and immediately determine the status of any manuscript at any time. If his wall begins to appear particularly barren, it serves as an incentive for him to spend more time writing.

Form a Writing Group. Many university faculty members have found it useful to meet regularly with colleagues about professional writing. In some writing groups actual manuscripts are copied and distributed beforehand for subsequent critique and discussion. Other groups have found it more useful to instead offer general suggestions and an overall level of professional support and encouragement.

Pick a Writing Time. Most of us have found that there are certain times or periods of the day (for example, early morning, midafternoon, evenings) when we are most productive. It is important to find a time that is best for you, and then stick with it. Many prolific researchers establish a writing time and stay with it daily by closing the office door, not answering the phone, and so forth. College professors sometimes are tempted to use these most productive times for teaching their classes. However, we have found that our personal prime times are best reserved for writing. We have learned that the presence of students in a class serves to stimulate us and our teaching even during our nonproductive hours. In contrast, the inherent difficulty of writing requires the commitment of our peak times of energy and productivity.

Many of us also have found that writing is easier when approached in small, manageable pieces, that is, regular small amounts of writing are preferable to and more productive than binge writing. Setting aside a habitual time for writing, and actually sitting down at that time and writing helps our overall scholarly productivity.

Stretch. One way to stay stimulated, and therefore more likely to generate ideas for manuscripts, is to stretch oneself a bit. We have found it useful to accept or even seek out assignments other than those we encounter routinely. Teaching a new class, visiting programs that are different from those to which we are accustomed, and accepting outside consulting work all serve to encourage the creative juices successful scholarly writing requires. Such professional pushing of our limits keeps us active and growing.

Lower Your Standards. Although this suggestion initially may seem questionable, it is often the best way to overcome the early writing inertia that paralyzes so many of us early on. One way of thinking about writer's block is to see it as a discrepancy between our desired performance standards and our actual performance. A means of reducing that discrepancy is to lower our expectations until the discrepancy is resolved. This can be done if we remember and take to heart the reality that no manuscript will ever be the last word on anything. Also, by considering and submitting to smaller journals with higher acceptance rates, we can establish some scholarly self-confidence and success.

Another way we can begin to get our writing into print is to volunteer to be book reviewers for journals, especially smaller journals. Most journals receive copies of professional books to be reviewed, and seek scholars in the field to do this. One of the advantages for us is that the paper is in essence accepted even before it is written; that is, once a journal has sent the book to you as a reviewer, the subsequent review, assuming it conforms to the journal's guidelines and timelines, is almost certain to be published.

Persevere. When a manuscript is returned from a journal with a note that it will not be accepted, most of us stumble, at least momentarily. However, to be successful we simply must take the suggestions on the reviewed manuscript, incorporate those suggestions into the paper, and resubmit it.

Experienced researchers often have identified ahead of time the first two or three journals to which they will submit any given manuscript. Thus, when one is returned, they quickly revise it according to the editorial suggestions, prepare a new cover letter, and immediately send it out, either back to the journal or to the next journal on the list. One of our most productive colleagues has as a personal rule the dictum that no returned manuscript will stay on her desk for more than 24 hours. Few manuscripts are accepted for publication never having left the author's desk.

Handling Rejection

Every one of us who has ever submitted papers for publication has received letters of rejection. Most successful writers have found that their letters of rejection outnumber their acceptance letters. What we must keep in mind is that, even with that rejection letter, we are still far ahead of many colleagues who have never gotten to the point of even sending a paper out. When a paper is not accepted, there are several options to consider.

If the criticisms are not too severe, the paper might be immediately sent to the next journal on the predetermined list. Some researchers even prepare such a cover letter ahead of time and have it waiting, so that it becomes that much easier through the disappointment to immediately send the paper to the next journal.

If specific concerns were noted, we should incorporate those. The presence of many reviewer suggestions is actually good. What this means is that the reviewer(s) found the paper salvageable. It is more difficult for a reviewer to read a paper that is good but has problems than it is to review a paper that is weak. The former situation will require more reviewer work and thoughtful comment, whereas the latter can more easily be dismissed. Thus a paper returned with many comments was seen by the reviewers as having significant value, and should be rewritten along the suggested lines.

Most journals will welcome the resubmission of such a rewritten paper, especially if it is returned with a cover letter explaining how each of the reviewers' comments has been incorporated into the revision. Even if we do not necessarily agree with the reviewers' comments, it is usually a good idea to accept this objective feedback, and revise accordingly. Once the journal editor sees how the paper has been revised following reviewer comments, he or she may simply accept it at that point without sending it out for re-review.

It is always best to have several manuscripts out at once. That way, if one paper is rejected, we can still have hopes for the others, instead of having all our hopes pinned on one.

On a lighter note, some of us have found it fun and useful to have contests with colleagues to see who can collect the most letters of rejection. Obviously, those of us with the most manuscripts out being considered will collect the most rejections, and also will collect the most acceptances.

Appearances sometimes to the contrary, editors look for, enjoy, and cherish good manuscripts. Although it is difficult not to personalize rejection, we must remember that the editor does not know us personally. After reading a harsh and disappointing letter from a journal editor rejecting a paper, we sometimes find it useful to immediately sit and write a letter back to the editor, pointing out how flawed the review was, how the editor clearly does not understand the field, questioning his or her lineage, and so forth. Then we throw that letter away, having vented our anger harmlessly. Rather than continuing to brood, we then can return to more productive scholarly functions.

Success Breeds Success

Most of us have found that the most difficult publication of our career was the first one. As we establish a growing record of published scholarship, the disappointment we feel when a paper is not accepted is reduced. Instead, with our growing success we see ourselves as productive scholarly writers. Through the process we learn much about the skills needed to publish a paper, which are quite different from the skills needed to write a paper. We learn which journals are likely to accept which kinds of papers, and also learn of more journals. This gives any manuscript that many more possibilities for publication.

A good concluding philosophy we keep in mind is that no manuscript should be an orphan, unable to find a journal home. Any manuscript worth writing in the first place can and should find a home somewhere. When we give birth to a manuscript, we also have the responsibility of then finding it this home.

REFERENCES

Cabell, D. W. (Ed.). (1989). *Cabell's directory of publishing opportunities in education*. Beaumont, TX: Cabell.
Heward, W. L. (1979). *The writer's guide to educational journals*. Columbus, OH: Special Press.

15

The Impact of New Developments in Information Technology on Postgraduate Research and Supervision

David Squires
King's College London

Academics now have access to an increasingly wide range of IT-assisted information systems that they can use to support information seeking in research. The extent and variety of access to online IT-assisted information systems have both increased radically with the advent of the World Wide Web. A measure of the diversity of these systems is indicated by the links to a range of library catalogs, bibliographic databases, directory services and archive services provided by the U.K. National Information Services and Systems (NISS) gateway (http://www.niss.ac.uk/datahosts). In March 1997, 21 datahosts that required registration were available, as were 14 unrestricted access datahosts. Figure 15.1 indicates the range of available datahosts.

In addition to online services, an increasing range of CD-ROM-based bibliographic services have become available. For example, PsycLIT, the American Psychological Association bibliographic database, has been available in CD-ROM format for some time. It consists of two databases that provide access to literature relevant to psychology and the psychology in the related areas of education, medicine, business, sociology, and psychiatry. One database covers journals in 30 languages from 45 countries published from 1974 onward, whereas the other relates to books written in the English language that have been published since 1987.

The combination of online and CD-ROM-based information systems is making a phenomenal amount of information potentially available to researchers. And it is not just the amount of information that is changing. The diversity of the material that can be accessed and searched is also increas-

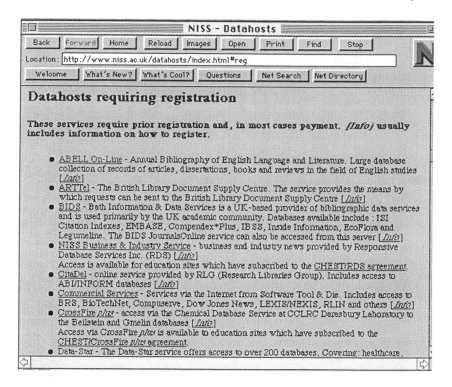

FIG. 15.1. Datahosts available via the NISS Gateway.

ing. Postgraduate research students have access to both "conventional" refereed material and to so-called "grey material," such as reports, departmental discussion papers, and conference papers. In addition there are discussion lists and bulletin boards (see chapter 16 by Rillero and Gallegos in this volume) that feature debates and position papers posted by academics throughout the world.

Although the advent of IT-assisted information systems in a research context is still relatively recent, it is clear that the information explosion fostered by these systems will have significant effects on the way in which research is carried out and the way in which it is reported. These effects will be influential throughout the research process. Using IT-assisted information systems can help students and supervisors to be more informed during the initial periods of a research program when critical decisions are being made about what area to research. During the completion of a research program, using such systems can help them to develop a comprehensive awareness of a chosen field, clarify methodological issues, and check the accuracy of information. In this chapter, the use of IT-assisted information systems for postgraduate research and supervision is discussed in terms of these two broad contexts—namely, initially establishing an area of research, and carrying out a research program.

Clearly, these effects will have implications for both postgraduate students and their supervisors. Postgraduate research supervisors are typically practicing researchers. As such, they will need to appreciate the information-seeking potential of using IT systems and utilize them in their own research programs. In turn, they will need to recognize the potential for the use of these systems in the research programs they supervise and advise students on their appropriate use. Supervisors will often need to train students in the use of specific techniques or arrange for them to attend suitable training programs.

Research training in science and mathematics education has its own information-seeking needs:

• Although science and mathematics education have their own research literature, workers in these fields will need to draw on the literature in other related areas such as psychology, curriculum theory, and mathematics or science themselves. In addition, the notion of adopting a mixed-methodology approach is well established in science and mathematics education: It is often the case that researchers will use both qualitative and quantitative methods in a supportive fashion. Science and mathematics education researchers need to be eclectic in their information seeking approaches, and adopt a broad, open approach in searching for information.

• Research students in science and mathematics education often have a limited scholarly background when they start their research programs. Their expertise is typically firmly rooted in classroom work, and they may find the norms and expectations of academic research alien to the practical ethos of the classroom. In particular, critical appraisal of academic literature, involving the related skills of information searching and synthesis, may be poorly developed.

The discussion in this chapter about the effects of IT-assisted information seeking for postgraduate research and supervision is based on the findings of a British Library-funded research project concerned with the use of IT-assisted information systems in academic research (Barry, 1996a; Barry & Squires, 1995; Squires, Barry, & Funston, 1994). The project involved detailed case studies of the use of IT systems by academics within a university school of education who had established track records in research. Five of the nine academics (David, Mary, Nick, Simon, and Tony) participated in the project work in the areas of science education or mathematics education. The findings of the research are relevant to postgraduate supervision and research (Barry, 1996b, 1997). In essence, the research programs conducted by postgraduate students and by established researchers have the same information-seeking elements. In addition, the knowledge and techniques gained by supervisors through their use of IT-assisted information systems will enable them to help students use these systems.

In this chapter a set of guidelines for the use of IT-assisted information in postgraduate research and supervision is discussed. The application of these guidelines is illustrated with examples of techniques that can be applied when IT-assisted information systems are used. In conclusion, some suggestions are made on how supervisors can help students to develop expertise in IT-assisted information seeking.

ESTABLISHING A RESEARCH AREA

Postgraduate research students in education do not usually conform to the apprenticeship model of research supervision that is typical in the sciences, medicine, and engineering. In these disciplines, it is common for research students to work on a large research project which determines the research area. Students are given a well-defined research problem, making the proposition of research questions relatively straightforward. In education, it is far more common for the researcher to work individually in areas chosen in terms of personal interest and classroom experience. Consequently, research students in education tend to start their research careers with vague ideas of what they would like to research. This leads to the initial stages of education research being characterized by two broad information-seeking activities:

- General browsing of the literature, including journals, books, conference proceedings and research reports.
- Exploratory discussions with colleagues and supervisors.

Browsing Publications

"Mary," a reader in science education, provides an example of how browsing the literature can act as an impetus for new directions in research (R = Researcher):

M: On *Cognition*, I'm up to date, I mean recently I had to go back to see an article which was '89 and I made certain that I got right up to date on everything. Now I don't have any reason to go and look at *Cognition* again, because I've got all the articles. So I'm disciplined, the next time I will look at a different journal and get up to date on that.

R: Oh, you mean the journal *Cognition*?

M: Yes. Sorry, I'm not up to date on "cognition," no. It's a question of browsing sensibly because otherwise you can spend a lot of time just looking through things, so each time I sort of bring myself up to date on one of the journals . . .

R: And did you find anything else while you were doing that?

M: About four good articles, yes. Well I found, quite a lot . . . if we do a new piece of research, I've got a lot of evidence in articles there. I had a good look at them, they're all very useful, so they're sort of sitting waiting for—there's a new piece of research I want to do, on the force and motion thing, on the theory of motion.

"Nick," a senior lecturer in education, provides two examples of IT-assisted browsing helping when researchers are making decisions about what area to study. He was interested in starting a new area of research concerned with gender and science education. The first example features his use of the PsycLIT CD-ROM database to explore rapidly the literature concerned with masculinity:

N: I've done some runs on boys and masculinity on PsycLIT before moving towards work in that area. Identity and masculinity turns up 20 of which 3 or 4 are useful. A half-hour job.

The second example features the use of PsycLIT and the Educational Resources Information Center (ERIC) CD-ROM databases:

N: So they asked me to do this, so what I immediately had to do was a literature search, so I did. Right through PsycLIT and ERIC and whizzing round the libraries and . . . to update myself. . . . I've always had a folder on cognitive learning styles, that's not new, but it needs drastic updating. So in the autumn I've really got to using these systems a lot, until I could get fairly clear what I had missed, what had been published in the last 2 or 3 years.

Mary provides another example of the use of the PsycLIT CD-ROM database to establish new research directions. She is a member of an interuniversity research group on mental models. The group was trying to decide on the number of new directions it wanted to pursue. Recent interpretations of consciousness, subjectivity, and tacit knowledge were being considered as possible new directions. By searching the CD-ROM database, she obtained a printout of 20 or 30 pages of the most recent material on consciousness. She then repeated it for the other areas in which the group was interested. The researcher asked Mary to comment on her decision to search for information in areas that she already knew very well. The usefulness of using the CD-ROM version of PsycLIT is evident in her reply:

> M: Yes ... when we get round to doing that area, I have got a search ... on this whole area of the nature of subjectivity, objectivity, consciousness, conscious knowledge, knowledge, tacit knowledge. ... I think the CD-ROM was invaluable for that.

Talking to Colleagues

"David," a senior lecturer in mathematics education, provides an example of talking to colleagues as a way of establishing new areas of research. He was convinced that the way teachers use examples to explain quite obscure mathematics is metaphorical. By implication it seemed to him that linguistics or semiology would give him a theoretical framework to describe how teachers use metaphor to help explain mathematics. This conviction led him to talk to colleagues who were more knowledgeable in linguistics:

> D: I don't know anything about linguistics really. ... Last week I spent half a day in the library looking at every single book under a class mark. I found a bit. I found bits and pieces. And I'll probably go to the Institute Library, and I'll talk to people here as well. I talked to Caroline and asked her if she had any ... and she found a general reference. ... She's also given me some names I might follow up on. ... I felt clearly that the three people I went to were William, Ronald, and Caroline.

Online discussion lists have the potential to increase the scope of collaboration, particularly from an international perspective. David's experience of contributing to an American Educational Research Association (AERA) discussion list illustrates how such lists can provide access to a range of opinions:

> R: Yeah. So what about the AERA one? Is that useful?
>
> D: There have been a couple of interesting debates. One of the ones about whether if in multiple choice testing, if you ask people to indicate their degree of faith in the answer, ... do you get more accurate assessments of people's ability? There are those who say that you should because you're cutting down the guess in effect. There are others who say that whether you're confident or not depends on ... you know, you might as well ask, are you male? [laughs] So that's been quite interesting.
>
> R: So, what, you've been listening in to other people's discussions?

D: Yeah. And launching in myself . . . occasionally, just to say . . .

In fact David's participation in the AERA list has led to the establishment of personal contacts:

D: A guy from somewhere in the midwest USA wrote, e-mailed me back directly, personally rather than via the board, saying, very interested to hear what you've got to say about the British context of multiple choice testing because it is very different . . . from the States. I just explained that. . . . One guy is actually coming over to do some workshops . . . and so he was asking me . . . about extra questions and said he found it very useful and could he write to me again and ask me some more questions, you know, when he gets over here. So I said, yes, sure. And I said . . . could you give me some references on what you've just said because they're embarking on a primary school testing program.

COMPLETING A RESEARCH PROGRAM

At various stages during a research program a range of information-seeking tasks need to be completed. Major tasks can be characterized as:

- Developing a comprehensive awareness of relevant literature.
- Keeping up-to-date with current developments in the chosen research field.
- Choosing a research methodology.
- Checking the accuracy of information.
- Checking the originality of research findings.

In this section, the use of IT-assisted information systems to help complete these tasks is discussed.

Comprehensive Awareness of Relevant Literature

After a research area has been established, students need to make sure that they know their field. While an area is being established, browsing and talking to colleagues makes the students familiar with the literature in the chosen research area. However, it is important to expand and develop this familiarity into a comprehensive awareness.

David provides an example of how IT-assisted information systems can be used to complete a comprehensive literature search. With a colleague he was awarded a contract to review research in mathematics education with a focus on how research findings could help to improve teaching standards. They used a combination of an online library catalog (Libertas), a CD-ROM-based bibliographic database (PsycLIT), and traditional journals:

D: We said we'd use PsycLIT and ZDM

R: ZDM?

D: ZDM is Zentralblatt fur Didaktic Mathematik—a review—it's really a review of research in maths education. And just said the journals we'd look at, really, so it's a matter of finding out what we've got downstairs [in the departmental library], what's at the Institute [of Education Library]. So I've done quite a bit of work on that, going through—PsycLIT has been very useful. . . . I've used Libertas quite a lot in finding out where copies of things are.

The synergistic use of journals and CD-ROM-based resources is evident from David's description of how inspection of traditional journals was used to back up searches of CD-ROM-based materials:

D: We started with "teaching" and "teaching style" and "teaching method" and eventually we managed to get "teaching method and mathematics" to throw up some references that then led on to other things. But we're very far from clear that we've actually managed to tap the riches of PsycLIT in a sense. So we've—the keywording isn't very dependable. The two articles can be—to my purposes—[said to] cover the same field and end up with very different keywording. So you don't know you haven't missed it. So as well as more sophisticated searching techniques we've also been doing things like going through the *Review of Educational Research* in the library and looking at articles there . . .

After David and his colleague had completed this contract, "Simon" (a reader in science education) and "Tony" were offered a similar contract to produce a bibliography of research into an area in science education. This particular research area was new to Simon, and he was keen to utilize IT-assisted information seeking to help him get to know it.

Compiling this bibliography involved the complimentary use of various IT-assisted information systems:

- A range of bibliographic CD-ROMs.
- The Bath Information and Data Services (BIDS) system, which provides access to the Science Citation Index, the Social Sciences Citation Index, the Arts and Humanities Citation Index, and the Index to Scientific and Technical Proceedings.

- The Microsoft Word software.
- The EndNote reference management software package in association with the EndLink utility for importing the results of searches into EndNote.

Simon started a literature search using PsycLIT to assist in writing a proposal for the contract. This search identified the titles of a few books, which he checked in the Institute of Education Library. This gave him an entry into the literature, but most of his literature searching was based on a combination of using Libertas and PsycLIT. In parallel, Tony looked at copies of journals and indexes of recent journals that he had ready access to in his office. "Learning strategy" or "learning style" were used as keywords in BIDS searches. Simon requested BIDS to e-mail the results of his searches to him and then transferred them into a Word document. EndLink was used to import the Word documents into an EndNote library.

Simon was convinced that the use of IT-assisted information systems had made a radical difference. Asked how useful he thought the use of these systems had been, he speculated on how he would have conducted the search without access to them:

S: I would have looked into ERIC. I did actually use ERIC, I didn't find it gave me a lot somehow. I suppose I would have physically searched journals. [This area] comes into everything, so there's no telling where the stuff's going to turn up. [I could have started] from all the journals in [the departmental library] and just looked at the last five issues—in the indexes—which would have been very laborious. But even if I'd done that, there may still be streams of research in the area which I would have missed.

Keeping Up-to-Date

Developing a comprehensive awareness of research is not a one-off activity. As students read around their subject, new areas of concern will become apparent and they will need to explore the literature in these areas. In addition, a research program will typically last for at least 3 years and students will need to keep up with current developments in research.

The huge amount of information of varying quality that is available militates against attempts to keep up-to-date. However, it is possible to develop information seeking techniques which can help. For example, David describes how searching based on entries in the bibliography of a seminal journal article can be used in this context:

D: I'm doing work on using Messick's theoretical framework for validation of assessments, and it just so happens that nobody could write an article about this field without quoting Messick, I mean there's no way they'd get published if they didn't and so that single article generates defines a field. So therefore you can keep [up-to-date] with any of the literature by just doing a citation search on that one paper, because if it's not put in a paper then it's not about your field.

Choosing a Research Methodology

At an early stage decisions need to be made about what methodology or methodologies will be adopted during the research program. Research in education features an eclectic mixture of methodologies, ranging from qualitative to quantitative approaches (Tesch, 1990). It is quite common for research studies to employ a range of quite diverse but complementary methodologies. Such a mixed methodologies approach is reflected in a recent research study conducted jointly by King's College London, the University of Birmingham, and the Cambridge Institute of Education to evaluate the implementation of the U.K. National Curriculum for Mathematics (Johnson & Millett, 1996). This project used questionnaires distributed to teachers, publishers, and in-service education providers; teacher interviews; inspection of work conducted by teacher groups; case studies of classroom work; discussions with advisers; informal meetings with school inspectors; and inspection of documents and reports. Similarly the *Effective Teachers of Numeracy* project recently completed by King's College London employed a mixed-methodologies approach, that is, questionnaire administration, classroom observation, teacher and head teacher interviews, concept mapping, and the elicitation of personal constructs (Askew, Rhodes, Brown, Wiliam, & Johnson, 1997).

David provides an example of how information seeking can lead to methodological insights:

D: The Swets books I actually got hold of on interlibrary loan. These are two papers, general articles.

R: You became aware of those because . . .

D: The Swets ones I became aware of when I realized that the Signal Detection Theory. . . . I don't know when I first came across the idea of the label Signal Detection Theory, but as soon as I realized that it was relevant I then did a search on PsycLIT and became aware of Swets, because all the papers that were on Signal Detection referred to Swets—Green and Swets' book. So then I did a search on Swets. Green doesn't appear to have written anything since this classic text. . . . But these two Swets articles are very useful because they're for a lay audience, a more general audience—the *American Psychologist* journal. So those were very useful in formulating my ideas about how to use the Signal Detection Theory . . . as a way of evaluating reliability within National Curriculum testing.

Checking for Accuracy

The information used and quoted in research studies needs to be checked for accuracy. Although this can be conceptually straightforward, it can also be both time consuming and tedious, as Simon's experience testifies.

Simon frequently refers to a quote from Edith Niemark (note his spelling) that he first used in his PhD thesis. He has given the reference as Niemark (1975), published in *Genetic Psychology Monographs*. Recently he used the quote in a journal article and he wanted to check the page numbers. When he was next near the Institute of Education Library, he looked for issues of *Genetic Psychology Monographs* on the shelves only to find that they were not there. He checked with the librarian, who said that the journal was on restricted access, but that the volume Simon wanted could be obtained in a few hours' time. Simon asked if the journal was available in the university library. The librarian told him that it was. Simon duly went to the university library and located the appropriate volume, but found that the quote did not come from the paper he was referencing.

Simon then decided to use the PsycLIT CD-ROM in the university library. He searched on "Niemark" in the author field, but this yielded no hits. However, a search on "Neimark" gave eight hits. He identified two likely papers that the quote could have come from. He located the journal corresponding to the first paper in the university library, but could not find the quote in the paper. He had to return to the Institute of Education Library to look at the second journal, but again the quote was not in the paper from this journal. However, he noticed a citation in the paper to a book chapter by Neimark (1975). Using Libertas he located the book (edited by Horowitz), and found the appropriate chapter and the quotation. He noted the reference and returned to his own college.

Simon noticed that he had forgotten to record the initials of the editor. He accessed the bibliographic CD-ROMs available in the college to try to find the missing initial. Horowitz is a very common name, and his search resulted in 136 hits. The next day he used Libertas to check the book in the college library, but to no avail. He then used Libertas to check the London Consortium of Libraries and finally located the book.

Despite the difficulties that Simon experienced in obtaining these page numbers, it is important to stress that without the use of IT-assisted information systems, he would probably not have been able to locate them at all.

David provides an example of how IT-assisted information can be used more successfully to improve the efficiency of checking the accuracy of information. He wanted to refer to a concept he had first heard about on the radio, but could not remember the details of the program:

D: In one part of the article I've used a concept that I actually heard on the radio. It's about arbitration—you know this new kind of arbitration that they use in the United States. . . . I actually thought it was quite a nice model for explaining how you might reconcile schools' internal judgments about kids' grades versus external test marks. You might use the same model. And I've actually cited this, which was called, in this radio program I heard, "Full-Scale Pendulum Swing Arbitration." . . . And of course one of the referees said, please cite a reference for this. . . . I actually started with PsycLIT and I looked at "pendulum"—nothing. And eventually I think I just tried "arbitration" and got a lot of things and eventually found what I was calling "Full-Scale Pendulum Swing Arbitration" is now called "Final Offer Selection Arbitration."

David was convinced that without the use of IT-assisted information systems that he would not have been able to locate the details of the radio program reference:

D: And that was something I could not have done before the eras of [IT-assisted information systems]. Think of that, you know, there's no way I could have actually found out. I would have had to go through hundreds of journals to find it at all. So that was very important, because I didn't want to lose the idea but I couldn't actually publish it without the reference.

Checking for Originality

Checking for originality presents conceptual problems. The notion of work being original is crucial to the concept of research. However, what constitutes originality is open to question and can be interpreted in various ways. For example, Phillips and Pugh (1994) identified 15 ways in which PhD candidates may have been considered to show originality, ranging from setting down a major piece of new information in writing for the first time to being cross-disciplinary and using new methodologies.

The critical importance of originality in research is illustrated by David:

D: I've also just discovered that I'm not the first one to do it. There's an article in *Educational Researcher* in 1994.

R: Oh dear.

D: It's all right (whispers).

R: (laughs) . . .

D: It's all right. I mean, I did feel scooped at one point but then I realized what I've actually got to say is more, more powerful, than what this person's already said. So I'll be okay.

David found out about competing research by reading a traditional journal, but IT-assisted information systems can be used very effectively to check for originality, as the following example illustrates.

Simon was considering whether to write a paper on progress and science education. He was concerned that there might already be a mass of literature that he was unaware of on this topic. After he had made some rough notes on the proposed article, he conducted a PsycLIT search using "science education" and "progress" as the keyword search criteria. This search produced 45 hits, which he then looked at to see if the ideas that he intended to present would be original:

> S: I went through them all, they all seemed to not be relevant at all to what I was thinking about, my concept of progress. In retrospect I can see that it's much too general a sort of word.... If I had defined it [with respect] to concept or ... cognitive development, that is imposing my model of progress on the research, ... I'm only going to find the things that I expect to find, which I know about anyway. I'm trying to look for something different.

IMPLICATIONS FOR POSTGRADUATE RESEARCH AND SUPERVISION

The discussion in the previous sections of this chapter indicates that the use of IT-assisted information systems can help researchers to be more effective. In principle, the availability of extensive and accessible information should lead to more comprehensive, timely and accurate information seeking. Paradoxically, however, the use of IT-assisted information systems can also hinder research. Information overload can lead to unproductive information seeking and the use of information of dubious quality. Research students need advice from their supervisors on how to use IT-assisted information systems so that they can realize their advantages and not their disadvantages.

In this section, some guidelines for the effective use of IT-assisted information systems are proposed:

- Focus on the information-seeking task in question.
- Be critical of the quality of information.
- Use a variety of IT-assisted information systems in an integrated fashion.
- Use a variety of searching techniques.
- Automate information seeking wherever possible.

Some illustrative information seeking techniques are described here to show how these guidelines can be used in practice.

Focus on the Information-Seeking Task in Question

With access to extensive and diverse information systems, it is very easy for researchers to lose a sense of direction when completing an information-seeking task. New and potentially fascinating nuggets of information appear all the time, and it is very tempting to just "have a quick look at them." In turn this may lead to other potentially fascinating information and so on. Before long, the original information-seeking task has been deferred or forgotten, and the information-seeking process has become unproductive. This danger is particularly apparent when students are browsing, as this type of information seeking is inherently eclectic and discursive.

There are some simple focusing techniques that are well established. For example, follow up the references in a seminal article or complete a citation search on a well-known author. As more comprehensive and extensive information systems become available, other techniques will be developed.

The emergence of a simple new focusing technique can be illustrated by considering information seeking in the World Wide Web. With its massive network of information sources related to each other by associative hypermedia links, information seeking can rapidly degenerate into unstructured and unproductive experiences. A simple focusing technique is to go to the home page of an institution or department that is well known for work in the area of interest. This will then provide a conduit to information about this topic.

To illustrate the use of this technique, consider a hypothetical research student who is trying to establish a research focus in the general area of misconceptions and learning in science, and in the particular area of misconceptions in understanding photosynthesis. The School of Education at Cornell University is internationally renowned for its research in misconceptions in science and mathematics education, so a sensible first step would be to access the home page of Cornell University. This would typically be a relatively straightforward process from the home page of the student's own university World Wide Web site. Accessing the Cornell University web home page in fact leads automatically via a Gopher to the options shown in Fig. 15.2.

The penultimate option, referring to the proceedings of the Third International Seminar on Misconceptions and Educational Strategies in Science and Mathematics as seen in Fig. 15.2, would clearly be of interest. Selecting this option leads to the options shown in Fig. 15.3. Figure 15.4 shows part of the table of contents, from which it is clear that there are papers concerned with photosynthesis.

A keyword search (sixth option) using "photosynthesis" as a keyword yields a list of 18 papers:

- "Misconceptions in Photosynthesis: The Use of Novel Database Software."

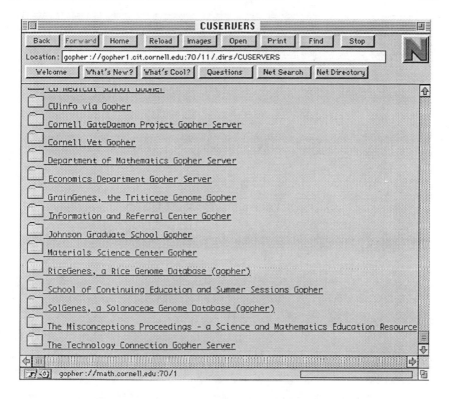

FIG. 15.2. The Cornell gopher providing access to the papers presented at the Third International Seminar on Misconceptions and Educational Strategies in Science and Mathematics.

- "The 'Light' and 'Dark' Reactions of Photosynthesis—Terminology as a Source of Misconceptions."
- "Understanding Cellular Respiration."
- "Some Sources of Students' Misconceptions in Biology: A Review."
- "Students' Misconceptions in Biological Subject Areas and Consequences in Teaching Biology."
- "Student Misconceptions of Ecology: Identification, Analysis and Instructional Design."
- "Research on Students' Conceptions—Developments and Trends."
- "Different Uses of Learners' Conceptions from Constructivist Models to the Allosteric Model."
- "Pupils' Understanding of Ecological Processes and Their Conceptions of Matter."
- "Development of a Diagnostic Test to Detect Misconceptions in Mendelian Genetics and Meiosis."

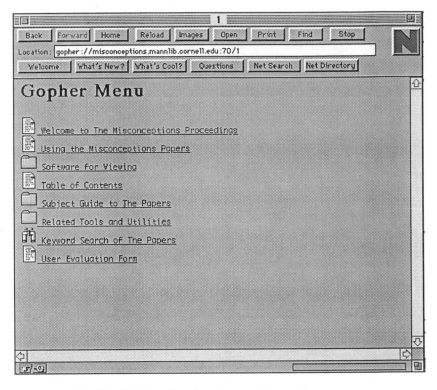

FIG. 15.3. The Cornell gopher misconceptions conference page.

- "Children's Misconceptions and Cognitive Strategies Regarding the Understanding of the Ozone Layer Depletion."
- "Contextual Settings, Verbal Argumentations, and Science Stories: Toward a More Humanistic Science Education."
- "Children's Ideas About the Nature of Science From Age Nine to Age 16."
- "Assessing Conceptual Understanding in Science Through the Use of Two- and Three-Dimensional Concept Maps."
- "Freshman Biology Non-Majors' Misconceptions About Diffusion and Osmosis."
- "Concept Mapping and Gowin's Categories as Heuristics Devices, in Scientific Reading of High School Students."
- "Cultural Factors in the Origin and Remediation of Alternative Conceptions."
- "Helping Middle School Students to Learn the Kinetic Particle Model."

Clicking on a paper title results in the full text of the paper being downloaded.

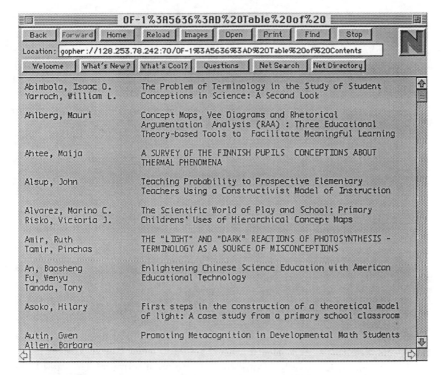

FIG. 15.4. Table of contents of the Cornell gopher misconceptions conference page.

Be Critical of the Quality of Information

Conventionally the major criterion by which an academic paper is judged is whether it has been published in a refereed journal. There is a pecking order among journals and it is more prestigious to published in some journals than others. These simple guidelines, although crude, may in fact be quite effective in policing the quality of academic research and debate.

If refereed publication is accepted as a criterion, IT-assisted information systems may be able to help researchers assess the quality of materials. For example, during the previously cited compilation of a literature review for the Office for Standards in Education on research in mathematics education, David and his coresearcher had decided that they would only cite references that came from a refereed journal. David used FirstSearch, an online catalog of bibliographic databases, to check whether a vocal member of the research community had actually published in refereed journals. He commented that "Well ... it's confirmed my prejudice that this [named researcher] had not written anything in the academic literature—in the refereed journals—which is why I'd missed her the first time."

However, with the advent of an increasing diversity of information about research, it is difficult universally to apply these simple guidelines. In particular, the increasing amount of grey literature, such as the recently published CD-ROM System for Information on Grey Literature in Europe (SIGLE), which is largely unrefereed, makes the critical evaluation of the quality of information difficult.

If a general evaluation is being made of the research reported by an identified person, the following criteria may be useful:

- Does the researcher only report research in one forum?
- Has the researcher published in established referred journals in the past?
- What is the research tradition and reputation of the institution that the researcher comes from?
- To what extent and in what ways does the researcher comment on issues posted in discussion lists?
- Is the unrefereed material commonly cited by other people?

An example of the application of these guidelines can be provided by considering the following quote from the introduction to a message about software evaluation that was submitted by Jacob Nielsen to the Internet-based discussion list of the Computer Systems Technical Group of the Human Factors and Ergonomics Society of the United States (CSTG-L) on February 24, 1994:

> Regarding usability inspection and heuristic evaluation, I should mention that I have revised my set of recommended heuristics. It is now as listed below. ... For more information see my chapter on heuristic evaluation in the forthcoming book: Nielsen, J., & Mack, R. L. (Eds.). (1994). *Usability inspection methods.* NY: Wiley. (ISBN 0-471-01877-5).

Nielsen is internationally respected in the field of Human–Computer Interaction. He has published widely in respected journals and conference proceedings, including papers on the subject of the discussion list topic. He is also based at a prestigious center for the study of human–computer interaction. Hence, it would seem that this entry to a discussion list should be taken seriously.

A more general approach to assessing unrefereed materials is to ask colleagues for their opinion of the materials. Of course, this can be done informally, but it may be worthwhile to circulate materials among other researchers in a department asking for critical comments. These materials can even form the focus of a research seminar. The opinions of other researchers could be sought more widely by posting a request on an electronic discussion list asking for critical comment. In essence these techniques establish an informal peer review mechanism.

Use a Variety of IT-Assisted Information Systems in an Integrated Fashion

Different IT-assisted information systems have different strengths and weaknesses. If researchers rely on only one system they will not realize the advantages of the full range of IT-assisted information systems. To capitalize on the full potential of IT-assisted information seeking, researchers need to use a mix of systems, choosing a combination that provides a profile of advantages geared to the information-seeking task at hand.

Some systems are comprehensive at a relatively superficial level. For example, FirstSearch has information on nearly 12,500 education and social science journals, but the bibliographic entry for a record is quite limited, as illustrated by the following example of a FirstSearch record:

AUTHOR: Geary, David C.

TITLE: Reflections of Evolution and Culture in Children's Cognition: Implications for Mathematical Development and Instruction.

JOURNAL NAME: *The American Psychologist.*

VOL, ISSUE: Volume 50, Number 1

PAGES: 24

PUB DATE: January

YEAR: 1995

TYPE: Article

ABSTRACT: Academic achievement is based on biologically primary and biologically secondary cognitive abilities. The co-option of primary abilities for learning mathematics depends on culture and didactic techniques. Although we know how to produce high-achieving mathematics students, available techniques go unused.

SSN: 0003-066X

J ALT NAME: *Proceedings of the annual convention of the American Psychological Association*

The PsycLIT record corresponding to the same publication is as follows:

Title: Reflections of evolution and culture in children's cognition: Implications for mathematical development and instruction.

Author(s): Geary,-David-C.

Institutional affiliation of first author: U Missouri, Dept of Psychology, Columbia, US

Journal: *American-Psychologist*; 1995 Jan Vol 50(1) 24–37

ISSN: 0003066X

Language: English

Publication Year: 1995

Abstract: An evolution-based framework for understanding biological and cultural influences on children's cognitive and academic development is presented. The utility of this framework is illustrated within the mathematical domain and serves as a foundation for examining current approaches to educational reform in the United States. Within this framework, there are two general classes of cognitive ability, biologically primary and biologically secondary. Biologically primary cognitive abilities appear to have evolved largely by means of natural or sexual selection. Biologically secondary cognitive abilities reflect the co-optation of primary abilities for purposes other than the original evolution-based function and appear to develop only in specific cultural contexts. A distinction between these classes of ability has important implications for understanding children's cognitive development and achievement. (PsycLIT Database Copyright 1995 American Psychological Assn, all rights reserved)

KP: evolution based framework of biological & cultural factors; cognitive & academic & mathematical development; children

Descriptors: COGNITIVE-DEVELOPMENT; MATHEMATICS-ACHIEVEMENT; SOCIOCULTURAL-FACTORS; THEORY-OF-EVOLUTION; CHILDREN-; BIOLOGY-; ACADEMIC-ACHIEVEMENT

Classification Code(s): 2820; 28

Population: Human

Composite Age Group: Child

Update Code: 9505

Psychological Abstracts Volume and Abstract Number: 82-16916

Journal Code: 1055

Note, in particular that the PsycLIT entry includes a much fuller abstract. Thus a useful technique is to employ extensive systems like FirstSearch to uncover likely articles, and then use a subject-specific (but more detailed system) like PsycLIT to get more information on chosen articles.

Use a Variety of Searching Techniques

The experience of Tony highlights how it is sometimes difficult for researchers to know how to search for the information they want. Tony sought the help of a colleague, "Tina" (Ti in the following), who was qualified as a librarian in the use of IT-assisted information systems. Initially they started an information search by focusing on some citations that Tony provided:

> Ti: Tina and I must have spent a couple of hours, if not more, looking for references to do with pupil learning, self-learning, and we started by . . . I had some references which had been given to me, but wanted more information and we tried to find them, and we had a lot of difficulty, eventually I think we must have found one or possibly 2, from a list of about 10.

However, as this approach was relatively unsuccessful, and they decided to try another way round:

> To: Then the other way round was to feed in some key words, and we were getting information, but it was about . . . it wasn't about the group of pupils that I was particularly interested in, not to do with special needs and . . . not . . . that's not the emphasis that we were looking for so . . . when it's talking about problems of pupils' learning, of course you end up with special needs, and what I was after was . . . how do you teach pupils to learn, and it was very difficult narrowing it down, getting the right references.

David provides another example of the need to be imaginative and flexible in refining search techniques. He decided to write a journal article on technical issues associated with the translation of tests from English to Welsh. First he completed searches using BIDS and CD-ROM versions of ERIC and PsycLIT:

> D: So I knew what I wanted to say but I had no idea of how to go about it. So I started with BIDS—didn't get far with that—PsycLIT and ERIC. [I] compiled some very complex search terms, because I was trying to get hold of everything that was to do with testing and assessment. So I had testing or assessment or measurement and bilingualism, or Welsh or Wales. So I wanted to tap into those two broad nexuses

However, his searches were too broad. He was locating too many references, many of which referred to material in subject areas that he was not interested in, such as children with special educational needs who did not speak very much English. He then used EndNote to help him refine his searches:

> D: I downloaded them [PsycLIT references] into EndNote so that I could look at the titles in a row, rather than wade through the abstracts and the journal stuff. And then I began looking at the key words. I

began to see that this term test translation came up in the articles I wanted so I realized that in fact test translation was the key word, for the area I was interested in, even though I was not interested in translating tests.

As these examples illustrate, there is a need to learn good information handling skills, and to be flexible and imaginative in their use. There is a tendency to base literature reviews on simple keyword searches, often simply on the author's name. Other techniques that may be useful include:

- Try a citation search on a seminal work by a well-known author.
- Search by institution of an author if it has a reputation for good work in relevant areas.
- Scan recent contributions in relevant discussion lists.
- Send a request for references to a discussion list.
- Use an online directory system such as Paradise to locate the e-mail number of an author and contact the author directly.
- Find a relevant article and search on the descriptor terms on which it is indexed.

Automate Information Seeking Wherever Possible

Information seeking can be time consuming, particularly for a students who are trying to maintain a current in-depth knowledge of a field. It is a tremendous help if information can be sieved and presented in a clear, condensed fashion. For example, a very popular service that is provided for students in my department is to simply copy the current contents pages of major journals and pin them to the science education and mathematics education noticeboards. In this way the students can keep a watch on these journals and visit the library to look at any article in which they are particularly interested.

As "Mary's" attempt to get up-to-date with the articles published in *Cognition* demonstrates, it is common practice for researchers to browse through a journal to identify articles of possible interest. However, with rapidly increasing numbers of journals it is difficult to find the time to do this in a systematic and comprehensive way. Mary originally visited the library to look at an article published in 1989, not to systematically review the articles published in *Cognition* from 1989 onward.

There are benefits from the systematic journal browsing and it makes sense to see if IT-assisted information systems can help researchers to organize this in a more reliable and effective way. Using the BIDS online citation indexes provides researchers with a technique that can help in these respects. It is possible to have the results of a BIDS search automatically downloaded into an e-mail mailbox. Thus the results of a simple search that results in listing the contents of a journal can be automatically downloaded for a set of journals defined by the user. As new journals appear this set can be increased. If the title of an article looks interesting, the researcher can look at it in the library. If the journal is not taken by the library the researcher can use a system such as Libertas to order a copy through interlibrary loans. Thus, not only does this technique provide a fast review mechanism for journals to which the researchers have access in their own library, it also makes them more aware of publications in journals to which they do not have immediate access.

CONCLUSION

IT-assisted information systems are now pervasive, and they are fast becoming an established aspect of academic research. The observations of the use of these systems by academic researchers in science and mathematics education indicates that there are significant benefits which accrue from their use, particularly in an eclectic field such as this. However, these observations also highlight the fact that IT-assisted information seeking is not trivial. Information overload can lead to an unstructured and unproductive research and the citing of poor research. New information-handling concepts need to be acquired, software application skills must be learned, and an appreciation of the advantages and disadvantages of the use of these systems in a research context needs to be developed.

There is a clear implication for postgraduate research supervisors: Not only will they need to use these systems in their own research, but they will also need to advise and help their students in the use of such systems. This support can take number of forms:

- Through their use of IT-assisted information seeking in their own research programs, supervisors should act as good role models for research students.
- Supervisors should be active in establishing training courses and workshops on the use of IT-assisted information systems as part of research training programs.
- Practical advice on the application of IT-assisted information systems in individual students' research programs should form an integral part of research supervision sessions.

The findings of the British Library-funded research imply that ensuring this sort of support may be problematic. The research indicates that the level of support provided by supervisors is low. Barry (1996b, 1997) suggested two reasons for this: The supervisors have low levels of expertise and, more fundamentally, information skills are tacit, making it difficult for the supervisor to realize that they need to be articulated to research students. If the potential benefits of IT-assisted information systems are to be realized, supervisors need to be encouraged to reflect on their own use of IT in information handling and consciously consider how they can both develop this use and convey good practice to research students.

REFERENCES

Askew, M., Rhodes, V., Brown, M., Wiliam, D., & Johnson, D. (1997). *Effective teachers of numeracy*. London: King's College.

Barry, C. A. (1996a). The digital library: The needs of our users. In *Proceedings of the International Summer School on the Digital Library, 5 August 1996*. The Netherlands: Tilburg University.

Barry, C. A. (1996b, April). *Training the next generation of academic researchers to operate in an electronic world*. SIG ENET roundtable presentation at the annual meeting of the American Educational Research Association, New York.

Barry, C. A. (1997). Information skills for an electronic world: Training doctoral research students. *Journal of Information Science, 23*(3), 225–238.

Barry, C., & Squires, D. (1995). Why the move from traditional information-seeking to the electronic library is not straightforward for academic users: Some surprising findings. In D. I. Raitt & B. Jeapes (Eds.), *Online information 95* (pp. 177–187). London: Meckler.

Johnson, D. C., & Millett, A. (Eds.). (1996). *Implementing the mathematics national curriculum*. London: Paul Chapman.

Phillips, E. M., & Pugh, D. S. (1994). *How to get a PhD: A handbook for students and their supervisors*. Buckinghamshire, England: Open University Press.

Squires, D., Barry, C., & Funston, T. (1994). *The use of IT-assisted information systems in academic research* (Rep. 6215). London: British Library Research and Innovation Department.

Tesch, R. (1990). *Qualitative research: Analysis types and software tools*. London: Falmer.

16

Databases: A Gateway to Literature in Mathematics and Science Education Research

Peter Rillero
Bee Gallegos
Arizona State University West

Huge databases exist for literature and information in almost every professional field of study. "End-users need to be aware of these sources and have the skill to exploit the information environment effectively ... or they will become its peasants" (Omaji, 1994, p. 46). With the increasing sophistication of computer hardware and software, it has become easier to rapidly find a needle of information in a haystack of data. These needles of information point researchers to information that enables them to understand a field, design research projects, write grant proposals, and develop theories.

The ease of using some databases may make novices feel like experts. This can be advantageous because it gives confidence in conducting searches. The confidence may, however, be a disadvantage if it prevents novices from learning more efficient and effective techniques. A study of ERIC searches by faculty members and graduate students indicates they are finding only one-third of the items that would be useful for their topics (Lancaster, Elzy, Zeter, Metzler, & Low, 1994). Furthermore, inefficient searches waste time. Few people have the time to wade through a few hundred records from a poorly designed search—full of unneeded items and missing relevant records. Science and mathematics education researchers must know how to efficiently access information in literature databases, and which databases are important and relevant for their research.

This chapter begins with a discussion of the benefits of using databases for finding materials for science and mathematics education research. The structure of databases is described and generalities of searching and retrieving database information are discussed. Database searches are further illustrated by examples from the world's largest and most used educational database—the Educational Resources Information Center (ERIC) database. In the quest to maximize the procurement of information and minimize the investment of time and money, the following areas are explored: free text searches, controlled vocabulary, narrowing and broadening searches, finding instruments, and finding printed materials from their bibliographic records. The ERIC example will be a springboard into an annotated bibliography of other key databases for mathematics and science education researchers. The chapter concludes with a discussion of the Internet—an unorganized, ever-changing, and rapidly growing database. Tools and techniques for searching this database are described, and pointers to Internet resources are presented.

THE VALUE OF COMPUTERIZED DATABASES

Databases contain gold for educational researchers. Abstracts of articles, tests, instruments, literature reviews, conference papers, curricular materials, and books are all found on databases pertaining to science, mathematics, social science, and education. A goldmine is only valuable if the gold can be efficiently retrieved. The value of a database lies only partly in what it contains; equally important is the ability to efficiently access the information stored in it.

With a well-designed database, computers provide researchers with the ability to efficiently find needed information. Fast computer search mechanisms have provided the ability to scan through data rapidly. This allows the user to be flexible and innovative in database searches. Linear limitations of searching indexes—page by page and volume by volume—have been replaced by a system that retrieves information from decades of research. No longer are researchers limited to looking up one descriptor or index term at a time; the ability to combine multiple terms has resulted in a revolution in database retrieval. Boolean logic can make the search narrower or broader and creates possibilities for highly efficient searches. If the information we seek is gold, the computer software is our lightning-fast pickax. However, the user must know how to swing it.

A knowledge of bibliographic databases and efficient searching ability are important for everyone in education, including students, teachers, researchers, and supervisors. We have developed a list of essential database competencies for educators (Gallegos & Rillero, 1996). Educators should be able to:

1. Describe the structure of databases.
2. Define goals for their search.
3. Choose appropriate databases.
4. Operate computer software to conduct a search.
5. Search with controlled vocabulary and with free text or natural language.
6. Narrow or widen a search with Boolean logic.
7. Retrieve records identified in a search.

DATABASE SEARCHING

Database Structure

Databases contain records of data. The records are organized into fields (Fig. 16.1). A bibliographic database contains data describing published literature. Each record pertains to one piece of literature. Many fields exist within that record including the author, title, and abstract of the work.

Databases are designed for users to easily access data. The software for sifting through the data is composed of a user interface and a search engine. There are some generalities that transcend most types of software used in database searching.

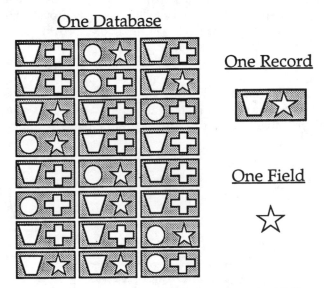

FIG. 16.1. Databases are composed of records made of fields.

Goals

In doing any kind of search, it is important for researchers to know what they want. One of the habits in the book *The 7 Habits of Highly Effective People* (Covey, 1989) is to begin with the end in mind. In database searching, as in life, goal definition facilitates goal achievement. It is important to crystallize the research focus into a clear statement identifying the main concepts involved. Researchers must also ask an important question, "Do I want all the information in these areas, or will I be satisfied with the seminal work?" The answer to this question is critical for planning a search strategy.

Boolean Logic

Thanks in part to the English mathematician George Boole (1815–1864), a search can be expanded or narrowed, according to the researcher's needs. The "and," "or," and "not" commands are the most useful Boolean operators in database searches. Combining terms with "and" or "not" gives a more narrow focus (Fig. 16.2). Combining terms with "or" gives a broader focus.

The use of Boolean logic is illustrated with an imaginary database and the terms "force" and "kinetics." Suppose our database contains three bibliographic records. Record A contains the terms "force" and "kinetics." Record B contains only the term "force." Record C contains only the term "kinetics" (see Fig. 16.3).

Table 16.1 combines the three records with Boolean operators. Using the Boolean operator "and" provides a narrower focus, because both terms must be present. The command, "force and kinetics" will only provide bibliographic records that contain both terms. It will, therefore, provide fewer records than either "force" or "kinetics" alone. In the example in Table 16.1, only one record (Record A) is found using "and" for combining the two terms.

The use of "or" gives a broader focus. For example, "force or kinetics" will provide records that have at least one of these terms. Thus, this selection will have a greater number of records than either of these terms alone. In the example in Table 16.1, all three records are found when the two terms are combined with "or."

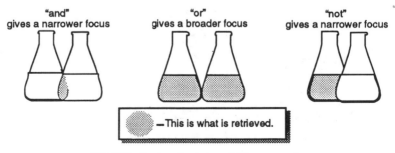

"and" gives a narrower focus   "or" gives a broader focus   "not" gives a narrower focus

—This is what is retrieved.

FIG. 16.2. Boolean Logic in a database search.

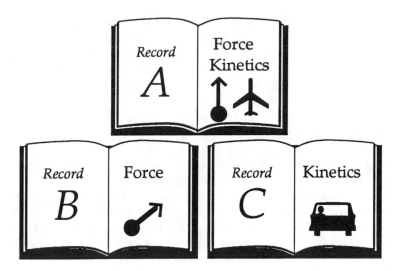

FIG. 16.3. Imaginary database composed of three records.

The "not" command is similar to the "and" command in that it narrows a search. The command "force not kinetics" will reduce the number of force records by removing those that contain the term "kinetics." In the example in Table 16.1, only Record B is found using "not" to combine the two terms. Record C was eliminated because it did not have "force." Although Record A did have "force," it was eliminated because it contained the term "kinetics." The use of "not" can be useful in narrowing a search, but researchers should be careful not to eliminate necessary items.

Boolean logic can help researchers find items of interest based on their needs. Most searches are done with "and," but efficient searches will frequently use a variety of Boolean commands. If researchers wish to reduce the number of records found on topics of interest, they should use "and" or "not" to make their searches more specific. Researchers doing exhaustive

TABLE 16.1
Boolean Operators Connecting Force with Kinetics

| Label | Terms in Record | Boolean operators for statement "Force ____ Kinetics" | | |
		AND	OR	NOT
A	Force	Yes	Yes	No
	Kinetics			
B	Force	No	Yes	Yes
C	Kinetics	No	Yes	No
	Number of Records Retrieved	1	3	1

literature reviews should use "or" frequently to give broader searches. The biggest mistake inexperienced users make is not using related terms in searches and joining them with "or" (Lancaster et al., 1994). For example, similar search terms can be joined, such as "educational research or program evaluation" and "science education or science instruction." This increases the likelihood of finding what is needed.

Searching Database Fields

As we mentioned earlier, databases are composed of records. Information in these records is placed into particular fields. Pickens (1994) described three commonalties of all databases. A database field or fields will contain key words or descriptors that describe the contents of the document or article. Second, there will be fields giving factual information about the document or article, such as title, year of publication, and author. Third, databases will contain information on how to obtain a document or article.

Search engines will look in these fields to find a match for the data entered by the user. An expert designated as a "super searcher" described her strategies in searches: "I use codes and controlled vocabulary wherever they're available. Then I might supplement it with free text in the title field. I really rely on the print thesauri" (as quoted by Basch, 1993, pp. 54–55). The use of controlled vocabulary and codes restricts the search to specific fields. This is an efficient way to conduct a search.

An inefficient, yet commonly used approach is a full-text or free search, by which the search engine looks in all the fields for the words entered. It is usually a better strategy to search only specific fields. The issue is not one of computer time. The search engines are so rapid that the time spent is insignificant. The issue is one of people time; a researcher can spend a great deal of time wading through records that aren't needed. A full-text search of a term such as "university" reveals the problems of this mode of searching. To be sure, bibliographic records for publications dealing with universities will be found. However, the user will also get many records only remotely related to universities, including works produced by universities, documents produced by persons with a university affiliation, and reports of meetings held at a university. A researcher will soon realize it is not an efficient use of time to read through all these records to find pertinent information. The most efficient way to avoid this problem is to search specific fields using the controlled vocabulary and codes of a particular database.

Getting the Literature

In the future, more literature databases will provide bibliographic records as well as complete text, tables, graphs, and pictures. Several of these new "virtual libraries" are being developed (Broering, 1994; Krumenaker, 1993).

Difficulties in handling the huge volumes of data need to be overcome. Beyond technical difficulties there are practical issues—one of which is that many publishers will not allow their materials to be disseminated electronically.

Although change might occur, present bibliographic databases are mostly pointers to literature. Users need to go and get the information the records describe. The information to find the literature is contained in one or more fields in the record. For example, a journal article will have a field giving the name of the journal and its volume, issue number, and page.

SEARCHING ERIC

To demonstrate the specifics of a database search and the fruits of retrieval, a case study of searching ERIC (Educational Resources Information Center) is presented. This U.S. government-funded database was "established in 1966 to make educational research and practice available from a single source" (ERIC, 1991).

ERIC is the largest and most used educational database in the world. Over 500,000 people use ERIC each year (U.S. Department of Education, 1997). According to the 1996 ERIC Annual Report (Smarte, 1997) more than 1,000 institutions in 27 countries provide access to the database and the ERIC microfiche collection. The database contains over 900,000 records. More than 900 journals are indexed each year.

ERIC can be accessed almost any place in the world. Six CD-ROM and four private online vendors offer this database (Smarte, 1997). The database can be searched for free on the World Wide Web through the AskERIC site (ericae.net/scripts/ewiz/amain2.asp).

In the CD-ROM search category, ERIC is the most used database in public libraries and information centers throughout the world (Stonehill, 1992). Our discussion of searching ERIC includes instructions (usually in parentheses) for using SilverPlatter search software. The SilverPlatter software is widely used for searching ERIC and other databases throughout the world.

Controlled Vocabulary

ERIC uses two types of controlled vocabulary, called *descriptors* and *identifiers*. All the articles and documents in the ERIC database have been given subject indexing terms called descriptors. The descriptors can be found in the *Thesaurus of ERIC Descriptors*, which is available in book form, online, in CD-ROM format (for SilverPlatter, the F9 key in DOS version and the Thesaurus button in WinSpirs version), and in experimental form on the Internet (ericae.net/scripts/ewiz/amain2.asp).

An analyst assigns a major descriptor if the article or document substantially addresses that topic. A maximum of eight major descriptors may be assigned to an article or document. A major descriptor search on "science-education-research in DEM" (SilverPlatter example) will uncover articles or documents that significantly address science education research.

Minor descriptors are assigned to articles or documents if they address an area but it is not the major focus of the work. Minor descriptors are also used for describing the type of research used in a study. A report of a study using qualitative research techniques would receive the minor descriptor "Qualitative Research." However, an article *about* qualitative research would have "Qualitative Research" as a major descriptor. Minor and major descriptors can be searched at the same time (in DE). A researcher who wants everything on a subject is advised not to restrict the search to only major descriptors.

Using the controlled vocabulary of the descriptor field, and searching only in that field can save a researcher from sorting through hundreds of irrelevant records. A search can be narrowed by using specific descriptors and broadened by using more general descriptors. The use of descriptors with Boolean logic is also a powerful way of broadening or narrowing a search.

In Table 16.2, an ERIC search using SilverPlatter software is presented. A researcher is interested in the use of ethnography in mathematics instruction. In Step 1, the researcher requests a search on "ethnography" as a descriptor (in DE). This request provides 674 bibliographic records. The researcher feels the articles and documents of interest might also have been labeled with the "Naturalistic Observation" descriptor. This request in Step 2 provides 145 records. Using "or" to combine Steps 1 and 2 provides 804 records, more than either Step 1 or Step 2 alone. The researcher has broadened the search. A similar strategy is used for mathematics instruction and mathematics education. Step 6 uses "or" to broaden the search and provides 4,922 records. Finally, in Step 7 "and" is used to combine the ethnography/naturalistic observation (Step 3) with the mathematics instruction/education (Step 6). The total number of records provided is 14.

TABLE 16.2
ERIC SilverPlatter Search Illustrating the Use of "and" and "or"

No.	Records	Request
#1	674	ETHNOGRAPHY-in DE
#2	146	NATURALISTIC-OBSERVATION in DE
#3	804	#1 or #2
#4	3,579	MATHEMATICS-INSTRUCTION in DE
#5	3,659	MATHEMATICS-EDUCATION in DE
#6	4,922	#4 or #5
#7	14	#3 and #6

Age-Level Descriptors

Educational researchers are frequently interested in finding literature about teaching or learning at a certain grade level. "For most database users *who* the information is about is, initially at least, often just as important as *what* it is about" (Pickens, 1994, p. 39). Although dozens of descriptors describe age level, there is a smaller list called the Mandatory Age-Level Descriptors (Table 16.3). These are the only age-level descriptors needed to search ERIC. The reason for this is the analyst *must* assign one of these descriptors to each document that is abstracted.

Many people interested in research concerning mathematics instruction at Grade 4 would use the descriptor "Grade 4." However, to only use this descriptor would be a mistake. "Grade 4" is not a mandatory age-level descriptor. Therefore, in many cases the abstractor would not use it—especially if the article or document being abstracted addressed more than one grade. Thus, for age level, it is best to use a descriptor that the abstractor is required to use. The most specific mandatory age-level descriptor encompassing Grade 4 would be "intermediate grades." If a researcher was not concerned with finding everything on a topic, the use of this descriptor would be sufficient. However, researchers who want everything should use all the mandatory age level descriptors that include Grade 4. The search command would be "intermediate grades or elementary education or elementary secondary education." Although it does no harm to use other age-level descriptors in conjunction with the mandatory age-level descriptors, the mandatory descriptors are the only age or grade descriptors researchers need to use.

TABLE 16.3
Mandatory Age-Level Descriptors

- Early childhood education . . . . (birth to Grade 3)
  Preschool education . . . . (birth to K or 1)
  Primary education . . . . (K–3)
- Elementary secondary education . . . . (1–12)
  Elementary education . . . . (K–8)
     Adult basic education
     Primary education . . . . (K–3)
     Intermediate grades . . . . (4, 5, & 6)
  Secondary education . . . . (7–12)
     Junior high schools . . . . (7–9)
     High schools . . . . (9–12)
     High school equivalency programs
- Postsecondary education
     Higher education (leading to a degree)
     Two-year colleges

Identifiers

The identifier field is another field in the database that uses controlled language. " 'Identifiers' are terms not found in the thesaurus that would be familiar to individuals who work in a particular area or who are familiar with a topic" (Blosser & Helgeson, 1986, p. 4). Identifiers are used for geographic locations (e.g., South-Africa), tests (e.g., Second-International-Science-Study), programs (e.g., Educational-Leaders-In-Mathematics-Project), teaching methods (e.g., learning-cycle), people (e.g., Vygotsky-Lev-S) and subjects (e.g., radical-constructivism). In time, some frequently used subject identifiers are promoted to descriptor level. Identifiers are found in the ERIC Identifier Authority List. The use of both identifiers (in ID) and descriptors creates possibilities for more efficient searches.

Searchable Fields

Other fields in an ERIC record are also useful for searches. Searches in the field "Publication Year" can restrict the search to records of a certain year (PY = 1997) or time interval (PY > 1992). Searching on publication types is also a useful way of narrowing the vast database and finding what is needed. For example, "publication type 143" (DTN = 143) may be used to focus the search on articles and documents that are research and technical reports. Publication types (also know as "document types") can help researchers find legal or regulatory materials, conference papers, teaching guides, and evaluation instruments.

Researchers who have looked for an instrument in the literature know there are many articles and documents discussing instruments, but finding an actual instrument can sometimes be very difficult. If "publication type 160" (DTN = 160) is entered, only records for articles and documents that actually contain instruments should appear. About 5% of the ERIC database have this publication type.

Obtaining Materials From Bibliographic Records

ERIC and ERIC vendors have also been investigating the possibility of full-text delivery. In fact, ERIC digests are currently available in full text online and in CD-ROMs. To experience full-text availability of these digests in the ERIC database, search by "publication type 073" (DTN = 073). The trend seems likely to continue, making full-text resources increasingly available in a variety of databases. For now, however, the majority of what researchers seek will not have full-text availability. The computerized database usually contains records of materials and the user must go beyond the database to obtain the actual literature cited in the records.

ERIC is actually composed of two files: "Resources In Education" (RIE) and "Current Index of Journals in Education" (CIJE). CIJE records provide information about journal articles. The RIE contains everything else, including conference papers, manuscripts, congressional reports, and teachers' guides. The accession number is used to determine whether a record is for a CIJE or RIE citation. Accession numbers, such as EJ476611 and ED372923, are the first numbers listed in the records. If they begin with an "EJ," they are for CIJE records, and if they begin with an "ED," they are for RIE records.

Table 16.4 shows one of the eight records from the search presented in Table 16.2. The accession number (AN) begins with an EJ, so the researcher knows this is a journal article. Reading the journal field (JN), the researcher can find the name, volume, and issue of the journal. The journals in the citations from the CIJE can often be found in university and research libraries. If accessible libraries don't have a particular journal, some journals will supply researchers with requested articles. Journal articles can also be obtained from University Microfilms International (1-800-248-0360, interna-

TABLE 16.4
ERIC Record From Search Presented in Table 16.1

AN (ACCESSION NUMBER): EJ491808
CHN (CLEARINGHOUSE NUMBER): SE553080
AU (PERSONAL AUTHOR): Voigt,-Jorg
TI (TITLE): Negotiation of Mathematical Meaning and Learning Mathematics.
PY (PUBLICATION YEAR): 1994
JN (JOURNAL CITATION): Educational-Studies-in-Mathematics; v26 n2-3 p275-98 Mar 1994
SN (INTERNATIONAL STANDARD SERIAL NUMBER): ISSN-0013-1954
AV (AVAILABILITY): UMI
DT (DOCUMENT TYPE): Reports-Research (143)
LA (LANGUAGE): English
DE (MINOR DESCRIPTORS): Ambiguity-; Case-Studies; Ethnography-; Grade-1;
   Interpersonal-Relationship; Mathematics-Education; Primary-Education; Social-Influences;
   Teaching-Methods
DE (MAJOR DESCRIPTORS): *Elementary-School-Students; *Elementary-School-Teachers;
   *Learning-Processes; *Mathematics-Instruction; *Number-Concepts; *Social-Cognition
ID (MINOR IDENTIFIERS): Mathematics-Education-Research
ID (MAJOR IDENTIFIERS): *Mathematical-Communication
IS ABSTRACT ISSUE: CIJFEB95
AB (ABSTRACT): Presents a case study of a first-grade class and their teacher who were
   observed as they ascribed mathematical meanings of numbers and of numerical
   operations to empirical phenomena. Differences in ascriptions led to negotiation of
   meanings. Discusses some indirect relations between social interaction and mathematics
   learning. (Contains 60 references.)
(MKR)
CH (CLEARINGHOUSE): SE
FI (SOURCE FILE): EJ
DTN (DOCUMENT TYPE NUMBER): 143; 080

---

tional Fax +1-313-973-7007, www.umi.com/infostore) or the Institute for Scientific Information (1-800-523-1850).

RIE documents begin with an ED accession number. Approximately 95% of RIE documents are available on microfiche at locations with ERIC microfiche collections (Smarte, 1994). As of 1994, there were 942 microfiche collections, 114 of which were outside the United States. Visiting these sites is a free way of accessing the needed documents (call 1-800-LET-ERIC to find your nearest site). Microfiche or paper copies can be bought at a reasonable price ($1.18 for five or fewer microfiche cards) from the ERIC Document Reproduction Service (7420 Fullerton Road, Suite 110, Springfield, VA 22153-2852; phone: 1-800-443-ERIC or 1-703-440-1400; e-mail: edrs@inet.ed.gov, www.edrs.com/).

Other Databases

ERIC has been used as a case study in learning about databases. Many students "tend to think one-dimensionally and focus on one database or index as the answer to all their questions and research needs" (Blumenthal, Howard, & Kinyon, 1993, p. 14). However, ERIC is not the only database that needs to be searched. ERIC does have articles and documents from countries around the world, but the majority of its records are directly related to education in the United States. Other databases may provide better resources for locating educational research from other countries. For example, *Francis CD-ROM* contains educational materials for French-speaking countries (Bruce & Hamalian, 1992). ERIC also tries to avoid duplication of materials in its database and the *Dissertation Abstracts International* database. There is only a 4% overlap between the RIE database and the *Dissertation Abstracts International* database (Morehead & Fetzer, 1992). Therefore, it is essential that researchers seek information in a variety of databases.

Appendix A contains an annotated bibliography of important databases for research in the social sciences, science education, and mathematics education. A brief description and availability information is provided for each database. There is a wide variety of useful databases available. Education databases from various countries can provide a more global perspective on a topic and databases from other content areas may provide additional resources. Databases in natural sciences and mathematics may also provide researchers with important information.

THE INTERNET

The Internet is a worldwide network of computer networks. These dissimilar networks can be found in universities, businesses, organizations, and government agencies. With thousands of networks worldwide, the number of individual users of the Internet is in the millions. This high level of connectivity fosters an unparalleled degree of communication, collaboration, resource sharing, and information access (Tennant, 1992, p. 1).

The Internet links many data sources together, making it a database of databases. It provides a mechanism for the storage of huge amounts of information and a means for immediate sharing new data and resources with colleagues and interested researchers. Information on the Internet can be searched, sometimes using Boolean logic, but its disorganized nature makes searches less efficient than those on CD-ROM databases. The Internet is like a giant library that makes books, journals, and multimedia available, but these resources are not cataloged and organized for systematic access as in a traditional library. Rather, the information is as disorganized as a pile of materials on the floor of a library after an earthquake tossed them from the shelves.

Although there are increasing attempts to get some control over the Internet, there is virtually none at this time. No one individual, country, or organization is in charge. Individuals, as well as schools and universities, businesses, organizations, and governments are free to establish an Internet site and make whatever files they wish available to Internet travelers. The Internet is always changing; new sites appear daily, with older sites being revised and updated, moved to a new address, or simply dropped completely. All of these characteristics create both the fantasy and the frustration of traveling on the Internet. The dynamic nature of the Internet does not diminish, but rather increases the need for skilled searches and critical evaluation of Internet sites and the information they contain.

For individual computers and networks to communicate easily, a set of agreements on communication protocols has been established. Some of the most commonly used tools for accessing the Internet include Telnet, File Transfer Protocol (FTP), Gopher, and the World Wide Web.

World Wide Web

The World Wide Web (WWW) allows connections to be made with other computers or sites transparently through a single point of entry. Unlike other Internet tools, the Web uses a combination of hypertext and full-text searching that allows the researcher to access information. The system of hypertext-linked sites throughout the world allows researchers to "point and click" on the site or document names rather than knowing Web addresses or URLs (uniform resource locator). Based on the technology that incorporates hypermedia, the Web can facilitate connection to sound, video, and graphic images as well as text. With the hypertext system, one or more words in a document or the entire document itself are linked to words or groups of words in other documents. This linking allows the user to move back and forth between the linked documents. Words or phrases that provide the user with links to other sites or documents are generally highlighted in red, blue, or another color for quick identification and easy pointing and clicking. Web connections can be made to Telnet and Gopher sites, Usenet newsgroups, or e-mail servers.

Software programs or browsers such as Netscape Navigator and Microsoft Explorer have made access to the Web easier. These programs are used to navigate the Web and the various types of resources available on the Internet (Gophers, newsgroups, interactive connections, file archives, and WWW servers). Mosaic, developed by the National Center for Supercomputing Applications (NCSA), was the original Web browser that helped popularize the World Wide Web. Netscape Navigator, developed later, became the overwhelming favorite of the majority of users. It provided all the features of Mosaic, one of which is allowing the screen to be manipulated as though it were a printed page. Its speed in accessing sites and documents was greater than Mosaic and its greater number of on-screen "buttons" allowed the user to take full advantage of the point-and-click capabilities of the Web. The Macintosh and Windows versions of this software are virtually identical allowing the researcher flexibility in moving between platforms.

Web sites such as Yahoo, which is arranged by subject, were an attempt by developers to "put the books back on the shelf" in our earlier analogy of a pile of books on the floor. They provide wonderful road maps for Internet travelers to easily begin their journeys. Subject-arranged sites identify relevant sites without the need for a specific address. The Web, along with FTP and Gopher, has software programs for searching by subject. Search engines such as Alta Vista, Lycos, Excite, InfoSeek Guide, and the WebCrawler serve as indexes to data available anywhere on the Web. The Netscape Navigator program also offers net search capabilities, as does Yahoo. Keywords and Boolean searching are common features of these programs. MathSearch out of the University of Sydney offers a similar service by searching keywords or phrases. However, its purpose is to specifically search mathematics and statistics servers across the Web rather than searching a broad range of topics.

One report estimated that the Web was doubling in size approximately every 4 months (Venditto, 1996). With this rate of growth in the amount of information available to Internet users, more sophisticated search engines are increasingly necessary to locate resources. Many of the current search engines available are still in relative infancy as to what they are capable of delivering to the searcher. Some offer limited Boolean searching. Search engines in common use are described and compared in the section following.

Alta Vista (altavista.digital.com) performs best when queries are kept simple; it does not allow for truncation—rather, it requires searching on the exact word or phrase keyed. It gives the searcher access to information found on nearly half a million servers throughout the world, although, it does not include FTP or Gopher sites. Its powerful search option allows for the use of Boolean operators ("and," "or," "not," or "near") but searches are case sensitive and cannot be modified or refined. Alta Vista is the best engine to use when the searcher is looking for everything available on a given topic.

Lycos (www.lycos.com) accesses information in FTP and Gopher sites but searches are only of headers, titles, and links, rather than the full text of pages. Lycos offers "and" and "or" Boolean searches only. These cannot be modified but case sensitivity is not a concern. A search using Lycos often is more comprehensive, picking up some sites not located using alternative search engines, but these are not always relevant and the search is not executed and completed quickly.

Excite (www.excite.com) offers concept searching. Although this might be considered essentially the same as keyword searching, the Excite developers say that their search goes beyond the word entered and looks for ideas linked to the words. Its searches are not case sensitive but searchers looking for a proper name are advised to capitalize the first letter of each word in the same way as if it were being used in a document. Use of the plus (+) and minus (−) signs tells the Excite search engine which words must and must not be present. The Boolean operators include "and," "or," and "not" as well as parentheses. They must be typed in upper case and have a space on either side in order to work. Searches cannot be modified or refined. Excite is at its best if the searcher is looking for current information, the topic is in the mainstream, and speed of searching is crucial.

InfoSeek Guide (guide.infoseek.com) does not offer Boolean capability but does provide full-text proximity searching. Searches can be refined and narrowed. When adding more words under the "search only under these results" option, InfoSeek will search again within the original set of results. Quotation marks around words or hyphens between words enable this search engine to locate sites containing those words adjacent to one another. Capitalizing the first letter of a word allows InfoSeek to distinguish between proper names and other groups of words. As with Excite, InfoSeek Guide uses the plus and minus to identify words that must or must not be present. InfoSeek is an excellent choice when the searcher needs to locate a specific site or piece of information.

When searching the WebCrawler (webcrawler.com), one of the original search engines available, the searcher is actually searching an index of the Web rather than the Web itself. The index is updated daily to maintain its currency. WebCrawler assumes all words in a search phrase are important; therefore it will look for sites that contain them all but it also returns pointers to sites that only contain some of the words in the search. Sites containing fewer than all words in the search phrase are distinguished from the others and listed lower in the retrieval results. WebCrawler offers the widest range of Boolean operators of any of the search engines discussed, including "and," "or," "not," "near," "adj," and quotations for phrases and parentheses for more complex searches. Searches are not case sensitive.

Hot Bot (www.hotbot.com), which conducts full-text searches, is composed of two parts, a website that responds to queries by consulting its database of the web and a web-crawling robot that maintains a database of new or changed documents on the web. It scans every word of these documents and adds the information to its own index. Searches can be narrowed by using the "all of the words" option which is equivalent to a Boolean AND search. Searches can also be narrowed by selecting the "exact phrase" option, which requires search terms to appear in the order specified. If a broader search is the choice, use the "any of the words" option which is the same as a Boolean OR search. The Boolean operators or notations (( ) and, or, not, &, |, !) can also be utilized in search queries.

MetaCrawler (www.metacrawler.com) does not maintain a database as most search engines do, rather, it relies on the databases of others such as a majority of the search engines discussed earlier. One of the advantages of searching MetaCrawler is that their query language is standardized, thus saving the requestor time in learning the search techniques and language of each engine. When the results are returned from those engines queried, MetaCrawler formats them and returns them to the requestor in rank order according to relevance and by search engine. In addition to searching all words using the "any words" option, the "as a phrase" option is also available.

Search engines offer the best opportunity for sorting out what is available on the Internet, but, with increasing information to search and the addition of bibliographic databases with their accompanying thesauri and Boolean capabilities, they will continue to be pressed to increase their level of sophistication and the variety of features offered.

The World Wide Web provides the Internet traveler with a seamless interface for accessing all types of sites: Web, Gopher, Telnet, or FTP. This accounts for its tremendous growth and popularity and the diminishing importance of other Internet protocols such as those in the following sections.

Telnet and File Transfer Protocol

Telnet allows individual researchers to establish a connection with a computer in another location as if it was in their own office. As soon as the connection is made with the remote computer, the two computers can send and receive messages as though they were hardwired. Telnet is most commonly utilized to make connections with bibliographic databases or online library catalogs; however, it can also be used for accessing a variety of data files and online services such as DIALOG.

File Transfer Protocol, or FTP as it is commonly known, allows for the transfer of files from one Internet computer to another. Virtually any kind of file stored on a computer can be transferred whether it is text, graphic, sound, or a software program. FTP is similar to Telnet in that it allows users to connect with remote computers, but it can only perform functions directly related to locating and transferring files. The software program Fetch is commonly used for transferring files. In order to transfer a file you must first know that it exists and where it is located. Archie provides the user with this information by indexing FTP archives. Archie servers do not store the actual documents themselves, but index only the directory names and filenames. Using a set of commands that are not user-friendly, Archie software searches the database in a given archive and relays back descriptions of the files, such as the name and the path name to follow, along with the location of the files which match the search query.

Gopher

Gopher was developed as an easy-to-navigate system of hierarchical menus to allow the researcher to access information resources on the Internet. With its standard presentation of information, Gopher is user-friendly. Travel through Internet space is transparent to the user with the menu system because the connections are made behind the scenes. This makes knowing specific Gopher addresses less important. Through the progression of menus utilized by Gopher, the researcher sees folders and various icons providing access to specific documents or files or facilitating links to other Gopher sites. With the speed, graphics, and sound of the Web this approach now appears cumbersome. Veronica (*Very Easy Rodent-Oriented Net-wide Index to Computerized Archives*) serves as the indexing tool for searching Gopher servers on the Internet. The researcher accesses Veronica directly from within Gopher. The Veronica server searches Gopher for information by subject and by incorporating the use of Boolean operators ("and," "or," and "not"). Veronica searches only the title for matches, not the full text of the document. A nice feature of Veronica is that it delivers the document to the researcher rather than displaying the location address of a item as Archie does. Gopher is rapidly becoming like the dinosaur with the conversion of many of its original sites to the Web sites.

The current search mechanisms of Gopher, FTP, and even the Web, with its variety of search engines, are rudimentary at best when compared to the sophisticated search software and controlled vocabulary of a biblio-graphic database. Consumer demand for more powerful searching capabili-ties for accessing Internet databases will cause search engine developers to develop their software. This can only benefit the educational researcher trying to locate resources on the Internet quickly and efficiently.

The annotated bibliography of Internet sites (Appendix B) is a starting point to the many Internet resources available for science and mathematics education researchers.

SUMMARY

Using databases as gateways to literature in mathematics and science edu-cation allows researchers to "stand on the shoulders of giants" in developing their own research questions and projects. The staggering amount of infor-mation in databases is only an asset if the researcher knows how to efficiently search and find needed information. The use of controlled vocabulary and Boolean logic are essential for conducting efficient searches. There are a variety of databases with information pertinent to science and mathematics education researchers, so researchers should not restrict their search to only one database.

The Internet—a network of networks—has characteristics of being a data-base of databases. Searching the Internet is not yet efficient compared to searching an organized database; nevertheless, the resources that the In-ternet contains are extremely useful for educational researchers. The use of information in the Internet and in databases will assist mathematics and science education researchers in developing important research projects. Hopefully, their published work will contribute to the field and become part of a database on which other researchers can build.

APPENDIX A
DATABASES WITH MATHEMATICS OR SCIENCE
EDUCATION INFORMATION

Australian Education Index. Camberwell, Victoria: Australian Council for Edu-cational Research.

Comprehensive coverage with some abstracts of published and unpub-lished Australian literature including journals, conference papers, theses, research reports, legislation, and monographs related to education.

Available: Online Vendor(s): Ausinet, 1978– ; Paper, 1957–

Bibliography of Education Theses in Australia. Hawthorn, Victoria: Australian Council for Educational Research.

> Coverage of dissertations awarded at Australian universities. Available online with the *Australian Education Index.*

> Available: Ausinet; Paper, 1982– ; WWW: http://www.informit.com.au

Biological Abstracts (BIOSIS). Philadelphia, PA: BIOSIS.

> Nearly 6,500 international journals are monitored to provide comprehensive coverage of the biological and biomedical literature.

> Available: Online Vendor(s): DIALOG, File 5 & 55, 1969– ; DataStar; STN International; European Space Agency. CD-ROM Vendor(s): SilverPlatter, 1985– ; Paper, 1927–

Biological and Agricultural Index. Bronx: H.W. Wilson Co.

> Indexes over 240 English-language journals covering popular to professional literature pertaining to biology and agriculture.

> Available: Online Vendor(s): OCLC, Wilsonline; CD-ROM Vendor(s): Silver-Platter, 1983– ; WilsonDisc; Paper, 1964–

British Education Index. Leeds: University of Leeds.

> Subject and author indexing is available for approximately 250 education journals published in the British Isles with some international titles included. The online version is available in a combined database with the British Education Theses Index.

> Available: Online Vendor: DIALOG File 121, 1976– ; Paper, 1961–

British Education Theses Index. London: Librarians of Institutes and Schools of Education.

> This microfiche collection records all theses relevant to education and deposited at universities within the United Kingdom and Ireland. The online version is available in a combined database with the British Education Index.

> Available: Online Vendor: DIALOG File 121; Microfiche, 1950–

CA Search (Chemical Abstracts). Columbus, OH: Chemical Abstracts Service.

> This database provides indexing for journal articles, patents, reviews, technical reports, monographs, dissertations, and conference or symposium proceedings in the principal areas of chemistry.

> Available: Online Vendor(s): DIALOG, 1967– , Orbit Search Service, STN International, European Space Agency; Paper, 1907–

Canadian Education Index/Repertoire Canadien Sur l'Education. Toronto: Canadian Education Association.

Contains indexing to more than 200 periodicals, monographs, dissertations, teachers' association publications, and federal and provincial government reports related to education in Canada, with text in English and French.

Available: Online Vendor(s): Info Globe Online, 1976– ; CD-ROM Vendor(s): MicroMedia Ltd.; Paper, 1965–

Dissertation Abstracts International. Ann Arbor, MI: University Microfilms International.

Subject, author, and title index to essentially every U.S. dissertation granted at an accredited North American university since 1861. Also includes selected masters theses since 1962, and since 1988 has provided citations for dissertations from 50 British universities and citations and abstracts from European dissertations. Abstracts of doctoral dissertations are only available since 1980 and masters theses since 1988 in the online version.

Available: Online Vendor(s): DIALOG File 35; CD-ROM Vendor(s): UMI, SilverPlatter; Paper, 1861–

Education Index. Bronx: H.W. Wilson Co.

Focus is on providing coverage of approximately 350 U.S. education journals using an author and subject approach.

Available: Online Vendor: Wilsonline, December 1983– . OCLC; CD-ROM Vendor(s): SilverPlatter, 1983– ; WilsonDisc, December 1983– ; Paper, 1929–

ERIC (Educational Resources Information Center). Rockville, MD: U.S. Department of Education.

Combined database of *Current Index to Journals in Education* and *Resources in Education* provides coverage of literature of education and related disciplines. In addition to journals, coverage is provided for conference papers, research reports, bibliographies, curriculum materials, legal/legislative/regulatory materials, guides, and limited theses. Although coverage primarily focuses on the United States, publications from Australia, New Zealand, and Canada are also indexed.

Available: Online Vendor(s): DIALOG, File 1, 1966– ; DataStar; OCLC/EPIC. CD-ROM Vendor(s): SilverPlatter, 1966– ; National Information Services Co. (NISC), 1966– ; Oryx Press (CIJE on Disc), 1969– , EBSCO; Paper, 1966–

General Science Index. Bronx: H.W. Wilson Co.

Cumulative subject index to approximately 140 English language periodicals covering the sciences.

Available: Online Vendor(s): Wilsonline, 1984– ; CD-ROM Vendor(s): SilverPlatter; WilsonDisc, 1984– ; Paper, 1978–

INSPEC (Physics Abstracts, Electrical & Electronic Abstracts and Computer & Control Abstracts). Piscataway, NJ: Institution of Electrical Engineers.

International coverage of over 4,100 journals with cover-to-cover indexing of 750. Although approximately 16% of the source literature is non-English, all articles are abstracted and indexed in English.

Available: Online Vendor(s):CEDOCAR; Orbit; STN; DIALOG, File 2,3,4, 1969– ; CD-ROM Vendor(s): UMI, 1989– ; Paper, dates vary by index

MathSci. Providence, RI: American Mathematical Society.

Provides international coverage of literature on mathematics, statistics and computer science, with indexing of approximately 600 journals cover-to-cover and 2,500 journals selectively.

Available: Online Vendor(s): DIALOG, File 239, 1959– ; OVID; European Space Agency; CD-ROM Vendor(s): SilverPlatter, 1940– ; Paper, dates vary, earliest date 1910–

PsycLit/PsycInfo/Psychological Abstracts. Washington, DC: American Psychological Association.

International coverage of all areas of psychology. Indexes over 1,300 journals, as well as technical reports, dissertations, and other items. *PsycLit*, the CD-ROM, edition also contains indexing to book chapters from 1987.

Available: Online Vendor(s): Orbit, OVID, DataStar, DIALOG, File 11, 1967– ; CD-ROM Vendor(s): SilverPlatter, 1974– ; Paper, 1927–

SciSearch (Science Citation Index). Philadelphia, PA: Institute for Scientific Information (ISI).

This international, multidisciplinary index to science, technology, biomedicine, and related disciplines indexes all significant items from approximately 4,500 major scientific and technical journals.

Available: Online Vendor(s): DataStar, Orbit Search Service, DIALOG File 34 & 434, 1974– ; CD-ROM Vendor(s): ISI; Paper, 1961–

Social Science Citation Index (SSCI). Philadelphia: Institute for Scientific Information.

International, multidisciplinary index to the literature of the social, behavioral, and related disciplines. Indexes all significant items from over 1,500 social sciences journals.

Available: Online Vendor(s): DataStar, DIALOG File 7, 1972– ; DIMDI; OVID; CD-ROM Vendor(s): ISI, 1981– ; Paper, 1969–

UnCover. Denver, CO: The UnCover Company.

Indexing of table of contents information from over 16,000 magazine and journal titles covering all disciplines and at all levels of interest and readership from 1989, this database also has a companion document delivery service whereby users can have articles faxed to them for a fee.

Available: Telnet: database.carl.org; WWW: http://www.uncweb.carl.org

APPENDIX B
INTERNET RESOURCES FOR MATHEMATICS
AND SCIENCE EDUCATION

Argus Clearinghouse for Subject-Oriented Internet Resources. Ann Arbor, MI: University of Michigan University Library, and School of Information and Library Studies (SILS).

Collection of subject-based Internet resources produced by members of the Internet community and students participating in the SILS Internet resource discovery project. Guides are typically identify relevant listservers, electronic journals, Gopher and World Wide Web sites. Examples of science guides include those on biology, botany, computer science, ecology, geology, mathematics, and physics.

Available: World Wide Web: http://www.clearinghouse.net.

AskERIC Virtual Library. Syracuse, NY: ERIC Clearinghouse on Information & Technology.

U.S. government–funded, Internet-based question-answering service available to educators. This site provides access to the ERIC database and serves as a link to other ERIC clearinghouses and educational resources on the Internet.

Available: Gopher: ericir.syr.edu; WWW: http://ericir.syr.edu; Telnet: ericir.syr.edu; e-mail: askeric@ericir.syr.edu.

Australian Mathematical Society. Kensington, New South Wales: AMS

This site contains information about the society, its publications and conferences as well as providing links to other sites of interest to mathematicians around the world.

Available: World Wide Web: http://www.maths.unsw.EDU.AU/amsweb

British Geological Survey. Nottingham: BGS

This organization, which serves as the national geological survey of the United Kingdom, provides geological information for the land and offshore areas of the United Kingdom. It also points to BGS publications, archives and data sets.

Available: WWW: http://kwum.nkw.ac.uk/bgs

Canadian Mathematical Society. Burnaby: Canadian Mathematical Society.

Access to conferences, journals, research funding and educational resources in mathematics are provided through this site. Links to the

Canadian Mathematical Society and other mathematical services including Canadian universities, are also provided.

Available: WWW: http://camel.math.ca/CMS

E-Math. Providence, RI: American Mathematical Society.

Resource of the American Mathematical Society for the delivery of electronic products and services including books, print and electronic journals, and other products of interest to mathematicians. Serves as a link to other mathematical resources on the Internet.

Available: Gopher: e-math.ams.org; WWW: http://e-math.ams.org

EE-Link: Environmental Education on the Internet. Ann Arbor, MI: National Consortium for Environmental Education and Training.

This site is dedicated primarily to providing K–12 resources in environmental education. Multimedia resources, classroom activities, and teaching tips are a part of this site. Links to other Internet sites of interest such as professional organizations, grants and conferences can also be found here.

Available: Gopher: nceet.snre.umich.edu; WWW: http://nceet.snre.umich.edu

EPA. Washington DC: U.S. Environmental Protection Agency.

Access is provided to the EPA national library catalog, a database of hazardous waste materials, the Access EPA database of directory information and several other databases.

Available: Gopher:gopher.epa.gov; WWW: http://www.epa.gov; Telnet: telnet://epaibm.rtpnc.epa.gov. Enter 4 for public applications then 1 for library systems.

ERIC Clearinghouse for Science, Mathematics and Environmental Education. Columbus, OH: ERIC/CSMEE.

Clearinghouse for the retrieval and dissemination of printed educational material at all levels related to science, mathematics and environmental education.

Available: Gopher: gopher.ericse.org; World Wide Web: http://www.ericse.org

ERIN: Environmental Resources Information Network. Canberra: Australian Department of the Environment.

Provides environmental data, including information on endangered species, vegetation types and heritage sites. Data about the Australian environment are drawn from a range of disciplines including ecology, geography and geology.

Available: WWW: http://kaos.erin.gov.au/erin.html

Institute of Mathematics and its Applications (IMA). Essex, UK: The Institute.

Provides a forum for mathematicians and a means of promoting mathemaatics and its applications in all sectors of society. Has links to academic, industry, and organization sites.

Available: WWW: http:www.ima.org.uk

Institute of Physics. London: the Institute

Wonderful resource for anything related to physics. One exciting aspect of this site is the availability of full the texs of all its journals, including *Physics Education*.

Available: WWW: http://www.iop.org

Los Alamos National Laboratory Education Programs. Los Alamos, NM: Los Alamos National Laboratory.

Contains information on science and mathematics programs, including National Teacher Enhancement, Science Outreach, National Geographic Kids Net, Preservice Research Institute for Science and Math, Science Bowl, and Science Education Online.

Available: WWW: http://www.education.lanl.gov/EPO/PROGRAMS /programs.html

MAA Online. Washington, DC: Mathematical Association of America.

Provides links to other mathematics sites, and includes information on fellowships, grants, workshops, and mathematical publications.

Available: WWW: http://www.maa.org

Math Forum. Swarthmore, PA: Swarthmore College

Resources on the web for mathematics education with pointers to NCTM Standards, electronic journals, conferences, and other internet sites of interest to math educators.

Available: WWW: http://forum.swarthmore.edu

Mathematics Archives. Knoxville, TN: University of Tennessee Department of Mathematics, National Science Foundation, State of Tennessee Science Alliance, and Calvin College.

Provides access to most public domain and shareware software that can be used in teaching mathematics in higher education. It also provides links to various Internet links of interest to mathematicians.

Available: Gopher: archives.math.utk.edu; WWW: http://archives.math. utk.edu

Mathematics Education at Nottingham. Leeds: University of Nottingham, School of Education.

This site includes information about the Shell Centre for Mathematical Education, a university center established for research and development within mathematics education. A bibliography of their publications is linked to this site. Information about the Maths Team and links to other international mathematical sites of interest are provided.

Available: WWW: http://acorn.educ.nottingham.ac.uk/Maths

National Academy of Sciences. Washington DC: The Academy

The National Academy of Science, National Academy of Engineering, Institute of Medicine and National Research Council have a combined internet site with an education section. In the section are online publications, news, events, and books in print. Online publications including National Science Education Standards, Research–Doctorate Programs in the United States, Continuity and Change, and Reshaping the Graduate Education of Scientists and Engineers.

Available: WWW: http://www.nas.edu

NASA. Washington DC: National Aeronautics and Space Administration.

Provides access to scientific and technical literature relating to space and other NASA endeavors. Good resource for K–12 educational materials.

Available: Gopher: gopher.gsfc.nasa.gov; WWW: http://www.nasa.gov

National Oceanic & Atmospheric Administration. Washington DC: National Oceanic and Atmospheric Administration (NOAA).

Provides access to data related to climate, fisheries, the environment, and oceanic and atmospheric resources for researchers around the world.

Available: WWW: http://www.noaa.gov

NSF. Washington DC: National Science Foundation

The NSF site offers access to the publications of the agency along with information regarding grant funding and links to external research centers, laboratories, and agencies.

Available: World Wide Web: http://www.nsf.gov

National Space Science Data Center. Washington DC: National Aeronautics and Space Administration.

Menu-driven interactive online system that provides a brief overview of information about NASA and important non-NASA space and earth science data.

Available: Telnet: telnet://NSSDC@nssdca.gsfc.nasa.gov; WWW: http://nssdc.gsfc.nasa.gov/nssdc

School of Mathematical Sciences, Australian National University. Canberra, Australian Capital Territory: Australian National University.

This website provides information about the school, its programs, staff, and students in addition to links to electronic and printed journals in the field, preprint servers, mathematical software, mathematical organizations, and other mathematical sites worldwide.

Available: WWW: http://wwwmaths.anu.edu.au

Science Education Resources. Vermillion, SD: University of South Dakota, School of Education, Interactive Technologies in Education and Corporations.

Provides an excellent listing of science education resources classified by content area.

Available: WWW: http://www.usd.edu/intec/science.html

TALMPAGE(Technology Assisted Learning in Math). Tampa, FL: University of North Florida.

Good source for topics in the use of technology in teaching and learning mathematics at the college level.

Available: WWW: http://www.unf.edu/~ramm/talmpage.html

USGS. Reston, VA: U.S. Geological Survey.

The home page includes announcements, news reports, a publications catalog and full text of some USGS items. In addition to providing agency information, it serves as a link to many other sites around the world which are affiliated with USGS or cover related topics.

Available: WWW: http://www.usgs.gov

Yahoo. Stanford, CA: Yahoo.

Subject-arranged website providing links to sites over the world. One of the best Internet sites as far as ease of use and links provided.

Available: WWW: http://www.yahoo.com

Young Mathematicians Network WWW Site. Lexington, KY: University of Kentucky.

Provides information on publishing, grant proposals, obtaining jobs and other matters of interest to mathematicians in graduate school.

Available: WWW: http://www.ms.uky.edu/~cyeomans

REFERENCES

Basch, R. (1993). Secrets of the super searchers. *Online, 17*(5), 52–58.

Blosser, P. E., & Helgeson, S. L. (1986, November). *Using ERIC for curriculum development.* Paper presented at the Annual Meeting of the School Science and Mathematics Association, Lexington, KY.

Blumenthal, C., Howard, M. J., & Kinyon, W. R. (1993). The impact of CD-ROM technology on a bibliographic instructional program. *College and Research Libraries, 54*(1), 11–16.

Broering, N. C. (1994). A digital full-text biotechnology system at Georgetown University. *Library Hi Tech, 12*(2), 85–91.

Bruce, E., & Hamalian, A. (1992, May/June). *From Vancouver BC (1974) to Charlottetown PEI (1992): Achievements, challenges, and opportunities of Canadian bibliography in education.* Paper presented at the Third National Conference on Canadian Bibliography, Charlottetown, Canada. (ERIC Document Reproduction Services No. ED 352 034)

Covey, S. R. (1989). *The 7 habits of highly effective people.* New York: Simon & Schuster.

Educational Resources Information Center. (1991). *All about ERIC.* Washington, DC: Author.

Gallegos, B., & Rillero. P. (1996). Bibliographic database competencies for preservice teachers. *Journal of Technology and Teacher Education, 4*(3/4), 231–246.

Krumenaker, L. (1993). Virtual libraries, complete with journals, get real. *Science, 260,* 1066–1067.

Lancaster, F. W., Elzy, C., Zeter, M. J., Metzler, L., & Low, Y. M. (1994). Searching databases on CD-ROM: Comparisons of the results of end-user searching with results from two modes of searching by skilled intermediaries. *RQ, 33*(3), 370–386.

Morehead, J., & Fetzer, M. (1992). *Introduction to the United States government information sources* (4th ed.). Washington, DC: Libraries Unlimited.

Omaji, A. (1994). Non-use of CD-ROM databases in an academic environment. *Computers in Libraries, 14*(9), 45–46.

Pickens, K. (1994). The relationship of bibliographic database design to the structure of information: A case study in education. *Journal of Documentation, 50*(1), 36–44.

Smarte, L. (1994). *ERIC annual report 1994.* Washington, DC: U.S. Department of Education.

Smarte, L. (1997). *ERIC annual report 1996.* Washington, DC: U.S. Department of Education.

Stonehill, R. M. (1992, June). *Myths and realities about ERIC.* Syracuse, NY: ERIC Clearinghouse on Information Resources. (ERIC Document Reproduction Services No. ED 345 756)

Tennant, R. (1992). *Internet basics* [ERIC Digest]. Syracuse, NY: ERIC Clearinghouse on Information Resources. (ERIC Document Reproduction Services No. ED 348 054)

U.S. Department of Education. (1997). *Programs and services.* Washington, DC: Author. (Available WWW: http://www.ed.gov/programs.html)

Venditto, G. (1996, May). Search engine showdown. *Internet World, 7*(5), 78–86.

About the Authors

Holly Anderson is Department Chair of the Department of Foundations, Technology, and Secondary Education in the College of Education at Boise State University, Boise, Idaho. She teaches graduate and undergraduate courses in pedagogy, educational issues, and foundations of education. She has directed numerous graduate committees, and was the codirector of a technology-based support program for beginning teachers. Her professional writing has focused on such areas as teacher induction, issues in teacher literacy, professional development for practicing teachers, and gender issues in higher education.

Annette Baturo is a lecturer in the School of Mathematics, Science and Technology at Queensland University of Technology, Brisbane, Australia, and is a mathematics education researcher within the Centre for Mathematics and Science Education at the same institution. Her main research interest is in probing students' mental models of mathematics concepts, processes, and principles, particularly in elementary probability, decimal-number numeration and area, and in developing descriptive tools to represent and describe explanations for how students acquire and access those mental models. Annette has a particular expertise in scholarly writing principles that allow for clear expression of coherent arguments.

Andy Begg is a senior lecturer in mathematics education at the University of Waikato in New Zealand where he teaches and supervises graduate work. He has been a high school teacher, a textbook author, and a curriculum developer. His research interests include curriculum and professional development.

Beverley Bell taught in several secondary schools before coming to the University of Waikato in 1979 to do a masters and doctoral degree in science education. While a graduate student, she worked on the first Learning in Science Project team. She then worked as the project coordinator for the Children's Learning in Science Project, University of Leeds. On her return to New Zealand, she joined the curriculum development division in the Department of Education and had responsibility for the revision of the F1-5 science syllabus. In 1989, she joined the Centre for Science, Mathematics, Technology Education Research at the University of Waikato, where she is currently Director. She has supervised more than 30 masters and doctoral research theses and dissertations. Her research interests include teaching, learning, and assessment in science education, and curriculum and teacher development.

Robert Bleicher is a part-time lecturer in science education at Queensland Institute of Technology. Since 1994 he has worked full time on large-scale professional development projects focusing on classroom interactions between teachers and students, and has been assisted in this task by postgraduate students with whom he has established a close rapport. His research has also enabled him to work closely with researchers and teachers, assisting them to gain deeper insights into classroom discourse.

Vicki Compton is a teacher educator specializing in technology and science education. She has taught science at high school and at a polytechnic in New Zealand, and for the last four years she has been at the University of Waikato where she contributed to the masters degree technology education courses. She is involved in research and development in technology education. Her current interests include the development of inclusive curricula and the processes of curriculum development, teacher development, and curriculum implementation.

Tom Cooper is an associate professor and Head of the School of Mathematics, Science and Technology Education at Queensland University of Technology, Brisbane, Australia, and is a mathematics education researcher within the Centre for Mathematics and Science Education at the same institution. Tom has extensive experience in the supervision of higher degree students and has special expertise in research design and thesis structure and presentation. His research interests include knowledge acquisition and access to the concepts, processes, and principles related to algebra and fractions, mental computational strategies, the social context of the classroom, professional development and teacher change. Tom has been a recipient of major Australian research grants related to these interests.

Frank Crawley is Professor and Chair in the Department of Science Education, East Carolina University, Greenville, North Carolina. For more than two decades he has been a highly active science teacher educator and has authored or coauthored numerous research publications, chapters, and reports. His research examines science teacher and student attitudes, how they are formed and changed, and he has extensive experience working with science teachers on projects designed to change their teaching practice. Frank's current research focuses on job-embedded learning and the design of graduate study and professional development programs that support teacher inquiry.

Vaille Dawson is a full-time doctoral student at the National Centre for School Science and Mathematics at Curtin University in Perth, Western Australia. She worked for a number of years in medical research before becoming a science teacher. Her doctoral thesis is concerned with the teaching of ethics in science. Her research interests include constructivism, feminism, genetics, and ethics.

Helen Forgasz is a research fellow in the Graduate School of Education at La Trobe University in Melbourne, Victoria. Before embarking on further studies, she was a high school teacher of mathematics, physics, and computing. Her research interests include: mathematics education (secondary and tertiary), mature-age students, gender issues in education, attitudes and beliefs, and learning settings. Helen has written the book, *Society and Gender Equity in Mathematics Education,* and has published widely in scholarly and professional journals.

Bee Gallegos is the Education Librarian at Arizona State University West in Phoenix, Arizona. Bee has collaborated with colleagues in the organization of workshops on the integration of information competencies into the curriculum, with faculty in providing classroom instruction on the use of databases, and has conducted workshops for faculty and students on use of the Internet. With colleague, Peter Rillero, Bee has done national presentations on database searching and recently published an article on core competencies required for students to successfully search databases.

Leonie Harris is a writing specialist and researcher within the Centre for Mathematics and Science Education at Queensland University of Technology, Brisbane, Australia. She has expertise in scholarly writing principles and in proofreading and editing masters and doctoral theses for students. As a writing specialist, she works with higher degree students identified as having writing problems that place their dissertations at risk. Since 1995, she has successfully assisted 20 such students. Her main research interest is in children's verbalizations of their knowledge and affects in numeracy and literacy.

Jack Hourcade is a professor in the College of Education at Boise State University, Boise, Idaho. He has been active in scholarly writing for two decades, having published more than 50 papers in professional journals. Over the years he has worked with undergraduate and graduate students on hundreds of research projects, a number of which have been published in professional journals. He presently serves as an associate editor of the journal, *Teaching Exceptional Children.* His major research interests include teacher collaboration, and the use of technology for students with disabilities. Recent publication include his coauthored book, *Cooperative Teaching: Rebuilding the Schoolhouse for All Students,* and several papers on professional collaboration in the schools.

Julie Landvogt is currently Post-Doctoral Fellow at La Trobe University and Resident Consultant (Research in Practice) at Methodist Ladies' College in Melbourne. Her PhD, *So Much to Do! So Little Time! A Study of Teachers at Work,* won the 1997 Outstanding Dissertation Award from the American Association for Research in Education, and explored the complexity of teachers' knowledge and the impact of teachers' beliefs on classroom action. She is the author of *Teaching Gifted Children: Developing Programs for Schools,* and *Probing Deeper: Issues in Gifted Education.* Her research seeks to combine the areas of reflective practice and gifted education.

Gilah Leder is a professor in the Graduate School of Education at La Trobe University-Bundoora. She has previously worked at Monash University, the Secondary Teachers College (now The University of Melbourne) and at secondary schools in Victoria and South Australia. Her teaching and research interests embrace the interaction between teaching, learning, and assessment of mathematics, affect, gender issues, and exceptionality. She has published widely in each of these areas. Gilah serves on various editorial boards and educational and scientific committees and is a frequent presenter at scientific and professional meetings. She is Past President of the Mathematics Research Group of Australasia and current President of the International Group for the Psychology of Mathematics Education.

John Malone is Professor of Mathematics Education and Coordinator of the doctoral program at the National Centre for School Science and Mathematics at Curtin University in Perth, Western Australia. He has almost 20 years' experience in research and supervision in his discipline, and has fulfilled the role of examiner for numerous doctoral and masters theses over that period. He has published extensively in the area of mathematics teaching and learning generally, and is currently President of the Mathematics Education Research Group of Australasia (MERGA).

Michelle McGinn is a doctoral student in the Faculty of Education at Simon Fraser University, Burnaby, British Columbia, Canada. Her dissertation research investigates everyday mathematical and scientific practices of working scientists, as well as her own apprenticeship in mathematical and scientific practices and educational research. She teaches an introductory course intended to provide prospective teachers with basic knowledge and skills for reading, interpreting, and evaluating educational research, so that they can make instructional decisions based on research results. She continues to lead the research support group for new mathematics teachers completing their masters theses in education.

Elizabeth McKinley's background is in teaching and administration in secondary schools and primary and secondary preservice teacher education in New Zealand. She has been involved with the recent national science curriculum development in both English and Maori. Currently she contributes to courses in research methodologies and science education. Her research interests include the influence of culture and language in science and science education, feminism and science education, and curriculum policy and development. Elizabeth's current research looks at the role of colonization in the underrepresentation of Maori women in science.

Peter Rillero is an assistant professor of science education at Arizona State University West in Phoenix, Arizona. As a former science education analyst at the ERIC Clearinghouse for Science, Mathematics, and Environmental Education, Peter read, analyzed, and abstracted hundreds of science education articles, books, curricula, and conference papers for the world's largest educational database.

Working with Bee Gallegos, Peter has done national presentations on database searching and recently published an article on core competencies required for students to successfully search databases.

Wolff-Michael Roth is Lansdowne Chair of Applied Cognitive Science and Science Education in the Faculty of Education, University of Victoria, Victoria, Canada. The notion of "coparticipation in practice" is central to his research on learning and his practice of working with graduate students. He has written two books and numerous research articles showing that coparticipating in activities, regardless of whether the participants are students and/or teachers in science classrooms with different degrees of experience and competence, allows learning to occur in explicit and implicit modes. He directs a multimedia analysis and interaction laboratory that facilitates and scaffolds learning by coparticipating.

John Schaller has been teaching biology and environmental science at SAIL High School in Leon County, Florida, for the last 10 years. Among the curricula John has developed and implemented are the Tropical Ecology and Research Academy, the Environmental Science Magnet Program, the Russian and Costa Rican Sister School Exchange programs, and the Marine Science Under SAIL program. He received his PhD in 1996 from Florida State University and continues to teach graduate courses in research methodology for the Science Education Department. His research interests include ethnographic studies in general and he particularly enjoys his experiences working with student interns.

David Squires is a reader in educational computing within the School of Education, King's College, London. He has extensive experience of the design, development, and use of software in schools and universities. His research supervision features specific links to his own research, for example, the use of Logo relative motion microworlds; mature students as multimedia composers; the use of multimedia tools by primary school children; and the design of help systems in educational software. He is a past codirector on the Computers in the Curriculum Project, a UK national curriculum development project featuring the use of education software in the sciences and humanities, and he has directed a British library-funded research project concerned with the use of interactive information systems in academic research.

Peter Taylor is a senior lecturer in the National Centre for School Science and Mathematics at Curtin University. His major research interest is the epistemological reform of school science and mathematics teaching, especially through the agency of action research. Peter is a member of the Self-Study of Teacher Education Practice (S-STEP) Special Interest Group of the American Educational Research Association (AERA) where he presents research on his own teaching and supervision practice. Key referents shaping both his pedagogy and research are constructivism, feminism, postmodernism, and phenomenology. Peter serves on the editorial review board for the *Journal for Research in Science Teaching*.

KennethTobin is a professor in science education and Director of Teacher Education at the University of Pennsylvania. He has been involved in interpretive research since the mid 1980s and has explored a variety of contexts associated with teaching, learning, teacher education, and policy implementation. Ken's research since 1984 has involved groups of researchers, including teachers, and has employed a variety of genres within the umbrella of interpretive research. In that time he has supervised 20 doctoral dissertations and a similar number of masters theses. He is the author of numerous papers, chapters, and books, including the *International Handbook of Science Education*, which he coedited with Barry Fraser.

John Truran is a mathematics educator in private practice and a PhD student at the University of Adelaide, South Australia. His research interests are in the teaching and learning of probability and statistics and in interpreting the forces operating on curriculum change in mathematics education. He has had extensive experience as a one-to-one teacher, and used clinical interviews as the basis for his masters thesis, which examined children's probability learning. He is a coleader of an international group concerned with studying the psychology of stochastics education.

Kathleen Truran is a lecturer in mathematics education at the University of South Australia. Her research interest is in teaching and learning of probability at the primary level and she regularly presents papers at international conferences in this field. The masters thesis that she is currently preparing and on which many of her papers are based integrates qualitative and quantitative approaches by using both group testing and clinical interviews for building up a broad picture of children's understanding. She is a coleader of an international group concerned with research into the teaching and learning of probability and statistics.

Loren White is a doctoral student at Curtin's National Centre for School Science and Mathematics. The focus of his research is on ways that students make sense of mathematics, with particular attention to the dynamics of classroom social relations. His research is being conducted from the perspective that mathematics is a culturally constructed artifact and that mathematics curricula are a product of conflicting and competing cultural value systems. Loren has been a teacher of high school mathematics since the early 1980s and is actively researching his own teaching practice while, at the same time, maintaining a critical reflectivity on his multiple roles as teacher, researcher, collaborator, and student.

Dylan Wiliam is Dean and Head of the School of Education at King's College, University of London. After eight years teaching in London schools he took up a post in mathematics education at Kings, and in 1989 was appointed Academic Coordinator of the Consortium for Assessment and Testing in Schools, developing innovative materials for assessing English, mathematics, science, and technology for the national curriculum of England and Wales. He teaches research methods and quantitative data analysis at both masters and research degree level and is coordinator of a new taught doctorate in education assessment.

Robyn Zevenbergen is a Senior Lecturer in Mathematics Education at Griffith University, Gold Coast Campus, in Queensland. Her particular area of interest is in the context of mathematics education--social, cultural, and political--and the impact this has on the learning of mathematics. She is actively involved in social justice issues associated with mathematics teaching and learning, particularly as they apply to primary school education. The methodologies used for her research are qualitative, preferring ethnography and action research projects. She is heavily involved in school-based research and projects. Current research includes workplace numeracy, early childhood intervention, and autonomous learning of preservice teacher education.

Author Index

Subject Index